# MIRACLE AT PHILADELPHIA

*The Story of the Constitutional Convention*
*May to September 1787*

BOOKS BY CATHERINE DRINKER BOWEN

FRIENDS AND FIDDLERS

BELOVED FRIEND
The Story of Tchaikowsky and Nadejda von Meck
(*In Collaboration with B. von Meck*)

FREE ARTIST
The Story of Anton and Nicholas Rubinstein

YANKEE FROM OLYMPUS
Justice Holmes and His Family

JOHN ADAMS AND THE AMERICAN REVOLUTION

THE WRITING OF BIOGRAPHY

THE LION AND THE THRONE
The Life and Times of Sir Edward Coke

ADVENTURES OF A BIOGRAPHER

FRANCIS BACON
The Temper of a Man

MIRACLE AT PHILADELPHIA
The Story of the Constitutional Convention,
May to September 1787

GEORGE WASHINGTON
(bust by Houdon)

# MIRACLE AT PHILADELPHIA

*The Story of the Constitutional Convention
May to September 1787*

*by* CATHERINE DRINKER BOWEN

*Foreword by* Warren E. Burger

*with illustrations*

*An Atlantic Monthly Press Book*

LITTLE, BROWN AND COMPANY · BOSTON · TORONTO

REPUBLISHED IN 1986

*Sixth Printing*

The Library of Congress has cataloged the first printing of this title as
follows:
   Bowen, Catherine (Drinker) 1897–
     Miracle at Philadelphia; the story of the Constitutional Convention,
   May to September, 1787. [1st ed.] Boston, Little, Brown [1966]

     xix, 346 p.   illus., ports.   22 cm.
     "An Atlantic Monthly Press book."

     1. United States.   Constitutional Convention (1787)   I. Title.
JK146.B75 *1986*  342.7302     66-20798
                                 MARC
LIBRARY OF CONGRESS [8510r85]rev

ATLANTIC—LITTLE, BROWN BOOKS
ARE PUBLISHED BY
LITTLE, BROWN AND COMPANY
IN ASSOCIATION WITH
THE ATLANTIC MONTHLY PRESS

RRD-VA

*Published simultaneously in Canada*
*by Little, Brown & Company (Canada) Limited*

PRINTED IN THE UNITED STATES OF AMERICA

*for*
EDWARD WEEKS

*Foreword by*

Warren E. Burger
Chairman of the Commission on the Bicentennial
of the United States Constitution

I first read *Miracle at Philadelphia* upon its publication twenty years ago. I sensed at that time that it was a singular work of narrative history. The years, and more frequent use of the Constitution, have confirmed my initial impression. Mrs. Bowen's book remains for me the best single popular work on how the "miracle" of our Constitution came to pass, how difficult it was to achieve, and what a boon it was to the cause of freedom everywhere.

Mrs. Bowen draws from sources well known to historians and students of constitutional law, but — at least in my view — no one has ever told this remarkable story so well. A reader can almost hear Patrick Henry's fuming that he would not accept appointment as a delegate to the Philadelphia Convention because he "smelt a rat." The "rat" he smelled was the replacement of the Articles of Confederation with a Constitution creating a strong national government. In his view we had not fought a revolution to rid ourselves of one distant despot only to set up a domestic version of the same — more republican in form, perhaps, but nonetheless a despotism of centralized power.

The effect of Henry's great debating powers and fiery oratory is reflected in the narrow margin of the Virginia Ratifying Convention's final vote of 89 to 79 in favor of the document — despite the fact that the document bore the signatures of three most prominent Virginians of the day, George Washington, James Madison, and John Blair.

One shudders to think what would have happened had Patrick Henry prevailed in Richmond. Earlier, there had been close votes in Massachusetts and New Hampshire in favor of ratification; Rhode Island had emphatically rejected it by popular referendum. With the Anti-Federalist views of Governor Clinton leading the opposition, sentiment in New York was sharply divided. Only when Alexander Hamilton managed to delay New York's vote until after the results in Virginia were received did New York ratify by a vote of 30 to 27.

Reaching across two centuries, the author reveals the parochial views of those who were content with each state issuing its own currency and free to exclude commerce from other states. Where would we be had not Chief Justice Marshall in 1824, using the Commerce Clause, made us a "common market" even before that phrase had currency? And think what Europe might be like today if it had had a common market in 1824.

Mrs. Bowen makes these great events come alive for us almost as if she were reporting on contemporary events. Of course she was working with one of the greatest stories in our history — indeed in the history of human liberty. I suppose the book initially attracted me because of the interest in history all lawyers share. A judge dealing often with the meaning of the Constitution needs to understand its origins. But Mrs. Bowen's book exerted a fascination for me well beyond the concerns of a lawyer. I had read and admired her previous work, such as her books on Oliver Wendell Holmes, John Adams, Lord Coke, and Francis Bacon. Concerned as all these books were with law and history, with the never-ending search for freedom and security, there seems to have been a natural culmination in this most compelling account of the creation of our Constitution.

Our Constitution has had as great an impact on humanity as the splitting of the atom. As Chairman of the Commission on the Bicentennial of the United States Constitution, I applaud the republication of this extraordinary work, and recommend it to anyone who wants to know about the creation of the oldest existing national constitution, and who enjoys the excitement of world-historic drama told by a master storyteller.

# *Author's Preface*

MIRACLES do not occur at random, nor was it the author of this book who said there was a miracle at Philadelphia in the year 1787. George Washington said it, and James Madison. They used the word in writing to their friends: Washington to Lafayette, Madison to Thomas Jefferson.

Every miracle has its provenance, every miracle has been prayed for. The wine was first water in Cana; there was a wedding and a need. If miracles are men's wishes fulfilled, so with the miracle at Philadelphia. Since the beginning, the country had moved toward this moment, toward self-government, toward union. One can count the experiments: The Fundamental Orders of Connecticut in 1639; West New Jersey's Fundamental Laws of 1677; the Albany Plan of Union in 1754; the Resolutions, Instructions, Declarations, Articles and Ordinances that ran throughout the Revolution, from the year 1765. Trial, error, success, retreat. Plans of union and plans of government, until, four years after the Peace of Paris, Americans attempted the grand national experiment.

My book celebrates that experiment. Its aim throughout is evocation, suggestion. I greatly desire that my readers may see Convention delegates as they rise and address the Chairman, Washington, or face each other in committee. Above all I want to call back the voices: James Wilson's cold, cutting logic; Gouverneur Morris's easy ironic flow, Roger Sherman's drawling Yankee common sense; Madison's quiet, extraordinary performance day after day. When I stop the narrative to inform on some point, it is only in order to clarify the scene, remind readers of historical facts which make the story pertinent.

It will early be plain that I wrote in admiration of the Convention and the delegates. Their very failings appeared interesting; that certain members were moved by self-interest only made the scene more credible and more dramatic. No doubt I shall be charged with an outmoded romanticism — this writer is an Old Whig, she has Bancroftian notions. It is true, and I count myself in good company, notably with that intellectual skeptic, Justice Holmes, who, after reading Beard's *An Economic History of the Constitution*, wrote in protest to his friend Pollock in England, "You and I believe that high-mindedness is not impossible to man."

*Miracle at Philadelphia* is a narrative, taken from source, from contemporary reports of the Federal Convention, from newspapers, diaries, the letters and utterances of delegates and their friends. To these men the situation in the states was critical and they said so, repeatedly and often; they believed the Union needed saving and needed it quickly. No one can read their speeches in Convention and miss the tenseness of the moment, miss the delegates' dread lest the Convention dissolve with nothing accomplished. In the fifth Convention week, Washington wrote to Hamilton that he almost despaired. His words on the page carry conviction. The General meant what he said, was wrung by it and sought support. Washington did not protest that the Union would founder without a new constitution and a firmer government. But there had been times when he so protested, and Madison and Hamilton with him.

Historians have suggested that these fears were mistaken and that the thirteen states were doing well enough in 1787, respected by Europe and recovering at home from the devastation of a six-year war. The evidence as I see it does not bear this out. And no field has been more thoroughly explored. From Bancroft to Charles Warren to McLaughlin to E. S. Corwin (whose wonderful book weighs five pounds on the bathroom scales) everyone has tried his hand. And from Charles Beard in 1913 to Benjamin Wright, McIlwain, Nevins, Jensen, Mason, Morris, Handlin, Nettels, Hacker, Main, Brown, Morgan, McDonald, Rossiter, Bailyn *et alii*, historians disagree. One group says the Convention was shockingly "conservative," a body of prosperous landholders and merchants out to solidify their interests. Another group (the current revisionists) reverts to the old Bancroft-Beveridge idealism which looked on the Convention delegates as men fired by conviction, eager to create a new government that would be acceptable to the people.

Having read the volumes concerned and in large part studied the evidence on which these works are based, I make my own interpretation and shall stand by it; my book does not enter into academic controversy. About twenty years ago, I first read Max Farrand's *Records of the Federal Convention,* four volumes of speeches as reported by delegates, together with elaborately footnoted letters and speeches made later. At the time, I had published a biography of Justice Oliver Wendell Holmes and was preparing to write about John Adams. The Federal Convention did not come into either book, but the delegates and that extraordinary scene stayed in my mind. As years went by and I wrote biographies of Chief Justice Coke and Lord Chancellor Bacon, things began to fall into place: the story turned to Independence and America's break with the past—to what was retained of English political heritage and what was rejected in the fateful year 1787.

But I did not write my book in order to pronounce Gladstonian eulogies over the United States Constitution. Said Justice Holmes, "The Constitution is an experiment, as all life is an experiment." It is the men who made this experiment with whom I am concerned, and the fortunate moment when they met. Considering the immense amount of literature on the subject, it is surprising how little the average American knows about the making of our Constitution. He confuses the Federal Convention with the Confederation Congress, sitting in New York at the same time. He even confuses the Constitution with the first ten amendments — the Bill of Rights. He forgets for how many years thirteen states had existed under the Articles of Confederation before that document was supplanted by the United States Constitution. Most books on the Constitution begin *after* the Convention of '87, going on to show the development of our Constitution through Supreme Court decisions in the nineteenth century.

My book, on the other hand, begins in May of 1787 and finishes in September, except for three chapters on ratification, ending a year later. In the midst of summer and at the heart of argument

I have a digression. The reader leaves the State House and in company with various genial foreigners is taken on a "Journey through the American states." It seemed pertinent to let readers see at first hand this country for which the Convention was creating a government. For much the same reason I have used off-stage voices throughout: Jefferson and John Adams and Tom Paine from Europe, Sam Adams from Boston — all intensely concerned with what was going on in Philadelphia. John Adams said something I did not include. Writing about history, he asked a friend, "Are not these facts as new to you as any political tale that could be brought to you from Arabia, or by special messenger from Sirius, the dog-star?"

The Federal Convention, viewed from the records, is startlingly fresh and "new." The spirit behind it was the spirit of compromise, seemingly no very noble flag to rally round. Compromise can be an ugly word, signifying a pact with the devil, a chipping off of the best to suit the worst. Yet in the Constitutional Convention the spirit of compromise reigned in grace and glory; as Washington presided, it sat on his shoulder like the dove. Men rise to speak and one sees them struggle with the bias of birthright, locality, statehood — South against North, East against West, merchant against planter. One sees them change their minds, fight against pride, and when the moment comes, admit their error. If the story is old, the feelings behind it are new as Monday morning.

If all the tales are told, retell them, Brother.
If few attend, let those who listen feel.

CATHERINE DRINKER BOWEN

# Contents

Foreword by Warren E. Burger     IX

Author's Preface     XI

Delegates Who Attended the Convention     XVIII

### THE CONSTITUTIONAL CONVENTION

I.   *The scene. Origins of the Convention.*     3

II.   *The delegates and the State House. Washington and Madison.*     16

III.   *In Convention. Randolph introduces the Virginia Plan.*     32

IV.   *Federal versus national. The "two supremes." The city of Philadelphia.*     40

V.   *The Chief Executive. Wilson of Philadelphia, Dickinson of Delaware. Dr. Franklin speaks his mind. June 1-6.*     54

VI.   *"Life, liberty and property." The people at large. The method of electing congressmen. June 6-7.*     69

VII.   *The congressional veto. Proportional representation. The delegates write home.*     80

VIII.   *America divided. Sherman's Compromise. The Committee of the Whole makes its Report. June 11-13.*     91

IX.   *The New Jersey Plan. Alexander Hamilton makes his speech. June 15-19.*     104

X.   *The Great Debate. June 19-28.*     116

XI.   *The tension mounts. Europe and America.*     128

XII. *Journey through the American states. The physical scene.* 141

XIII. *Journey through the American states, continued. The people.* 153

XIV. *The Western Territory, the land companies and the Northwest Ordinance. Manasseh Cutler.* 168

XV. *The Great Compromise. A king for America. Ten-day adjournment. General Washington goes fishing.* 185

XVI. *Committee of Detail. The slavery compromise.* 197

XVII. *Foreigners in Congress. The "ten miles square."* 205

XVIII. *Test oaths, Deism and tolerance. A standing army. Treason defined.* 212

XIX. *Who shall ratify? The people or the states?* 225

XX. *Drafting the Constitution. The Committee of Style and Arrangement take hold. September 8-12.* 234

XXI. *A bill of rights rejected.* 243

XXII. *The Constitution is signed. The dissidents.* 254

THE FIGHT FOR RATIFICATION

XXIII. *The Constitution goes before the country.* 267

XXIV. *Massachusetts. The people speak.* 282

XXV. *Virginia and New York. The Federal Procession.* 293

Chapter Notes 311

The Constitution 313

Author's Note 327

Acknowledgments 331

Index 333

It appears to me, then, little short of a miracle, that the Delegates from so many different States (which States you know are also different from each other), in their manners, circumstances, and prejudices, should unite in forming a system of national Government, so little liable to well founded objections.

WASHINGTON TO LAFAYETTE, *February 7, 1788*

# Delegates Who Attended the Federal Convention

| | |
|---|---|
| New Hampshire | John Langdon<br>Nicholas Gilman |
| Massachusetts | Elbridge Gerry ✓<br>Nathaniel Gorham<br>Rufus King<br>Caleb Strong |
| Rhode Island | No appointment |
| Connecticut | William Samuel Johnson<br>Roger Sherman<br>Oliver Ellsworth |
| New York | Robert Yates<br>Alexander Hamilton<br>John Lansing, Junior |
| New Jersey | David Brearley<br>William Churchill Houston<br>William Paterson<br>William Livingston<br>Jonathan Dayton |
| Pennsylvania | Thomas Mifflin<br>Robert Morris<br>George Clymer<br>Jared Ingersoll<br>Thomas Fitzsimons<br>James Wilson<br>Gouverneur Morris<br>Benjamin Franklin |

| | |
|---|---|
| Delaware | George Read |
| | Gunning Bedford, Junior |
| | John Dickinson |
| | Richard Bassett |
| | Jacob Broom |
| | |
| Maryland | James McHenry |
| | Daniel of St. Thomas Jenifer |
| | Daniel Carroll |
| | John Francis Mercer |
| | Luther Martin |
| | |
| Virginia | George Washington |
| | Edmund Randolph |
| | John Blair |
| | James Madison, Junior |
| | George Mason |
| | George Wythe |
| | James McClurg |
| | |
| Georgia | William Few |
| | Abraham Baldwin |
| | William Pierce |
| | William Houstoun |
| | |
| North Carolina | Alexander Martin |
| | William Richardson Davie |
| | Richard Dobbs Spaight |
| | William Blount |
| | Hugh Williamson |
| | |
| South Carolina | John Rutledge |
| | Charles Pinckney |
| | Charles Cotesworth Pinckney |
| | Pierce Butler |

# THE
# CONSTITUTIONAL
# CONVENTION

# I

*The scene. Origins of the Convention.*

It is much easier to pull down a government, in such
a conjuncture of affairs as we have seen, than to build
up, at such a season as the present.
JOHN ADAMS TO JAMES WARREN, *January, 1787*

OVER Philadelphia the air lay hot and humid; old people
said it was the worst summer since 1750. A diarist noted
that cooling thunderstorms were not so frequent or violent as formerly. Perhaps the new "installic rods" everywhere
fixed on the houses might have robbed the clouds of their electric
fluid. French visitors wrote home they could not breathe. "At
each inhaling of air, one worries about the next one. The slightest
movement is painful."

In the Pennsylvania State House, which we call Independence
Hall, some fifty-five delegates, named by the legislatures of
twelve states (Rhode Island balked, refusing attendance), met in
convention, and during a summer of hard work and high feeling
wrote out a plan of government which they hoped the states
would accept, and which they entitled *The Constitution of the
United States of America.*

It was May when the Convention met, it would be September
before they rose. Here were some of the most notable names in
America; among them Washington, Madison, Hamilton, Benjamin
Franklin; John Rutledge and the two Pinckneys from South Caro-
lina; the two Morrises — Robert and Gouverneur; John Dickinson
of Delaware; George Wythe, George Mason and John Blair of
Virginia; Roger Sherman of Connecticut; Rufus King and Elbridge
Gerry of Massachusetts. The roster reads like a Fourth of July

oration, a patriotic hymn. It was a young gathering. Charles Pinckney was twenty-nine; Alexander Hamilton, thirty. Rufus King was thirty-two, Jonathan Dayton of New Jersey, twenty-six. Gouverneur Morris — he of the suave manners and the wooden leg — was thirty-five. Even that staid and careful legal scholar, James Madison of Virginia, known today as "father of the Constitution," was only thirty-six. Benjamin Franklin's eighty-one years raised the average considerably, but it never went beyond forty-three. Men aged sooner and died earlier in those days. John Adams at thirty-seven, invited to give a speech in Boston, had said he was "too old to make declamations."

Richard Henry Lee wrote from Virginia that he was glad to find in the Convention "so many gentlemen of competent years." Yet even the youngest member was politically experienced. Nearly three-fourths had sat in the Continental Congress. Many had been members of their state legislatures and had helped to write their state constitutions in the first years after Independence. Eight had signed the Declaration, seven had been state governors, twenty-one had fought in the Revolutionary War. When Jefferson in Paris read the names he said it was "an assembly of demi-gods."

Even so, the Convention was a chancy thing. Delegates showed themselves nervous, apprehensive, but only to each other. Sessions were secret and very little news leaked out; members wrote guardedly to their friends. Neither to the delegates nor to the country at large was this meeting known as a *constitutional* Convention. How could it be? The title came later. The notion of a new "constitution" would have scared away two-thirds of the members. Newspapers announced a Grand Convention at Philadelphia, or spoke of the "Foederal Convention," always with the nice inclusion of the classical diphthong. Within doors and without, men were tentative as to what they were devising and what they wanted devised. Congress, meeting in New York during the previous February, had sanctioned this Philadelphia convention *"for the sole and express purpose of revising the Articles of Confederation."* Congress had said nothing about a new constitution. To the thirteen states the Articles of Confederation were constitution enough; since 1781 they had made shift under its aegis.

"The said states hereby severally enter into a firm league of friendship with each other." So ran Article III of the Confederation. Yet if friendship sufficed to hold a nation together during a war — and to win a war — in peacetime it seemed that friendship was not enough. The Confederation, resting only on good faith, had no power to collect taxes, defend the country, pay the public debt, let alone encourage trade and commerce. On that day of 1781 when a messenger brought news of the victory at Yorktown, there was not sufficient hard money in the treasury for the man's expenses; each member paid a dollar from his pocket. In desperate need, Congress sent out *requisitions*. "A timid kind of recommendation from Congress to the States," Washington called these. Often enough there was no response; New Jersey and New York had been especially recalcitrant. A notice was printed in the *New York Packet* for October 1, 1787, terse and to the point, twice reprinted:

THE SUBSCRIBER has received nothing on account of the quota of this State for the present year.

(Signed) ALEXANDER HAMILTON
Receiver of Continental Taxes

The states which paid were bitter against the states which did not, and said so. "New Hampshire," wrote a Virginian in '87, "has not paid a shilling since peace and does not ever mean to pay one to all eternity. In New York they pay well because they can do it by plundering New Jersey and Connecticut. Jersey will go to great lengths from motives of revenge and interest."

The country was by no means blind to the fact that the Articles of Confederation were inadequate and needed mending. Successive presidents of Congress sent letters to the state legislatures, urging them not only to pay their requisitions but to vote additional powers to Congress. State executives asked their local legislatures to recommend that Congressional powers be strengthened. Yet nothing happened, every effort fell through. Among those who began early to work for reform, three names stand out: Washington, Madison and Hamilton. And of the three, evidence points to Hamilton as the most potent single influence toward calling the

Convention of '87, though historians still argue the point and Madison's biographers are at pains to give him the palm. Yet if Madison saw logically what ought to happen and if Hamilton expressed it brilliantly, Washington from the first had felt the situation most deeply; his letters during the war were hot with anger and indignation. His troops lacked shoes, meat, gunpowder, clothing, barracks, medicines. "Our sick naked," he wrote; "our well naked, our unfortunate men in capitivity naked." Was Congress then helpless in the face of the army's plight? Express riders went out from camps at Cambridge, Harlem Heights, Morristown, Valley Forge, bearing messages signed by the Commander in Chief: "Morristown, May 27, 1780. It is with infinite pain that I inform Congress that we are reduced again to a situation of extremity for want of meat." Congress, powerless, unsupported by the state assemblies, said stubbornly: "Last war, soldiers supplied their own clothing."

Last war, last war . . . Washington was bedeviled by the phrase. But the last war, with the French, before Independence, had been local, sporadic — and paid for by the Crown. Could not Congress understand that this war was continental, and the expense and responsibility must be borne by all the states, by *the continent?* It was no time for local jealousies, local evasions and contests for power. To the Commander in Chief it seemed the states in Congress showed themselves more concerned over naming new officers and generals, the distribution of rich plums to constituents, than over the army's needs.

Washington owed his own title to Congress, which had elected him by ballot as General of the Continental Army. (Some called it the Grand American Army.) Civilian control of the military was a cardinal principle of the Revolution. "We don't choose to trust you generals with too much power for too long a time," John Adams told Horatio Gates. It was Congress that had enacted the Rules and Regulations for the Government of the Army. But Washington complained that until and unless these rules were altered the army might as well disband — he could not discipline his men, shoot deserters, or properly punish soldiers who stole horses and hospital stores from the army or who burned and plundered houses near the camps. Among the troops, local attachments were fierce and easily aroused. Washington tried to persuade his New Jersey troops to swear allegiance to the United States. They refused. "New Jersey is our country!" they said stubbornly. In Congress a New Jersey member denounced the General's action as improper.

Washington saw what lay behind all this. With Independence, America had indeed achieved a continental dimension and must learn to govern itself accordingly. The General possessed a quite cynical, pragmatic grasp of politics and the political temper of his country, together with a talent — usually thought of as intellectual — for putting into precise words the heart of a problem. "For heaven's sake, who are Congress?" he wrote in '83. "Are they not the creatures of the people, amenable to them for their conduct, and dependent from day to day on their breath? What then can be the danger of giving them such powers as are adequate to the great ends of government, and to all the general purposes of the Confederation?"

As disorders among the states increased, the General's irritation grew. "*Influence* is no *government*," he wrote not long before the Convention met. And even earlier: "I do not conceive we can exist long as a nation without having lodged somewhere a power which will pervade the whole Union in as energetic a manner as the authority of the state governments extends over the several states."

Alexander Hamilton during the war had acted as Washington's aide-de-camp. It was an extraordinary friendship between the young lawyer, foreign-born, impatient, quick, and his Commander in Chief, infinitely steady, with a slow prescience of his own. Concerning Congress and the states, the two saw eye to eye. Moreover, Hamilton worked on Washington, urging him to a strong stand, frequently drafting the General's public statements toward that end. From headquarters at Liberty Pole,* New Jersey, in September of 1780, Hamilton wrote his friend Duane a now famous letter — his first clear exposition of the need for a constitutional convention. Covering seventeen printed pages, the letter is an amazing document from anybody's pen, let alone a man in his early twenties, born outside the continent. It was impossible,

* Now Englewood.

wrote Hamilton, to govern through thirteen sovereign states. A want of power in Congress made the government fit neither for war nor for peace. "There is only one remedy — to call a convention of all the states." And the sooner the better, Hamilton said. Moreover, the people should first be prepared "by sensible and popular writings."

For the ensuing seven years, Hamilton never stopped driving and pushing for a convention. He wrote letters private and public, made speeches, published a series of newspaper articles entitled "The Continentalist" — the title alone betrayed his position. The crying need, Hamilton urged, was for a government suited, not to "the narrow colonial sphere in which we have been accustomed to move." Rather, he wished for "that enlarged kind suited to the government of an independent nation." Although not a member of the New York state legislature, in 1782 he persuaded them to pass a resolution urging a convention. Elected to Congress that same year, Hamilton drafted a similar proposal, but with no success.

The states would not listen. Why go outside of Congress? Rufus King, representative from Massachusetts, declared that Congress was "the proper body to propose alterations." To John Adams, King wrote that Congress could "do all a Convention can, and certainly with more safety to original principles."

Original principles signified Revolutionary principles; the Federal Convention was to find the phrase very useful. And it meant whatever men chose it to mean: to men like Governor Clinton of New York, Judge Bryan of Pennsylvania, Patrick Henry, young James Monroe or Congressman Grayson of Virginia, original principles signified as little government as possible, a federation wherein each state would remain sovereign, with Congress at their disposal. Had not the Articles of Confederation been written with this idea uppermost? It had taken five years, beginning in 1776, to write the Articles, argue and vote on them in Congress, modify them, compromise, and finally persuade the last state to ratify. The Articles were in fact America's first constitution. "The Stile of this Confederacy," said Article I, "shall be 'The United States of America.'" Nothing less than the perils of war would have induced the states to make even this tenuous union at a time when

John Adams referred to Massachusetts Bay as "our country," and to the Massachusetts representatives as "our embassy." Danger had proved a strong cement. Only through the persistence and skilled maneuvering of a few men did the Federal Convention meet at all. It happened that Maryland and Virginia were engaged in a strenuous quarrel over the navigation of the Potomac River; in the spring of 1785, their respective legislatures sent commissioners to Mount Vernon for a discussion of the subject, bearing on the question of east-west communication in general. Seeing the chance to enlist the cooperation of neighboring states, the commission was enlarged, and met at Annapolis in September of 1786. Madison attended; Hamilton came down from New York.

Before the Annapolis Commission rose it had recommended to Congress (Hamilton wrote the report) that all thirteen states appoint delegates to convene at Philadelphia "on the second of May next, to take into consideration the trade and commerce of the United States."

Commerce was a far-reaching word; it covered a multitude of troubles. The war debt still hung heavy; states found their credit failing and small hope of betterment. Seven states had resorted to paper money. True, the postwar depression was lifting. But prosperity remained a local matter; money printed by Pennsylvania must be kept within Pennsylvania's own borders. State and section showed themselves jealous, preferring to fight each other over boundaries as yet unsettled and to pass tariff laws against each other. New Jersey had her own customs service; New York was a foreign nation and must be kept from encroachment. States were marvelously ingenious at devising mutual retaliations; nine of them retained their own navies. (Virginia had even ratified the peace treaty separately.) The shipping arrangements of Connecticut, Delaware and New Jersey were at the mercy of Pennsylvania, New York and Massachusetts.

Madison saw the picture clearly. "New Jersey," he wrote, "placed between Philadelphia and New York, was likened to a cask tapped at both ends; and North Carolina, between Virginia and South Carolina, to a patient bleeding at both arms." When Virginia passed a law declaring that vessels failing to pay duty in her ports might be seized by any person and prosecuted, "one half to the use of the informer and the other half to the use of the commonwealth," she was not aiming at Spain or England but at the cargoes of Pennsylvania, Maryland and Massachusetts. "Most of our political evils," Madison wrote, "may be traced to our commercial ones." It was true, as it is true today between nations at large. The little states feared the big states and hated them. "The people are more happy in small states," Roger Sherman was to say in Convention — though, he added, "states may indeed be too small, as Rhode Island, and thereby too subject to faction." Ellsworth of Connecticut declared that "the largest states are the worst governed. Virginia is obliged to acknowledge her incapacity to extend her government to Kentucky. Massachusetts cannot keep the peace one hundred miles from her capital and is now forming an army for its support."

It was a telling shaft. Since '86, Massachusetts had suffered public humiliation over Shays's Rebellion in the west. Desperate farmers, ruinously taxed — "by Boston," they said — and seeing their cattle and their land distrained by the bailiffs, had risen in revolt. With staves and pitchforks they had marched on county courthouses after the best Revolutionary technique, frightening sound-money men out of their wits and rousing General Washington to express disgust and anger that a country which had won a difficult war was not able to keep order in peacetime. By January, 1787, fourteen rioting leaders, earlier condemned to death, had been pardoned; a newly elected Massachusetts legislature would enact many of the reforms the Shaysites had demanded. Yet the stigma of insurrection remained, and in the Federal Convention sat men who had themselves suffered at the hands of mobs: James Wilson, Robert Morris and John Dickinson knew well that rebellion can be contagious.

Shays's Rebellion had been in the public mind when Congress, after debating the Annapolis report, had voted in favor of a convention at Philadelphia. Even so, Congress proceeded cautiously. The Annapolis report had hinted that not only trade and commerce but the entire federal system might need adjusting. Congress resolved that the Convention was to meet "for the sole and express purpose" — the phrase was soon to become a byword and a strength to anti-Constitutionalists — "the sole and express purpose of revising the Articles of Confederation." Throughout the country the opposition was strong; its roots lay deep from Maine to Florida. Sovereign and independent of each other the states had fought through six years of war. They had won the war, they had beat the enemy. Why fight a war and achieve independence only to be taxed by a powerful Congress instead of by a powerful Parliament? Let the states govern themselves! It was the prevailing notion. States still showed something of the anarchical spirit of the little town of Ashfield, Massachusetts, which in 1776, intoxicated by "freedom," had voted in town meeting *that we do not want any Goviner but the Goviner of the univarse, and under him a States Ginaral to Consult with the Wrest of the united States for the Good of the Whole.*"

John Adams had not been far wrong when he said that from the beginning he had seen more difficulty from our attempts to govern ourselves than from all the fleets and armies of Europe.

Seventy-four delegates were named to the Convention at Philadelphia; in the end fifty-five turned up. Two men of eloquence were absent; the Convention missed them but felt their hand. John Adams was in London, Thomas Jefferson in Paris, arranging treaties of commerce and foreign loans and trying to persuade the powers — France, Holland and the rest — that the infant United States could be trusted to meet obligations and pay her debts. Both men were vitally interested in the Convention; letters went back and forth. Adams's book on constitutions* past and present, just off the press, circulated among members, receiving praise or blame according to the reader's view of federalism in general and a bicameral legislature in particular.

Congress, sitting in New York, complained of losing members to the Convention at Philadelphia. Since the war ended it had been difficult enough to obtain a quorum. Members simply stayed home, preferring state interests to the general government. (When the treaty of peace had arrived from Paris in 1783, only seven states were represented — two short of the quorum neces-

---

* *A Defence of the Constitutions of Government of the United States of America*, Volume I (London, 1787).

sary for ratification.) Letters had to be dispatched, urging attendance. Congress was in bad enough case without its best-qualified men taking coach for Pennsylvania. In April of '87 a motion was actually brought to adjourn and move to Philadelphia. The measure failed, though it irked representatives not to know exactly what was brewing. At the moment, Congress sat upstairs in New York's City Hall, described as "a magnificent pile of buildings in Wall Street — more than twice the width of the State House in Boston, but not so long." New York was only one of many Congressional homes. Since the year 1774 a harried legislature had met in Philadelphia, Baltimore, Lancaster, York, Princeton, Annapolis, Trenton — chased from pillar to post by war or, in one case, by mutinying ill-paid soldiers of the Pennsylvania militia.

On the twenty-ninth of May, William Grayson of Virginia complained that Congress was very thin, and that he had heard the Convention at Philadelphia might sit as long as three months. "What will be the result of their meeting I cannot with any certainty determine, but I hardly think much good can come of it: the people of America don't appear to me to be ripe for any great innovations."

*Innovation* was a word that had been in bad repute for centuries. It meant something impulsive, a trifle addled, the work of an enthusiast and certainly an infringement on the law. "To innovate is not to reform," Edmund Burke said in England, and back in Chief Justice Coke's day, to accuse a politician of introducing innovations was to discredit him at once. Grayson's skepticism was shared by his colleagues, summed up by a congressman who had been named to the Philadelphia Convention: William Blount of North Carolina declared he could not be in favor of the Convention plans as they were developing; "I still think we shall ultimately and not many years [hence] just be separate and distinct governments perfectly independent of each other."

Delegates drifted slowly into Philadelphia. On May twenty-fourth, Rufus King wrote home that he was "mortified" because he alone was from New England. "The backwardness may prove unfortunate. Pray hurry on your delegates." New Hampshire delayed because she had no money in her treasury to pay expenses; it was nearly August when two out of her four appointees appeared. One of them, John Langdon, was a rich merchant from Portsmouth, formerly president of his state, described as a "large handsome man, and of a very noble bearing, who courted popularity with the zeal of a lover and the constancy of a martyr." Rhode Island stayed away. At Providence the agrarian party controlled the legislature; they had even contrived to pass a law punishing with fines any creditor who refused the inflationary state currency. It was common knowledge that certain politicians were feathering their nests under the system. A strong central government no doubt would force debts to be paid in specie: Rhode Island at the moment would have none of it. *Rogue Island*, a Boston newspaper called her in disgust, recommending that she "be dropped out of the Union or apportioned to the different States which surround her."

From everywhere came jibes and anger at this small and seemingly thriving state. A speaker in New Haven said publicly that "Rhode Island has acted a part which would cause the savages of the wilderness to blush. That little state is an unruly member of the political body, and is a reproach and a byeword among all her acquaintances."

"Rhode Island," wrote General Washington from the Convention on July first, "still perseveres in that impolitic — unjust — and one might add without much impropriety scandalous conduct, which seems to have marked all her public councils of late. Consequently no representation is yet here from thence." Jefferson called Rhode Island the "little *vaut-rien*."

James Madison rode over to the Convention from New York, where he had been sitting in Congress. It was typical of Madison to arrive in Philadelphia eleven days early; this was a man who liked to be ready. Long study had given him a prophetic quality; in a letter to Washington as early as April he had outlined the most important points that were to be debated in the Convention. Madison was a small man, slight of figure, "no bigger," someone said, "than half a piece of soap." He had a quiet voice. In meetings, members called out, asking him to speak louder, or the clerk omitted parts of his speeches, "because he spoke low and could not be heard." To his friends he was Jemmy.

But Madison, enormously pertinacious, was also flexible — two qualities not often found together. Of the entire delegation no one came better prepared intellectually. At his request Jefferson (eight years his senior) had sent books from Paris. Madison asked for "whatever may throw light on the general constitution and *droit public* of the several confederacies which have existed." The books arrived not by ones and twos but by the hundred: thirty-seven volumes of the new *Encyclopédie Méthodique*, books on political theory and the law of nations, histories, works by Burlamaqui, Voltaire, Diderot, Mably, Necker, d'Albon. There were biographies and memoirs, histories in sets of eleven volumes and such timely productions as Mirabeau on *The Order of the Cincinnati*. In return Madison sent grafts of American trees for Jefferson to show in France, pecan nuts, pippin apples, cranberries, though he failed in shipping the opossums Jefferson asked for, and the "pair of Virginia redbirds." Madison threw himself into a study of confederacies ancient and modern, wrote out a long essay comparing governments, with each analysis followed by a section of his own, entitled "Vices of the Political System of the United States." "Let the national government be armed with a positive and complete authority in all cases where uniform measures are necessary. Let it have a negative, in all cases whatsoever, on the legislative acts of the states, as the King of Great Britain heretofore had. Let this national supremacy be extended also to the judiciary department."

Small wonder that James Madison, in his methodical way, was to be the most formidable adversary the Virginia anti-Constitutionalists would encounter, especially the inflammable Patrick Henry. Madison knew the politics of his state as Hamilton knew them in New York, knew also that the actual writing of a constitution was only one step in a long and hazardous process. Madison understood the meaning and procedure of that Revolutionary discovery, the constituent convention. Already he had set down his ideas in letters to his friends. First, the states must appoint delegates. Then the convention must reach agreement and sign a document. Thirdly, the document would be submitted to Congress. If Congress approved, the states would be invited to call their separate ratification conventions, which meant that technically, the Philadelphia Convention sat in a position merely advisory.

Yet should it fail, what hope was there of calling another? In April, a full month before the Convention met, Madison had told a Virginia colleague that the nearer the crisis approached, the more he trembled for the issue. "The necessity," he wrote, "of gaining the concurrence of the Convention in some system that will answer the purpose, the subsequent approbation of Congress, and the final sanction of the states, presents a series of chances which would inspire despair in any case where the alternative was less formidable."

It was like Madison to declare that the situation was too serious for despair. It was like Washington, too, of whom the British historian Trevelyan was to write that he "had learned the inmost secret of the brave, who train themselves to contemplate in mind the worst that can happen and in thought resign themselves — but in action resign themselves never." At fifty-five, Washington was almost a generation older than Madison. Yet the two had known each other for years; Madison had been in the Virginia government since '76. It is hard to say which man was the more serious by nature. Reading Madison's long letters on politics, with their cool forceful arguments, or Washington's with their stately rhythm, one senses beneath the elaborate paragraphs a very fury of concern for the country. And one takes comfort in this solemnity. One rejoices that these men felt no embarrassment at being persistently, at times awkwardly serious, according to their natures.

# II

## The delegates and the State House.
## Washington and Madison.

We are, I think, in the right road of improvement, for
we are making experiments.
BENJAMIN FRANKLIN, *1786*

GEORGE WASHINGTON arrived in Philadelphia on May thirteenth, a Sunday; the Convention was scheduled for the following day. Bells chimed for the General, artillery boomed. He was escorted from Gray's Ferry on the Schuylkill by the City Troop, smart in their white breeches, high-topped boots and round black hats bound with silver. The General's first move was to call on Dr. Franklin, who lived just off Market Street above Third. The old man had laid in a cask of porter against the occasion. As president of Pennsylvania and one of the world's most celebrated savants, it was the Doctor's part to entertain the delegates. His new dining room, he wrote his sister, could seat twenty-four. Only two years ago, Franklin had come home, after nearly nine years abroad. Even before that he had traveled back and forth to London, as negotiator for Pennsylvania's interests in England, and during the Stamp Act troubles as agent for various of the colonies. After Independence he had been sent to France by Congress to try for an alliance. Nearly seventy at the time, Franklin had told Congress he was "only a fag end," and they could "take him for what they pleased." Before he sailed he lent his impoverished government four thousand pounds from his own purse. Paris adored him, with his simple clothes, his famous fur cap and unpowdered gray hair. Franklin was no Quaker but neither was he at pains to deny it; he knew the romantic French admiration for *les Quakeurs de Philadelphie.*

John Adams, who was at Paris with him, wrote that Franklin's reputation was "more universal than that of Leibnitz or Newton, Frederick or Voltaire, and his character more beloved and esteemed than any or all of them." The Convention did not take kindly to all of Franklin's notions of how a government should be run. His preference for a single-chambered legislature like Pennsylvania's was too democratic by half; on the other hand his notion that our highest officers should serve without salary smacked of England and the aristocratic tradition. The truth was that Franklin's character had always been puzzling. America was proud of the Doctor, proud that he had "tamed the lightning" and that he was everywhere received as a citizen of the world. Yet a citizen of the world is inevitably suspect at home. Sam Adams never rid himself of the belief that Franklin was a Tory at heart, and to certain circles in Boston and Philadelphia, no man could be so much at home in Europe and remain pure in his private morals.

Actually, Franklin's letters show him bitter against the Tories. He had suffered greatly when in 1776 his natural son, William, became an avowed loyalist. "Nothing," he wrote later, "has ever hurt me so much." Benjamin Franklin was inflexibly republican in principle; his faith in the people never wavered. "God grant," he wrote an English friend, "that not only the love of liberty but a thorough knowledge of the rights of man may pervade all the nations of the earth, so that a philosopher may set his foot anywhere on its surface and say, 'This is my country.' "

Whatever the Federal Convention thought of Franklin, few political assemblies have had at hand so prestigious and disarming a philosopher.

On Monday, May fourteenth — opening day — only Pennsylvania and Virginia were represented in the State House. That week it rained, the roads were deep in mud. Of Georgia's four delegates, two came over from Congress in New York; the other two had eight hundred miles to travel. It was the twenty-fifth of May before a quorum of seven states was obtained. Meanwhile the Virginians met every morning by themselves, and in the afternoons at three — dinnertime — joined the Pennsylvanians, "to grow into some acquaintance with each other." It was at these early meetings that the plan of the Convention was plotted; Virginia wrote out the fifteen Resolves which were to be the core and foundation of the United States Constitution.

Virginia's delegation was brilliant, socially as well as politically; the Old Dominion had a right to be proud of her showing. She had been the first state to appoint delegates, and she had sent seven. The Convention Journal listed them as two Excellencies (Washington and Governor Randolph), one Honorable (Judge Blair), and four Esquires (Madison, Mason, Wythe and James McClurg). Patrick Henry was conspicuous by his absence. Named to the Convention, he refused, saying he "smelt a rat." Fifty-one years old, a member of his local legislature, Henry was still a powerful factor in state politics. For all his celebrated rhetoric ("I am not a Virginian but an American"), he was the most Virginian of them all. At the moment, state politics with him were paramount. Madison said outright that Henry had stayed home to look after Virginia's interests along the Mississippi — a matter of life and death to the back settlements, with Spain in control of New Orleans. Samuel Adams too remained in Boston. He had not been named to the Convention; he was suspicious, he said, "of a general revision of the Confederation." Though he came round in the end, Sam Adams was to oppose the new Constitution vigorously. "I stumble at the threshold," he wrote. "I meet with a National Government instead of a Federal Union of sovereign States."

Patrick Henry, Sam Adams — the old firebrands of '76 were missing. The Violent Men, they had been called, skillful and dedicated in revolution and the intrigues of revolution, but lacking the qualities to erect a government. Better hands at pulling down than building, as John Adams had said. Nor was Tom Paine upon the scene. He had gone to Europe to promote his newly invented iron bridge, for which he had failed to find backers in America. To choose the delegates had not indeed been easy. "For God's sake be careful who are the men," Rufus King had admonished Gerry in Massachusetts. "Let the appointment be numerous, and if possible let the men have a good knowledge of the several states, and of the good and bad qualities of the confederation."

Virginia sent the biggest delegation next to Pennsylvania, which had eight members. No limit in numbers had been set. The tiny state of Delaware sent five deputies and so did New Jersey. Massachusetts sent only four. In population the largest states were Virginia, Pennsylvania, Massachusetts, in the order named. After them came North Carolina, New York and Maryland.

As delegates drifted into Philadelphia, local newspapers announced their arrival, pleased that the Convention was meeting in the Pennsylvania State House instead of in New York's City Hall, where Congress sat. Newspapers, plainly proud of the social and political distinction of the representatives, used an even more elaborate social classification than had the Secretary of the Convention: first, Excellency, for governors of states, then Honorable, for justices and chancellors, then honorable with a small *h* for Congressmen, and ending up with a list of "the following respectable characters." The traditions of the mother country were not easily shed.

On the fourth day of the Convention, a Thursday, the *Pennsylvania Packet* burst into poetry — a flowery ode of fifteen stanzas with six lines to a stanza, entitled "On the Meeting of the Grand Convention at Philadelphia." That the lines made little sense was beside the point. This was a greeting, this was goodwill and glory and no doubt the delegates appreciated it.

> Faction shall cease [the poem ended], Industry smile
> Nor next-door neighbors each revile,
> But friendly hands combine:
> The powerful league will all unite,
> Destroy invidious smiles and spite,
> As harmony doth join.

It happened that the Presbyterians were also holding a convention in Philadelphia, and more importantly the Society of the Cincinnati, composed of officers who had served in the Revolutionary War. The *Pennsylvania Packet* announced them exultantly: "Perhaps this city affords the most striking picture that has been exhibited for ages. Here, at the same moment, the collective wisdom of the continent deliberates upon the extensive politics of the confederate empire, a religious convention clears and distributes the stream of religion throughout the American world, and those veterans whose valour accomplished a mighty revolution, are once more assembled to recognize their fellowship in arms, and to communicate to their distressed brethren the blessings of peace."

Actually these valorous veterans were proving an embarrassment to General Washington. Any veterans' organization, then as now, is a potential political threat. Moreover, there had always been opposition to the Cincinnati. These gentlemen, "panting for nobility and with the eagle dangling at their breast," could well become the nucleus of an American aristocracy or of a Cromwellian military government. And Washington was president of the Cincinnati! Early in 1787, the General at Mount Vernon had told his friends that the accident of the Society's meeting at the same time as the Convention would be serious and sufficient reason for his staying away. It had required the combined efforts of Madison, Hamilton, Edmund Randolph and Washington's especial friend General Henry Knox to get the General to Philadelphia at all; he feared that as president of the Cincinnati his presence would inconvenience the Convention.

With the Convention under way, however, the public seemed disposed to overlook this particular threat, though the name of the Cincinnati came up more than once in Convention. Debating the method of electing a chief magistrate for the nation, Elbridge Gerry of Massachusetts feared "the Cincinnati would in fact elect the chief magistrate in every instance, if the election be referred to the people." The people's ignorance, he said, "would put it into the power of some one set of men dispersed throughout the Union and acting in concert." Gerry, who entertained no great respect for the multitude — he would have called it the *mobility* — declared he "could not be blind to the danger and impropriety of throwing such a power into their hands."

Washington, always slow to make up his mind, had been dogged by misfortune that winter of '87. In January his favorite brother died, John Augustine, companion of his youth — "by a fit of gout in the head, my beloved brother," says the General's diary. His letters were troubled, it was plain he had little wish to risk his reputation in a movement that might fail. In March, Washington was attacked by rheumatism so severe he could scarcely move in bed, or, wrote Madison, raise his hand to his head. But he recovered, made his journey by carriage, and on his arrival at Philadelphia was at once seized upon by the ladies of the city and invited out. His diary records drinking tea "in a very large circle of ladies," or tea "at Mrs. Bingham's in great splendor." Mrs. Bingham was young, pretty and vivacious. She had lived abroad and liked to entertain lavishly; she had pretensions to a salon. Philadelphia was the first city of America, with about forty-three thousand inhabitants; its growth had been phenomenal. The city moreover was looked on as urbane, cultured. Newspapers made much, that May, of poetry readings at the College Hall by a widowed lady, a Mrs. O'Connell. The "innocence and rationality" of her performance were applauded, as also the personnel of the audiences, comprising "gentlemen of the three learned professions and ladies of the most elevated rank and fortune." Washington went, and noted merely that the lady's performance was "tolerable."

During the entire summer the General stayed with Robert Morris as his guest. Dining there one evening in what Washington called "a large company," he was witness to an embarrassing incident. A man arrived at the door with news that Morris's bills had been protested in London. Considering that Morris, a member of the Federal Convention, was known as the richest man in Philadelphia, and that from 1781 to '85 he had acted as superintendent of finance for all thirteen states, the incident seemed more than "a little mal-apropos," as Washington said in his diary. And it proved indicative of what was to come. Robert Morris was, of course, a notoriously controversial figure. During the war and later it was said he had accomplished marvels in keeping the government solvent. But he had been violently abused in the press, his business methods publicly investigated, forcing him to resign his office. Morris's rise had been spectacular, his fall would be no less so. He was to spend three years in the Prune Street debtors' prison, ruined, like many another businessman, by speculation in the Western territories, unable to sell his lands or to pay the taxes on them.

This, however, lay in the future. That spring of '87, when Washington was his guest, Robert Morris and his family lived splendidly. They had an icehouse and a hothouse and stable room for twelve horses. Moreover, Morris had bought as his summer residence the Shippen mansion on the wooded banks high above the Schuylkill. A French visitor declared that Morris's luxury was not to be outdone "by any commercial voluptuary of London." Robert Morris was a big, good-humored man, direct and forceful in conversation, though in the Federal Convention he spoke seldom; a hard worker, with a quick, sympathetic warmth of manner. Born in England, he had come to America as a youth and had been in business at sixteen. Washington had always liked and respected Morris and would one day offer him the position of Secretary of the Treasury.

General Washington, watchful of his political fences and his public character, did not stop with dining at the houses of his friends. He reviewed the City Troop, attended high mass at St. Mary's on Fourth Street — "the Romish church," he called it — and dined with the Sons of Saint Patrick as well as the Cincinnati. (A contemporary foreigner asked why it was that while French and German immigrants were always described as French and German, Irishmen became "Americans" overnight.)

With all this entertaining of delegates and geniality in tavern and parlor, it must have been difficult to maintain the rule of secrecy. Delegates were questioned on all sides; one meets it in their letters. Pierce of Georgia was apt to be talkative, especially when he went over to the meetings of Congress in New York. As for old Dr. Franklin, it seemed impossible to keep him quiet; it is said a discreet member attended the Doctor's convivial dinners, heading off the conversation when Franklin in one of his anecdotes threatened to reveal secrets of the Convention.

There was criticism of the secrecy rule; Jefferson did not like it when he heard. Yet it is difficult to see how a Constitution could have evolved had the Convention been open to abuse and suggestion from the public. Sentries were placed at the State House doors; members could not copy the daily journal without permission. Secrecy in legislative assemblies was no new thing. All the Revolutionary colonial assemblies were secret; the first Continental

Congress had been so of necessity, and Congressional debates still were not reported. American politicians knew that for centuries unauthorized vistors had not been allowed in the British House of Commons.

The State House was cool and the hallway dark after the baking summer streets — cool certainly at ten in the morning when delegates entered. On the right one saw through arches the chamber where the state supreme court held its sessions. Across the hall was the east room where the Federal Convention met. Here the Continental Congress had been used to sit and here the Declaration of Independence was signed. The Pennsylvania legislature looked on this room as theirs. They had lately risen, to meet again in September; their actions were regarded locally with an immediate interest scarcely equaled by the doings of the Federal Convention and Congress combined. Along Chestnut Street the City Commissioner had strewn gravel to deaden the sound of wheels and horses passing.

The east chamber was handsome and inviting, designed as if for a gentleman's town house, but large, forty feet by forty with a plaster ceiling twenty feet high and no supporting pillars to break the floor space. A wooden bar had been placed across the room from north to south, with a gate for members, as in the House of Commons. Wide, lofty windows ranged on two sides. Slatted blinds kept out the summer sun but the room was light even in winter. The east wall was paneled and painted gray; on a bright morning the panels showed a bluish tinge. Against this wall the presiding officer's chair (visitors called it the throne) was high-backed; behind it rose a tall smooth panel surmounted by a cockleshell, carved in deep relief. Two wide fireplaces were faced in marble; to the right a door led to a committee room lined with bookcases and known as the library.

Delegates sat at tables covered in green baize — sat and sweated, once the summer sun was up. By noon the air was lifeless, with windows shut for privacy, or intolerable with flies when they were open. New Englandmen — "the Eastern gentlemen" — suffered in their woolen suits. Only the Southerners were suitably dressed in light camlet coats and breeches. The tables were wide, three or four members sat together. Attendance was uncertain; the last delegate, John Francis Mercer of Maryland, did not arrive till August sixth. Members disappeared toward home and business, or left in disapproval of the direction things were taking. So that in spite of fifty-five enrollments, no more than eleven states were represented at any one time and scarcely more than thirty delegates at any given meeting. On most mornings the room resembled a large committee gathering.

As each man was introduced, he presented the credentials from his state legislature. It is revealing to read these credentials; the states differed widely in their approach. Most of the documents were brief, cast in the ordinary form of a piece of enacted legislation, stating in the now familiar phrase that Congress had resolved a convention be held, "for the sole and express purpose of revising the Articles of the Confederation," and going on to name their deputies. New York went a bit further in speaking of possible "alterations and provisions adequate to the exigencies of government and the preservation of the Union." Massachusetts added a little flourish in the date at the end: "the ninth day of April A.D. 1787, in the Eleventh Year of the Independence of the United States of America."

Several of the states, however, decided to have their say and wrote out justificatory preambles, after the immemorial custom of the English Parliament in creating important laws. "*Whereas,*" wrote New Hampshire, "it was not possible in the infant state of our Republic to devise a system which in the course of time and experience, would not manifest imperfections that it would be necessary to reform . . . And Whereas Congress hath, by repeated and most urgent representations, endeavored to awaken this, and other States of the Union, to a sense of the truly critical and alarming situation in which they may inevitably be involved, unless timely measures be taken to enlarge the powers of Congress . . . And Whereas this State hath ever been desirous to act upon the liberal system of the general good of the United States, without circumscribing its views, to the narrow and selfish objects of partial convenience; and hath been at all times ready to make every concession to the safety and happiness of the whole. . . . BE IT THEREFORE ENACTED," etc. New Hampshire had a right to be a bit expansive; she had been the first colony to compose, in 1775, her own state constitution.

Virginia's preamble was even more explicit, referring to the Annapolis Convention and "the necessity of extending the revision of the federal System to all its defects." Virginia stressed a pertinent fact of which no other state took cognizance — answering insistent and quite reasonable queries as to why Congress itself could not revise the Confederation, thus doing away with the expense and trouble of a special convention. Because, said Virginia, Congress would be too much interrupted by their ordinary daily business; moreover they would lack the valuable counsels of certain individuals who were not congressmen. The statement was much to the point — the very core and *raison d'être* of a constituent convention, though Virginia might have added (as did Lord Bryce a century later) the beneficent absence of jobbers and office-seekers, and the prospect of short duration, which permitted the attendance of men of large interests.

Virginia's credentials continued on a rising note — hortatory, with an undercurrent of indignation that was reminiscent of the old "instructions" of Revolutionary times, sent by towns or colonial assemblies with their delegates. "The Crisis is arrived," said Virginia, "at which the good People of America are to decide the solemn question whether they will by just and magnanimous Efforts reap the just fruits of that Independence which they have so gloriously acquired and of that Union which they have cemented with so much of their common Blood, or whether by giving way to unmanly Jealousies and Prejudices or to partial and transitory Interests they will . . . furnish our Enemies with cause to triumph."

Not a man in the Convention but knew the humiliations of our position with respect to Europe, knew that Spain and England looked on the disorganized infant republic with a hungry eye, calculating their own interests in Louisiana, Florida, the Ohio country and the long, vital trade route of the Mississippi River. The British still occupied posts south of the Canadian border, to the great disadvantage of the American fur traders and frontier settlers. These complained to Congress about the warlike designs of the Indians and their British guardians. In New Orleans and Natchez, Spain throttled southern outlets to the sea and to European commerce, bribed politicians in the back country to her purpose, used the Indians — Creeks, Choctaws, Chickasaws — to harass the border from Nashville to southern Georgia. Every delegate knew moreover that neither England nor Spain believed the states could achieve an effectual union. Britain met such plans with indifference or contempt. In London, John Adams had recently been told that His Majesty's government could negotiate only with the thirteen separate states, the Confederacy having proved unreliable. "It will not be an easy matter," wrote Lord Sheffield, "to bring the American States to act as a nation. They are not to be feared as such by us."

Small wonder Virginia believed that disunion would furnish our enemies with cause to triumph. Moreover, having herself abandoned all claim and title to an immense region north of the Ohio, Virginia had reason for urging other states to make concessions — in order, said her credentials, to secure "the great objects for which that government was instituted," rendering the United States "as happy in peace as they have been glorious in war."

It was James Madison who wrote the Virginia Act approving a Federal Convention: "The preparation of the document fell on me," he said later. Somehow the bill does not sound like the product of Madison's cool pen. There is fire in it, and the pride of Virginia's consciousness of her position as a leader among the states. Was she not the Ancient Dominion, America's first colony, by whose early charter the boundaries ran "from Sea to Sea, West and Northwest"? If Virginia could "make concessions" — so the document implied — others would follow. As against such leadership, what price the notions and ambitions of a minuscule state of Delaware, or of Georgia with her unpeopled swamps? What price, indeed, the habitual arrogance of that cocksure and vigorous commonwealth of Massachusetts Bay?

Once the delegates had presented their credentials and settled into living quarters at Philadelphia, an unfortunate practical item threatened to cut down their style considerably. City life was expensive and the Convention seemed likely to drag out; it might be harvest time before members got home to their estates, their farms, their law practices or tobacco businesses. When his wife's illness forced George Wythe to leave the Convention and return to Virginia, he left fifty pounds of treasury funds with the delegates, "to be distributed to such of his colleagues as should require it." Delegations from distant states ran in debt to their landladies; the North Carolina deputies sent an official plea to Governor Caswell at Kinston: "Your Excellency is sufficiently informed that the Money of our State is subject to considerable Decrement when reduced to Current Coin . . . we submit to your consideration the Propriety of furnishing us with an additional Draught for two months' services."

During an especially trying week of disagreement, Franklin proposed that a chaplain be invited to open the Convention every morning with prayers. Williamson of North Carolina replied bluntly that the Convention had no money to pay a chaplain. It is hard to remember how slim the state budgets were in 1787, and the shifting finances of the group of brilliant men who led the states. Washington was to leave property worth $530,000. Elbridge Gerry held public securities to the amount of $50,000; Robert Morris's land speculations, his continental securities and stock transactions involved millions. But in 1787 Morris was already on the road to bankruptcy; Washington two years hence would have to borrow money to go to New York and assume the Presidency. George Mason, for all his great plantation, came to the Convention by virtue of sixty pounds lent him by Edmund Randolph. Young Charles Pinckney, with an income of $5000, was perhaps the most secure financially of his Convention colleagues. The grandest of them boasted more land than money.*

On the twenty-fifth of May, when a quorum was obtained, Washington was unanimously elected president of the Convention and escorted to the chair. From his desk on the raised dais he made a little speech of acceptance, depreciating his ability to give

---

* These figures are taken from Forrest McDonald's *We the People* (Chicago, 1958). McDonald got them from family papers, loan offices, land books, the census of 1790, etc. Conversion from pounds to dollars is dubious, considering the fluctuation of the dollar. Nonetheless the figures afford some basis for comparison. Incidentally, it was the genial habit of Southern gentlemen to borrow money frequently from their friends.

satisfaction in a scene so novel. "When seated," wrote a member, "he declared that as he never had been in such a situation he felt himself embarrassed, that he hoped his errors, as they would be unintentional, would be excused. He lamented his want of qualifications."

There is something touching in the way Washington always lamented his want of qualifications and called on God to help, whether it was a nomination as Commander in Chief of the army, as president of the Federal Convention or as President of the United States. One feels he meant it, this was not false modesty. To his colleagues it must have been reassuring. Washington was everywhere known as "the greatest character in America" — a man of prestige, with a landed estate and a magnificent physical appearance. An English traveler, impressed, wrote a detailed account, beginning with the General's commanding height and going on to say that "his chest is full and his limbs, though rather slender, well shaped and muscular. His head is small . . . his eyes are of a light grey color . . . and, in proportion to the length of his face, his nose is long. Mr. Stewart, the eminent portrait painter, told me there are features in his face totally different from those he had observed in that of any human being. The sockets of the eyes, for instance, are larger than what he ever met with before, and the upper part of the nose broader. All his features . . . were indicative of the strongest passions, and had he been born in the forest . . . he would have been the fiercest man among the savage tribes."

A person of such passions had need of control. "This Vesuvius of a man," the biographer Beveridge has called him. Washington's self-discipline is legendary, as is his anger when aroused. Officers who served under him in the war testified they had never seen him smile, that his countenance held something austere and his manners were uncommonly reserved. Certainly, Washington was not a ready talker. "He speaks with great diffidence," wrote a foreign observer, "and sometimes hesitates for a word. . . . His language is manly and expressive."

It is odd that such a man should come down in history marked with a slight taint of the Sunday school; perhaps Parson Weems will never be lived down. Yet in spite of the General's almost glacial reserve and dignity, one sensed that he would never be overbearing, power would not turn his head. One knew it by the troubled lines in his brow, a quality of melancholy when his face was in repose.

Through four months, Washington was to sit silent in the Convention, even when they went into Committee of the Whole and he came down from the chair. He voted with the Virginians; before the Convention met he had made clear that his sympathies lay with a national government. Yet only on the last day, September seventeenth, did Washington rise to take part in the debates. Silence in public debates was, it seems, natural to him. Jefferson, who served with Washington in the Virginia legislature and with Dr. Franklin in Congress, testified afterward that he "never heard either of them speak ten minutes at a time, nor to any but the main point which was to decide the question. They laid their shoulders to the great points, knowing that the little ones would follow of themselves."

Washington showed himself firm, courteous, inflexible. When he approved a measure, delegates reported that his face showed it. Yet it was hard to tell what the General was thinking and impossible to inquire. In his silence lay his strength. His presence kept the Federal Convention together, kept it going, just as his presence had kept a straggling, ill-conditioned army together throughout the terrible years of war.

In the front row near the desk, James Madison sat bowed over his tablet, writing steadily. His eyes were blue, his face ruddy; he did not have the scholar's pallor. His figure was well-knit and muscular and he carried his clothes with style. Though he usually wore black, he has also been described as handsomely dressed in blue and buff, with ruffles at breast and wrist. Already he was growing bald and brushed his hair down to hide it; he wore a queue and powder. He walked with the quick bouncing step that sometimes characterizes men of remarkable energy.

As a reporter Madison was indefatigable, his notes comprehensive, set down without comment or aside. One marvels that he was able at the same time to take so large a part in the debates. It is true that in old age Madison made some emendations in the record to accord with various disparate notes which later came to light; he has been severely criticized for it. Other members took notes at the Convention: Hamilton, Yates and Lansing of New York, McHenry of Maryland, Paterson of New Jersey, Rufus King of Massachusetts, William Pierce of Georgia, George Mason of Virginia. But most of these memoranda were brief, incomplete; had it not been for Madison we should possess very scanty records of the Convention. His labors, he said later, nearly killed him. "I chose a seat," he afterward wrote, "in front of the presiding member, with the other members on my right and left hand. In this favorable position for hearing all that passed, I noted in terms legible and in abbreviations and marks intelligible to myself what was read from the Chair or spoken by the members; and losing not a moment unnecessarily between the adjournment and reassembling of the Convention I was enabled to write out my daily notes during the session or within a few finishing days after its close in the extent and form preserved in my own hand on my files . . . I was not absent a single day, nor more than a casual fraction of an hour in any day, so that I could not have lost a single speech, unless a very short one."

It was, actually, a tour de force, not to be published — and scarcely seen — until thirty years after the Convention. "Do you know," wrote Jefferson to John Adams from Monticello in 1815, "that there exists in manuscript the ablest work of this kind ever yet executed, of the debates of the constitutional convention of Philadelphia . . . ? The whole of everything said and done there was taken down by Mr. Madison, with a labor and exactness beyond comprehension."

Always, the notes refer to himself as "Mr. M," and Madison set down everything, even remarks uncomplimentary to Mr. M. Actually, Major Jackson of South Carolina had been engaged as official secretary, elected by ballot over William Temple Franklin, the Doctor's grandson. Above his military uniform Major Jackson's portrait shows a face bland yet puzzled, wearing the slight frown of the talkative man who finds it hard to keep up with his clever acquaintances. Jackson had asked Washington to recommend him for the job and he was to receive $866.60 for his pains.

His bare official outline tells us little. Madison seems simply to have ignored him.

When the Convention was in full swing, Francis Hopkinson of Philadelphia — signer of the Declaration, pamphleteer, musician, designer of the American flag — wrote to Jefferson outlining some of the troubles into which the states had fallen, and expressing his feelings about the secret transactions which were taking place within the State House walls. Matters were more serious even than Hopkinson reported. Martial law had been declared in Georgia. Savannah was fortified against the Creek Indians, supposed to be incited by Spain. There was a rumor that a certain group in the New York legislature — "the seditious party" — had "opened communications with the Viceroy of Canada." No doubt, said Hopkinson, Jefferson had read in the papers about the insurgents in Massachusetts. Rhode Island at present was "governed by miscreants . . . A serious storm seems to be brewing in the South West about the navigation of the Mississippi."

Hopkinson went on to tell of the Convention. "From all the states," he wrote, "except Rhode Island, delegates are now setting in this city. George Washington president. Their business is to revise the Confederation, and propose amendments. It will be very difficult to frame such a system of Union and government for America as shall suit all opinions and reconcile clashing interests. Their deliberations are kept inviolably secret, so that they set without censure or remark, but no sooner will the chicken be hatch'd but every one will be for plucking a feather."

# III

## In Convention. Randolph introduces the Virginia Plan.

> We are in a peculiar situation. We are neither the
> same nation nor different nations.
>
> ELBRIDGE GERRY, *in Convention*

"THE *State of Georgia, by the grace of God, free, Sovereign and Independent*" . . . On Friday morning, May twenty-fifth, as soon as Washington had finished his little speech of acceptance from the chair, Major Jackson rose to read aloud the credentials — so carefully worked over at home — of the nine states present. It was noticeable that the smallest states spoke out with the loudest voice. Georgia, referred to as "small and trifling" because of her sparse population, announced herself to the Convention with a proud resounding orchestration which left little doubt of her position . . . "*Sovereign and Independent.*"

Certain members of the Convention were already heartily sick of the word sovereign. The monster, sovereignty, Washington had called it. The General knew well from what sanction Georgia derived the word. "*Each state,*" the Articles of Confederation had said, "*retains its sovereignty, freedom and independence.*" Without such a clause the Confederacy never would have been achieved. Back in '77 the larger states had threatened to leave the union if their weight in Congress were not equal in votes to "the numbers of people they had added to the Confederacy, while the smaller ones declared against a union if they did not retain an equal vote for the protection of their rights." Men who had sat through those long debates remembered it well. Was this Convention then to hammer it all out once more, with the same old arguments? Before the Declaration of Independence, no colony had pretensions to independent sovereignty, nor were the states mentioned by name in the body of that document. Yet from the moment peace had been signed, states flaunted their sovereignty as an excuse to do as they pleased. "Thirteen sovereignties," Washington had written, "pulling against each other, and all tugging at the foederal head, will soon bring ruin on the whole."

A General of the Army is not expected to possess so direct and merciless a political eye. Already on May 25, 1787, it looked as if the Federal Convention were to have its fill of sovereignty. The reading aloud of these state credentials was a matter for strict attention; here were signs portent of which way the states were leaning. Madison and Hamilton thought they already knew. Madison had canvassed exhaustively; both men were personally acquainted with many delegates, some of whom had themselves drafted these documents and no doubt would stand by what they had written. Delaware, for instance, whose credentials forbade her deputies to change Article V of the Confederation, giving to each state one vote in Congress and one only. Proportional representation was no part of Delaware's scheme. Should the old rule be altered to voting by population, the small states would be blanketed out. Delaware had come prepared to oppose it.

Small states against large, the planting interests of the South against the mercantile money of the North, the regulation of the Western Territory — these were immediate problems. Not every delegate brought to Philadelphia a comprehension of how thirteen independent states could share a government of tripartite powers: legislative, judicial, executive. James Wilson of Philadelphia understood it and so did Wythe of Virginia. Wilson and Wythe were scholars like Madison. Not only had they acted a part in government but they had thought, read, pondered on the subject; they knew the theory behind the practice. "I am both a citizen of Pennsylvania and of the United States," Wilson told the Convention.

Time would pass before members realized how far the plans of such men as Madison and Hamilton reached, and what the Constitution promised to be. It would be misleading to name thus early the Constitution's "enemies," or to set down this name or that as "against" the Constitution. Five delegates in the end would refuse to sign — Elbridge Gerry of Massachusetts, Yates and Lansing of New York, George Mason and Edmund Randolph of Virginia — all men of decided views and each with a different reason for his action. More vociferous than any of these would be Luther Martin of Maryland, who, though out of town on private business at the moment of signing, later declared that had he been present he would have given the document his "solemn negative," even had he "stood single and alone."

Martin did not arrive at the Convention until nearly a month after it met; for the moment, members were spared his boisterous and interminable harangues. On this first Saturday of a quorum the Convention faced a twofold problem: the theoretic question of what kind of government best suited America — a democracy, a limited monarchy, a republic? — and the practical problem of creating such a government with all its untried component parts. It was good to review, by way of the state credentials, the aims of the Convention as declared by twelve legislatures. Major Jackson's voice droned on:

*"To take into consideration the state of the union . . . as to trade and other important objects . . . to render the Foederal Government entirely adequate to the actual situation . . ."* When Jackson ceased there was time only to name a committee to prepare standing rules and orders, and to appoint a doorkeeper and messenger. The meeting adjourned for the weekend.

On Monday, Dr. Franklin appeared. Stormy weather had hitherto kept him away. The Doctor suffered greatly from gout and stone; he came to the State House in a sedan chair which he had brought from Paris, as the only mode of transportation that did not jostle him painfully. The first such vehicle in Phildaelphia, the Doctor's chair was one of the city's sights. There were glass windows on both sides. The poles, ten or twelve feet long, were pliant, allowing the chair to give a little with the bearers' footsteps — vibrate gently, a contemporary said. Four husky prisoners from the Walnut Street jail bore the cheerful cargo, measuring their pace as smoothly as they could. Up five steps to the State House went the little procession and into the east room, where the bearers set down their burden beside the bar. The Doctor was helped out and made his way through the gate to his nearby armchair at the Pennsylvania delegates' table. The prisoners, having placed the sedan close by the west wall, took their leave until the afternoon.

On that same Monday, May twenty-eighth, the last of Pennsylvania's eight delegates arrived — Jared Ingersoll, who was to remain silent during the entire four months, an extraordinary feat for a man who was described as "the ablest jury lawyer in Philadelphia." The fourth of Delaware's five members came in also: Gunning Bedford, Jr., tall, sociable, very fat, known as an impetuous speaker who did not hesitate to make trouble if trouble was in order. Bedford was attorney general of his state. He had been named to the Annapolis Convention but neglected to go, and he came to Philadelphia as a champion of the small states, prepared to accept any workable system which gave these states their due — but defiant, suspicious of Pennsylvania.

Two more Massachusetts delegates appeared on Monday: Nathaniel Gorham and Caleb Strong. Gorham (Madison usually spelled it Ghorum) was one of the old patriots, a Boston merchant, indifferently educated but likable. "Nothing fashionable or elegant in his style," a member noted. Gorham had just stepped down from being president of Congress and wished to see that body strengthened by a new government. Caleb Strong was the son of a tanner and had risen through the law; he had helped to draft the Massachusetts Constitution. His manners were easy, plain.

Of the four Massachusetts delegates, Rufus King was the most impressive, though only in his thirty-third year. A lawyer, born in Maine, he had sat in the Massachusetts legislature and in Congress; it was he who in 1787 had moved the resolution (originally Jefferson's) providing there should be "neither slavery nor involuntary servitude" in the Northwest Territory. He had, wrote contemporaries, "an handsome face, with a strong expressive eye and a sweet high-toned voice," also "the appearance of one who was a gentleman by nature and who had well improved her gifts."

Rufus King could, however, be rude when he chose, and abrupt; he had a talent for exposing the weak places in an opponent's argument.

The Rules Committee had done its work over the weekend; George Wythe of Virginia rose with his report. At sixty, Wythe looked like a sinewy old eagle. A long sharp nose nearly met a jutting chin, the head went into a point at the top. Wythe's eye was keen, his forehead deeply lined. Chancellor Wythe, he was called, because of his position in the Virginia courts. In Williamsburg his neighbors referred to him as "the Just" and said he was another Aristides. Wythe had signed the Declaration of Independence and helped to design the state seal of Virginia with its defiant motto, SIC SEMPER TYRANNIS. He was a notable classical scholar and served as first professor of law at the College of William and Mary. Although he left the Convention early, Wythe's influence was felt; he supported a strong national government.

The Convention rules were simple and took account of courtesy as well as convenience. It was an age of formal manners; an old Connecticut charter had specified that a voter must be "of quiet and peaceable behavior, and of civil conversation." "Every member," read Wythe, "rising to speak, shall address the President; and whilst he shall be speaking, none shall pass between them, or hold discourse with another, or read a book, pamphlet or paper, printed or manuscript. . . . A member shall not speak oftener than twice, without special leave, upon the same question; and not the second time, before every other, who had been silent, shall have been heard, if he choose to speak upon the subject. . . . When the House shall adjourn, every member shall stand in his place until the President pass him. . . ."

Seven states were to make a quorum, and all questions to be decided "by a greater number of these which shall be fully represented." There was an excellent rule providing for reconsideration of matters that had already been passed on by a majority. Young Spaight of North Carolina suggested it: "The House may not be precluded, by a vote upon any question, from revising the subject matter of it when they see cause." Again and again, in Committee of the Whole, the rule would go into action and a subject already voted upon would next day be reconsidered. Rufus King made this procedure the more effectual by objecting to a rule authorizing members to call for the yeas and nays and have them entered in the book. It would be binding to delegates, he said, and confusing if they later changed their minds. George Mason of Virginia seconded King and the rule was canceled. Madison, however, often included in parentheses the names of voters; it is thus we know of Washington's support of at least five measures.

There is something impressive about these rules. They show determination; the Convention was to be formal and parliamentary and behave as an authorized assembly. Moreover, a group of less experienced men would not have dared to be so simple, or would not have known how to free themselves from small and hampering considerations, leaving room for delegates to differ and change their minds. Reading the rules, one sees here a group of reasonable men, strong enough to yield. One knows what Madison meant when he wrote to Jefferson on June sixth: "The names of the members will satisfy you that the States have been serious in this business."

When Wythe had finished, Gouverneur Morris presented to the chair a letter "from sundry persons of the State of Rhode Island." Signed by thirteen leading merchants in Providence, it deplored the fact that Rhode Island was not represented at Philadelphia, hoped the state would suffer no commercial loss from "Sister States" on that account, and conveyed respect and best wishes for a favorable outcome of the meetings. Quite plainly the letter repudiated the victorious Rhode Island rural legislature which had voted against attending the Convention. "Deeply affected with the evils of the present unhappy times . . ." the letter began.

Nobody recorded what the Convention thought of this politic missive. It was Tuesday morning before Madison wrote in his notes: "Mr. Randolph then opened the main business."

Edmund Randolph, Governor of Virginia, was thirty-three years old, nearly six feet tall and noticeably handsome. He wore his dark hair loose, unpowdered and brushed back from the forehead; his big brown eyes rolled and flashed as he spoke. "The main business" was — in most delegates' minds — to revise the

Confederation. Randolph, however, went far beyond this. In the form of fifteen Resolves he outlined what amounted to an entirely new national government, with a national executive, a national judiciary and a national legislature of two branches: the "first branch" (the representatives) to be elected by the people; the "second branch" (the senators) to be elected by the first branch.

These were the famous Virginia Resolves, or Virginia Plan. The Randolph Plan, it is sometimes called, though Madison's biographers claim that he drafted it; certainly his influence is evident. Much later, Madison himself said the plan was the result of a "consultation among the deputies, the whole number, seven, being present." At any rate the document was hammered out in caucus at the Indian Queen or elsewhere. And on the morning of May twenty-ninth, when the Resolves were read to the Convention, not a man in the room but understood their import and felt they were indeed innovations. There was, however, no immediate expression of shock and very little protest. Members recognized the plan as only suggestive — "a mere sketch," Madison called it later, "in which omitted details were to be supplied, and the general terms and phrases to be reduced to their proper details." Delegates knew also that they must have something upon which to proceed, some agenda to follow. For the rest of summer the Virginia Plan would form the basis of the Convention's procedure — and the basis of the United States Constitution — to be debated clause by clause in Committee of the Whole, with every Resolve reconsidered, reargued, passed or discarded.

Randolph did not try to disguise his position. He candidly confessed, wrote Yates of New York, that his Resolves "were not intended for a federal government — he meant a strong *consolidated* union, in which the idea of states would be nearly annihilated."

Yates exaggerated; Randolph had said nothing about annihilation. He would not have been such a fool, moreover he had no such radical notion. He had started off tactfully enough, with an apology for his youth and inexperience, compared with other members. This task had been imposed on him, he said, because the Convention "had originated from Virginia."

Considering that Edmund Randolph had been, at twenty-three,

a member of the Virginia convention to adopt a state constitution; considering also that he had once been attorney general, had attended the Annapolis Convention and now served as governor of his state, he was an altogether suitable man to propose the Virginia Plan. Randolph was attractive, wellborn; he wore his honors with an easy modesty. Before proposing his Resolves, he outlined the defects of the Confederation, which he declared was not even "paramount to a state constitution, nor would any judge so pronounce it. . . ." "Look," Randolph said, "at the public countenance, from New Hampshire to Georgia! Are we not on the eve of war, which is only prevented by the hopes from this Convention?"

Randolph was three or four hours on his feet. When he had done, a delegate from South Carolina got up: Charles Pinckney, aged twenty-nine. He too, said Pinckney, had reduced his ideas of a new government to a system, which he confessed was grounded on the same principles as the one just proposed. Carefully drawn in articles and sections, Pinckney's plan had been drafted in Charleston without consulting his colleagues, though his ideas were known; he had proposed them in Congress a year ago. Young Pinckney read his document aloud to the Convention. But the hour was late, the paper not discussed. Years afterward, Charles Pinckney was to make extravagant claims concerning his plan and its part in the Federal Convention, managing thereby to earn for himself locally the nickname of Constitution Charlie.

"The house then resolved," wrote Yates of New York, "that they would the next day form themselves into a committee of the whole, to take into consideration *the state of the Union*."

## IV

## Federal versus national. The "two supremes." The city of Philadelphia.

I cannot conceive of a government in which there can exist two supremes.
GOUVERNEUR MORRIS, *in Convention*

EXT morning, Wednesday, May thirtieth, General Washington stepped down from the chair and Nathaniel Gorham of Massachusetts took his place, having been duly chosen by ballot. The Convention was now in Committee of the Whole, at liberty to debate measures and even to vote without binding themselves — without, as it were, pledge or engagement.

The Committee of the Whole House was an ancient device, invented long ago in England to give the Commons freedom of debate under an autocratic ruler. Down came the mace — symbol of royal authority — from the table before the Speaker. As long as the mace remained out of sight, votes were not recorded but counted merely as a test, a trial of opinion, a way of taking the sense of the meeting. Back in the 1590's, Queen Elizabeth's royal councilors had not liked this invention of the Commons. It gave plain men — merchants, lawyers, country squires — a leeway to discuss affairs of state, *grandia regni*, which properly were the concern of noblemen and princes. It was a point of view which died hard. During the American Revolution, Lord George Germain had remarked testily that he "would not have men of a mercantile cast every day collecting themselves together and debating about political matters."

The Convention in Philadelphia had no mace, and "men of a

mercantile cast" led the country. Yet from their experience in colonial assemblies or in their state legislatures, delegates knew well the Committee of the Whole and its uses. On May thirtieth, debate in the Convention opened by Randolph's suggesting an amended version of his first three resolves. Plainly, the Virginia members had been at work out-of-doors. A union of the states "merely federal," said Randolph, would not accomplish the object for which they were met. He therefore proposed "a *national* government, consisting of a supreme legislative, executive and judicial."

Silence followed, complete and ominous. A government of three separate parts was entirely acceptable; six of the new state constitutions specified such separation of powers. But a government *national, supreme?* How were the words to be defined, what powers did they comprehend? The small-state men seemed frozen by the words, stunned. There must have been a shifting of chairs, a restless movement in the room. Chancellor Wythe of Virginia was quick to seize advantage. "From the silence of the House," he said, "I presume that gentlemen are prepared to pass on the resolution?"

It was a shrewd move but it failed. The House was not so prepared! countered Butler of South Carolina. He desired Mr. Randolph to show that a "national" government was necessary to the continuance of the states. . . . But we *are* a nation! said John Dickinson of Delaware. "We are a nation although consisting of parts or states." Elbridge Gerry of Massachusetts expressed himself as wary of this distinction between a federal and a national government. To acknowledge it and to pass Mr. Randolph's resolution would be to destroy the Confederation, which this Convention had no right to do. He proposed therefore that "provision should be made for the establishment of a *federal* legislative, judiciary, and executive."

On these words, *federal* . . . *national* . . . *supreme*, the Convention would stick for days to come. Did gentlemen, it was asked at once, indeed propose to overthrow state governments? No! said Randolph. There was no such intention. Gouverneur Morris rose, attempting to explain the terms. A *federal* government, he said, was a mere compact, resting on the good faith of the parties; a *national* government on the other hand had "a complete and compulsive operation."

Gouverneur Morris has been called the most brilliant man of the Convention. Certainly he was a marathon talker — 173 speeches to Madison's 161. Yet Morris never said anything foolish or tedious. He was a big man physically. "The Tall Boy," they had called him in the Continental Congress; "an eternal speaker and for brass unequalled." His face was genial, fleshy, his eyes shrewd and his expression quizzical. Washington liked him, the two were close friends. Morris had injured his leg driving fast horses; it was said the amputation did not diminish his prowess with the ladies. New Englanders were suspicious of Morris. He was a man of pleasure, they said; it was recalled that at King's College in New York his graduate essays had been on "Wit and Beauty" and on "Love." To John Adams, Morris was a "man of wit and made pretty verses, but of a character *très légère*." Born on the manorial estate of Morrisania in New York, Morris had recently moved to Pennsylvania. He carried an easy air of wealth; actually his finances were in a precarious condition. Desiring a strong central government, he had little faith in the common man or his capacity to govern — a position in which he was by no means alone at the Convention. Yet there was no denying Morris's patriotism and his devotion to a republican government. He was impatient with the states. "This generation will die away," he said, "and give place to a race of Americans."

In the Convention, Morris's tactics were abrupt; first an eloquent, explosive expression of his position and then a cynical waiting while the Convention caught up with him. "When the powers of the national government clash with the states," he said, "only then must the states yield." This in itself was startling . . . What powers? And how implemented? With some heat Morris added that "we had better take a supreme government now than a despot twenty years hence, for come he must." He could not, however, conceive of a government "in which there could exist two supremes."

It was not surprising the Convention found itself confused. What they were attempting was to discover a new kind of federalism, controlled by a supreme power that was directly responsible to the people. Only eleven years ago, they had been subject to King and Council. The colonies had been of three kinds: royal or provincial, as Virginia; proprietary, as Pennsylvania; corporate, as Massachusetts. The Confederation and the state constitutions were a long step ahead, but even so, the Convention found no overall example to follow. "A very large field," the North Carolina delegation reported home, "presents to our view without a single straight or eligible road that has been trodden by the feet of nations." True, there had been federations in the world. Greece had had her city-states and the Convention was to hear much of them. Senators were no new thing nor was government by representation new. But never attempted on so large a scale, with a union comprising three and a half million people, thirteen states, a territory that reached, potentially, across a continent.

The term *federal* in the ensuing years would reverse its meaning. But when Randolph of Virginia declared on May thirtieth that "a union merely federal will not accomplish the objects proposed," he defined the word as the Convention was to use it. A federal government, Madison told the delegates, operates on states, a national government directly on individuals. It was a difficult concept for the Convention, state loyalty having been the American loyalty almost since the beginning. And what was the Confederacy, if not a league of states? James Wilson of Pennsylvania saw the problem at its heart. Was this government, he asked, to be over men or over imaginary beings called states? In 1777, Wilson had asked the same question in Congress, declaring that individuals — not states — were the objects of governmental care. Why should annexing the name of state give ten thousand men rights equal with forty thousand? This, said Wilson, was the effect of magic, not logic.

But magic has quicker appeal than logic, as any politician is aware. Nobody answered Wilson. Young Charles Pinckney suggested it would be advisable to divide the continent into four sections, from which a certain number of persons should be nominated, and from that nomination to appoint a Senate.

This brought the discussion out of theory into the practical consideration of how the national legislature was to be elected: Virginia's Resolves 4 and 5. Should the second house — the Senate — be elected by the state legislatures and the first house by popular vote? And if so, how was the vote to be apportioned? By numbers or by property? In what did the American wealth consist, in people or in land?

Characteristically, the Convention never stayed long upon theory. Its business was not to defend "freedom" or to vindicate a revolution. That had been done long ago, in July of 1776 and later, when colony after colony created its state constitution, flinging out its particular preamble of political and religious freedom. The Convention of 1787 would debate the rights of states, but not the rights of man in general. The records show nothing grandly declaratory or defiant, as in the French constituent assembly of 1789. America had passed that phase; had anyone challenged members, they would have said such declarations were already cemented with their blood. In 1787 the states sat not to justify the term United States but to institute a working government for those United States. One finds no quotations from Rousseau, John Locke, Burlamaqui or the French *philosophes*, and if Montesquieu is invoked it is to defend the practical organization of a tripartite government. When the Federal Convention discussed political power, governmental authority, they discussed it in terms of what was likely to happen to Delaware or Pennsylvania, New Jersey or Georgia.

Most members of the Philadelphia Convention, in short, were old hands, politicians to the bone. That some of them happened also to be men of vision, educated in law and the science of government, did not distract them from the matters impending. There was a minimum of oratory or showing off. Each time a member seemed about to soar into the empyrean of social theory — the eighteenth century called it "reason" — somebody brought him round, and shortly. *"Experience* must be our only guide," said John Dickinson of Delaware. *"Reason* may mislead us."

The practical matter of how the national legislature should be elected was to take up half the summer. Roger Sherman of Connecticut on May thirty-first declared the people "should have as little to do as may be about the government. They want information and are constantly liable to be misled." Elbridge Gerry, man of business affairs and money, agreed. "The evils we experience," he said, "flow from the excess of democracy. The people do not want virtue, but are the dupes of pretended patriots." There is small doubt that Gerry's mind turned as he said it to Captain Shays and his band of debt-ridden farmers, breaking up the meetings of county law courts and demanding "reforms" in the legislature. That the farmers had been badly treated did not enter into Gerry's philosophy. To this Boston merchant a mob was a mob. And were men of this stamp to be permitted authority in government?

Elbridge Gerry, friend of Samuel Adams, was one of the "old patriots"; he had signed the Declaration of Independence. Yet to the members of the Federal Convention the word *democracy* carried another meaning than it does today. Democracy signified anarchy; *demos* was not the people but the mob. When Paterson of New Jersey said "the democratic spirit beats high," it was meant in derogation, not in praise. Again and again we meet these phrases: if aristocracy was "baleful" and "baneful," unchecked democracy was equally to be shunned. Edmund Randolph desired, he said, "to restrain the fury of democracy," and spoke also of "the democratic licentiousness of the State legislatures."

Gerry went on with his speech. "I am still republican," he said. "But I have been taught by experience the danger of the levelling spirit."

Experience, in this connection, again meant Captain Shays. Much ink has been spent by historians in tracing the effect of Shays's Rebellion on the states. Some claim it as a major factor in the calling of the Convention. "Good God!" Washington had written. "Who besides a Tory could have foreseen, or a Briton predicted [these disorders]? . . . I am mortified beyond expression, when I view the clouds that have spread over the brightest morn that ever dawned in any country. . . . What a triumph for our enemies, to verify their predictions! What a triumph for the advocates of despotism, to find that we are incapable of governing ourselves, and that systems founded on the basis of equal liberty, are merely ideal and fallacious. Would to God that wise measures may be taken in time to evert the consequences we have but too much reason to apprehend."

Jefferson, on the other hand, took a lighthearted view of Captain Shays and the insurgents. "I like a little rebellion now and then," he wrote airily to Abigail Adams in London. "The spirit of resistance to government is so valuable on occasion that I wish it to be always kept alive. It will often be exercised when wrong, but better so than not to be exercised at all." And to Mrs. Adams's son-in-law, William Smith: "God forbid we should every twenty years be without such a rebellion! What signify a few lives lost in a century or two? The tree of liberty must be refreshed from time to time with the blood of patriots and tyrants. It is its natural manure."

Thomas Jefferson had been away from home for three years. What he saw of Europe convinced him that the less regulation, the better. "And we think ours a bad government!" he wrote to Rutledge of South Carolina. "The only condition on earth to be compared with ours is, in my opinion, that of the Indians, where they have still less law than we. The European, are governments of kites over pigeons. The best schools for republicanism are London, Versailles, Madrid, Vienna, Berlin." To Washington, Jefferson wrote that he was much an enemy to monarchy before coming to Europe, and that he had become ten thousand times more so. "There is scarcely an evil known in these countries which may not be traced to their king as its source, nor a good which is not derived from the small fibres of republicanism existing among them. I can further say with safety, there is not a crowned head in Europe whose talents or merits would entitle him to be elected a vestryman by the people of any parish in America."

Small wonder that Jefferson told Madison he believed the rebellion in Massachusetts "had given more alarm than it should have done." In Paris, Jefferson found himself brilliantly congenial with the crowd of *philosophes,* both male and female, by whom he was surrounded and with whom he conversed daily on government in its ideal state. If Jefferson appeared to shrug off those faraway local threats, it was natural; from Paris they seemed a puff of smoke. "They are setting up a kite," he wrote, "to keep the henyard in order."

But if Elbridge Gerry of Massachusetts had learned from Captain Shays "the danger of the levelling spirit," George Mason of

Virginia, sitting in Convention, shared none of these apprehensions. Mason had written his son from Philadelphia that the Easterners were some of them "anti-republican." And if this seemed extraordinary, considering their record in the Revolution, one must remember, said Mason, that the human mind runs to extremes. The Eastern states, having had too-sanguine expectations for "liberty," were suffering greater disgust from unexpected evils. Mason was sixty, Washington's neighbor on the Potomac and longtime friend, republican to the marrow and since youth a flaming patriot, part author of the Virginia Constitution and drafter of the Virginia Bill of Rights. On his family coat of arms, Mason had altered the motto, *Pro Patria Semper*, to read *Pro Republica Semper;* Jefferson spoke of him as "the wisest man of his generation."

White-haired, spirited, the proprietor of five thousand Virginia acres, Mason was a state-rights man and would be until the end, though he considered that America badly needed a better government. Skeptical about human nature in general, Mason had a firm faith in the common people. He rose now to answer Gerry. What he feared, said Mason, was that in turning away from too much democracy we should run into the opposite extreme. "We ought to attend to the rights of every class of the people . . . provide no less carefully for the . . . happiness of the lowest than of the highest orders of citizens." The word *slaves* had not yet been broached in the Convention. But Mason knew whereof he spoke, having been a fervent abolitionist before the word was coined. The first branch of our legislature, he went on, "so to speak to be our House of Commons . . . ought to know and sympathize with every part of the community." Will not our children, Mason finished, "in a short time be among the general mass?"

Already in this second week of meeting it was evident that whatever should divide the Convention, the division would not be on the basis of class. George Mason for all his broad acres and aristocratic bearing had faith in the people, while Roger Sherman, son of a shoemaker, had not, nor had Elbridge Gerry, the self-made merchant. Benjamin Franklin, humbly born but by all odds the man of greatest worldly experience in the country, from time to time "expressed his dislike," wrote Madison, "of every thing that tended to debase the spirit of the common people. If honesty was often the companion of wealth, and if poverty was exposed to peculiar temptation, it was not less true that the possession of property increased the desire of more property. Some of the greatest rogues he was ever acquainted with, were the richest rogues. . . . This Constitution will be much read and attended to in Europe, and if it should betray a great partiality to the rich, will not only hurt us in the esteem of the most liberal and enlightened men there, but discourage the common people from removing to this Country."

Before the Committee of the Whole adjourned on the last day of May, it had voted aye upon Randolph's original Resolve 3: *"That the national legislature ought to consist of two branches."* Among the states only two, Pennsylvania and Georgia, possessed one-chamber legislatures. Both would soon amend their constitutions to include both senate and representatives, though in Pennsylvania Dr. Franklin opposed the change; to the end of his life he would remain staunch in defense of the radical one-chamber house. Resolve 3 was agreed to, therefore, "without debate or dissent," wrote Madison, "except that of Pennsylvania, given probably out of complaisance to Docr. Franklin." On June twenty-first the question would, however, come up again in Committee of the Whole, and pass seven to three (with Maryland divided), after striking out the offending word "national."

Resolve 4 of the Virginia Plan, for popular election of the Federal House of Representatives, also passed — surprisingly — in the affirmative, though in a week's time it too would be reconsidered. It would seem that in these first days of the Convention, the small-state men were not ready, not organized for resistance. New Jersey and South Carolina had voted no to Resolve 4, with Connecticut and Delaware divided. Even more surprisingly, the first part of Randolph's Resolve 6, giving Congress authority over state laws, went through without dissent; this was later to cause heated disagreement and be voted down. It was well indeed that Convention rules allowed these repeated votes in Committee of the Whole, tests of what delegates thought and felt, before the entire body of Resolves should be presented for final official vote in full Convention, with Washington in the chair.

On the last clause of Resolve 6: *"to call forth the force of the Union against any member of the Union failing to fulfill its duty under the articles* [of Confederation]" — Madison asked for a postponement. He was, he said, strongly in favor of enumerated, distinct powers granted to Congress. The more he reflected, the more he doubted the practicability, justice and efficacy of using force against a state. It would look "like a declaration of war," Madison said.

On the motion of postponement, *"Agreed,"* said Madison's notes, *"nem. con."* In the end the Constitution was to contain no clause calling forth a national army against state or section. "The Committee [of the Whole]," wrote Madison, *"then rose and the House adjourned."*

It was three o'clock in the afternoon. Members left the State House, strolled out to Chestnut Street or through the south doors to the yard with its serpentine graveled walks, where the young trees were still too slight for shade. Here one could hope to feel air moving in from the river, six blocks to the east, or from green country to the westward; the city stopped at Ninth Street.

The State House was not at its best that summer. The steeple had been taken down some years ago when it grew shaky. Nevertheless the building was attractive with its two wings and the tall arcades between; the eighteenth century called them piazzas. In the narrow street the whole was set back from the brick sidewalk, giving it dignity and importance. There was a closed well in the pavement near each corner, with a wooden pump standing high. At the west end — Sixth Street — work had begun on the new county courthouse; so far it was no more than a large hole in the ground. Fifth Street was noisy with hammering, blocked here and there with piles of lumber; the Philosophical Society's building was going up. Across Walnut Street, fronting directly on the State House yard, rose the stone prison, four stories high. The city took pride in it and in its novel arrangements for the humane treatment of prisoners, after the notions of Philadelphia Quakers and the philosophy of the Italian reformer, Beccaria, who believed that evildoers should be helped as well as punished. The dark cells for solitary confinement were in a separate structure, and the debtors were housed apart from criminals.

As Convention members emerged from the State House yard, prisoners thrust through the barred windows long begging poles of reed, with a cloth cap at the end. Calling out for alms, they cursed any who ignored them. "Foul and horrid imprecations," some one said, from "this cage of unclean birds."

Convention members had not far to walk to their lodgings. Washington and Robert Morris were only a block from Morris's home on Market Street, just east of Sixth. Like many other delegates the General had brought his coach and horses, a servant and a groom. Elbridge Gerry had taken a house on Spruce Street and sent to Cambridge for his family: a handsome young bride and infant son. Other members boarded with the well-known landlady Mrs. Mary House, at Fifth and Market, or in hostels such as the Indian Queen on Fourth Street, often crowded two in a room.

Philadelphia was hospitable. Diaries show delegates dining with Dr. Franklin, with Jared Ingersoll and Robert Morris, or with those indefatigable Pennsylvania politicians Thomas Mifflin and George Clymer, themselves members of the Convention. There were bookshops and stationery shops, where one could buy, that May, Bell's edition of the *British Poets* in 109 volumes, or Blackstone's *Commentaries* in four. A new poem by Joel Barlow was advertised: *The Vision of Columbus*, ready now for its subscribers. The Library Company kept their books on the second floor of Carpenters' Hall, only a block from the State House: members found it convenient. Many of them knew well this brick building, where the Continental Congress first had met in '74. On the right as one entered were models of mechanical instruments and devices: plows, harrows, machines for cleaning grain and dressing flax. A Philadelphian wrote to Jefferson that the city abounded, that summer, with schemers and projectors. "One Fitch" had this twelvemonth been endeavoring to make a boat go forward by a steam engine. He had "spent much money in the project and has heated his imagination so as to be himself a steam engine." The writer Francis Hopkinson had "no doubt but that a boat may be urged forward by such means, but the enormous expense and complexity of the machine must prevent its coming into common use."

Philadelphia offered much to interest the delegates. One could visit Mr. Peale's Museum to view the fossil bones, the stuffed animals, the portraits, and not least Mr. Peale himself, an agreeable gentleman, described as "very complaisant," who had fought in the Revolutionary War, had taken active part in local politics and painted five portraits of Washington; he was shortly to be at work upon a sixth. The Delaware riverfront was a colorful sight; it reached for miles. The west side was lined with warehouses; dozens of quays were noisy with vessels loading and unloading. Three years ago the *Empress of China* had sailed to Canton — a pioneer voyage — and now one could find in the shops everything from tea, cocoa, China silk and ivory fans to Spanish oranges, French soap balls or South Carolina rice. Now and again a load of redemptioners came ashore, well advertised beforehand in the newspapers, strong young men or likely young women from Ireland, Scotland or the German states, indentured servants whose time would be sold to the highest bidder.

On Wednesday and Saturday mornings the market opened, a sight in itself. It was under cover and reached straight down Market Street to the river, "neat and clean as a dining-hall," with newly caught fish laid out, fresh meat, butter, vegetables, fruits, and by daylight so crowded a man could scarcely make his way through. America, restless to be self-sufficient, was more and more manufacturing her own products and proud of it. In the *Pennsylvania Packet*, Mr. Long, "Cabinet-Maker, late of London," advertised French sofas in the modern taste; the elegant product as pictured was enough to make a visitor's mouth water. Gordon on Arch Street would fashion a pair of boots complete in nine hours for any person choosing to leave his measure. Dr. Baker sold his "well-known antiscorbutic dentifrice and Albion essence." Toothbrushes were coming into fashion, though considered somewhat effete; if a gentleman wished to sweeten his breath he rubbed his teeth with a rag dipped in snuff. Along the streets at brief intervals stood the famous Philadelphia pumps with their iron handles. But the city was not healthy in summer and the drinking water far from tasty. Flies and mosquitoes were a continual torment, and when the wind was right it brought a whiff of the shambles, tainted and heavy. Nor were householders particular where they threw their slops, and there were complaints of dead animals lying in the gutters. Prisoners from the jail were put to cleaning the streets and privies. Known as "wheelbarrow men," they were shorn and wore fetters.

Evenings were spent by Convention members in talk at the City Tavern, the Indian Queen, the George, the Black Horse, often enough in preparation for tomorrow's meeting; the work before them was hard and continuous. There was much conviviality. After the fashion of the day and perhaps of conventions anywhere, large amounts of drink were consumed; an account of a dinner for twelve notes sixty bottles of Madeira ordered. To certain delegates Philadelphia was a city dangerously lax in morals and rife with luxury, fond of dancing, clamoring after a new theater to be built. George Mason had not been in town ten days when he wrote his son complaining that he began "to grow heartily tired of the etiquette and nonsense so fashionable in this city." To French visitors like Chastellux and Brissot de Warville, Philadelphia was alarmingly virtuous, its maidens unbelievably prim. "The men are grave, the women serious. There are no finical airs to be found here, no libertine wives, no coffee-houses, no agreeable walks." The Federal Convention, in short, found itself in a busy, thriving, growing town, where one met upon the streets all nations and all classes: Germans from the farms beyond the city, sailors jabbering in outlandish tongues, French noblemen returned since the peace to tour the country they had fought for, frontiersmen in fringed leggings, Quakers in their broad hats, Indians from the backlands — Shawnees or Delawares.

And always, bells rang and chimed above the city roofs. Twice a week, the evening bell announced next morning's market; after dinner a churchbell signaled that the library was open in Carpenters' Hall. Hawkers rang their handbells along the morning streets, and on Sundays the churchbells made the day seem even quieter. At night from bed one heard the watchman call the time and the weather every hour until dawn. If a man desired to catch the early coach for out of town at two or three after midnight, the watchman would wake him — a service peculiar to the city, and much appreciated by visitors.

# V

## The Chief Executive. Wilson of Philadelphia, Dickinson of Delaware. Dr. Franklin speaks his mind. June 1-6.

> Do gentlemen mean to pave the way to hereditary monarchy?
>
> GEORGE MASON, *in Convention*

MEMBERS knew it had been hazardous to attempt this Convention in the first place. Now, it seemed they were to endure the problems attendant upon Congress. When the first ten days went by without a quorum, delegates became anxious and wrote home urging their colleagues to set out without delay. New York's delegates had arrived promptly, but by July eighth all three had vanished; only Hamilton would return. Dr. McHenry of Maryland went home on June first because of family illness; he remained absent until August. New Hampshire was very late indeed. Chancellor Wythe left the Convention on June fourth because of a sick wife and never came back, though he strongly approved the Constitution and would support it in the Virginia convention for ratification. Other members came and went to the Congress at New York, absent from the Convention for days or weeks at a time, on public or private business.

No delegate confessed it in his letters home — the secrecy rule made for discretion — yet there was an ever-present danger that the Convention might dissolve and the entire project be abandoned. Every few days, as new delegates appeared, Washington recorded their arrival in his diary. It was good to see them come, and reassuring. On Friday, June first, William Houstoun of Georgia arrived — a young lawyer with little to recommend him save a distinguished family background and striking good looks. Nevertheless, the remotest of states now had three out of her eventual four delegates.

No sooner were William Houstoun's credentials examined than the House resolved itself into a Committee of the Whole, to take into consideration Virginia's Resolve 7: *"that a national executive be instituted . . ."*

Charles Pinckney rose at once to urge a "vigorous executive." He did not say a "President of the United States." It took the Convention a long while to come around to *President*. Always they referred to a chief executive or a national executive, whether plural or single. James Wilson followed Pinckney by moving that the executive consist of a single person; Pinckney seconded him.

A sudden silence followed. "A considerable pause," Madison wrote . . . *A single executive!* There was menace in the words, some saw monarchy in them. True enough, nine states had each its single executive — a governor or president — but everywhere the local legislature was supreme, looked on as the voice of the people which could control a governor any day. But a single executive for the national government conjured up visions from the past — royal governors who could not be restrained, a crown, ermine, a scepter!

As the silence lengthened, Franklin, always alert to the atmosphere of a meeting, said he wished gentlemen would deliver their sentiments. John Rutledge deplored the shyness of members on this and other subjects. It looked, Rutledge said, as if they feared that once they had declared themselves they could not change their opinions. James Wilson of Pennsylvania rose to explain why it was he favored a single executive. Energy, dispatch and responsibility, he said, were the prime necessities for the executive branch. And vigor and dispatch would best be found in a single person. Wilson, signer of the Declaration of Independence, was a lawyer and a student of jurisprudence — occupations by no means synonymous. Born in Scotland, Wilson had come to America at the age of twenty-one, bringing with him a mind well trained at Edinburgh and Saint Andrews Universities. As early as

1774, he had had a remarkable view of what the British Empire could be. "Distinct states," he wrote, "independent of each other but connected under the same sovereign." It was a view that Wilson carried over to 1787, modified and adapted to the Constitution of the United States.

James Wilson has been called the unsung hero of the Federal Convention. A century later, Lord Bryce was to put him down as one of the Convention's "deepest thinkers and most exact reasoners." Wilson believed in a strong central government and in the sovereignty of the people. He thought as he chose, independently of other men, a trait which invited some very stormy episodes. Shortly after the Federal Convention, Wilson was to be burned in effigy by an excited mob which hated his attitude toward Pennsylvania politics. A demon for financial speculation possessed James Wilson; to gamble was in his blood. Already over his depth in western land-company shares, he would one day be forced to fly his creditors, frantic with anxiety and crying out that he had been hunted like a wild beast.

Whether or no Wilson's land speculations influenced his statesmanship one cannot say, though he has been accused of special pleading in Congress and on the judicial bench: certainly western speculators were firmly of the opinion that a strong central authority would favor land values. Wilson was not the first dedicated statesman whose services to his country were strangely mixed with personal inability to manage his finances. One thinks of a far greater man, Lord Chancellor Sir Francis Bacon, impeached for bribery by Parliament in the year 1621. One thinks also of that other member of the Federal Convention, Robert Morris, cutting his wide swath in Phliadelphia society and dying in the disgrace of debt and poverty.

When James Wilson rose in June of 1787 to urge a single executive for the United States, his colleagues saw a man of forty-four, with sloping shoulders, a neat ruffled shirt and a studious, calm expression. His spectacles had round lenses; the steel rims were hooked into his powdered wig. Wilson's Scotch burr was pronounced; Philadelphians knew him as Caledonia James. His motion for "a single vigorous executive" met with instant opposition. Roger Sherman declared that the executive magistracy was "nothing more than an institution for carrying the will of the legislature into effect . . . the person or persons ought to be appointed by and accountable to the legislature only, which was the depository of the supreme will of the society." Randolph in his turn "strenuously opposed" a unity in the executive magistracy. He regarded it as the fetus of monarchy. He could not see why the great requisites for the executive department — vigor, dispatch and responsibility — could not be found in three men as well as in one man. We must not look toward "the British government as our prototype. The fixed genius of the people of America requires a different form of government."

James Wilson disagreed. Unity in the executive, he said, instead of being the fetus of monarchy, would be the best safeguard against tyranny. Plurality in the executive would probably produce a tyranny as bad as the thirty tyrants of Athens or the Decemvirs of Rome. Nor was he governed by the British model. "We must consider two points of importance existing in our country . . . the extent and manners of the United States." A country so large, said Wilson, "seems to require the vigor of monarchy." Yet "the manners are against a king, and are purely republican."

Already the Convention was becoming accustomed to certain phrases: *the fetus of monarchy . . . the fixed genius of this country . . . the sense of the nation . . .* Members were also growing used to references concerning the British form of government. . . . How is it in England? The question was insistent. How is it with the House of Commons? Have the judges of England a share in legislature or are they merely advisory? . . . It was natural enough. Even the youngest man present had been born under the British government; all of them had grown up in the belief that the English government and the English common law comprised the best and freest system on earth. Not until Great Britain betrayed her principles — they would have said — had the colonies gone to war. But the war was over. Why not therefore look to the British government as a model? Had not the celebrated Montesquieu done so when he advocated a tripartite system of judiciary, legislature and executive?

But there were Convention members who would have none of it. "We were eternally troubled," wrote Luther Martin afterward, "with arguments and precedents from the British government." On the second of June, John Dickinson, rising to declare for a single executive, said he considered a limited monarchy "as *one* of the best governments in the world," though, he added, in America it was out of the question. A House of Nobles could not be created by a breath, by a stroke of the pen. But "we must not despair."

Dickinson was fifty-four; he had been famous in America since the publication in 1768 of his *Letters from a Farmer in Pennsylvania to the Inhabitants of the British Colonies.* Everyone, high and low, had read these *Letters:* their author seemed conversant with both theory and practice, he knew the principles underlying English liberty and the impasse which the colonies had reached with the mother country. The *Letters* were written in a warm, simple style, as man to man; almost with the Franklin touch. Dickinson had studied law at the Middle Temple in London, married Speaker Norris's daughter and in the Continental Congress was numbered among the "cool Devils" (James Wilson was another) who in '76 had done their utmost to delay Independence, thus infuriating John Adams. It was Dickinson to whom John Adams had referred in the notorious intercepted letter of 1775, as "a certain great fortune and piddling genius." Nevertheless it had been Dickinson who in July of '75 had written the magnificent closing passages in the *Declaration of the Cause and Necessity of Taking up Arms,* and a year later had been chairman of the committee that wrote the Articles of Confederation. In spite of voting against the Declaration of Independence, Dickinson had immediately marched to Elizabethtown with the militia. In the Convention of '87, he was one of the strongest advocates for a national government.

The debate on a single or plural executive began to mount high; members forgot their shyness. Randolph, although the Virginia Plan favored a vigorous Congress, rose again with objections to a single executive. The people, said Randolph, would never be brought to have confidence in any one man. Besides, no matter who was appointed, he would be sure to live somewhere near the center of population. "Consequently the remote parts would not be on equal footing." Whereas an executive of three members could be drawn from three different portions of the country.

Pierce Butler of South Carolina strongly objected. He said he had seen in Holland how a plurality of military heads distracted that little republic when threatened with invasion by the imperial troops. Members of a plural executive would be swayed by the interests of the locality from which they came. Pierce Butler was Irish-born, the son of a Member of Parliament. His mother had been a Percy, of the old nobility, a fact which her son never let people forget. Butler wore a powdered wig, a handsome stock, gold lace on his coat. Yet at home in South Carolina, instead of supporting the planter-merchant group to which he belonged, Butler championed the people of the back country, helped them when seaboard politicians tried to devalue their property or refused them proper representation in the state legislature. Butler was impulsive and a trifle cantankerous. In the Convention he strongly supported the national side; it was logical that he come out for a single executive. But when the debate shortly turned to Virginia's eighth Resolve — giving the chief executive a veto on the legislature — Butler abruptly altered his position. Gentlemen seemed to think, he said heatedly, that we had nothing to apprehend from an abuse of the executive power. "But why might not a Catiline or a Cromwell arise in this country as well as in others?"

The Federal Convention was to hear much of Catilines and Cromwells. Though nobody mentioned George III by name, it was plain that unfortunate monarch was in the minds of all. "Do gentlemen mean," asked Mason, "to pave the way to hereditary monarchy? Do they flatter themselves that the people will ever consent to such an innovation?"

The presidential veto — the Convention called it the executive negative — was a vital matter. Experience had caused citizens to be chary of the executive power whether in state or nation, and whether single or plural, one man or three. Virginia's Resolve 8 suggested that the chief executive, together with "a convenient number of the National Judiciary," should compose a council of revision to examine acts of Congress before they became operative. Benjamin Franklin possessed decided views on the subject.

Having been a member of the old Assembly when Pennsylvania was still a proprietary colony under the Penn family, Franklin had had experience, he said now, of this check of the executive upon the legislature, when "the negative of the Governor was constantly made use of to extort money. No good law whatever could be passed without a private bargain with him. An increase of his salary or some donation was always made a condition; till at last it became the regular practice to have orders in his favor on the Treasury presented along with the bills to be signed, so that he might actually receive the former before he should sign the latter."

When the Indians, went on Franklin, were scalping the Western people and notice of it arrived, the governor would not countenance any means of self-defense until it was agreed that Proprietary estates should be exempt from taxation. . . . Were the executive to have an elected council to help him, his power would be less objectionable. "It was true the King of Great Britain had not . . . exerted his negative since the revolution [of 1688]; but that matter was easily explained. The bribes and emoluments now given to the members of Parliament rendered [the royal negative] unnecessary, everything being done according to the will of the ministers." He feared, the Doctor added, that if the executive were given a negative on acts of the legislature, he would demand more power and more until at last the legislature would be in "complete subjection to the will of the executive."

Dr. Franklin had lived many years abroad. He knew the British, he knew the French and spoke their language — and he knew the state of Pennsylvania of which he was president. He wished for a plural executive, he said. Not only might a single executive be overambitious or "fond of war," but he might fall ill. Who then would conduct public affairs? If the chief magistrate should die, who would serve until a new election? Why not elect a council for life? As for a single chief magistrate, "The first man put at the helm," said Franklin, "will be a good one. Nobody knows what sort may come afterwards."

Franklin was very old and his voice soft. Sensible of his age, he said now, and of an untrustworthy memory, he had reduced to writing his ideas on the subject of compensation for the executive. James Wilson offered to read the paper and Franklin gave assent. . . . The Doctor, it developed, was much opposed to salaries for the executive branch, whether single or plural. "Sir," read Wilson, "there are two passions which have a powerful influence on the affairs of men. These are ambition and avarice, the love of power and the love of money." Salaries that began by being moderate would soon be augmented; applicants would struggle one against another for places and position. In England, men served in high place without compensation. Here at home there was an example in the Quakers, who in cases of public service considered the less profit, the greater honor. Moreover, a salaried executive would lead the sooner to a monarchy in America. There was a natural inclination in mankind to kingly government. It sometimes relieved them from aristocratic domination. They had rather have one tyrant than five hundred. "There is scarce a king in a hundred who would not, if he could, follow the example of Pharaoh, get first all the peoples' money, then all their lands and then make them and their children servants forever."

And if it were Utopian to think that valuable men would serve without pay — had we not seen "the great and most important of our officers, that of General of our armies, executed for eight years together without the smallest salary, by a patriot whom I will not now offend by any other praise. . . . and shall we doubt finding three or four men in all the United States, with public spirit enough . . . to preside over our civil concerns and see that our laws are duly executed?"

During all this time, Washington, having come down from the chair, had been with the Virginians at their table. Everyone in the State House, perhaps everyone in America, knew that General Washington would in some guise or other be at the head of the new government. Yet here he sat, his strong back erect as ever, his powdered pigtail stiff on his collar, while men debated whether a single chief magistrate could be trusted for America, and trusted moreover with a salary from the people. The whole question, Madison wrote later to Jefferson, was "peculiarly embarrassing."

Franklin's paper ended with a motion that the executive not be paid. Alexander Hamilton rose to second it. No discussion followed and the motion was postponed — "treated with great respect," wrote Madison, "but rather for the author of it than from any apparent conviction of its expediency or practicability."

James Wilson now remarked that the people in their state governments were "accustomed and reconciled to a single executive." The Convention was not impressed. Who was to restrain an ambitious chief executive, how was he to be checked or controlled? By impeachment? George Mason, like Randolph, spoke out strongly for a threefold executive, one person from the Northern, one from the Middle and one from the Southern states. Would not this quiet the minds of the people, Mason asked, and would not three men so chosen bring with them into office a more perfect and extensive knowledge of the real interests of this great union?

Seven to three, the states voted in Committee for a single executive; New York, Delaware and Maryland voting no; "*Gen.W. ay*," wrote Madison.

"I consider," said George Mason darkly, "the federal government as in some measure dissolved by the meeting of this Convention." Mason exaggerated: Congress was sitting; the offices of war, treasury and foreign affairs still carried on their business, as did the land office. Yet it was true that already the Convention had greatly exceeded its instructions. (The time would come when a President of the United States — Martin Van Buren — would refer to the writing of the Constitution as "an heroic and lawless act.")

Resolve 8 now came up, concerning the executive veto; it suggested that the "judicial should be joined with the executive to revise the laws," when necessary. Rufus King at once objected. The judges, he argued, when cases came before them, would surely stop the operation of such laws as were repugnant to the Constitution; they should therefore have no part in making them, not even the negative power of veto. Dickinson agreed. The national judiciary must not be blended with the executive, "because the one is the expounder, the other the executor of the laws."

Dr. Franklin thought in any case it was improper to give one person power to negative a law passed by the legislature. Madison, "in a very able and ingenious speech," wrote Mason, came out strongly in favor of the judges joining with the executive as a council of revision. Such a move would be strictly proper, Madison said, "and would by no means interfere with that independence so much to be approved and distinguished in the several departments." Elbridge Gerry, however, remarked testily that he did not wish to see the executive "covered by the sanction and seduced by the sophistry of the judges."

Did the judges present smile when he said it — Rutledge of South Carolina, Blair of Virginia, Yates of New York, Brearley of New Jersey, Read of Delaware, Ellsworth, Sherman and Johnson of Connecticut? Among the fifty-five delegates, thirty-four were lawyers. Congress showed an even greater proportion; lawyers had written the Declaration of Independence and the Articles of Confederation. Yet lawyers were aware of the American prejudice against them, especially since the Revolution. About lawyers there was a taint of England, of the Middle Temple and the Inns of Court — above all there was the taint of authority. Lawyers required debtors to pay. Lawyers threw honest men into prison for debt in cases that were not the debtors' fault but the fault of depreciation, bad times, a requirement of specie payment, when all a farmer had was a trunkful of worthless paper.

It has been said that revolutions, like utopias, always believe they can manage better without courts. Shakespeare knew it: "The first thing we do, let's kill all the lawyers!" cries one of Jack Cade's rebels. . . . A beautiful anarchy, the courts closed, the prisons emptied, the rich brought low and no bailiffs knocking at the door with summonses. Shortly after the meeting of the Continental Congress in '75, John Adams, that fervent lover of the law, had an ominous encounter. Returning from Philadelphia he met in Boston an old client, one of those men who are forever being sued in court. The man was full of enthusiasm. "Oh, Mr. Adams!" he cried. "What great things have you and your colleagues done for us! We can never be grateful enough to you! There are no courts of justice now in this Province, and I hope there never will be another!" This incident, said Adams, threw him into a fit of melancholy. Was it for this he risked his life and fortune in a revolution? He had thought he was fighting for law, not against it.

To Captain Shays's men, lawyers were "savage beasts of prey," who moved "in swarms." (People who dislike lawyers are apt to have them moving in swarms.) Moreover, since the peace in '83, lawyers had made themselves extremely unpopular by defending former Tories in court, retrieving for them their lands and houses which had been seized by the patriots. Alexander Hamilton had been active in this, as had Yates of New York. Hamilton had even written newspaper articles urging his position. The mobbing of James Wilson's house had been partly due to his defense of Tories.

When Elbridge Gerry spoke of the sophistry of the judges, he was expressing a widespread prejudice. Gerry would have much to say at this Convention, and he was in a position to say it, having signed both the Declaration of Independence and the Articles of Confederation. Gerry had in fact been busy in politics since the day of '72 when he came under the influence of Samuel Adams. Politically, Gerry was a thoroughly inconsistent man; all his life he would veer between federalism and anti-federalism. He was thin and small and worried-looking, with a long nose, a way of squinting up his eyes when he talked and a slight stutter; for some mysterious reason he had a reputation as a ladies' man. He took offense easily. John Adams said Gerry had the kind of obstinacy that would "risk great things to secure small ones." Not only was Gerry full of maneuvers but he possessed the energy to carry them out.

On the question of an absolute veto for the executive, the Committee voted no, ten states to none. At some point in the discussion, Madison had suggested that a proper proportion of Congress be allowed to overrule the executive veto. No chief executive, Madison said, would have firmness enough to go against the whole of Congress. Even the King of Great Britain in all his splendor could not withstand the wishes of both Houses of Parliament!

On these variations of the executive revisional power the states voted, but no agreement was reached, nor would be until June eighteenth, when the Committee finally granted the veto power to the executive, subject to overruling by two thirds of Congress. So it would stand in the Constitution.

Next morning, Tuesday, William Livingston arrived. He was nearly sixty-four and, wrote a delegate, "remarkably healthy." Governor of New Jersey since the year '76, Livingston had sat in the first two Continental Congresses and was celebrated for the active part he had taken in the Revolution; a Tory paper had called him "the Don Quixote of the Jerseys." Wellborn and well-placed, he was known for a stout integrity, boundless energy and a tendency to grow excited when his political principles were assailed. Oddly enough — with such a disposition — Livingston took little part in debates on the floor of the Convention. He was however named to various committees where, Madison said later, "it may be presumed he had an agency and a due influence." In person Livingston was tall, thin, awkward in movement; somebody had once called him "the whipping post" and the epithet stayed. His was one of the best-known names of the Convention.

On the morning of Livingston's arrival, debate turned on Randolph's ninth Resolve, concerning the appointment of inferior tribunals. Who was to name the federal judges for the states? Should the executive do it, or should Congress? James Wilson thought the appointment would best be made by a single responsible person; experience showed that appointments by large bodies resulted in "intrigue, partiality and concealment." Rutledge was vehement in disagreement. As Chancellor in South Carolina he had carried enormous weight. Dictator John, they had called him during the Revolution; he was used to being listened to. By no means, he said now, should the chief executive appoint the judges. "The people," said Rutledge, "will think we are leaning too much towards monarchy" (an argument the Convention kept always in mind). Rutledge was against establishing any national tribunal except a single supreme one.

Roger Sherman argued that the existing state courts would serve the same purpose. A new set of federal courts would be too expensive. Rufus King disagreed; he thought these courts would in the end save more by preventing appeals than they would cost to establish. Pierce Butler was strongly against the setting up of federal tribunals. The people would not bear this innovation; the states would revolt at such encroachments. Even were the tribunals useful, the Convention should not venture on it. "We must follow the example of Solon, who gave the Athenians not the best government he could devise but the best they would receive."

As the debate mounted, Dr. Franklin interposed mildly. Only two modes of choosing the judges, he said, had so far been mentioned; it was a point of great moment and he wished other modes might be suggested. He would like to mention one which he understood was practiced in Scotland. He then, wrote Madison, "in a brief and entertaining manner related a Scotch mode, in which the nomination proceeded from the lawyers, who always selected the ablest of the profession in order to get rid of him, and share his practice among themselves." Here in America, on the other hand, it was the interest of the electors to make the best choice.

Old men can be tedious. Yet when this particular old man told a story it was impossible not to be diverted. Madison moved that in the ninth Resolve the words "appointment by the legislature" be struck out, and a blank left "to be hereafter filled on maturer reflection." In Committee of the Whole the states voted, approving nine to two.

The rest of Tuesday, June fifth, was taken up by a rapid review of the remaining six Virginia Resolves, the sense of the meeting being revealed as usual by vote. Resolve 10 was affirmed without dissent: "*that provision ought be made for the admission of States lawfully arising within the limits of the United States.*" Resolve 11 guaranteed a republican government to all states. It was postponed on a motion made by New Jersey, whose Attorney General Paterson — small-state champion — desired "the point of representation" first to be decided. Paterson, like Patrick Henry, "smelt a rat." Virginia's twelfth Resolve went through without debate: "*for the continuance of Congress . . . until a given day after the reform of the articles of Union shall be adopted, and for the completion of all their engagements.*" Congress, after all, was still highly necessary. Resolve 13 provided for amendment of the Constitution, without requiring the assent of Congress. It was postponed on the oppositon of three states — and Elbridge Gerry. The next proposition, requiring state officers to take oaths supporting the national government, was also postponed — "after," wrote Madison, "a short uninteresting conversation."

Virginia's last Resolve, number 15, concerned ratification. Here the debate was anything but uninteresting. "*That the amendment,*" wrote Yates, "*which shall be offered to the confederation, by the Convention, ought at a proper time . . . after the approbation of Congress, to be submitted to an assembly or assemblies of representatives, recommended by the several legislatures to be expressly chosen by the people, to consider and decide thereon.*" As every delegate knew, the method of ratification was enormously important; by it the Constitution could stand or fall. Roger Sherman thought popular ratification unnecessary. Did not the Articles of Confederation provide for changes and alterations with the assent of Congress and nine states? To Madison, however, popular ratification was essential. The Articles of Confederation, he argued, were "a treaty only of a particular sort," wherein the breach of any one article absolved the other parties from obligation to the whole. The new Constitution needed, said Madison, a ratification "in the most unexceptionable form, and by the supreme authority of the people themselves."

Elbridge Gerry characteristically "seemed afraid," wrote Madison, "of referring the new system to the people." According to Gerry, people in the New England states had "the wildest ideas of government in the world." (Once more the ghost of Captain Shays!) In Massachusetts, Gerry said, they were for abolishing the Senate and giving all powers of government to a one-chamber legislature. But Gerry's colleague Rufus King disagreed; he was for ratification by popular convention. These special conventions, said King, had only one house, whereby adoption could the more easily be pushed through.

James Wilson rose now with a solemn warning and reminder of the dangers ahead. In the ratification period the new Constitution might well be defeated "by the inconsiderate or selfish opposition of a few states." He hoped, said Madison, that whatever the provision for ratifying, it would not require unanimity but permit at least a partial union, "with a door open for the accession of the rest of the states."

The question of ratification — Resolve 15 — was postponed for future consideration. But Charles Pinckney, doubtful if the country would accept a system of government so bold, so filled with innovations, rose to say he "hoped, that in the case the experiment should not unanimously take place, nine states might be authorized to unite under the same government."

# VI

*"Life, liberty and property." The people at large. The method of electing congressmen. June 6-7.*

If no state will part with any of its sovereignty, it is in vain to talk of a national government.
JAMES WILSON, *in Convention*

THE Committee of the Whole House, having reviewed all fifteen Virginia Resolves and having agreed upon, negatived or postponed them severally, took up once more on Wednesday morning, June sixth, that thorniest of their problems, Resolve 4: *"that the members of the first branch of the National Legislature ought to be elected by the people of the several States."* The first branch was of course the House of Representatives. A week ago, in Committee of the Whole, the vote had gone six to two for popular election: New Jersey and South Carolina voting no, Connecticut and Delaware divided. But the small states, by no means satisfied, did not intend to let the question rest. Did popular election signify proportional representation and the snuffing out of ten states by three? Moreover, certain delegates were not ready to trust such responsibility to the people.

On the morning of June sixth, Charles Pinckney of South Carolina opened by moving that the first branch—the representatives—be elected, not by the people at large, but by the state legislatures, on the now familiar argument that "the people were less fit judges." If the state legislatures felt excluded from all share in the new government, they might refuse to adopt it, decline to ratify. Every delegate recognized the prestige of local politicians in his state. It remained to be seen if these were more powerful than the nationally minded men, continentalists like Hamilton, Madison, Washington, Wilson.

Elbridge Gerry agreed with Pinckney that the state legislatures should appoint the representatives in Congress. But could not the people first nominate certain persons from their districts, who in turn would do the final appointing? Like Pinckney, Gerry did not wish to rob the people of all confidence in the new government; they must be permitted to feel their share in it. In England, said Gerry, the people were in danger of losing their liberty because so few had the right of suffrage. Whereas here, the danger was the opposite. Look what was happening in Massachusetts! "The worst men get into the legislature . . . Men of indigence, ignorance and baseness spare no pains, however dirty, to carry their point . . ."

To most of the Convention there is no doubt that *indigence* was a bad word. We meet the phrases often: persons without property or character . . . men without character and fortune . . . "The most dangerous influence," said John Dickinson, "of those multitudes without property and without principle with which our country, like all others, will soon abound." If today the words are shocking, almost absurd, it is well to recall that they were spoken in an America where, for a few generations at least, poverty very likely did mean sloth and idleness. America in 1787 was three-quarters agricultural, with land abundant and labor scarce. The poorest immigrant could soon earn enough to buy his plot of ground, cut down his trees, erect his log hut and plant his seeds against the coming spring. When those who governed Revolutionary America spoke of "men of the better sort," or "men of the baser sort," they did not refer to men with character or without it but to men with property or without it. And if the word property today carries sinister philosophical overtones, to the Convention of 1787 it had an altogether different connotation: property was not a privilege of the higher orders but a right which a man would fight to defend. Men had indeed died to defend it in the war with England.

*Liberty, property and no stamps!* It had been the first slogan of the American Revolution. New York at one strategic point had even altered it to *Liberty, property and prudence*. In the English tradition a man's house was his castle, unassailably his own. Had not Magna Carta declared that of his own should no man him disseise except by lawful judgment of his peers?

"Liberty and property," Voltaire had written, "is the great national cry of the English. It is certainly better than 'St. George and my right,' or 'St. Denis and Montjoie.' It is the cry of nature." Stephen Hopkins, arguing from Rhode Island against the proposed stamp tax in the year 1764, had announced that "they who have no property can have no freedom." The famed Massachusetts Circular Letter of 1768 had declared it "an essential, unalterable Right, in nature . . . ever held sacred and irrevocable . . . that what a man has honestly acquired is absolutely his own." Even Jean Jacques Rousseau had held property sacred (though he wished it more equably distributed). The Continental Congress, composing its first Declaration and Resolves (1774), had said the colonists were entitled to "life, liberty and property." In the Declaration of Independence, Jefferson altered it to read, "life, liberty and the pursuit of happiness." If nobody knew exactly what that meant, they did not need to know. They felt it, breathed it in the Revolutionary air. To pursue happiness signified that a man could rise in the world according to his abilities and his industry.

For John Adams, property was a "right of mankind as surely as liberty." Even John's cousin Samuel Adams spoke in one breath of "right and property," and declared that "to render right and property precarious tended to destroy both property and government." A rebellion which is launched over the principle of no taxation without representation is hardly a proletarian revolution. Nor does a proletarian revolution include a Commander in Chief from whose tongue there trips easily the phrase "men of reflection, principles and property." Here was no quarrel, as today, between human rights and property rights. Madison said that "a man has property in his opinions and the free communication of them, he has property in the free use of his faculties, in the safety and liberty of his person." To the eighteenth century, property gave a man a stake in society, made him responsible, worthy of a vote and a voice in government. "The true foundation of republican government," wrote Thomas Jefferson, "is the equal right of every citizen, in his person and in his property. . . . In the American States," Jefferson said further, "every one may have land to labor for himself, if he chooses." And "every one, by his property, or by his satisfactory situation, is interested in the support of law and order."

*By his property, or by his satisfactory situation.* Jefferson owned, at one time or another, about ten thousand acres and from one to two hundred Negroes: the pursuit of happiness did not start from scratch. "Such men," Jefferson went on to say, "may safely and advantageously reserve to themselves a wholesome control over their public affairs, and a degree of freedom which in the hands of the *canaille* of the cities of Europe, would be instantly perverted to the demolition and destruction of everything public and private."

The Federal Convention was not interested in the redistribution of property, nor did it meet for such a purpose. Threatened with anarchy, the founders desired order, and to blame the Convention as "conservative" is to look on 1787 with the eyes of today. John Jay, no member of the Convention, but soon to be a potent champion of the Constitution, would not have offended delegates when he said that "the people who own the country ought to govern it."

The Convention of '87 discussed America not in terms of social philosophy but in relation to the country as they saw it around them. In the fields were no wretched peasant tenants, subsisting by their lord's favor. These men owned the land they cultivated. Even the mean desolate cabins of the frontier were inhabited by settlers who had gone west of their own free will. The states had indeed their poor, their ill, their aged destitute. Care of these the Convention looked on as a local responsibility; Philadelphia had her Alms House and her twenty Overseers and Guardians of the Poor. That a large part of America rested upon slavery was again no part of the Convention's immediate problem; they were met not to reform society but to create a government for society as it existed. The idle rich were as yet almost nonexistent. An American worked for what he owned; Southern planter as well as Northern merchant was aware of it.

America, in short, was middle-class, and Jefferson's "assembly of demi-gods" was for the most part an assembly of middle-class demigods, to whom the word "people" meant respectable forty-shilling freeholders. "The people" were men who had fought in the Revolutionary War, who sat in their local legislatures or town meetings or whose authorized representatives sat for them. "The people at large — the freeholders of the country," said Gouverneur Morris, debating who should elect the chief executive. Richard Henry Lee of Virginia — later a leading anti-Constitutionalist — defined "the solid, free and independent part of the community" as "the men of middling property, men not in debt on the one hand, and men on the other content with republican government and not aiming at immense fortunes, offices and power."

The Federal Convention was composed of propertied men; more than half owned public securities which could be expected to rise in value under a new, strong government. Madison told his colleagues that the United States had not reached the stage of a closely peopled Europe, where the propertied and the poor were natural enemies. In 1787, as today, the propertied men of America differed greatly in their sympathy with the common people. To George Washington, Captain Shays and his men had been "misled"; to Jefferson they signified a healthy republic; to Gerry they were incorrigible and should be allowed no part in government.

For the next three months the Convention would debate, argue, quarrel over the nature and disposition of the American people, the "people at large." What did the people desire in the way of government, what did they deserve, what would they accept? Most of the state constitutions required their voters to own property, in sums ranging from twenty pounds in New York to sixty pounds in Massachusetts, though Pennsylvania, Delaware and New Hampshire had already come out for free elections. In the end the Convention left this matter to the state legislatures. But concerning property qualifications for federal officeholders, the Convention took a bolder step. In many states such conditions were severe. To be governor of Massachusetts a man must own a freehold amounting to a thousand pounds. South Carolina required of her chief executive "a settled plantation or freehold of the value of at least ten thousand pounds currency, clear of debt"; representatives in the South Carolina state legislature must own three thousand five hundred pounds currency. In North Carolina the governor had a salary but must be proprietor of a freehold worth a thousand pounds. Members of the lower house — North Carolina called it their House of Commons — were required to possess "not less than one hundred acres of land in fee."

It is significant that the Convention simply overrode these traditions and that in the end the United States Constitution required no property qualifications for the men who were to govern the country, whether senators, judges or chief executive. This was achieved not without struggle. "It is exhilarating," a historian has said, "to trace the growth of reasonableness in society."

The question of popular elections was indeed at the heart of republican government — a test of how far men trusted their fellows, how much power they dared grant to the people. Elbridge Gerry and Charles Pinckney met the question bluntly, making no secret of their distrust. James Wilson of Philadelphia — James the Caledonian — was of another mind. Rising to reply, Wilson did not mince his words. He wished for a vigorous government, he said. To the Convention the words vigorous, energetic, as applied to government, meant a government with strong central powers. Wilson wished to see that vigorous authority "flow immediately from the legitimate source of all authority — the people. . . . The government," said Wilson, "ought to possess not only first the *force* but secondly the *mind* or *sense** of the people at large. The legislature ought to be the most exact transcript of the whole society." Why was representation necessary? Only because the people could not act collectively. Opposition to popular elections would come not from the citizens at large but from the state governments.

George Mason agreed. "Under the existing Confederacy," he said, "Congress represents the *States*, not the *people* of the states." It was natural for Madison to underline the words; after all, this had been largely his idea. "The case will be changed in the new plan of government," George Mason went on. "The people will be represented; they ought therefore to choose the represent-

* Madison's italics.

atives. The requisites in actual representation are that the representatives should sympathize with their constituents, should think as they think and feel as they feel, and for these purposes should even be residents among them. Much has been alleged against democratic elections. . . . But it is to be considered that no government is free from imperfections and evils, and that improper elections in many instances are inseparable from republican governments."

Madison here interposed firmly that the people must elect at least one branch of the legislature. This, he said, was "a clear principle of free government."

George Read of Delaware now rose with a statement which, from a small-state man, was startling, a presage of what was to come. "Too much attachment," said Read, "is betrayed to the state governments. We must look beyond their continuance. A national government must soon of necessity swallow all of them up. They will soon be reduced to the mere office of electing the national Senate."

George Read was fifty-three, a signer of the Declaration, a lawyer who had been in politics all his life. He lived at New Castle in a mansion on the Delaware, with lawns and stables in substantial style, though it was said he had not much money. Read was tall, slightly built and pleasant but with an austerity about him; there were pouches under his eyes as though his nights were restless. He spoke emphatically, on the edge of anger. Rather than see the small states overshadowed by the large, he preferred all boundaries to be erased. He was against patching up the old federal system. "It would be like putting new cloth on an old garment," he said. "The Confederation was founded on temporary principles. It cannot last; it cannot be amended. If we do not establish a good government on new principles we must either go to ruin or have the work to do over again. The people at large are wrongly suspected of being averse to a general government. . . . The state governments must be swept away! We had better speak out."

It was dramatic, threatening, and there was no doubt that Read meant what he said. On the heels of this outburst, General Charles Cotesworth Pinckney of South Carolina arose. The General was eleven years older than his brilliant cousin Charles Pinckney, and had fought through the war. He was very much of a swell, having been educated in England, first at Westminster School, then at Oxford University, where he had attended Blackstone's famous course of lectures. After reading law at the Middle Temple, Pinckney had been called to the English bar, and even rode circuit with one of the judges before he went to Europe on the grand tour. He spoke French fluently, he was wealthy, he had married advantageously and he must have had the speech and manner of an Englishman. When he was a prisoner at Charleston, the British officers had done their courteous best to win him from the American cause. In his own state General Pinckney was much beloved, known to be as staunch a republican as George Mason, given moreover to marvelously rhetorical flourishes that were entirely genuine: "If I had a vein which did not beat with the love of my country, I myself would open it. If I had a drop of blood that could flow dishonourably, I myself would let it out!"

But in Convention, answering Read of Delaware, Pinckney gave voice to no such resounding statement. Instead, he delivered one of those irrelevant but quite practical remarks which at times relieve the more intense moments of public debate. Some states, the General said a trifle plaintively, had not enough people in them for a popular election. "In South Carolina the inhabitants are so sparse that four or five thousand men cannot be brought together to vote."

After this the General sat down. Yet if his brief and homely statement did little to enlighten the Federal Convention, to modern readers it is a vivid reminder of the extensively rural nature of the delegates' America, of the great stretches of unoccupied country — delegates would have called it savage country — and the simplicity of the inhabitants. Not many years earlier, during a critical time in the Revolution, assemblymen of Salem, Massachusetts, had been sent home when it was learned they were elected by a count of corn kernels and peas in a hat. John Adams, hearing of it, had said Nonsense! Let Salem elect by a count of dead codfish if they pleased — but let them get on with the business of government.

When General Pinckney delivered himself, it was late in the day; the Convention adjourned. Nothing positive had been achieved. Votes had been negative, eight to two against popular election of the House of Representatives. Plainly, this Wednesday's work was all to do over again. It was on such evenings that Washington felt constrained to write in his journal: "Attending in Convention and nothing being suffered to transpire, no minutes of the proceedings has been or will be inserted in this diary."

All that day it had rained. The General dined with Dr. Franklin and remained for tea. Then he went home to Robert Morris's and wrote to Lafayette in France. The Marquis would be surprised, said Washington, to hear that his friend was once more — contrary to all he said and wished for — "on a public theatre." Attendance at the Federal Convention, however, could not be resisted. These meetings would determine whether America was to have a government which guaranteed life, liberty and property, or whether the country was to drift into anarchy, confusion and the dictation of "some aspiring demagogue."

The *Pennsylvania Packet* reprinted an article from the *New York Journal*, on the advisability of newspapers being given information as to what was transpiring in the Convention. The tone of the article was lofty but its complaint was cautious: "At this awful moment, when a Council is convened to decide the fate of the Confederation, would it not be dangerous and impolitic to divert or destroy that great channel which serves at once to gratify the curiosity and collect the voice of the people?"

Into the turbulent waters of that great channel, the public press, delegates had no wish to be hurled. The rules of secrecy remained. At ten o'clock next day — Thursday — sentries stood as usual before the State House doors, saluting members, perhaps exchanging greetings or a comment on the weather. No sooner was the meeting convened, with delegates in their seats and the doors closed into the hall, than Resolve 5 came up again, concerning the United States Senate. How many senators would be suitable, and how should they be elected? John Dickinson moved that the Senate be chosen by the state legislatures; Sherman of Connecticut seconded him. The Senate's usefulness, argued Madison, lay in their proceeding with more coolness, more system and wisdom than the popular branch. (This was generally acknowledged as the function of the British House of Lords.) "Enlarge the Senate," said Madison, "and you communicate to them the vices which they are meant to correct." Elbridge Gerry now reminded the Convention that four modes of choosing the Senate had so far been considered: election by the House of Representatives, by the national executive, by the people, by the state legislatures. Let delegates recall that America was divided into the landed interest and the commercial interest. Gerry favored election of the Senate by the state legislatures, where "the commercial and monied interest would be more secure than in the hands of the people at large." The state legislators "have more sense of character and will be restrained . . . from injustice. The people are for paper money when the legislatures are against it."

Elbridge Gerry was one of those politicians who can conceive of new legislation only in terms of their own interests. This is not to accuse Gerry of chicanery or lack of patriotism; few men had been busier in the Revolution than he. But Gerry had days when he could not see beyond his nose. Blinded by occurrences of the moment — Shays's Rebellion, the paper-money men in Massachusetts — Gerry desired a Constitution that would cure the ills of the moment. Luther Martin, soon to arrive from Maryland, would be just such another, and equally persistent. In the Federal Convention it seemed that money men, of "the commercial interest," showed themselves least useful. So far it had been the scholars — Madison, Wythe, James Wilson — who took the longer view and were willing to assume calculated risks for the sake of the future.

John Dickinson, forever moderate and forever knowledgeable, was ready now with two pronouncements. The first was unacceptable and highly characteristic; the second a happy figure of speech which suddenly clarified, for the Convention, the heretofore baffling conception of a national federation — that enigma of "two supreme governments," which Gouverneur Morris had found incomprehensible.

He wished, Dickinson began, the American Senate to consist of the most distinguished characters — distinguished for their rank in life and their weight in property, and bearing as strong a likeness to the British House of Lords as possible. Such characters were more likely to be selected by the state legislatures than by any other mode. In America there existed a variety of interests to be reconciled. This however could be a strength rather than a weakness, as in Great Britain, where the constitution embraced a diversity. It was impossible to abolish the American states and consolidate them into one government. "Let our government," said Dickinson, "be like that of the solar system. Let the general government be like the sun and the states the planets, repelled yet attracted, and the whole moving regularly and harmoniously in their several orbits."

The Convention seized upon the figure, the note-takers' pens were busy. Dickinson had also mentioned "thirteen small streams, pursuing one course." Judge Yates of New York set this down as the "union of several small streams [which] would at last form a respectable river, gently flowing to the sea."

Dickinson's metaphor — without the respectable river — was to be often repeated, very useful in the ratification debates next winter. But James Wilson, after politely acknowledging his colleague's happy imagery (Wilson himself needed no such clarification of the problem), at once denied that the British government could stand as a model. "Our manners, our laws, the abolition of entails and of primogeniture, the whole genius of the people are opposed to it. But I know that all confederations have been destroyed by the growth and ambition of some of their members. . . . I therefore propose that the Senate be elected by the people."

Wilson was voted down. Unanimously, on Dickinson's motion, the Committee agreed that members of the national Senate should be appointed by the state legislatures. The question was settled once and for all. On June twenty-fifth the Convention would adopt the motion officially, nine states to two, Virginia and Pennsylvania dissenting. In the Constitution of 1787 it would so stand.

# VII

*The congressional veto. Proportional representation.
The delegates write home.*

> Federal liberty is to states what civil liberty is to
> individuals. . . . I do not see the danger of the states
> being devoured by the national government. On the
> contrary, I wish to keep them from devouring the na-
> tional government.
>
> JAMES WILSON, *in Convention*

ROM Crèvecoeur and de Tocqueville to Lord Bryce, it
would seem that the shrewdest observers of the American
scene have been foreigners, or at any rate, men born and
educated abroad. At the Federal Convention James Wilson's was a
clear and powerful voice; behind it lay a wide experience in
American politics and law. Franklin liked to refer to Wilson as
"my learned colleague." Wilson cannot be called an eloquent man;
he had none of Patrick Henry's magnetism and poetry. Rather, he
was dry, powerful, persistent. Yet the intellectual clarity of his
view is in itself dramatic.

On June eighth, Wilson was to be particularly effectual. The
Committee of the Whole moved that morning to reconsider the
next to last clause of Virginia's Resolve 6 — in Pinckney's words,
"that the national legislature should have authority to negative all
laws which they should judge to be improper." Elbridge Gerry
declared himself strenuously opposed. In his opinion, Congress
with such a power could enslave the states. "The negative will be
abused," Gerry said heatedly. "New states having separate views
from the old states will never come into the Union. They may even
be under some foreign influence. Are they in such case to partici-
pate in the negative on the will of the other states?"

Spanish intrigues in the Southwest — Natchez, New Orleans — New York loyalists plotting with the British across the Canadian border. Over the minds of delegates lay always the threat of European influence. *Foreign gold!* The phrase was to come up often. Some modification of the congressional veto might be expedient, yet discretion must be left to the one side or the other. Consider individuals, James Wilson said: there are no laws to say that individuals shall be bound to obey in one case and at liberty in another to say if they will obey or disobey. "Federal liberty is to states what civil liberty is to private individuals." The savage emerging from a state of nature purchases civil liberty by a surrender of his personal sovereignty. Should states be less willing to purchase *federal* liberty by a like sacrifice? Wilson reminded the delegates that Congress itself had at first been as one state, with dissensions and separate interests unknown. "We must remember the language with which we began the Revolution: 'Virginia is no more, Massachusetts is no more, Pennsylvania is no more. We are now one nation of brethren, we must bury all local interests and distinctions.'"

Once again the Convention was being reminded of Patrick Henry's famous words. But "the tables," Wilson went on, "at length began to turn. No sooner were the state governments formed than their jealousy and ambition began to display themselves. Each endeavored to cut a slice from the common loaf to add to its own morsel, till at length the Confederation became frittered down to the impotent condition in which it now stands. Review the progress of the Articles of Confederation through Congress," said Wilson, "and compare the first and last draught of it! . . . One of its vices is the want of an effectual control in the whole over its parts. What danger is there that the whole will unnecessarily sacrifice a part? But reverse the case, and leave the whole at the mercy of each part, and will not the general interest be continually sacrificed to local interests?"

It was natural for speakers to refer back in time, recalling the difficulties of the Confederation and the war years which were still so recent — only four years since peace was signed, eleven since the Declaration of Independence and still less since most of the state constitutions were created. Members of the Convention recognized that during this period the states had been growing stronger, the Congress and the Confederacy weaker. They knew also that the Federal Convention had two sets of documents to use as guide: the state constitutions and the Articles of Confederation. Beyond these lay unknown territory — *terra incognita* — into which they must daringly venture, into which indeed the Convention had already stepped. Beyond and outside the State House waited the people, those millions whose sense and mind must somehow be divined, considered, in the making of this new government.

John Dickinson agreed with Wilson in giving Congress power over state laws. "We must take our choice of two things," Dickinson argued. "We must either subject the states to the danger of being injured by the power of the national government, or the latter to the danger of being injured by that of the states. I think the danger greater from the states."

Again one imagines a wave of disturbance sweeping the room. Gunning Bedford of Delaware, plainly angry, declared that Dickinson's words only proved the impossibility of "such a system as that on the table." Bedford must have gestured toward the Virginia Resolves. Was it intended, he asked, to strip the small states of their right of suffrage? Delaware might then be injured at pleasure. She would have about one ninetieth share in the general government, "whilst Virginia and Pennsylvania would possess one third of the whole!"

Gunning Bedford was stout and fiery. "His form was goodly," the epitaph says on his tombstone at Wilmington. And Bedford's loyalty lay within the boundaries of Delaware. "Will not these large states," he demanded, "crush the small ones whenever they stand in the way of their ambitions or interested views? It seems as if Pennsylvania and Virginia wish to provide a system in which they will have an enormous and monstrous influence." And how could the proposed negative be exercised? Were the state laws to be suspended until they could be sent seven or eight hundred miles from home, and then undergo the deliberations of a body which might be incapable of judging local interests? "Is the national legislature," Bedford finished, "to sit continually in order to revise the laws of the states?"

Throughout the Federal Convention one senses the members' consciousness of America's size, of the distance between states, the long, expensive journeys from south to north. From South Carolina it was as easy to go to England as to Boston. Newspapers from London reached Savannah faster than mail sent overland from Massachusetts or Connecticut. Every delegate's thinking was colored by these facts. In their mind's eye were relays of horses, the hazard of vessels beating their slow way down the coastline.

Concerning the small states, Madison answered Gunning Bedford: "If the large states possess the avarice and ambition with which they are charged, will the small ones in their neighborhood be more secure when all control of a general government is withdrawn?" And what would be the consequence to the small states of a dissolution of the union, which seemed likely if no effectual substitute was made for the defective system now existing?

South Carolina, mindful of geography, now interposed in the person of Pierce Butler, proud and — wrote Madison — "vehement." Mr. Butler "was vehement against the negative . . . as cutting off all hope of equal justice to the distant states. The people there would not, he was sure, give it a hearing." According to Alexander Hamilton's brief notes of the proceedings, Butler was indeed emphatic. "Will a man throw afloat his property," Butler demanded, "and confide it to a government a thousand miles *distant?*"

"On the question for extending the negative power to all cases as proposed by Mr. P. & Mr. M.," wrote Madison:

| Mas. | | |
|------|------|------|
| Pa. | | |
| Va. | } Ay | |
| Del. divd. | | Mr. R[andolph] Mr. Mason no. Genl. W. |
| | | not consulted. |

| Conn. | | |
|-------|------|------|
| N.Y. | | |
| N.J. | | |
| Maryd. | } No. | |
| N.C. | | |
| S.C. | | |
| Geo. | | |

The measure, defeated, would not come up again.

Next morning, Saturday, June ninth, was to prove a dangerous day for the Federal Convention. Once more they took up Virginia's hazardous Resolve 4. Paterson of New Jersey made the motion: *"that the Committee* [of the Whole] *resume the clause relating to the rule of suffrage in the national legislature."* How were the states to be represented in Congress? By equal votes, as in Congress to date? Or by a representation proportional to inhabitants or to wealth of states, as the Virginia Resolves had suggested? Judge Brearley of New Jersey seconded Paterson's motion, but rose to say he was sorry the question had to come up. Representation "by ratio" seemed fair on the face of it; in Brearley's estimation it was both unfair and unjust. "The large states — Massachusetts, Pennsylvania and Virginia — will carry everything before them. Virginia with her sixteen votes will be a solid column indeed, a formidable phalanx, while Georgia with her solitary vote and the other little states will be obliged to throw themselves constantly into the scale of some large one in order to have any weight at all."

It was an issue which would block proceedings for days, even weeks. Brearley went on to say he had come to the Convention prepared to support a more energetic and stable government. But now he was astonished, he was alarmed. What was the remedy for this inequality of representation? "One only, that a map of the United States be spread out, that all the existing boundaries be erased and that a new partition of the whole be made in thirteen equal parts."

The small-state men were closing in. Paterson of New Jersey followed his colleague at once. Proportional representation, he said, struck at the existence of the lesser states. He would ask the Convention to consider under what auspices they met here — under an Act of Congress which had been recited in several of the state commissions. Let the Massachusetts credentials be read again!

It was done: *"For the sole and express purpose,"* Massachusetts had said, *"of revising the Articles of Confederation . . ."*

"We shall be charged by our constituents with usurpation," Paterson went on hotly. "We are met here as the deputies of thirteen independent, sovereign states, for federal purposes. Can we consolidate their sovereignty and form one nation, and annihilate the sovereignties of our states who have sent us here for other purposes? . . . The people of America are sharpsighted and not to be deceived. The idea of a national government as contradistinguished from a federal one never entered into the mind of any of them. . . . We have no power to go beyond the federal scheme, and if we had, the people are not ripe for it."

It is the age-old caution: the people are not ripe for change, for reform, for the franchise, for "innovation." Paterson was a brilliant man, much admired at home by his colleagues. At this stage of the proceedings he was acting logically enough. It was impossible to see further ahead; the small states indeed seemed threatened. Gentlemen had hinted, Paterson went on, that if the small states would not agree to any plan, the large states might confederate among themselves. Let them unite thus if they pleased! They could not compel others to unite.

"I therefore declare," finished Paterson, "that I will never consent to the present system, and I shall make all the interest against it in the state which I represent that I can. Myself or my state will never submit to tyranny or despotism!"

There must have been a stir when Paterson ceased, a murmur; surely his voice had risen and rung out. Yates, King, Madison took down his words, and we have Paterson's notes of his own speech. One longs for more, for some echo of the excited defiance felt by the small-state delegates and the corresponding dismay of such men as Randolph, Wilson, Madison. James Wilson answered Paterson; one feels anger in his words and, at the end, a hint of desperation. "Shall New Jersey have the same right or council in the nation with Pennsylvania? I say no! It is unjust — I never will confederate on this plan. The gentleman from New Jersey is candid in declaring his opinion. I commend him for it. I am equally so. I say again I never will confederate on his principles. If no state will part with any of its sovereignty it is in vain to talk of a national government."

At this point and indeed throughout the month of June, one marvels the Convention did not dissolve and the members go home. The large states were if possible more stubborn than the small. After all, it had been Read of Delaware and Brearley of New Jersey who suggested erasing boundaries and redistricting the Union. But Delaware could afford the gesture; she had little to lose by new boundaries and much to gain. The basic issue remained small states against large, ten against three. Rhode Island was not present to be counted, but everyone knew she would have to come into the new government sooner or later — if there was to be a government.

When James Wilson finished speaking, the morning was gone. The State House clock outside struck noon. The question of proportional voting was postponed, the Committee of the Whole rose and the House adjourned until Monday. Delegates went home to inn or dwelling house. Washington dined at the City Tavern. Afterwards he "drank Tea," says the diary, "and set till 10 oclock at Mr. Powell's."

Luther Martin, the firebrand antinationalist from Maryland, had arrived in Convention that morning. He took his seat, surprisingly silent. The weekend was badly needed for rest and reconsideration before Monday. Judge Brearley and after him William Paterson had today been impressive, forceful in their arguments against a consolidated government. No matter what system the Convention had in mind, the small states would never consent to proportional representation as the Virginia Plan had it. So far, New York had said little, though Hamilton had been present and silence was not one of his characteristics. His two colleagues were openly against him. Yates and Lansing, fierce against a national system, were very influential at home. They desired no "energetic government" outside of New York State. Yet Hamilton, as everyone knew, was immensely skillful; perhaps his silence meant only that he was biding his time.

Delegates were by now aware that the Convention was to be no brief thing; it might drag out until autumn. Huge and vital questions had not been touched on. *Slavery!* How should slaves be counted in the franchise — as population or as property? The Western country! How would the Western people vote, according to numbers — population — or by some plan that took into account the value of property? Both subjects were touchy. Washington wrote home that there was no chance of his return to Mount Vernon before harvest, "and God knows how long it may be after." He would like his umbrella sent on — the new one in his study — also his "Blew Coat with the Cremson collar." The honeysuckle against the house should be nailed up and made to spread. "P.S.," wrote the General to his farm manager. "Have you thinned the Carrots which were too thick?"

No planter but remembers his land, especially in the growing season, and no farmer but looks at the sky each morning, no matter where he is, to see what the weather will bring. Washington was in love with Mount Vernon; each journey from it was a sorrow, each return a joy. During all his mature life, whether he wrote from the Federal Convention, from camp in the war or from the President's mansion, the General's letters are filled with farming instructions. This summer of '87 the letters were gloomy. Washington retained his doubting mood of the spring, when he had written to John Jay that he feared the *monster* — sovereignty — would put all to rout. As the Convention proceeded, the General wrote a friend, David Stuart, how ardent was his wish to know "what kind of government is best calculated for us to live under." Yet he was confirmed in his conviction that "the primary cause of all disorders lies in the different state governments and in the tenacity of that power which pervades the whole of their systems. . . ." Local views, the desire for independent sovereignty, separate interests — all these refused to yield to the general good. "Weak at home and disregarded abroad is our present condition," finished Washington, "and contemptible enough it is."

At no time during the Convention do Washington's letters convey much hope. The passion of anger which had sustained him in his struggles for congressional support during the war, seemed now suspended. Washington never wrote, as did other members, of the "importance" of this Convention, or declared the eyes of the world were upon Philadelphia. On the contrary, the General seemed simply to endure, to bear it out. He sat in his place before the delegates and descended from the chair when they went into Committee of the Whole. Twice during the summer he was to manifest grave displeasure. Except for that, Washington maintained the reserve that was natural to him and that people had come to expect.

The General's old friend, George Mason of Gunston Hall, reacted differently. Mason wrote to his son in Virginia that he had never felt himself in such a situation. From a man with his patriotic record, this was strong language. "The eyes of the United States," wrote Mason, "are turned upon this assembly and their expectations raised to a very anxious degree. May God grant we may be able to gratify them by establishing a wise and just government. For my own part I . . . declare I would not, upon pecuniary motives, serve in this convention for a thousand pounds per day. The revolt from Great Britain and the formations of our new governments at that time, were nothing compared to the great business now before us; there was then a certain degree of enthusiasm, which inspired and supported the mind; but to view, through the calm, sedate medium of reason the influence which the establishment now proposed may have upon the happiness or misery of millions yet unborn, is an object of such magnitude, as absorbs, and in a measure suspends the operations of the human understanding."

It was the fashion of the century to look toward posterity, asking quite frankly for its support and applause. "*That the world may know, in all present and future generations,*" John Adams, at the age of thirty, had written in Braintree's Instructions against the Stamp Act. A sense of destiny is no comfortable thing, nor does a man feel easy when he confesses that posterity will bless or curse him for what he is about to do or leave undone. Often, on the floor of the Convention, delegates so confessed. "We should consider," said James Wilson, "that we are providing a Constitution for future generations and not merely for the circumstances of the moment." Rutledge of South Carolina remarked that "as we are laying the foundation for a great empire, we ought to take a permanent view of the subject and not look at the present moment only." Madison declared that the plan now being digested would "decide forever the fate of republican government." Even Elbridge Gerry, cautious, shrewd, narrow in his views, reminded the Convention that "something must be done or we shall disappoint not only America but the whole world."

Strange words for propertied gentlemen, intent, as some historians have hinted, only on commerce and their own financial security. "The eyes and hopes of all are turned towards this new assembly," wrote Madison to William Short in Paris. And to Jefferson on that same day of June: "The attendance of Genl. Washington is a proof of the light in which he regards it. The whole community is big with expectation; and there can be no doubt but that the result will in some way or other have a powerful effect on our destiny."

*In some way or other.* Young James Madison, Father of the Constitution, was not given to overstatement.

Jefferson's transatlantic mail, this summer, was large, his friends eager to tell what they could. Dr. Benjamin Rush of Philadelphia was hopeful, more so perhaps than circumstances warranted. To that celebrated American sympathizer in London, Dr. Price, Rush wrote that Mr. Dickinson had told him the delegates "are all *united* in their objects, and he expects they will be equally united in the means of attaining them. . . . Mr. Adams' book* has diffused such excellent principles among us, that there is little doubt of our adopting a vigorous and compounded federal legislature." Rhode Island, Rush went on to say, had acted infamously, but she was so insignificant in point of numbers, strength and character that her defection would be of no consequence. As for Price's old friend Dr. Franklin, he "exhibits daily a spectacle of transcendent benevolence by attending the Convention punctually, and even taking part in its business and deliberations. He says it is the most august and respectable assembly he ever was in in his life."

The vividest comment of all came from that cheerful, valiant, downright general of artillery Henry Knox, onetime bookseller and hero of the Revolutionary War. Henry Knox weighed three hundred pounds. He and his lady were known as "the largest couple in New York," where they lived lavishly and enter-

* *A Defence of the Constitutions of Government of the United States of America.*

tained much. Generous, profane, persistently sanguine, Knox, like James Wilson, was a speculator in lands, a reckless borrower, continually in litigation. People who did not like him called his figure Bacchanalian and said Knox talked too much, but he held the deep affection of such men as Washington and Lafayette. Knox was passionately interested in the Federal Convention and wrote that his hopes were founded on it. "Should they possess the hardihood to be unpopular and propose an efficient National government, free from the entanglements of the present defective state systems we may yet be a happy and great nation. But I have no expectations if their propositions should be truly wise, that they will be immediately accepted. I should rather suppose that they would be ridiculed . . . as was the ark of old, while building by Noah. . . . But should the Convention be desirous of acquiring present popularity; should they possess local and not general views; should they propose a patch work to the present wretchedly defective thing called the Confederation, look out ye patriots, supplicate Heaven! for you will have need of its protection!"

# VIII

*America divided. Sherman's Compromise. The
Committee of the Whole makes its Report.
June 11-13.*

> There are great seasons when persons with limited
> powers are justified in exceeding them, and a person
> would be contemptible not to risk it.
> EDMUND RANDOLPH, *in Convention*

IT was hard for a Southerner to become used to the "Eastern"
ways. Edmund Randolph, governor of his state, was Virginian to the core. His native good manners made it possible for him to get on with the New Englandmen. Yet they
seemed a race apart — crabbed, foxy, with a rasping whine to
their speech which was a continual irritant to anyone from below
the Pennsylvania line. A South Carolinian, not a member of the
Convention, was heard to say that before he really knew them he
had disliked all New Englandmen because they wore black
woolen stockings. These were the damned Yankees,* and had
been since the first volunteers marched out of Carolina to join
Washington's army. From the Continental Congress in Philadelphia, John Adams had written home that "the characters of gentlemen in the four New England colonies differ from those in the
others . . . as much as several distinct nations almost." He
dreaded, said Adams, the consequences of these differences.
"Without the utmost caution on both sides and the most consid-

---

* A letter from a Massachusetts officer to his brother, dated "Camp at Crown
Point, July 8, 1776," mentions a skirmish where the American troops came
off badly. "But it gives me pleasure," the writer says, "to acquaint you that
none of the 'dam'd Yankees' were there, as the Southern troops are pleased
to term us."

erate forbearance with one another and prudent condescension on both sides, they will certainly be fatal."

This was written in 1775. Yet even in June of '87, with the Federal Convention well on its way, regional divisions seemed insurmountable. Jefferson had said that certain proposals to close the Mississippi made him seriously apprehend a "severance of the eastern and western parts of our confederacy." Pierce Butler of South Carolina wrote home that the interests of Southern and Eastern states were "as different as the interests of Russia and Turkey." What did Connecticut know about growing rice or indigo? What did Pennsylvania know about an economy based on slave labor? In the peace treaty with England, John Adams had made it a basic condition that Massachusetts could cure and dry fish caught off the Grand Banks. But what did Georgia care about the sacred codfish that was carved above the speaker's dais in Boston State House? A Southern nose would not recognize the indigenous cherished tang of an acre of rich cod, split and drying in the sun. Even James Madison, as well informed as any man in America, confessed that of the affairs of Georgia he knew as little as those of Kamchatka. Thomas Jefferson once wrote his friend Chastellux, describing the characters of the states:

| *In the North they are* | *In the South they are* |
|---|---|
| cool | fiery |
| sober | voluptuary |
| laborious | indolent |
| persevering | unsteady |
| independent | independent |
| jealous of their liberties and those of others | zealous for their own liberties but trampling on those of others |
| interested | generous |
| chicaning | candid |
| superstitious and hypocritical in their religion. | without attachment or pretensions to any religion but that of the heart. |

On Monday, June eleventh, the star of the Convention was to be a New Englandman, altogether true to type. Roger Sherman of

Connecticut looked the part and acted it. At sixty-six he was tall, lean, sharp-nosed. His dark hair, streaked with gray and cut straight across the forehead, hung to his collar; he was plainly dressed. His hands and feet were big; his gestures, someone noted, "rigid as buckram." Yet in the craggy face was dignity, the wide-spaced brown eyes had depth behind them. "That old Puritan, honest as an angel," John Adams said of Sherman. Jefferson, pointing him out to a visitor in Congress, had remarked, "That is Mr. Sherman of Connecticut, who never said a foolish thing in his life." The son of a shoemaker and in youth apprenticed to his father, Sherman had risen through farming and the law and had been a signer of the Declaration of Independence. People liked to tell stories about him, how as a young politician he used to advise his colleagues, "When you are in a minority, talk; when you are in a majority, vote." How, when he was asked one time to make a speech at the opening of a new bridge, he walked onto the bridge, turned around and came back. "I don't see but it stands steady," he told a waiting audience — and that was all he said.

Yet here in the Convention, Sherman spoke 138 times; only Madison, James Wilson and Gouverneur Morris outdid him. There is no delegate of whom we have a more vivid description. Major Pierce of Georgia wrote that Sherman "exhibits the oddest shaped character that I ever remember to have met with. He is awkward, unmeaning and unaccountably strange in his manner . . . The oddity of his address, the vulgarisms that accompany his public speaking . . . make everything that is connected with him grotesque and laughable. And yet he deserves infinite praise. He is an able politician and extremely artful in accomplishing any particular object. It is remarked that he seldom fails."

Sherman had arrived in Philadelphia on May thirtieth; he showed no haste to cast in his lot with the national government men. Jeremiah Wadsworth wrote down from Hartford that he feared Sherman was disposed to patch up the Confederacy, "the old scheme of government," rather than create something stronger. "He is as cunning as the devil," said Wadsworth, "and if you attack him you ought to know him well; he is not easily managed, but if he suspects you are trying to take him in, you may as well catch an eel by the tail."

Wily as the devil, honest as an angel, slippery as an eel, rigid as buckram — only a politician could attract to himself such contradictory adjectives. On that very warm Monday morning of June eleventh, the Convention had barely opened when Roger Sherman was on his feet with a proposal which, while it lost the day, was eventually to save the Convention. The question — postponed from Saturday — was the critical problem of how to apportion votes in Congress. The small states wished an equal vote; the large states, for obvious reasons, a proportional one.

"Mr. Sharman proposed . . ." wrote Madison.

Madison was, for his day, an excellent speller; no doubt he wrote Sherman's name as it was pronounced. He was also apt to write Rutlidge with an *i*, Dickenson with an *e*, Pinkney without a *c*, the word "secresy" with an *s*, the word "probaly" with one *b* too few. . . . "Mr. Sharman proposed that the proportion of suffrage in the 1st branch [the House] should be according to the respective numbers of free inhabitants; and that in the second branch or Senate, each state should have one vote and no more."

It would be a month before the Convention came round to this solution, which was to go down in history as the Connecticut, the Great, or the Sherman Compromise. Roger Sherman cannot be given entire credit; the idea had been talked of before. Sherman is on record as hinting at it as far back as 1776, when the Continental Congress was preparing the Articles of Confederation. Should the colonies vote in proportion to population or "according to what they pay"? Sherman said the vote should be taken two ways: by colonies and by individuals. Nobody listened. "When a great question is first started," John Adams once had said, "there are very few, even of the greatest minds, which suddenly and instinctively comprehend it in all its consequences."

The Federal Convention, like the old Congress, met Sherman's proposal with suspicion, though Sherman explained that his plan would protect the small states. "The House of Lords," he said, "have an equal vote with the House of Commons that they may be able to defend their rights."

At this point even the cold print of the record lets the excitement through. Everyone was talking. Motions and amendments followed pell-mell. Rutledge of South Carolina said the vote in the lower house should be according to the "quotas of contribution" — according to taxes paid and the tribute each state brought into the national treasury. Rutledge's colleague Pierce Butler declared bluntly that money is power and the states should have weight in the government according to their wealth. If taxation were to be the basis for representation, Elbridge Gerry interposed — then what about slaves? "Blacks are property," said Gerry, "and are used to the southward as horses and cattle to the northward." Why then should not horses and cattle have the right of representation in the North?

It was a bitter, stinging question, to be echoed and repeated down the years. James Wilson met it by moving that the "three-fifths rule" be adopted, as proposed by the Confederation Congress of 1783, whereby the vote should be in proportion to the "whole number of white and other free citizens and three-fifths of all other persons except Indians not paying taxes . . ." All other persons were of course slaves — a word carefully excluded from the Constitution, though the three-fifths rule was to be adopted and to remain law until the Fourteenth Amendment was passed (1868).

Nor was the problem wholly regional, North against South. George Mason of Virginia, owner of two hundred slaves, was openly and urgently abolitionist; he wished to see all slaves freed. Whereas certain New England shipowners who had profited by the importation and sale of slaves to the Southern states were soon to argue that slavery was not a moral but an economic issue and should be left to the states severally for decision.

It would be August before the slavery question came to full issue; in June the quarrel stood on proportional representation, small states versus large. Dr. Franklin had been sitting, quietly scribbling. Now he asked to be heard, and James Wilson rose to speak for him. . . . He had observed, Franklin stated, that small states are more easily governed than large ones. Therefore he would not be averse to diminishing Pennsylvania by giving part of it to New Jersey and part to Delaware.

Coming from the President of Pennsylvania, this was a startling offer. Was the Doctor serious? Franklin went on to say that until today he had noted with much pleasure that debates were carried on with great coolness and temper. "We are sent here to *consult*, not to *contend* with each other; and declarations of a fixed opinion, and of determined resolution never to change it, neither enlighten nor convince us. Positiveness and warmth on one side, naturally beget their like on the other; and tend to create and augment discord and division in a great concern, wherein harmony and union are extremely necessary to give weight to our councils, and render them effectual in promoting and securing the common good."

Concerning representation, the Doctor said he had no fears that the greater states would swallow the smaller. What advantage would they gain thereby? He recalled that when at the beginning of the century a union was proposed between Scotland and England, the Scotch patriots were full of like fears; they thought they would be ruined in Parliament by the English having a greater representation. Yet nothing of the kind had happened. Moreover, in the mode of representation which this Convention had proposed, it would be in the power of the smaller states to swallow up the greater.

Franklin therefore suggested a more extended version of Rutledge's plan — complex and very long in telling. When the Doctor was done no motion on his proposal was made. But the recital had gained time, allowed tempers to cool. Roger Sherman asked for the question on his motion for an equality of votes in the Senate. Six to five, the states voted Sherman down — a near thing — then voted six to five in favor of proportional representation in both houses. The matter would come up again.

It was closing time. Members went out into the afternoon heat, walking wearily through the streets to lodgings which afforded little relief. In Dr. Franklin's garden the mulberry tree gave hospitable shade. Yet on days like this, if a breeze stirred it was from the southwest, a breath from the furnace. The city sweltered and the delegates endured.

The heat held overnight; with one brief respite it was to hold for nine days. We know it from the diary of a Connecticut delegate — William Samuel Johnson, the new president of Columbia College in New York. Always known as Dr. Johnson, this was an engaging personality, modest, scholarly. There were those who remembered that he had stood aloof from the Revolution — from Tories and rebels alike — and had declined to serve in the Continental Congress after election. Yet the Convention respected Johnson; he was named to important committees. Every evening he noted down the weather; he had arrived in Philadelphia on June first and was staying at the City Tavern on Second Street.

For anyone who knows Philadelphia summers, Dr. Johnson's diary makes painful reading; this is a city where the damp heat lies heavy on the spirit. Visitors from abroad despaired of it. "A veritable torture during Philadelphia's hot season," wrote a Frenchman, "is the innumerable flies which constantly light on the face and hands, stinging everywhere and turning everything black because of the filth they leave wherever they light. Rooms must be kept closed unless one wishes to be tormented in his bed at the break of day, and this need of keeping everything shut makes the heat of the night even more unbearable and sleep more difficult. And so the heat of the day makes one long for bedtime because of weariness, and a single fly which has gained entrance to your room in spite of all precautions, drives you from your bed."

French visitors were irritated also by what they called Philadelphia's "ridiculous custom of using guillotine windows," which came crashing down and could not be opened full, like casement windows. . . . How busy this city by day, and how noisy! — wrote a young Englishman this summer of '87. And at night, how extraordinarily still! By eleven o'clock "there is no city in the world, perhaps, so quiet; at that hour you may walk over half the town without seeing the face of a human being except the watchman." There were mosquitoes, and there were bedbugs even in daylight, wrote Moreau de St. Méry; elder-flower powder was thought to be the best insecticide. As for Philadelphia Sundays, they were purgatory. "What a gloomy silence reigns!" wrote that cheerful Parisian, Chastellux. "One could imagine that some violent epidemic or plague had obliged every one to shut himself up at home." Yet French and English visitors alike were charmed by the beauty of the Schuylkill westward beyond the city, by the fireflies at night, the hummingbirds in the gardens by day. The roaring of bullfrogs in the claypools, the violence of thunderstorms — to outlanders these were curiosities worth noting.

For the delegates, sleep must have been fitful. Lodging-house rooms were small, a man woke unrefreshed. Yet delegates did little complaining. Certainly their evenings were busy, and their afternoons when they left the State House. Much of maneuver, caucus, political planning took place after hours. Delegates dined together, exchanged visits, noting the fact briefly in letters or diaries, always and surprisingly mindful of the secrecy rule. William Pierce of Georgia paid a morning call one June day upon Dr. Franklin and they sat in the garden. The conversation, Pierce noted, was "gay and cheerful." Someone mentioned the Doctor's great age. "I have lived long enough," Franklin said pleasantly, "to intrude myself on posterity."

Pierce's notes, together with his descriptions of delegates, his son later saw fit to bind stylishly in red leather, with an elegant borrowed title, tooled in gold, *Pierce's Reliques*. But it is Washington's diary, meticulous, spare, which best indicates how the delegates occupied their time. Monday evening, June eleventh — the day of Sherman's Compromise — the General spent in his room at Robert Morris's; Dr. Johnson had dined with them earlier. On Tuesday the General attended a concert at the City Tavern, where the two clubrooms were elegant, each room fifty feet long at the least. . . . Close-fitting wigs and woolen coats, closebuttoned; mosquitoes and bad water — delegates endured it all. Perhaps in the State House they removed their coats, loosened cravats. On such points history is silent and the heroes suffer.

One anecdote, again from Pierce, shows the seriousness with which the secrecy rule was regarded, shows also the awe in which delegates held their chairman, the President of the Convention. As the meeting rose one afternoon, a member dropped a paper on the floor. It was picked up and handed to Washington. Pierce tells how, next day, when debate was over and the question for adjournment called for, the General rose from his seat. "Gentlemen!" he said. "I am sorry to find that some one member of this body has been so neglectful of the secrets of the Convention as to drop in the State House a copy of their proceedings, which by accident was picked up and delivered to me this morning. I must entreat gentlemen to be more careful, lest our transactions get into the newspapers and disturb the public repose by premature speculations. I know not whose paper it is, but there it is [throwing it down on the table], let him who owns it take it."

"At the same time he bowed," Pierce's notes continue, "picked up his hat and quitted the room with a dignity so severe that every person seemed alarmed; for my part I was extremely so, for putting my hand in my pocket I missed my copy of the same paper, but advancing up to the table my fears soon dissipated; I found it to be in the handwriting of another person. When I went to my lodgings at the Indian Queen, I found my copy in a coat pocket which I had pulled off that morning. It is something remarkable that no person ever owned the paper."

If indeed men were abashed by the General, their diffidence in his presence was salutary; it kept tempers within bounds, curbing tongues loosened by anger. In the State House chamber the weight of problems unresolved grew with the hours. How long a term should be fixed for members of the House of Representatives? Sherman and Ellsworth were for one year, Rutledge for two, Madison and Jenifer of Maryland for three. Because of the country's size, Madison argued, it would take three years for members to acquaint themselves with the needs of states other than their own. One year, moreover, would be "almost consumed in preparing for and travelling to and from the seat of national business."

It was true enough. America's magnitude, the distance between states, remained the pivot on which great questions hung. But Elbridge Gerry would have none of Madison's argument. Annual elections, Gerry insisted, were "the only defense of the people against tyranny." Gerry was "as much against a triennial House as against a hereditary executive." It "savored of despotism," he said. "The people will be alarmed."

This was an old cry of libertarians everywhere. In England, politicians whom the conservative Edmund Burke called "gentlemen warm in a popular cause" had always come out for annual parliaments. "Where annual election ends, slavery begins," it had been said, and the phrase became a slogan. Elbridge Gerry's own position in the popular cause was a trifle shifty; he backed and he filled. His words, however, quite palpably irritated James Madison, whose answer was cold, quick. Members, Madison said, were continually referring to *the people* and taking the people's opinion as a guide. How could this Convention know what the people thought at the moment, much less what the people would think if they had "the information and lights possessed by the members here"? Surely, the best procedure was to consider what was necessary to attain a proper government; the most enlightened citizens would support it. Gerry renewed his argument. But when the question was put, he lost the vote. Seven to four, the sense of the meeting was for a triennial House.

And how were congressmen of both Houses to be paid? Certainly, urged Madison, not by the states, whose parsimony toward their local legislators was notorious. The best men would not serve if underpaid. Dr. Franklin in the end was willing to agree that salaries be "fixed," as in Virginia's third Resolve. But he preferred the word *moderate* stipend rather than *liberal*. Always, abuses crept in. The Doctor made his point with a little story, "related very pleasantly," wrote Madison. The twelve apostles were not paid, said Franklin, in effect. Yet observe how ecclesiastical benefices had grown and swollen, down to the whole complex edifice of the papal system!

When the vote was taken, eight to three the states favored paying congressmen out of the national treasury. Concerning the term of senators, Spaight of North Carolina moved for seven years. Roger Sherman demurred: "If they are bad men it is too long, and if good they may again be elected." Pierce of Georgia proposed three years. "Great mischiefs had risen in England from their septennial act, which was reprobated by most of their patriotic statesmen." Pierce was exaggerating the facts, but he made his point. Edmund Randolph was for seven years. "The democratic licentiousness of the state legislatures," he said, "proves the necessity of a firm Senate. The object of this second branch is to control the democratic branch of the national legislature. If it be not a firm body, the other branch being more numerous and coming immediately from the people, will overwhelm it. . . . A firmness and independence may be the more necessary also in this branch, as it ought to guard the Constitution against encroachments of the executive, who will be apt to form combinations with the demagogues of the popular branch."

Madison here reminded the Convention of how greatly the new government needed stability, that quality "which the enemies of the republican form allege to be inconsistent with its nature." It was much to be lamented, said Madison, that we had so little experience to guide us. Maryland's constitution was the only one which bore any analogy to this part of the plan. Elbridge Gerry next moved to restrain the Senate from originating money bills; in the British Parliament only the Commons had this power. Pierce Butler said impatiently that we were "constantly running away with the idea of the excellence of the British parliament, and with or without reason copying from them. . . . With us, both Houses are appointed by the people, and both ought to be equally trusted." Gerry said he saw no reason for repudiating everything the British government did, merely because we hated them for their oppressive measures toward us.

Seven to three, the Committee voted down Gerry's measure.

Four weeks had passed since the Convention first met. All their debates had been based on the Virginia Resolves of May twenty-ninth. "Mr. Randolph's Resolves," delegates called them; by division and subdivision these had grown from fifteen to nineteen. The Committee of the Whole had finally gone through them, voted down some Resolves, agreed to others and postponed several of the most important. One June thirteenth, Nathaniel Gorham of Massachusetts, chairman, announced that the Committee of the Whole was ready with its report. What this meant was that the Virginia Resolves, as amended, would tomorrow be presented to the Convention for official consideration, official vote.

Gorham read the nineteen Resolves aloud, as they now stood, then laid them on the table. It was agreed that members might copy them and take copies home. (Very likely it was these Resolves which the offending member dropped on the State House floor.) Several copies survive, differing slightly, but clear and explicit. "*State of the resolutions* [says the first paragraph] *submitted to the consideration of the House by the honorable Mr. Randolph, as altered, amended, and agreed to in a Committee of the Whole House.*"

Reading these Resolves, one sees the firm outline of a government. In spite of obstacles the Convention had indeed made progress. Actually this was only a beginning; the Virginia Resolves were still no more than a map for the Convention to follow. Since May twenty-ninth, delegates had become familiar with this map. They knew the territory to be covered and had glimpsed as it were the end of their journey. Yet a summer of hard work lay ahead, of friction, increasing hazard and the wavering of hope. New Jersey had a plan of her own up her sleeve, a states-rights plan, drastic, federal not national, and counter to the Virginia Plan. She needed time to consolidate her forces, enlist the other small states in support.

The *Massachusetts Centinel* that day burst into exhortation, addressing such citizens as had become restive under the Convention's secrecy: "Ye men of America, banish from your bosums those daemons, suspicion and distrust, which have so long been working your destruction. Be assured, the men whom ye have delegated to work out, if possible, your National salvation are the men in whom ye may confide — their extensive knowledge, known abilities, and approved patriotism warrant it. . . . Consider, they have at their head a Washington, to describe the amiableness of whose character would be unnecessary."

Next morning, a Thursday, Paterson of New Jersey announced that several of the deputations wished to prepare another plan, "purely federal and contradistinguished from the reported Plan." He asked that time might be given for the purpose. Everyone understood: the dissident states desired a day in caucus by themselves. It was granted and the Convention rose without further business.

"*Hot,*" wrote Dr. Johnson in his diary. "*In Convention but adj.*" The North Carolina delegates took occasion to write to their governor, Caswell: "Though we sit from day to day, Saturdays included, it is not possible for us to determine when the business before us can be finished, a very large Field presents to our

view without a single Straight or eligible Road that has been trodden by the feet of Nations. An union of Sovereign States, preserving their Civil Liberties and connected together by such Tyes as
to Preserve permanent & effective Governments is a system not
described, it is a Circumstance that has not Occurred in the History of men. Several members of the Convention have their Wives
here and other Gentlemen have sent for theirs. This Seems to
promise a Summer's Campaign. Such of us as can remain here from
the inevitable avocation of private business, are resolved to Continue whilst there is any Prospect of being able to serve the State
& Union."

## IX

## The New Jersey Plan. Alexander Hamilton makes his speech. June 15-19.

> Why should a national government be unpopular?
> . . . Will a citizen of *Delaware* be degraded by becoming a citizen of the *United States?*
> JAMES WILSON, *in Convention*

IT was Friday, June fifteenth, when William Paterson laid the New Jersey Plan before the Convention. "Mr. Paterson's Plan," delegates called it. There was discussion of how the document could be most fairly considered; members agreed it should be referred to a Committee of the Whole, and that "Mr. Randolph's Plan" be recommitted, so as to place the two in due comparison. Lansing of New York asked for another day's delay, permitting friends of the new plan to take copies and be better prepared to explain and support it. At the Indian Queen, the City Tavern, delegates must have sat late that night.

As soon as the meeting convened on Saturday, Lansing called for a reading of the first resolution of both plans, which he said involved principles that were "directly in contrast." They were indeed, as at once became apparent. "*Resolved* [said the Virginia Plan] that a national government ought to be established, consisting of a Supreme Legislative, Judiciary, and Executive." "*Resolved* [said the New Jersey Plan] that the Articles of Confederation ought to be so revised, corrected and enlarged as to render the federal Constitution adequate to the exigencies of Government, and the preservation of the Union."

Mr. Paterson's Plan, Lansing said fervently, "sustains the sovereignty of the respective states, that of Mr. Randolph destroys it." Not only, Lansing continued, had the Convention no power to propose or discuss Randolph's Plan, but it was improbable the states would ratify it. "The scheme is itself totally novel. There is no parallel to it to be found." The one plan was federal, the other national. "The States will never sacrifice their essential rights to a national government." Had New York suspected — Lansing finished — a consolidation of the states and the formation of a national government, she would never have sent delegates to this Convention.

The two sides were in the open now, openly aligned. It was the resumption of a classic battle, begun even before Independence and marked by convictions that are basic, native it would seem to the bloodlines of American citizens. In 1787, states-sovereignty partisans had no desire to leave the Union, as it was loosely defined by the Articles of Confederation. But like the "old patriots" and the "men of original principles," Paterson's supporters mistrusted a strong central government and preferred some version of the old Confederacy, where Congress could be ordered by the states. Of this belief the most convinced and industrious Convention champions were Lansing and Yates of New York, Gunning Bedford of Delaware, Paterson and Brearley of New Jersey, Luther Martin of Maryland. Following along, each with his reasons, were Elbridge Gerry of Massachusetts, Sherman and Ellsworth of Connecticut and George Mason of Virginia. Read of Delaware occupied a position all his own — someone has called him a small-state man with big-state ideas. Among these, Mason appears as the most disinterested, purest in his motives. In Mason's eyes a strong central government lay counter to the republican ideals for which the American Revolution had been fought. Thomas Jefferson spoke in like manner. "I am not a friend to a very energetic government," Jefferson wrote to Madison from Paris. "It is always oppressive. It places the government more at their ease, at the expense of the people . . . With respect to everything external, the politics of Europe make it indispensably necessary that we be one nation firmly hooped together; interior government is what each state should keep to itself."

Jefferson, of course, viewed America as an agricultural country, a nation of small farmers, sturdy freeholders, though he fore-

saw, in a phrase now famous, that when the American people became "piled upon one another in large cities," another system
might be necessary. It is tempting to speculate on what Jefferson
might have said and done had he been present at this stage of the
Federal Convention. Certainly he was no anti-Constitutionalist
like Luther Martin, Yates or Lansing — the last of whom was to
call the Constitution "a triple-headed monster, as deep and wicked
a conspiracy as ever was invented in the darkest ages against the
liberties of a free people."

The most striking feature of the New Jersey Plan was a Congress with a single legislative chamber in which the states voted
equally, without regard to population or wealth. In a brilliant,
concise summation, given while debate was in full progress, James
Wilson explained the differences between the two plans. All the
note-takers wrote it down:

> Virginia Plan proposes two branches in the legislature.
> Jersey, a single legislative body.
> Virginia, the legislative powers derived from the people.
> Jersey, from the states.
> Virginia, a single executive.
> Jersey, more than one.
> Virginia, a majority of the legislature can act.
> Jersey, a small minority can control.
> Virginia, the legislature can legislate on all national concerns.
> Jersey, only on limited objects.
> Virginia, legislature to negative all state laws.
> Jersey, giving power to the executive to compel obedience by force.
> Virginia, to remove the executive by impeachment.
> Jersey, on application of a majority of the states.
> Virginia, for the establishment of inferior judiciary tribunals.
> Jersey, no provision.

Alexander Hamilton had already declared that he was "not in
sentiment with either plan," possibly saving his fire for next Monday. Paterson rose to defend his plan. As he progressed, his speech
gathered intensity. A tiny man, only five feet two, Paterson, now
in his early forties, possessed an unobtrusive personality, "of
great modesty," it was said, "whose powers break in upon you

and create wonder and astonishment." Paterson's portrait shows a big nose, high-bridged, an eye penetrating and steady, a neat wig above the lawyer's gown. "If the Confederacy was radically wrong," he began, "let us return to our states and obtain larger powers, not assume them of ourselves . . . We have no power to vary the idea of equal sovereignty. The only expedient that will cure the difficulty is that of throwing the states into hotchpot. Let it be tried and we shall see whether the citizens of Massachusetts, Pennsylvania and Virginia accede to it." The Virginia Plan, moreover, would be "enormously expensive," went on Paterson. "Two hundred and seventy members [of Congress] coming once at least a year from the most distant parts as well as the most central parts of the republic! In the present deranged state of our finances, can so expensive a system be seriously thought of?"

Paterson's phrase — from medieval law — about throwing the states "into hotchpot" caught on at once; it would be argumentative currency throughout the summer, along with such favorites as *the dangers of a cabal . . . the temptations of foreign gold . . . the jury trial, palladium of our liberty.* James Wilson, whose deadly, incisive style needed none of these ornaments, got up now to answer Paterson in one of the most telling speeches of his career. After his outline of the two plans with their essential differences, Wilson said that as he conceived the Convention, it was authorized to conclude nothing, but to propose anything. As for the sentiments of the people, was it not true that the sentiments of one's particular circle are commonly mistaken for the general voice? He could not persuade himself, said Wilson, that the state governments and sovereignties were so much the idols of the people, nor a national government so obnoxious to them as some supposed. "Why should a national government be unpopular? Has it less dignity? Will each citizen enjoy under it less liberty or protection? Will a citizen of *Delaware* be degraded by becoming a citizen of the *United States?*"

General Charles Cotesworth Pinckney of South Carolina here remarked with pertinence and some acidity that if New Jersey were given an equal vote — one out of thirteen — she would have no objection to a national government. For his part he thought delegates were authorized to go to any length in recommending whatever they found necessary to remedy the evils which produced this Convention.

Edmund Randolph concurred, only with more heat. When the salvation of the Republic was at stake, it would be treason to our trust not to propose that we found necessary. "View our present deplorable situation," he said. "France, to whom we are indebted in every motive of gratitude and honor, is left unpaid the large sums she has supplied us with in the day of our necessity. Our officers and soldiers, who have successfully fought our battles, and the loaners of money to the public, look up to you for relief. . . . The bravery of our troops is degraded by the weakness of our government." The true question, Randolph went on, was whether we should adhere to the federal plan or introduce the national plan. Only a national government, properly constituted, would answer the purpose. He begged it to be considered "that the present is the last moment for establishing one. After this select experiment, the people will yield to despair."

It was noon — a Saturday — when Randolph finished. Concerning his final word, despair, this was not the last time the Convention would hear it.

*Then adjourned,* wrote Yates, *to Monday morning.*

Eleven states were represented in Convention on Monday, and Hamilton was first on his feet. He was to speak for nearly six hours — all day, in fact. When he rose in his place, delegates saw one of the most extraordinary of the citizens America had produced and would produce in the future. Everyone in the room knew Alexander Hamilton and his reputation. Born in the West Indies, he had come to America as a youth. At thirty-two he was already famous and already hated in certain quarters. Impatient with the slow-witted, humble with those he loved, fiery yet capable of a cold arrogance, Hamilton carried always some slight air of his foreign, mysterious birth — something not truly of America and its thirteen sturdy provincial states. To John Adams, Hamilton was "the bastard brat of a Scotch pedlar." "His manners," wrote a Convention delegate, "are tinctured with stiffness, and sometimes with a degree of vanity that is highly disagreeable."

Perhaps no man in American annals has been so variously characterized. A contemporary historian, from New England — a political enemy — chose to describe Hamilton as "a young officer of foreign extraction, an adventurer of a bold genius, active talents and fortunate combinations." Talleyrand, on the other hand — a diplomat of no mean powers of perception, himself the intimate of state leaders in Europe and America — selected Hamilton as the greatest of the "choice and master spirits of the age." Lord Bryce was to declare that Hamilton, alone among the founding fathers, had not been done full justice by Americans. Theodore Roosevelt went further and placed Jefferson "infinitely below Hamilton." Brilliant, daring, politically ruthless, Hamilton had a vision of the United States as a single, unified nation, rivaling Britain and France and powerful also on the sea. Hamilton would have been at home in the modern industrial world. Moreover he was convinced that he knew the way to achieve his end, where to begin and what to do.

Small wonder that such a man suffered distrust in his time. In person Hamilton was slight, only five feet seven. "The Little Lion," they had called him in the army. He wore his chestnut hair brushed back loosely; his complexion was fair, his cheeks pink as a girl's, the nose high-bridged, nostrils and mouth sensitive as in a blooded horse. Hamilton held his head high, his blue eyes were said to turn black when he was angry. It was a handsome, mobile face, full of light when its owner was speaking, expressive of the energy which caused Jefferson, later his enemy, to say that this man "without numbers is an host within himself."

Here in the Convention, Hamilton stood in a peculiar position, frustrating and embarrassing. Mason wrote afterward that "Yates and Lansing never voted *in one single instance* with Hamilton, who was so much mortified at it that he went home." Actually, it was surprising that Hamilton had got to the Convention at all. The New York legislature never would have named him had it not been for the political prestige of his father-in-law, Philip Schuyler, of the great patroon family. New York State was divided sharply into two political parties. George Clinton, now serving his sixth term as governor, was on the rural, agrarian side, for paper money and states' rights. In June of '88 he was to preside over the ratifying convention at Poughkeepsie.

Clinton had beaten Philip Schuyler for governor in '77; the Clintonian faction was very powerful among the mechanic and artisan groups of the town. But Schuyler had a faction of his own, backed by the old landowning families: Van Rensselaers, Morrises, Van Cortlands, Livingstons, Bayards, together with the urban financial interests of the state — bankers, lawyers and merchants. Supporters of a strong national government, these men saw to it that at least one nationalist went to Philadelphia. Members of the Federal Convention knew these things; many of them had sat in Congress with Alexander Hamilton. They knew also that Hamilton had fought the Clintonians openly and bitterly in the matter of loyalist lands and properties, a vital point in politics. To declare such property forfeited, ready for sale in public bidding, was a sure road to popularity; Governor Clinton had used it to the full. At least four members of the Philadelphia Convention had openly protested this policy, which they said was not only unjust, contravening express terms of the peace treaty, but it was bad for the country. Why force valuable citizens, men of property and education, to continue enemies to the government? It was "mischievous and absurd," Hamilton wrote in the New York newspapers.

All this had counted against him when the New York legislature elected its delegates for Philadelphia. Hamilton would have liked a large representation, say of five, with a Jay, a Duane, a Livingston to support him. Yet here he stood alone, a man who had done much to bring the Convention about, and who almost single-handed would swing a hostile New York State to ratification of the United States Constitution. Hamilton called himself a highflyer and he was; he liked aristocracy and admired the British constitution above all governments on earth. Jefferson later accused Hamilton of being "bewitched and perverted by the British example." It was a passion which in a few years would lead Hamilton into highly questionable behavior, endeavors to override and undermine government plans which he considered unfavorable to Anglo-American relations. For all Hamilton's outward coolness, there seemed to be a nervous instability. Considering his absurd and stubborn quarrel with his Commander in Chief in the midst of war, one queries how the man was able to accomplish all he did for his country. Yet Washington trusted Hamilton. This restless ambition, he told John Adams, was never ignoble, but "of the laudable kind which prompts a man to excel in whatever he takes in hand."

It was typical of young Hamilton to marry advantageously, right into one of the richest, most powerful families of the state, and then to fall so deeply in love with his wife, his dark-eyed Betsy, that he feared himself incapacitated for business. "My Angel!" he wrote. "I told you truly that I love you too much. I struggle with an excess which I cannot but deem a weakness and endeavor to bring myself back to reason and duty. . . . 'Tis a pretty story indeed that I am to be thus monopolized by a little nut-brown maid." In his turn Hamilton won the affection not only of his family but of a diverse company of friends. This fervent personality, once encountered, could not be forgotten. "I feel within myself," wrote Lafayette from France in '85, "a want to tell you I love you tenderly."

Alexander Hamilton was never to know old age. He died, as the world knows, in his late forties, shot in a duel with Aaron Burr. Somehow it is impossible to imagine Hamilton as an old man. Even his hardheadedness and relentless skepticism showed a quality not of caution but of youthful daring, careless defiance. Hamilton read voraciously. His statesmanship, his plans for the restoration of public credit, were to contemporaries tempting but wildly imaginative.

Yet something about his person, his bearing and disposition made him bait for suspicion; Hamilton was bound to be defeated in his day. So much of him was foreign! — even the circumstance that he loved painting, possessed a rich voice and liked to sing. He felt no loyalty to New York, did not know the meaning of state pride, was not born to it and looked on it as stupid provinciality. It was the Union that Hamilton admired; it was the Union whose glorious illimitable future his rich imagination soared to meet. When such a man stood up before the Federal Convention on Monday morning, June eighteenth, what he said was bound to meet with doubt, uneasy praise. In the minds of members a Virginia Plan had been debated and digested, a New Jersey Plan had been introduced and awaited the vote. What then had this impeccably dressed son-in-law of Philip Schuyler to offer, what was he about to propose?

The Convention knew that Hamilton was a nationalist, a continentalist, and that he desired a government "tuned high," a strong central power that would pervade the whole. Yet what he proposed today outdid in audacity any former statement. He would read to the Committee, Hamilton said, the sketch of a plan which he preferred to the two plans under consideration. He "almost despaired" that republican government could be established over so great an extent of country. Yet what he suggested was, he said, republican in form, a government elected "by a process originating with the people." His plan was offered not as a proposition to the Committee but merely as a correct view of his own ideas — amendments that might be later offered to Mr. Randolph's plan.

He would like to see in America, said Hamilton, a single executive, chosen for life by electors and given the power of absolute veto. Senators also were to be chosen for life. A lower house or assembly would be elected by the people for a term of three years. State governors were to be appointed by the national government. Thus the senate and executive (Hamilton called him the governor) would balance against a democratic assembly. Such a government would derive from the people, but the rage for liberty would be checked, restrained. "Men love power," said Hamilton. "Give all power to the many, they will oppress the few. Give all power to the few, they will oppress the many."

Without hesitation, Hamilton pointed to Great Britain, whose House of Lords he called a most noble institution. "I believe," Hamilton said, "the British government forms the best model the world ever produced . . . This government has for its object *public strength* and *individual security* — said with us to be unattainable. All communities divide themselves into the few and the many. The first are the rich and well born, the other the mass of the people. The voice of the people has been said to be the voice of God. . . . it is not true in fact. . . . Can a democratic Assembly, who annually revolve in the mass of the people, be supposed steadily to pursue the public good?"

Popular passions, Hamilton went on, "spread like wild fire and become irresistible." He would ask the New England states whether experience did not bear this out? And why should we fear an elective monarch for life more than one for seven years? Were not the governors of the states elective monarchs? Hamilton's own notes for his speech went even further. "The monarch must have proportional strength," he had written. "He ought to be hereditary and to have so much power that it will not be his interest to risk much to acquire more. The advantage of a monarch is this — he is above corruption. He must always intend, in respect to foreign nations, the true interest and glory of the people." To the Convention, Hamilton repeated his doubts concerning a republican government for so large a country. "States," he said, "will prefer their particular concerns to the general welfare . . . What in process of time will Virginia be? She contains now half a million of inhabitants — in twenty-five years she will double the number. . . . The national government cannot long exist when opposed by a weighty rival." History was rife with warnings on this point, said Hamilton. In ancient Greece the Amphictyonic Councils had failed.

That Hamilton was not interrupted seems extraordinary, considering the tenor of his remarks, their boldness, the growing unpopularity of this "British example." *Annihilate state distinctions and state operations?* In the whole gathering, perhaps only Read of Delaware and Butler of South Carolina would have agreed. *A single executive, elected for life?* It came close to monarchy. Paradoxically, Hamilton's idea of a lower house elected directly by the people went beyond what most delegates were ready to concede to "democracy." Even Madison was against it. *A general and national government, completely sovereign?* Nothing less, Hamilton had argued, could establish American power at home and American prestige abroad.

It was enough to make James Madison's hair turn gray. Hamilton was going to antagonize every small-state man in the Convention. Messieurs Yates, Lansing and Luther Martin must have writhed in their seats. The day was fearfully hot. Hamilton could not have finished speaking before three in the afternoon. Nathaniel Gorham, who had presided, confessed that he was "quite overcome with the heat of the weather." Hamilton's final sentence became famous, a byword, though only his opponent, Judge

Yates, included it in his notes. The New Jersey Plan, said Hamilton in peroration, was perhaps nearest to the peoples' expectations. His own plan and the Virginia Plan were, he knew, "very remote from the idea of the people. But the people," finished Hamilton, "are gradually ripening in their opinions of government. They begin to be tired of an excess of democracy. And what even is the Virginia Plan but democracy checked by democracy, or pork still with a little change of the sauce?"

*Then adjourned,* wrote Yates succinctly, *to tomorrow.*

Alexander Hamilton at the Federal Convention cuts a disappointing figure, at odds with his previous and subsequent magnificent performance in support of the Constitution. His long speech — a day's work — was out of tune, unacceptable to both sides. It is true that George Read of Delaware later declared in Convention that he would like to see Hamilton's plan substituted "in place of that on the table." It is true also that Gouverneur Morris called the speech "a generous indiscretion." But Morris, from his own inclinations, probably discounted Hamilton's British predilections, putting them down to his foreign birth; Hamilton confessed himself "an exotic." Fifty years later, John Quincy Adams, coming across a copy of the speech in Madison's papers, pronounced it to be "of great ability," and Hamilton's plan for a constitution theoretically better than that which was adopted. "But energetic," Adams added, "and approaching the British Constitution far closer, and such as the public opinion of that day never would have tolerated."

The striking fact is that there occurred no argument with Hamilton on the floor. No delegate stood up next morning in rebuttal, nor was any action taken on Hamilton's recommendations. Dr. Johnson of Connecticut probably voiced the general feeling when he said openly a few days later that "a gentleman from New York with boldness and decision proposed a system totally different from both; and though he has been praised by everybody, he has been supported by none." It would seem that Hamilton's speech was too radical for rebuttal, too extreme, though quite palpably he meant every word; his future conduct proved it. Perhaps he deliberately outlined to the Convention a system of government so "national," so "consolidated," that it would make the Virginia Plan look tame and the New Jersey Plan impossible.

Yet Hamilton must have anticipated the effect of his words. He was far too experienced to be led, and at such a time, into rash or uncalculated statements. Had the Convention been public rather than secret, surely Hamilton would not have ventured so far. In spite of his audacity there was a hesitation to his delivery, an uncertainty which came through the reports. And there are five reports, from Madison, Yates, Lansing, Rufus King — and Hamilton's notes. Judge Yates has Hamilton say that he is "greatly embarrassed"; he "despairs" — and twice, he is "at a loss."

Alexander Hamilton was to pay a price for his speech of June eighteenth; for the rest of his life it would rise to harass him. When the moment came his enemies made much of it. They said the Constitution had "an awful squinting towards monarchy," and that Hamilton wanted an American king. Hamilton denied it, declared that what he said that day had been compounded of "propositions made without due reflection," then denied even that he had advocated a President with life tenure. Such a denial, Madison wrote blandly from Virginia, was due "to a want of recollection."

"Mr. Hamilton left Town this morning," Lansing was to write on June thirtieth. Ten days afterward, Lansing himself, with Yates, spurned the Convention forever and returned to New York, resolutely opposed to the proceedings and prepared to fight whatever "national" system the delegates should produce. Hamilton, however, came back to Philadelphia from time to time during the summer. And always he had something pertinent to say, something striking. In September he was to arrive at the State House by himelf, without his two colleagues, to sign the Constitution — an act of no small courage, defying the political powers of his own state.

# X

## The Great Debate. June 19-28.

The situation of this Assembly, groping as it were
in the dark to find political truth.
BENJAMIN FRANKLIN, *in Convention*

JAMES MADISON was on his feet almost as soon as the
meeting opened. It was Tuesday, June nineteenth, and the
Convention still in Committee of the Whole. Madison was
primed and ready for what he had to say. He did not so much as
mention Hamilton or his six-hour speech of the previous day,
which certainly had been no help to the nationalists. Hamilton
had gone too far; such extreme statements would scare off possible adherents. The talk must have been busy, Monday night, in
tavern and club. Had delegates rebuked young Hamilton for his
rashness? Had they agreed that the best strategy was to ignore
what he had said and press on to the matter at hand — the vote,
the final choice between the New Jersey and Virginia Plans?

In any event, Madison on Tuesday morning did not waste a
minute, but proceeded to tear the New Jersey Plan to pieces,
coldly, logically, point by point, with each point phrased as a
question. Would the New Jersey Plan prevent the states from
trespassing upon each other, as debtor states had done by issuing
paper money in retaliation against creditor states? Would the Plan
prevent internal state turmoils such as Massachusetts had experienced in Shays's Rebellion? Would it protect the Union against
the influence of foreign powers? Had the small states considered
the expense of the New Jersey Plan, by which each state must
pay its entire delegation to Congress? Could a nation survive under
a compact which did not bind the whole?

And had the small states stopped to think where they would be if their stubborn adherence to Mr. Paterson's Plan prevented the adoption of *any* plan? New Jersey delegates had declared it would not be "safe" — that was their language — to allow Virginia sixteen times as many votes as Delaware. These gentlemen preferred to throw all the states into one mass and make a new partition into thirteen parts. Were they not, Madison hinted, becoming entangled in their own self-spun cobwebs? The history of confederations was filled with such snares and hazards.

When Madison had finished, Rufus King of Massachusetts at once put the question: Was Mr. Randolph's Plan preferable to Mr. Paterson's? The states voted. Seven to three the motion won, with Maryland divided. The New Jersey Plan was dead, finished. Madison had given it the crowning blow. Had the plan been introduced to the Convention earlier, it might have prevailed — who knows? But delegates had had three weeks to think things over, talk, argue, become used to what at first seemed shocking, impossible. Henceforward the Convention would proceed according to Virginia's nineteen Resolves — though much would be altered before September seventeenth. The Constitution as signed was to be very different from Randolph's original proposals — a far more flexible instrument.

But when on June nineteenth delegates voted down the New Jersey Plan, it did not mean the small states had capitulated. The battle over Congressional representation would rage for another month, right up to July sixteenth when the Convention adopted the Great Compromise, giving equal representation in the Senate — two votes to a state whether large or small — and in the House, proportional representation. Until then, the drama in the Pennsylvania State House would heighten week by week, the tension increasing and the atmosphere darkening until it seemed there could be no solution, no daylight at the storm's end, no strong new Constitution for thirteen harassed, vigorous, quarreling American states.

Next morning, June twentieth, delegates met in full Convention. Washington resumed the chair; it would be the first day he had sat through a full debate since the fateful May twenty-ninth when Randolph and Charles Pinckney presented their separate plans. Nathaniel Gorham, having acted all this time as chairman in Committee of the Whole, stepped down to take his place among the Massachusetts delegates. A plain, forceful speaker, Gorham now could have his say.

The Convention's initial move that morning was to expunge the word "national" from the First Virginia Resolve. Instead of reading, "Resolved, that a national government ought to be established, consisting of a supreme Legislative, Judiciary, and Executive," Ellsworth of Connecticut moved the resolution read, "that the Government *of the United States* ought to consist. . . ."

It was a highly politic suggestion; Gorham seconded it. This word national, Ellsworth pointed out, would frighten people. The states would not ratify a constitution — any constitution — unless it appeared as an amendment to the old Articles of Confederation. Leave out the word national! The motion went through. *"Nem. con.,"* wrote Madison.

At this point John Lansing of New York rose with a long, heated protest against things in general. Lansing was not easy to listen to; he had what Pierce of Georgia called "a hisitation in his speech." This Convention, Lansing said, had no powers to create a two-branch legislature. Concerning the proposal that Congress should have a negative on the state laws — "Is it conceivable," demanded Lansing, "that there will be leisure for such a task? There will on the most moderate calculation, be as many acts sent up from the states as there are days in the year. Will the members of the general legislature be competent judges? Will a gentleman from Georgia be a judge of the expediency of a law which is to operate in New Hampshire? Such a negative would be more injurious than that of Great Britain heretofore." This general government now under consideration, Lansing insisted, was "utterly unattainable, too novel and complex."

George Mason of Virginia, with the fierce vigor of an old man, spoke out against the extensive powers being granted to Congress. "Is it to be thought that the people of America, so watchful over their interests, so jealous of their liberties, will give up their all, will surrender both the sword and the purse to the same body, and that, too, not chosen immediately by themselves?" How were the national taxes to be gathered in? — Mason demanded. "Will the militia march from one state to another in order to collect the arrears of taxes from the delinquent members of the Republic?" Fire and water themselves are not more incompatible than such a mixture of civil liberty and military execution! "Will not the citizens of the invaded state assist one another till they rise as one man and shake off the Union altogether?" He was struck with horror at the prospect, Mason concluded.

It was now that Luther Martin of Maryland stood up with the first of his intolerably long-winded speeches, which were to be a feature of the Convention until Martin's angry — and merciful — departure on September fourth, thirteen days before the Constitution was signed. Martin was about forty, broad of shoulder, carelessly dressed, with short hair, a long nose, a rough voice and a convivial liking for the bottle which later was to lead him into insolvency and disgrace. He was impulsive, undisciplined, altogether the wild man of the Convention, furious defender of state sovereignty, by no means foolish in all he said, though he could talk fatuously about "the rights of free men and free states." That perceptive historian Henry Adams described Martin as "the rollicking, witty, audacious Attorney General of Maryland, drunken, generous, slovenly, grand . . . the notorious reprobate genius."

This however was said a century later. In the Federal Convention it is to be doubted if anyone would have called Luther Martin a genius. Delegates were too irked by his verbosity, which chose to erupt on the hottest of Philadelphia days, when the Convention sat in moist discomfort. What Martin actually said was that he saw no necessity for a Congress with two branches. One was preferable. . . . A national judiciary extended into the states would be ineffectual and resented. . . . To grant unnecessary powers to the general government might well defeat "the original end of the Union." Congress represented and was meant to represent not the people but the state legislatures. Also, he was against state conventions for ratification of the Constitution.

"This," wrote Madison, "was the substance of a very long speech" — and then crossed out the sentence.

Unable to agree or even discuss the paramount issue — proportional representation in Congress — a stalemated Convention referred back to lesser questions, hashing them out, arguing, wrangling, in the process finding out about their country and inching slowly toward the day when compromise must be reached, or — every delegate knew it in his heart — the Convention dissolve in failure. Much was said that had been heard before; to the more experienced delegates this repetition was plainly irritating. Even so, new arguments were raised, old issues approached from a fresh viewpoint, and things said that would influence court decisions generations later.

On the question of pay for congressmen, James Wilson suggested Congress itself should fix the amount and pay it from the national treasury. . . . But this was indecent, Madison countered. The legislature should not put their hands in the public purse to convey it to their own. Let the stipend be fixed by the Constitution. If the state governments decided the amount, what of "the poor states beyond the mountains"? Western states hereafter arising ought to be considered as equals and brethren, and provision made so they could send their best men to Congress. . . . As for senators, they ought not to be paid at all. (This from General Pinckney.) Senators were supposed to represent the wealth of the country; *ergo*, they should themselves be wealthy. Dr. Franklin repeated that he was against payment for all government officers. In this chamber, he said, were young men who no doubt would be elected senators. The Convention might be charged with having carved out lucrative places for themselves.

There was hot discussion over the question of whether congressmen should be permitted to hold other government offices during their terms. Many delegates present did hold such offices, state and national; it was the accepted custom, people were used to it. James Wilson was in favor, not wishing to discourage merit. Had not our Commander in Chief of all the armies been selected out of Congress?

It was a telling argument. Did Washington permit himself to smile? Although Rufus King agreed with James Wilson, Pierce Butler of South Carolina objected, warning of Great Britain, where men got into Parliament in order to secure place and office for themselves and their friends. The English government had been ruined by this practice. George Mason was of like mind; he said the door must be shut against corruption. Nathaniel Gorham disagreed. The corruption of the English government could not be applied to America. Our elections were frequent, we had no rotten boroughs.

The argument ran back and forth, Madison saying flatly that it was hard enough in Virginia to persuade the best citizens to serve in the legislature. Were the states then to rely on *patriotism?* "If this be the only inducement," said Madison, "you will find a great indifference in filling your legislative body."

Elbridge Gerry spoke bluntly, after his fashion. (It was once remarked of Gerry in Congress that he was always satisfied to shoot an arrow without caring about the wound he caused.) "At the beginning of the war we possessed more than Roman virtue. It appears to me it is now the reverse. We have more land and stock-jobbers than any place on earth. . . . We have constantly endeavored to keep distinct the three great branches of government. But if we agree to this motion," Gerry finished, ". . . legislators will share in the executive [branch], or be too much influenced by the executive, in looking up to him for offices."

Young Charles Pinckney declared fervently that Americans were perhaps "the only people in the world who ever had sense enough to appoint delegates to establish a general government." Why, therefore, imitate older governments, endeavoring to create in our Senate a body like the House of Lords? In the United States, property was more evenly divided. Few could be called rich, as men were esteemed rich in Europe, or whose riches might have dangerous influence. Perhaps there were not a hundred such on our Continent. "The genius of the people . . . is unfavorable to the rapid distinction of ranks." The people of the United States, said Pinckney, may be divided into three classes: professional men, commercial men, and the landed interest. Why not bear this in mind and make a government for our people as they are, and as we know them? With unconscious arrogance, Pinckney ignored the artisans and mechanics, whose sole property was in their labor. The state governments, finished Pinckney, must remain. They must not be erased.

The Convention seized upon this point with as much zeal as though it had never been broached. The senatorial ratio of representation would determine whether the small states were to be rendered powerless. Once more, delegates voted to postpone this vital question, then voted aye to the motion that senators be chosen by the state legislatures, and voted unanimously that senators must be not less than thirty years old. On the motion for a nine-year senatorial term the Convention voted no, eight to three. Nathaniel Gorham's motion for a six-year term — one-third to go out biennially — carried, seven to four. (Six days earlier, the Convention had voted a two-year term for representatives.)

Here James Madison lost out; he had favored a nine-year term for senators, just as from the beginning he had wished the Senate elected by the state legislatures, as balance against a popular House. He was also for Congress having a negative on state laws. Only one of these three measures was to go into the Constitution — the method of Senate election — and that would last until the Seventeenth Amendment (1913). Looking ahead, Madison saw a United States peopled very differently from the year 1787. "In framing a system which we wish to last for ages," he told the Convention, "we should not lose sight of the changes which ages will produce. An increase of population will of necessity increase the proportion of those who will labor under all the hardships of life, and secretly sigh for a more equal distribution of its blessings. These may in time outnumber those who are placed above the feelings of indigence." Power, Madison said, could then slide into the hands of the numerous poor rather than the few rich. Symptoms of a leveling spirit had already appeared in certain quarters. How was this danger to be guarded against "on republican principles"? A body in the government (a senate) "sufficiently respectable for its wisdom and virtue," with an elective term of nine years to render it stable — surely this would provide a safeguard for liberty.

Present-day readers may be a trifle dashed to find the Father of our Constitution urging, in effect, that the American rich put up barriers against the American poor, who with power in their hands could be dangerous. By symptoms of a leveling spirit, Madison meant riots and rowdyism under Pennsylvania's popular government, the recent unrest in Maryland, the agrarian paper-money troubles of Rhode Island, and of course Shays's Rebellion. Yet it is unfair to make judgment in terms of today. In the year 1787 the Convention's proposals were essentially new, untried. And before they could take effect the people must approve them.

That senators should be paid was now finally agreed, ten states to one, though on the source of payment the vote was close; six to five on its coming from the national treasury rather than the state legislatures. George Mason (he of the fertile Virginia acres) suggested a property qualification for senators. Nobody seconded him and the question was dropped. That both houses should have the right to originate bills was agreed on, and that members of both houses were eligible to state office but not to office in the United States government.

All this was progress and looked encouraging. Beneath it however still lurked the prime question before which the Convention stood embattled: How was America to be represented in Congress — by population or equally, state to state? On June twenty-seventh, debate on this question began in earnest, with the delegates still sitting in full Convention, Washington in the chair.

The weather continued hot. In the past two weeks there had been only three cool days. This Wednesday morning, delegates must have been tired to start with, and edgy. Luther Martin rose again — "chose this most inopportune time," wrote a member afterward, "to deliver a lengthy harangue." For over three hours, Martin contended "at great length and with great eagerness," Madison noted. All that Martin said was stale, a repetition of his earlier speech. . . . The powers of the general government must be kept within narrow limits, its function being merely to preserve the state governments, not to govern individuals. . . .

Martin paused to read passages from Locke, Somers, Vattel, Dr. Priestley, an exercise the Convention had thus far avoided. Every experienced politician knew of these authors and of their respected and well-worn arguments about the law of nature . . . man in a state of nature . . . the compact between ruler and ruled. During the Revolution the phrases had become almost as familiar as the Bible, and had been made the most of by every penny politician who could find a crowd to harangue. Was it necessary now to plow over this old ground? "I have never heard of a confederacy having two legislative branches," Martin went on. "Even the celebrated Mr. Adams, who talks so much of checks and balances, does not suppose it necessary in a confederacy." He would never, Martin argued, trust a government so organized for "all the slaves of Carolina or the horses and oxen of Massachusetts! . . . What are called human feelings in this instance are only the feelings of ambition and the lust for power."

At this point the speaker announced that he was "much too' exhausted to finish his remarks," and would resume them tomorrow. Delegates stumbled out into the street; it was time for adjournment. Wearily they faced the morrow. And on the morrow Martin made good his word. His discourse was delivered, wrote Madison, "with much diffuseness and considerable vehemence."

A long speech is a hazard on any count. But a long speech delivered with vehemence is scarcely endurable. If the three large states leagued themselves together, Martin shouted, then the other ten could do the same! For himself he would rather see such partial confederacies than submit to the Virginia Plan.

Luther Martin was to suffer for this speech. During the ratification battle in the ensuing winter, Ellsworth attacked Martin's anti-Constitutional stand via the newspapers, addressing his opponent directly, after the fashion of the era. "The day you took your seat [in the Convention] must be long remembered by those who were present . . . You had scarcely time to read the propositions which had been agreed to after the fullest investigation, when, without requesting information, or to be let into the reasons of the adoption of what you might not approve, you opened against them in a speech which held during two days and which might have continued two months, but for those marks of fatigue and disgust you saw strongly expressed on whichever side of the house you turned your mortified eyes."

Martin defended himself with equal vigor; it was not a time of nicety in the public prints. Newspapers today would not dare to publish insults such as the founding fathers hurled at each other with joyful abandon. In the Federal Convention, however, Martin's long effort provoked little reaction beyond disgust. The debate continued, baffling, seemingly getting nowhere, yet actually serving the purpose of airing all views. . . . If combinations of large states were to be feared, said Williamson of North Carolina, then what about the new states from the westward? Their distance from market would inevitably tempt them to combine, thus laying commercial burdens on the old states. . . . Madison here demanded which was more to be feared — a superior central force or the selfishness of feeble associates? What common interest could cause Virginia, Massachusetts and Pennsylvania to combine? None! In point of staple productions they were as dissimilar, said Madison, as any other three states in the Union. Tobacco, fish, flour: these were their respective products. And were not large states everywhere more apt to be rivals than partners? Great powers are always hostile. To the enmity and rivalry between England and France, said Madison, America perhaps owed her liberty.

Old Dr. Franklin, sitting with the famous double spectacles low on his nose, now broke silence; he had said little these past days. Addressing himself to Washington in the chair — "The small progress we have made," Franklin said, "after four or five weeks close attendance and continual reasonings with each other — our different sentiments on almost every question . . . producing almost as many noes as ayes, is methinks a melancholy proof of the imperfection of the human understanding. We indeed seem to feel our own want of political wisdom, since we have been running about in search of it. We have gone back to ancient history for models of government, and examined the different forms of those republics which, having been formed with the seeds of their own dissolution, now no longer exist. And we have viewed modern states all round Europe, but find none of their constitutions suitable to our circumstances.

"In this situation of this Assembly, groping as it were in the dark to find political truth, and scarce able to distinguish it when presented to us, how has it happened, Sir, that we have not hitherto once thought of humbly applying to the Father of lights to illuminate our understandings?" Franklin here reminded the Convention how at the beginning of the war with England, the Continental Congress had had prayers for divine protection — and in this very room. "Our prayers, Sir, were heard," said Franklin, "and they were graciously answered. All of us who were engaged in the struggle must have observed frequent instances of a Superintending providence in our favor. To that kind providence we owe this happy opportunity of consulting in peace on the means of establishing our future national felicity. And have we now forgotten that powerful friend? . . . I have lived, Sir, a long time, and the longer I live, the more convincing proofs I see of this truth — *that God governs in the affairs of men.*"

On the Doctor's manuscript of this little speech, the word God is twice underscored, perhaps as indication to the printer. But whether or no Franklin looked upon the deity as worthy of three capital letters, his speech was timely. . . . If a sparrow cannot fall to the ground unseen by him, Franklin continued, was it probable an empire could arise without his aid? "I firmly believe this, and I also believe that without his concurring aid we shall succeed in this political building no better than the builders of Babel. We shall be divided by our little partial local interests; our projects will be confounded and we ourselves shall become a reproach and bye word down to future ages. And what is worse, mankind may hereafter from this unfortunate instance despair of establishing governments by human wisdom and leave it to chance, war and conquest.

"I therefore beg leave to move that henceforth prayers imploring the assistance of heaven and its blessings on our deliberations, be held in this Assembly every morning before we proceed to business, and that one or more of the clergy of this city be requested to officiate in that service."

Benjamin Franklin was possessed of so much wisdom and political acumen that there is no telling which quality was uppermost, impelling this speech. Roger Sherman at once seconded Franklin's motion. But Hamilton "and several others" — wrote Madison — feared that calling in a clergyman at so late a stage might lead the public to suspect dissensions in the Convention. To this Franklin countered dryly that a measure of alarm out of doors might do as much good as ill. Williamson of North Carolina made the flat statement that everyone knew the real reason for not engaging a chaplain: the Convention had no funds.

There was general embarrassment. Nobody liked to move against the distinguished Dr. Franklin, and in such a matter. Later on, fantastic stories arose; it was rumored that Hamilton had said ironically the Convention was not in need of "*foreign* aid." This is palpable nonsense. Nevertheless the scene had urgency, danger, drama. A Georgia delegate, William Few, described that morning of June twenty-eighth as "an awful and critical moment. If the Convention had then adjourned, the dissolution of the union of the states seemed inevitable." Franklin's motion failed, though Randolph proposed tactfully that on the approaching Fourth of July a sermon be preached at the request of the Convention and that thenceforth prayers be used.

Yet whether the Doctor had spoken from policy or from faith, his suggestion had been salutary, calling an assembly of doubting minds to a realization that destiny herself sat as guest and witness in this room. Franklin had made solemn reminder that a republic of thirteen united states — venture novel and daring — could not be achieved without mutual sacrifice and a summoning up of men's best, most difficult and most creative efforts.

# XI

*The tension mounts. Europe and America.*

I do not, gentlemen, trust you!
GUNNING BEDFORD, *in Convention*

EVEN Elbridge Gerry, by nature combative, now began to lament the contentiousness of delegates. "Instead of coming here like a band of brothers, belonging to the same family," he said, "we seem to have brought with us the spirit of political negotiators." Dr. Johnson of Connecticut, affable, and known for his influence with certain Southerners, observed that the controversy must be endless while gentlemen differed in the grounds of their arguments. Concerning the fears of a strong union, Nathaniel Gorham reminded the Convention that Massachusetts herself had once been three colonies: Massachusetts Bay, Plymouth, and Maine. The same with Connecticut and New Haven, and with East and West Jersey. "The dread of union was reciprocal," said Gorham. Yet "incorporation took place, all parties were safe and satisfied, and every distinction is now forgotten." If his colleagues from Massachusetts saw the union of the states in the light he saw it himself, he would consider it his duty, finished Gorham, to stay here as long as any other state would remain with them and agree on some plan that could be recommended to the people.

Delegates had already voted against equality of representation in the House. After more than two weeks of debate the Convention voted again — and could not break the deadlock. The large states stood firm, though Madison had a way of placing the blame for obduracy always on the small states. Balloting now was taking place not in Committee of the Whole but in full Convention. The rules, however, made it possible to alter any decision by calling for another vote next day, slowing up procedure maddeningly. Yet in the end the rule was good, giving every delegate his chance. No one, when the time came, could say the United States Constitution had been muddled together in a hurry.

For the third time, Connecticut advanced the Great Compromise originally proposed by Roger Sherman, giving large and small states equal voice in the Senate. Should the great states refuse this plan, Ellsworth said, we would be separated. He was not in general a halfway man, yet he preferred to do half the good we could rather than do nothing at all. But Madison would not yield. State equality of representation was an unjust principle, he said. James Wilson agreed. *Why should the small states fear the large?* . . . It was the old, tired question, so often asked and never answered. Irritably, Wilson told the Convention that there were only two kinds of governments — the one which does too much and oppresses, the one which does too little and is weak.

Ellsworth was not convinced. The small states must be given power of defense against the large. Madison at this waxed uncharacteristically warm and resorted to something very close to insult. Did the gentleman, he inquired, forget that his state had declined to pay her share during the war? Had not Connecticut *"positively refused"* * her compliance to a federal requisition? "Has she paid," Madison went on, "for the last two years, any money into the continental treasury? And does this look like government, or the observance of a solemn compact?"

It was too much for Oliver Ellsworth. Like any American then or today he could not hear his state impugned; it was enough to make the eagle scream. Ellsworth turned to the chair: "I can with confidence appeal to your Excellency. . . . The muster rolls will show that Connecticut had more troops in the field than even the state of Virginia. We strained every nerve to raise them. . . . We feel the effects of it even to this day. . . . We are constantly exerting ourselves to draw money from the pockets of our citizens as fast as it comes in. . . . If my state has proved delinquent through inability only, it is not more than others have been, without the same excuse."

* Madison's italics.

Logically, this was no answer. Yet Ellsworth's warmth and loyalty were appealing. Surely Washington's face must have softened? Young Davie of North Carolina supported Ellsworth's motion for equal representation in the Senate. James Wilson suggested one senator for every hundred thousand souls, and for the smallest states not more than one member each — comprising about twenty-six in all, thus keeping the Senate expediently small. "I make this proposal," Wilson finished, "not because I belong to a large state but in order to pull down a rotten house and lay the foundation for a new building."

Dr. Franklin interposed. "When a broad table is to be made," he said, "and the edges of planks do not fit, the artist takes a little from both, and makes a good joint. In like manner here both sides must part with some of their demands, in order that they may join in some accommodating proposition." He had prepared such a proposition, Franklin added, to "lie on the table for consideration."

But it seemed, today, that not even Dr. Franklin could propitiate or soothe. Argument rose, took on an ugly tone. Rufus King declared he could not listen, nor would he ever listen to an equality of votes in the Senate; his feelings were harrowed, his fears agitated for his country. Jonathan Dayton of New Jersey, twenty-six years old, remarked acidly that declamation had been substituted for argument. "When assertion is given for proof," said Dayton, it ". . . will have no effect no matter how eloquently spoken. I consider the system on the table [the Virginia Plan] as a novelty, an amphibious monster, and I am persuaded it will never be received by the people."

Noontime approached. It was Saturday and again very hot; another week of inconclusive debate lay behind the Convention. It was now that Gunning Bedford of Delaware — fluent, fat and angry — rose and tore into the large states. Look, he said, at the votes of this Convention! Were they not dictated by ambition? Had not self-interest blinded the big states, and was it not evident they sought to aggrandize themselves at the expense of the small ones? Even Georgia had trailed after them, moved by the prospect of soon becoming a great state herself. So also with North and South Carolina — the latter being "puffed up with the possession of her wealth and Negroes." Were the small states, Bedford demanded, expected to act with greater purity than the rest of mankind? The great states cried out, Where is the danger in the coalition? "They insist . . . they never will hurt or injure the lesser states. *I do not, gentlemen, trust you!*" said Gunning Bedford, and the reporter underlined the words.

Bedford must have been looking straight at the delegates from Massachusetts, Pennsylvania and Virginia; he addressed them directly. "Where is your plighted faith?" he demanded. "Will you crush the smaller states?" Should the small states indeed confederate, "the fault will be yours, and all the nations of the earth will justify us. We have been told with a dictatorial air that this is the last moment for a fair trial in favor of a good government. It will be the last indeed, if the propositions reported from the Committee go forth to the people. The large states," said Bedford, "dare not dissolve the confederation. If they do, the small ones will find some foreign ally of more honor and good faith who will take them by the hand and do them justice. I say this not to threaten or intimidate. If we once leave this floor, and solemnly renounce your new project, what will be the consequence? You will annihilate your federal government, and ruin must stare you in the face!"

*Take a foreign power by the hand!* It was a wild, rash statement. And though there must have been other small-state men who had said the like in private, Bedford had put himself blatantly in the wrong; it is always easy for the other side to cry renegade. At once, Bedford was rebuked. Rufus King pronounced himself "grieved, that such a thought had entered into the heart" of the honorable member. He was "even more grieved" that such an expression had dropped from his lips. The gentleman could excuse it to himself only on the score of passion. "For myself, whatever may be my distress," finished the delegate from Massachusetts in his high clear voice, "I will never court a foreign power to assist in relieving myself from it." Later, Edmund Randolph also protested — "animadverted," wrote Madison primly, "on the warm and rash language of Mr. Bedford."

It would be interesting to know what Bedford's colleagues said to him that afternoon, when the meeting dispersed for the weekend and the Delaware members went out together into Chestnut Street. Bedford's outburst had forced into the open an issue that was at the back of everyone's mind: the dangers of foreign intervention and foreign bribes, though until today no state had used it as a threat against her sisters in the Convention. Alexander Hamilton had earlier remarked that "the weak side of republican government is the danger of foreign influence." And on the next day (June nineteenth) Madison had demanded whether the New Jersey Plan would "secure the Union against the influence of foreign powers over its members."

Europe was a fact of life. The states could not rid themselves of it merely by damning monarchical or aristocratic systems and praising their own. "We are a commercial people," Gouverneur Morris reminded the Convention, "and as such will be obliged to engage in European politics."

In the Convention were ten or a dozen men who had been born or educated abroad. Gouverneur Morris had never left American shores. Yet for him as for Hamilton and James Wilson it was possible to conceive some kind of peaceable and even advantageous political communication with Europe. Elbridge Gerry, however, expressed more clearly the spirit of most delegates. "If we do not come to some agreement among ourselves," he said, "some foreign sword will probably do the work for us."

Sooner or later the states as a nation would have to choose between a friendship with France or with England. At the moment they were closer to France, which after all had been their strong ally in the war. Without French troops and a French fleet — without General Rochambeau and Admiral de Grasse — Washington could not have beaten Cornwallis at Yorktown. France was the most powerful nation of Europe. French taste, the French example of monarchy dominated; every petty princeling tried to imitate the splendors of Versailles.

No delegate to the Federal Convention foresaw the French Revolution, felt its imminence or dreamed that only a few years hence the streets of Philadelphia would be loud with citizens in liberty caps, singing Ça ira. Yet America was aware that in certain circles French sympathy with the American Revolution had existed since the beginning. In Paris, les insurgents had been the rage, and following the tea riots, *philosophes* played a card game called *le Boston*. . . .

> Bon, bon, bon [sang certain brave spirits]
> C'est à Boston
> Qu'on entend soufflent les canons!

A French official gazette published the complete text of the Declaration of Independence; one news sheet even dared to reproduce long extracts from Thomas Paine's high diatribe against kingship, *Common Sense*. "It is really our cause the Americans plead," said the witty advocate Linguet. Jefferson, in Paris, wrote home to Madison that the Virginia Act of Religious Freedom had been translated into French and inserted in the famous *Encyclopédie*. Paris developed a romantic affinity with the Pennsylvania Quakers, referred to them as Quaqueurs, Kouakres or Trembleurs and extolled their founder, Guillaume Penn, a famous *illuminé*. It was understood that any Frenchman who believed in liberty and equality must of necessity admire this *Utopie de Pennsylvanie*. Poems were written about the Quaker —

> . . . un vrai sage, un homme de bien,
> Qui aime ni le jeu ni le vin ni les femmes.

Guillaume Penn was a modern Lycurgus who it seemed had established a Golden Age.

It was all delightful and inspiring. Yet it bore little relation to European state policy as the Federal Convention and the United States commissioners in Europe knew it. If the French people loved us, the French government preferred to see us weak and divided. Louis XVI had consented to an alliance more out of rivalry with England than sympathy with *les insurgents*. What an opportunity to disrupt the British Empire! And it had succeeded. "We may thank the perfidy of France," wrote the poet Cowper, "that pick'd the jewel out of England's crown."

France was our ally; we had not forgotten. Yet by blood and history the states were English; as Englishmen they had fought the French on American soil for a full century. *King Wil-*

*liam's War, Queen Anne's War, King George's War:* these were
American titles for struggles which in Europe went by names of
dynasties that rose and fell — the War of the Spanish Succession,
of the Austrian Succession. Europe was forever at war. And since
the founding of Virginia, European wars — civil, religious, dy-
nastic — had always and inevitably their reflection in America,
influencing the course of domestic affairs. Struggle as they might
to be free of "foreign entanglements," the states would never be
free.

Europe for her part kept a watchful eye on the American
states. Should their union be cemented by this new constitution,
as rumored, it was possible American credit might rise, and be
worth a commercial treaty here and there. Since the peace, only
Holland had come forward with a loan. All very well for *philosophes* and libertarians to applaud these successful rebels. But the
heads of states, the absolutist monarchs everywhere asked themselves why they should encourage revolutionaries, even at such a
distance. "I still fear," D'Alembert had written Frederick II of
Prussia, "lest this drop of oil spread till it reach us." Frederick II,
*der alte Fritz*, was dead a year ago, in 1786. In Russia, Catherine
the Great ruled; in Spain, Charles III. All across Europe, efficient
despotism was the style and the watchword. Social reform it is
true was in the air. But reform lay in the ruler's right hand;
men's hopes for betterment looked only to a better prince. East of
the Elbe the structure remained prince and peasant, master and
serf. And if Great Catherine flirted with the *philosophes* and the
principles of the Enlightenment, it was never to the point of
social or political risk.

That the Americans were successful rebels did not, thus far,
make them fit partners for the commercial favors they sought.
The states had not paid their debts; they could not even pay the
interest. A New Englander who traded with European countries
told his state convention that he found "this country held in
the same light by foreign nations as a well-behaved Negro
is in a gentleman's family." Cocky, defiant, yet altogether aware
of their financial and military weakness, the American states for
their part looked on Europe as a political desert, a howling waste

of darkness and oppression. "The nations of Europe," Washington had said, "are rife for slavery."

And in truth, representative government everywhere was on the wane. In Portugal the Cortes had disappeared a hundred years ago; the Spanish Cortes had convened but eight times in the century. In Denmark the Estates had not met since 1660, and nowhere in Germany were they much more than a survival. The Hungarian Diet had lost its authority. Joseph II of Austria labored hard for his country but he was soon to die disappointed — though knowing in his heart, he said, that he had been destined by Providence to wear his diadem. It was the accidents of royal birth that determined European wars, European boundaries and the fate of men. England it is true had her Parliament, her House of Commons; she lived in the long tradition of the common law. Yet the fact remained that in England, land was king. The common law had more regard for land than for human life. The great Whig landowners, arrogant, ruthless in their own interests, controlled Parliament. Reform would await a new century.

The population of Great Britain was fifteen million; of France, over twenty-five million; from Vienna were ruled some twenty-seven million. Monarchical absolutism in Europe had reached its peak. And it was now, in this fruitful New World summer, that a young nation of three and a half million souls had elected delegates to meet in Philadelphia and create a national, independent republican government, shaped to their own notions, without king, nobles, or hereditary fiefs. Actually, it was the one moment, the one stroke of the continental clock when such an experiment had a chance to succeed. Five years earlier and the states would not have been ready. Since then the creation and operation of their own state constitutions had taught them, prepared them. Five years later and the French Revolution, with its violence and blood, would have slowed the states into caution, dividing them (as it indeed divided them) into opposing ideological camps. Tom Paine had recognized the moment, had seen and felt it with his wild rash prescience, his eloquence of genius, and at the very start of hostilities with England. "*The Time hath found us,*" he wrote. "Freedom hath been hunted round the Globe. . . . Europe regards her like a stranger and England hath given her warning to depart. Now is the seed-time of Continental union, faith and honour. . . . A new era for politics is struck. . . . A new method of thinking has arisen. All plans, proposals etc. prior to the nineteenth of April * . . . are like the almanacs of the last year."

It was Benjamin Franklin, of course, who had discovered Tom Paine in London and sent him to America. And now Paine had gone back to Europe, and old Franklin sat in the Pennsylvania State House, watching his young compatriots struggle mightily with this "new method of thinking," this new form of government, half federal and half national, yet wholly republican. Having much experience with European courts, Franklin was aware that a change of government, reasonably and peaceably executed, could not take place in the Old World, built as it was like a pyramid based upon an illiterate, brutish mass of peasantry, and rising to a peak of long-accepted hereditary privilege. European aristocrats in plumed hats and powdered hair, wearing their swords to evening parties, were a race apart from the rest of mankind. Even at the university the nobility kept aloof, eating, sleeping and studying by themselves; in church and at the theater they sat in their privileged places. For Paine's "new thinking" a different citizenry was necessary. America possessed it in that class of persons, neither rich nor poor, which Franklin celebrated as our "happy mediocrity."

John Adams, in London, found himself miserable among the plumed hats. An exiled American loyalist, Samuel Curwen, heard that the new Minister chose to consider himself "as a plain American republican, his garb plain, without a sword." This was carrying transatlantic ideas too far, wrote Curwen. He trusted that Mr. Adams would not display his surly pertinacity to the point of appearing at a royal levee or a St. James's drawing room on a court day without his sword.

"I am not at home in this country!" Adams wrote angrily to Jefferson. He had taken a resolution to quit Europe, Adams continued. Thus far, England had sent no minister to America. It was therefore inconsistent with the honor and dignity of Congress to renew his commission to the Court of St. James's. Should Con-

* The battle of Lexington, 1775.

gress indeed renew it, Adams had a mind to send the commission back to New York. It was true King George had received him amiably. "Sir," said his Majesty, "I was the last man in my kingdom to consent to your independence, and I shall be the last to do any thing to infringe it." But after an evening spent with the aristocracy at a Mayfair ball, John Adams wrote in his diary, "There is an awkward timidity, in general. This people cannot look me in the face: there is a conscious guilt and shame in their countenances, when they look at me. They feel that they have behaved ill, and that I am sensible of it."

"Nothing American sells here," Adams wrote home to Massachusetts. "There is a universal desire and endeavor to forget America, and an unanimous resolution to read nothing which shall bring it to their thoughts. They cannot recollect it without pain." Adams's wife, the invincible Abigail, in spite of her Puritan background had enjoyed their years in Paris. But like her husband, she was uneasy in London. "This same surly John Bull," she wrote, "is kicking up the dust and growling, looking upon the fat pastures he has lost, with a malicious and envious eye, and though he is offered admission upon decent terms, he is so mortified and stomachful, that although he longs for a morsel, he has not yet agreed for a single bite."

Even Jefferson, who possessed not half of the Adamses' intransigence, wrote eloquently from Paris of "those rich, proud, hectoring, swearing, squibbing, carnivorous animals who live on the other side of the Channel." On Adams's pressing invitation to come to London and lend his help, Jefferson came, was presented to the King and Queen at a levee and declared "it was impossible for anything to be more ungracious than their notice of Mr. Adams and myself." The Minister for Foreign Affairs, Lord Carmarthen, confirmed Jefferson's belief in the British "aversion to have anything to do with us." For seven weeks, Jefferson waited in vain for a second interview with Carmarthen, then returned to the more congenial airs of Paris, where, he said, "a man might pass a life without encountering a single rudeness." He wished, wrote Jefferson, that his countrymen could adopt just so much of this politeness "as to be ready to make all those little sacrifices of self, which really render European manners amiable, and relieve society from the disagreeable scenes to which rudeness often subjects it."

In this critical summer, it was good that the United States (not yet truly united) had two such extraordinary — and dissimilar — representatives abroad: the one stubborn, combative, loyal, incorrigibly provincial in his New England ways; the other reared in the Southern ease of manner. Yet both men possessed highest intelligence, both men were studious by nature, insatiable readers, charged with perpetual curiosity concerning governments, agriculture, politics, and the nature of mankind. Jefferson, believing in the people, looked on the best government as that which governed least. John Adams saw every man in power as "a ravenous beast of prey," who must be checked, controlled, balanced by other governmental powers. When his cousin Samuel wrote grandly that the love of liberty was interwoven in the soul of man — "So it is," replied John, "according to La Fontaine, in that of a wolf." Hamilton and Madison would have agreed. It was the eighteenth-century view, skeptical, deistic, "reasonable," yet oddly optimistic, permitting the aim of government to be stated as the pursuit of happiness — or, as Adams had it, the best government is "that which communicates ease, comfort, security, or, in one word, happiness, to the greatest number of persons and in the greatest degree."

With the advent of July the Federal Convention, unfortunately, was no nearer a solution, no closer to the perfect government than they had been two months ago. July second fell on Monday. As soon as the meeting convened, the great question was put: should the states have equal vote in the Senate? To the general dismay the result was a tie: five states aye, five no, with Georgia divided. Gloom settled on the chamber, a sense almost of shock. Delegates could not vote on this question forever, day after day. "If we do not concede on both sides," said a North Carolina member, "our business must soon be at an end." "It seems we have got to a point," said Roger Sherman, "that we cannot move one way or another." "The world at large expect something from us," Gerry said. "If we do nothing, it appears to me we must have war and confusion." A committee was elected by ballot, with a member from every state, to try for some kind of compromise concerning representation in the Senate and House. No one had much hope, but at least the committee would have three days to work before the Convention met again.

Wednesday was Independence Day, the Glorious Fourth; the Convention did not meet. Philadelphia celebrated with pomp, bell-ringing and the salute of guns — a *feu de joie* from the Light Horse and three times three rounds from the Artillery. There was marching with fife and drum, there was an Independence Day sermon at the Lutheran Church. (To Washington, a Virginia Episcopalian, it was "the Calvinist Church.") Nobody mentioned the precarious state of the Federal Convention; nobody beyond the delegates knew about it. All over the country there were toasts and mutual congratulations: "The Grand Convention — may they form a Constitution for an eternal Republic!" "The Federal Convention — may the result of their meeting be as glorious as its members are illustrious!" At the London Coffee House, the City Tavern, at Oellers, the Indian Queen, and across the river on the Jersey shore, citizens met for revel, for song and rejoicing concerning a country where "forests are falling before the hand of labour, our fields doubling their increase . . . our cities thriving, and millions of freemen covering the shores of our rivers and lakes with all the arts and enjoyment of civilized life." Newspapers did their part. "With zeal and confidence," said the *Pennsylvania Herald*, "we expect from the Federal Convention a system of government adequate to the security and preservation of those rights which were promulgated by the ever memorable Declaration of Independency."

Next morning the Convention filed glumly to their places in the State House. The new committee was ready with a report. Nobody liked it, nobody agreed. Gouverneur Morris declared the form as well as the matter objectionable. The whole human race, he warned, would be affected by the proceedings of this Convention. Gunning Bedford tried to explain what he had meant the other day by the small states taking some foreign power by the hand. "No man can foresee," he said, "to what extremities the small states may be driven by oppression." Gouverneur Morris said savagely that "men don't unite for liberty or life . . . they unite for the *protection of property*.\* . . . There never was," he said further, "nor ever will be a civilized society without an aristocracy." Nathaniel Gorham of Massachusetts insisted that the large states should be cut up, their boundaries reduced. Benjamin Franklin interposed shortly that it was always of importance that the people should know who had disposed of their money, and how. "It is a maxim that those who feel, can best judge."

July fifth . . . sixth . . . seventh . . . eighth . . . ninth. "We were on the verge of dissolution," wrote Luther Martin, "scarce held together by the strength of an hair, though the public papers were announcing our extreme unanimity." It was on July tenth that Yates and Lansing departed the Convention. Their defection must have been depressing, a real blow; they were the first men to withdraw in protest, with expressed intention of not returning. George Mason had said he would bury his bones in Philadelphia rather than quit with no solution found.

In Philadelphia at about this time was present one of Washington's French officers, De Maussion. To his mother abroad, young De Maussion wrote that the General appeared very gloomy, coming from the State House. "The look on his face," said De Maussion, "reminded me of its expression during the terrible months we were in Valley Forge Camp."

That night of July tenth, Washington wrote to Alexander Hamilton in New York. "I am sorry you went away," the General said. "I wish you were back. The crisis is equally important and alarming." Our councils "are now, if possible, in a worse train than ever; you will find but little ground on which the hope of a good establishment can be formed. In a word, I almost *despair* of seeing a favorable issue to the proceedings of the Convention, and do therefore repent having had any agency in the business."

\* Yates's italics.

# XII

## *Journey through the American states.*
## *The physical scene.*

"GO, ye warrior peoples, ye peoples of slaves and of tyrants, go to Pennsylvania! There you will find every door open, all possessions unguarded, not a soldier, and many merchants and laborers." To French liberals, Pennsylvania was of all states the most admirable. The South was peopled by slaves. New England had been cruel to the honest Quakers, who in Philadelphia had the added virtue of being rich. Go, ye tyrant-ridden people, to Philadelphia!

All through the seventeen-eighties and -nineties they came, the French visitors to America — and after the Peace of '83 came the English for touring, trade or settlement — men like Dr. Priestley and Thomas Cooper, sympathetic to revolutionary ideals. It began even earlier, with the French Alliance of 1778, when six thousand French soldiers debarked on American shores. The inhabitants had dreaded their arrival, and why not? For generations, America had fought the French and their Indian allies. Moreover, since the first Jesuit missionary-explorer, the French had had a way with Indians, got on with them — palpably a treacherous trait in any white man. Yet here were six thousand French soldiers, magnificently dressed and equipped, surprisingly correct in behavior, keeping to their camps at night and disciplined against pillaging. Their officers, nobly born, wealthy, young, with none of the hauteur of their British counterparts, charmed wherever they went.

Chief among them was of course "the Marquis," Washington's favorite, young Lafayette. There were also Count de Rochambeau and Count de Noailles, de Maussion, the Chevalier de Chastellux and, much later, the civilian Moreau de St. Méry. The French consul general, the Marquis de Barbé-Marbois, lived six years in Philadelphia and won many hearts. And that shrewd chargé d'affaires Monsieur Otto reported to Versailles all that he could discover about the Federal Convention and its delegates.

Concerning possible European-American trade arrangements, "It would be useless to observe, my Lord," wrote Otto, "that in America as in all commercial republics, affections will follow very closely the transactions of money." Men seemed to think, said Otto, that it would be impossible to unite under one head all the members of the Confederation. "Their political interests, their commercial views, their customs and their laws are so varied that there is not a resolution of Congress which can be equally useful and popular in the South and the North of the Continent. Their jealousy seems an insurmountable obstacle. The inhabitants of the North are fishers and sailors; those of the Central States, farmers; those of the South, planters." Rhode Island — "*le Rhodeisland*" — was badly thought of by her sisters. Connecticut had sent as delegates two most typical citizens, the Messieurs Ellsworth and Sherman. "The people of this state," remarked Otto, "generally have a national character not commonly found in other parts of the country. They come nearer to republican simplicity; without being rich they are all in easy circumstances."

These French gentlemen traveled, kept diaries, wrote letters home, wonderfully descriptive and fresh, filled with the sharp yet lighthearted perceptions of men of the world who can afford to be amused by customs and foibles they need not share for long. Well disposed, the travelers saw what they chose to see and were ready to overlook the more uncomfortable aspects of this brave new society. The books later published by these visitors bore alluring titles, very French in style: *Rélation Fidèle* . . . *Promenades* . . . *Voyage Pittoresque*. And most famous of all, the classic *Letters from an American Farmer*, by Jean de Crèvecoeur, who loved America, named his daughter America-Frances and did his best to persuade the world to share his sentiments. It was Crèvecoeur who, when he read the United States Constitution in November of 1787, told Thomas Jefferson he would be willing to

fight for it, or return to Europe should it fail. No native American could have described his country so well. In these accounts,
these diaries and letters, we see the states for which the Federal
Convention was making a Constitution — and we see them not
only as they were but as the travelers had been led, at home, to
expect. Pennsylvania, for instance, was inhabited not only by the
honest *Kouakeur* in his broad hat, but by that child of nature, the
savage — open-hearted, beautiful in body, innocent of the corruption endemic to cities and to royal courts:

> I am as free as Nature first made man,
> Ere the base laws of servitude began,
> When wild in woods the noble savage ran.

It was the seventeenth-century ideal, Arcadian, Graeco-Roman.
Poets easily confused the pagan hero, the Aztec and the Iroquois.
When one has never seen a Mohawk or a Cherokee it is reasonable
enough to envision him as black rather than red. Moreover there
was a notion in Europe that Americans were proceeding, in their
government, upon Greek principles. President Willard of Harvard in 1788 received a letter from an English sympathizer, saying
the writer had heard there was to be a revival of the Olympic
games in America. "All her friends wish it and say they are capable of it, and having acted on Greek principles, should have
Greek exercises." The illusion reached even to Scotland, where
Lord Monboddo, the eccentric jurist and philosopher, extolled
the blessings of nature and urged the benefits of walking about
naked and eating one's vegetables raw.

From the American Indian to the pagan hero was a nice poetic
transference, but it irritated Dr. Johnson in London, who told
Boswell not to "cant in defense of savages." Thomas Hobbes had
seen the life of the savage as "solitary, poor, nasty, brutish, and
short." Americans living on Western borders could have wished it
even shorter. It is to be doubted if many eighteenth-century colonials looked on the Mohawk or the Cherokee as anything but
verminous, thieving and potentially ferocious nuisances. The
dusky maiden with the squash blossom in her hair . . . the
zephyr, the rill, the solitary glen . . . only the poets of Europe
could afford to indulge in such imaginings. As a rule Americans

hated red Indians, wished to see them exterminated, and for the most part treated them accordingly. A William Penn, a Franklin, a Benezet, a Weiser or even a William Johnson were few and far between. John Bartram the botanist, a Quaker, said the only way to deal with Indians was to "bang them stoutly." To Europe, however, the Indian had never been a "problem," but always a curiosity.

From Constantinople to London the notions of America as they appeared in print were marvelously ingenious. The Wakwak tree bore its fruit in the shape of young women, ripe and delicious. The reason it was so cold in America was because of the great forests which covered the interior from the first ridge of mountains to the Pacific Ocean. Dense-growing trees kept the sun from the earth, which naturally stayed frigid. Only on the seacoasts was the climate mild, and becoming milder as the land was cleared. In America grew wondrous plants which yielded two kinds of fruits in one harvest. As for the potato — "There," exclaimed the traveler Brissot de Warville, "is the food for the man who wants to be, and is capable of being, free!" This vegetable, says Brissot, springs up everywhere without being cultivated. Another curiosity among the Americans, who have neither priests nor masters, said Brissot, is the existence of "a great number of individuals known as 'men of principle'" — a type produced by the Americans' frequent exercise of *reason*, and "a type so little known among us," continues the Frenchman, "that it has not even been named. It is among these men of principle that you will find the true heroes of humanity." Brissot named as examples William Penn, Franklin and Washington.

Other European writers, purporting to scorn fantasy and look realistically upon the Western world, noted that the American continent, being only recently formed, had scarcely finished drying out; in places the land was still a deep swamp. Therefore the meager vegetation, the scentless plants, feeble animals and short-bodied men, hairless and discouragingly impotent in the marriage bed. Such were the conclusions of the redoubtable Abbé de Pauw. Even Buffon the naturalist declared the American animals to be inferior, due to the meager native grasses which were not nearly as large and succulent as those of Europe. It was said that dogs ceased to bark after breathing American air. Jefferson, reading all this in Paris, was irritated enough to send home for the skeleton of a moose.

Accounts of travels in America were so well received in France and so popular that men eventually began inventing them. One quite respectable scholar who had never set foot on a transatlantic ship wrote, under a pseudonym, an entire book about his adventures and fooled everybody. Not until the eighth edition did the author sign his real name, though his work was entertaining as well as perceptive.

It was natural for Europeans to speculate about this vast unpenetrated continent; the very exaggerations held an element of truth. Few men saw as yet the physical potential, the almost limitless resources for wealth and material expansion. Yet America's spiritual potential was recognized, at the same time feared by despots and celebrated by the enlightened. Here was indeed an asylum, a refuge for the downtrodden. If the noble savage was a fiction, the sturdy Quaker citizen was not, nor the husbandman tilling his own soil, free of church tithes and overlord, also the artisan or mechanic who dared to raise his voice at town meeting with his betters. In America the *âme républicaine* found vital airs for nourishment. German liberals echoed this enthusiasm. "In America," said a news sheet, the *Deutsche Chronik*, "thirteen golden gates are open to the victims of intolerance and despotism."

The friends of America were by no means numerous in Europe but they were vocal and enjoyed their defiance. La Rochefoucauld-Liancourt wrote warmly to Dr. Franklin about the constitutional principles of the Americans. That Europe did not "understand" us was clear to every American who went abroad. Yet it was clear also that certain circles looked to us with hope and good faith, equating their own revolutionary plans with the success of our experiment. These men studied our new state constitutions and watched with eager interest for the national constitution which they had heard was to be published in the near future.

But philosophy is one thing and day to day hard facts are another. Debarking from their ships, European travelers found in America less — or horrifyingly more — than they had been led to expect. There was a harshness to this land, this terrain, which poets and *philosophes* had neglected to mention. Instead of the glen, the rill, the zephyr, they met with an uneven climate, incredibly bad roads or no roads beyond a forest trail, swollen rivers unbridged, and everywhere the unsightly two-foot-high tree-stumps which the Americans looked on with indifference or even with pride, symbolic of the forest conquered. Here were storms of lightning and thunder unequaled at home, here were snows which fell for days running. In summer, most violent transitions from heat to cold were occasioned, wrote an English traveler, "by means of the N.W. wind, which in this country is the most keen and severe of any that is to be met with on the face of the globe. The wind is perfectly *dry*, and so uncommonly penetrating that I am convinced it would destroy all the plagues of Egypt." Here were fireflies, hummingbirds, bullfrogs that roared in the swamps like calves taken from their mothers. The flowering trees were entrancing. Barbé-Marbois rode out from Philadelphia to "a neighboring forest," where he saw magnolias, "whose flowers perfume the air . . . tulip trees, of which they say the shade rejuvenates old married couples; catalpas, sassafras . . . laurels of every kind with which we shall crown the heroes of America, but which are still waiting for her to produce a poet."

Nevertheless it was plain that in this country the forest was man's enemy. "Compared with France," wrote one traveler, "the entire country is one vast wood." Isaac Weld, a visiting Englishman, wrote of the American's "unconquerable aversion to trees." Another said his landlord "this day cut down thirty-two young cedars to make a hog-pen." The ground, says Weld, could not be tilled nor the inhabitants support themselves until the trees were destroyed. "The man that can cut down the largest number, and have the field about his house most clear of them, is looked upon as the most industrious citizen, and the one that is making the greatest improvement in the country. . . . I have heard of Americans landing in barren parts of the north west coast of Ireland, and evincing the greatest surprise and pleasure at the beauty and improved state of the country, 'so clear of trees!'" Considering the burning heats of summer, could not some few trees near the house be spared? Weld asked. Oh no, their owners replied, that would be dangerous.

Stumps were left to rot, a matter of years. In the front yards were no flowers; farmers grew their wheat and corn right up to the front door. Everywhere were the zigzag wooden barriers known as snake fences, a depressing sight, with none of the charm of the English hedges or French poplars. The farmhouses stood stark among the stumps and cornstalks. Twining round the larger trees, Weld noted poisonous vines which looked like grapevines but which, if handled, raised large blisters.

Europeans were shocked by the American destruction of trees and the resulting ugliness. Even so, travelers riding through Virginia, Ohio, western Pennsylvania, told of their hearts lifting at the sound of an axe against wood: it meant a habitation, human companionship. The American forest! Only a man who had made his own clearing, who in the face of hunger, wild animals, storms and savages had put his axe to the trees, plowed the land, and sown his first crop of corn — only he could know that in America "the forest" signified wilderness and "a clearing" meant civilization. To an American "the forest" was the backlands, the backwoods, pioneer country. John Marshall's grandfather was known as John Marshall of The Forest; he came from Fauquier County, on Virginia's western frontier, where store goods were hard to obtain and the Marshall women used thorns for pins. To Europeans however, "the forest" was synonymous with all America. As late as 1827, a Frenchman who had lived in the United States wrote of "those forests where I spent eleven years so free and independent . . . where one meets neither peasant nor pauper, where one enters without passport and leaves without permission." The redoubtable Abbé Robin, noting in Connecticut the elaborate headdresses of the ladies, declared himself surprised to find French fashions "in the midst of American forests." Thomas Jefferson in Paris varied the expression, inquiring of a correspondent if he would like to hear what "a savage of the mountains of America" thought of Europe.

The New World invited. "The river Ohio," wrote a British visitor, "is, beyond all competition, the most beautiful in the universe." The French called it *La Belle Rivière*. There was a grandeur to the American scenery, a wild awesome invitation. Yet the land proved inhospitable to any who would not claim it by hard work. "I do not think America the place for a man of pleasure," wrote Thomas Cooper. Cooper was a highly educated scientist and theologian, who in the early 1790's emigrated to Pennsylvania with Dr. Priestley and settled in Northumberland County. Even in Philadelphia, Cooper knew, he said, of only one "professed gentleman — i.e. idle, unoccupied person of fortune. Their time is not yet come." Cooper advised the prospective emigrant to avoid the seven-month winters of New Hampshire and Massachusetts, also the parching summers of New Jersey and the Carolinas. In New Jersey, Cooper reported, one found insects, reptiles, oppressive heat, fevers and ague. "The influence of a hot sun upon the moist and low land of the American coast almost infallibly subjects an European . . . to attacks of intermittents." Like the celebrated Dr. Priestley, Cooper preferred northwest Pennsylvania, the high clear Susquehanna country. In Kentucky one risked continual danger from Indians.

And how hard it was to clear the land! "Grubbing," the Americans called it. For grubbing, laborers received three shillings a day, victuals and a dram of whiskey morning and evening. To quench great thirst by water alone, without spirits, was said to be extremely hazardous. In summer men had been seen to fall dead on the streets of Philadelphia after drinking cold water from the pumps. Bleeding was suggested, Moreau said, for those who drank too fast; some pumps bore a sign reading, "Death to him who drinks too quickly." And what quantities of spirituous liquors the Americans consumed! When drunk they had a propensity to fight; in the Southern and Western country, fistfights were looked on as a frolic. No rules were observed of honor or sport, and men gathered to watch two champions gouge out eyes, break jaws and bite off fingertips with every appearance of ferocious pleasure.

French visitors were apt to view this landscape and its people more genially. One September, three French noblemen, including the Marquis of Lafayette, set out from Albany on an expedition.

James Madison happened to be one of the party. They planned to see the Oneida Indians and also a colony of Shakers in whom Lafayette, an ardent admirer of Dr. Mesmer in Paris, was especially interested because their practices resembled mesmerism. It was cold; Lafayette wore a rain cloak of gummed taffeta which had been sent him from France wrapped in newspapers. The papers had stuck to the gum, "so that," wrote Barbé-Marbois, "the curious could read, on his chest or back, the *Journal de Paris*, the *Courier de l'Europe*, or news from other places."

As for the Chevalier de Chastellux, he rode through the forests and the cities with a bluejay's feather in his cap, enjoying everything. It was natural to feel well disposed towards a people with whom one had fought side by side. In Connecticut the Chevalier went squirrel hunting, a diversion which he wrote was much in fashion in that part of the country. The animals, he said, were larger than those of Europe, with thicker fur, and very adroit in leaping from tree to tree. Should a squirrel be wounded without falling, it was only a slight inconvenience; somebody was usually within call to cut down the tree. "As squirrels are not rare," finished Chastellux, "one may conclude, and quite rightly, that trees are very common."

Squirrel ragout was tasty and gamy, though some preferrred their squirrels fried for supper, with coffee. Travelers frequently carried their food with them, meat or cornmeal. Innkeepers let them cook it over the fire. Visitors were impressed with the American wild turkey, its size and appearance. "Why do not the Americans domesticate this noble bird?" asked William Priest. Frenchmen complained unsparingly of the American bread, but remarked that in a surprisingly short time a landlord could produce little hot *galettes*, baked and kneaded. Chastellux found them to his taste.

Persons of all ranks, it was noted, drank coffee and tea. The Americans breakfasted on what they called "relishes" — salt fish, beefsteaks, broiled fowls, ham and bacon. Oysters were much eaten and the shad an excellent fish, but there existed "a fanatical law, passed by the Quakers," which prohibited catching shad on Sunday, a great waste, considering the fish remained in the river but a short time. The Bostonians ate fish every Saturday "to benefit their fisheries," and in private houses grace was said before meat. Barbé-Marbois noted that all the courses, even dessert, were put on the table at one time. Tablecloths fell over the knees and took the place of napkins, after the English style. In Boston — a town of eighteen thousand — everything reminded travelers of London: the brick and wooden houses, the customs, even the speech and accent. But it seemed odd that on a warm August day people paid calls dressed in velvet, satin and damask. In the country, stone fences divided men's property. New England churches were clean and well lighted; to the Frenchmen they did not look like churches. One found oneself in a room with benches, lacking paintings or ornaments — "no addresses to the heart and the imagination." Yet one met no beggars therein, "nor even," wrote Barbé-Marbois, "an untidily dressed man, no one from the hospital for the blind to hit you with his stick, nor verger to interrupt you with the noise of his halberd."

Connecticut, travelers noted, was as closely populated as England; one passed continually through towns and villages. Hartford had no galleries, public gardens or palaces, but Barbé-Marbois was shown the Charter Oak. "In this country," he wrote, "everything which has any connection with liberty is sacred." And what odd customs were attributed to liberty and equality! — even the barbarous custom of admitting another man to one's bed when one was asleep at an inn. Another sign of this so-called liberty, wrote Moreau, was the refusal of a carriage to alter its course when passing, unless threatened with collision by a heavier vehicle. It was charming to see schoolchildren, girls and boys, draw up in line along the road and salute the passing stranger by curtsies or doffing the hat, though some Americans protested the custom as servile, a relic of the old country.

New York (population thirty-three thousand) in 1787 still showed the ravages of war. The city had been occupied by the enemy for seven years, till the English left and the Tories with them. Now the wharves were tumbledown, bereft of ships; the great fire had swept away almost every building on Broadway, including Trinity Church. What remained was a collection of wooden hovels and gabled Dutch houses of yellow brick. In the

East and North Rivers one saw porpoises. Baltimore, with its thirteen thousand inhabitants, was badly paved, "with scarcely a dozen lamps in the whole town."

Nearly every French traveler commented on the high scale of living in America. Brissot de Warville remarked that it was not rare to see a carter driving his cart and eating a turkey wing and some white bread. Wages for laborers and servants were high, much higher than in Europe, and when a vessel loaded with Scotchmen landed in New York, "the next day there was not one who was not hired out and busy." Travelers agreed that the further south one went, the more this condition deteriorated. It was in Virginia that Chastellux saw poor people "for the first time," he said, "since I crossed the sea." Not only the Negro slaves but the wan and ragged whites in their miserable huts aroused his pity. In Virginia the horses were beautiful, finely bred to race. Gentlemen's houses were spacious, well furnished with linen and silver plate, but few had books or libraries and the plantation manors were crowded as to bedrooms: "they think nothing of putting three or four persons in the same room." The seed ticks made life miserable in summer, and the bedbugs which Virginia called chinches. With Southerners the drinking of spirituous liquors was a delightful — and frequent — ceremony which involved extraordinary mixtures: mint sling, pumpkin flip, bumbo, apple toddy.

In Virginia, Chastellux met with his first pioneer, a young man who had come from Philadelphia with his pretty wife and babe, and was setting out for "Kentucket." Chastellux was astonished at the easy manner in which this pioneer proceeded on his expedition, with but one horse, no cattle and no tools. "I have money in my pocket," the young man said stoutly, "and shall want for nothing." In Pennsylvania good lands were "too expensive to get." This nonchalance at moving about seemed indeed one of the most striking traits of Americans. "Four times running," wrote Moreau, "they will break land for a new home, abandoning without a thought the house in which they were born, the church where they learned about God, the tombs of their fathers, the friends of their childhood, the companions of their youth, and all the pleasures of their first society." The American clung to nothing. At a price, said Moreau, he would part with "his house, his carriage, his horse, his god."

It was the very antithesis of Europe, this repudiation of the past, and for the foreigner it repelled or inspired according to his personal philosophy.

# XIII

*Journey through the American states,
continued. The people.*

What then is an American, this new Man?
CRÈVECOEUR

THE slaughtered trees, the American "forests," the free
land waiting to be claimed, the Beautiful River and wild
romantic scenery; the rattlesnakes in the brush, the zigzag
fences, hummingbirds, squirrel ragout; the bridgeless streams to
be crossed, the clear cold northwest wind — in the accounts of
Europeans all this took second place to the Americans themselves,
to the men, women and children who inhabited this New World
and who themselves seemed a species of New People. "By the
term *American*," wrote William Priest, "you must understand a
white man, descended from a native of the Old Continent; and by
the term *Indian*, or *Savage*, one of the aborigines of the New
World." "Americans," noted Moreau, "are said to be a sort of
blend of Europeans and Indians. It is evident that they have progressed far beyond the Indians and are rapidly becoming more and
more like Europeans."

Perhaps the gentleman showed restraint, everything considered. The longer he stayed in America, the less European its inhabitants appeared. Moreau and his friends were continually surprised by the condition of equality between citizens of different
rank; nothing they had read at home prepared them for it. In
France, a man of the world would blush, said Brissot de Warville, to ride in so unworthy a vehicle as a public diligence. Yet
in America one saw a member of Congress seated in the stage-

coach beside a laborer "who had voted for him," the two talking busily. "You do not see people putting on airs, which you find so often in France," added Brissot. He had traveled through New Jersey in a coach of this kind with the son of Governor Livingston — nor would he have known it, had not the innkeepers at the stops saluted young Mr. Livingston "with an air of respectful familiarity." It was said the Governor himself frequently used the public stage.

All this was extraordinary; surely it stood as proof that the American experiment was succeeding? Here the equality of man was not a matter for philosophers, poets and the conversation of enlightened drawing rooms. Here it was put in practice, accepted as an everyday fact. One must, however, accommodate oneself — and accommodation was not always easy. Barbé-Marbois wrote home that his party had found it necessary to address innkeepers discreetly. An imperative tone was unsuccessful; more than one host had said he could be asked but not commanded. "People treat us very familiarly," said the Frenchman, "and they do it so innocently that we should be very hard to get on with if we took it in bad part." Wagoners, after putting their carts under cover and oating their horses, came and joined the company for dinner, without apology. At private houses were neither porters nor doorkeepers; in Boston the governor of the state himself answered their knock when they came to call one evening. After the call was over his Excellency showed them to the door, candle in hand. Often one met respected magistrates — Barbé-Marbois called them "senators" — returning from the market with greenstuffs or fish, not even trying to hide the parcels under their cloaks.

As for the stagecoach drivers, they were a phenomenon; they showed no surprise when addressed as Colonel, took part in the conversation, said Brissot, and passed on all kinds of questions as "a sort of magistrate." It was rare for anyone to remonstrate with the driver, even in the humblest way, on his manner of handling the reins. And if debates arose upon the length of the road, upon whether or not the journey was comfortable, upon horseflesh and the lineage thereof, or upon the private fortunes of gentlemen whose houses were seen along the road, the driver was consulted and listened to with deference. And how pleasant it was to travel with so little official interference! In New England, wrote Barbé-Marbois, "we went through pretty little villages, without ever having an official come up, hat in hand, and with a mawkish expression beg us in the name of the Thirteen States to get out of our carriages and let him inspect them." Here were no seignorial rights on entering or leaving districts, and no farm guards.

French noblemen who had served as officers under Washington were amazed to find retired captains and majors keeping inns, even an apothecary who had been a general. In Europe, war was a profession; a gentleman bought his commission as he would buy a place in the government. War moreover was a policy of princes, an instrument of power continually in use, to be reckoned with by men of ambition. And how, pray, could the American General Knox, a former bookseller, have functioned so well as an artillery commander during the strife with England? "These things," wrote Lafayette, "are very different from Europe. The master and the mistress sit down at table with you, do the honors of an excellent repast, and when you leave, you pay without bargaining. When you do not want to go to an inn, you find country-houses where you are received with the attentions which you would have in Europe from a friend."

For English visitors as well as French, it was hard to understand a people who had no tradition of feudality, no loyalty of peasant to the lord who protected him, or of tenant to landlord. Not only were the Americans without this tradition, handed down through the generations, but they had no acquaintance with it. Although born as colonials they seemed to have been born free of the class above them. An English traveler, Francis Baily, put it down to the fact of easy subsistence. Because land could be acquired cheaply, men's dependence on each other was "so trifling, that the spirit of servility to those above them so prevalent in European manners is wholly unknown, and the [Americans] pass their lives without any regard to the smiles or frowns of men in power." Thomas Cooper said much the same thing. There were no Americans of great rank, Cooper wrote, nor many of great riches. "Nor have the rich the power of oppressing the less rich, for poverty such as in Great Britain is almost unknown." The very term *farmer*, said Cooper, had in America another meaning. Whereas in England it signified a tenant, paying heavy rent to some lord and occupying an inferior rank in life, here in Pennsylvania a farmer was a land-owner, equal to any man in the state, "having a voice in the appointment of his legislators, and a fair chance . . . of becoming one himself. In fact, nine-tenths of the legislators of America are farmers."

Barbé-Marbois has an anecdote wonderfully illustrative of the incomprehensibility, to a highly placed European, of the American condition. One fine September day in Massachusetts, he and his French companion walked from their country inn to a nearby valley, where numbers of men were busy getting in the harvest. Barbé-Marbois selected one of them — a well-clothed fellow, he said, probably the head farmer — and put a series of questions. Who possessed the high and low justice in his district, how much rent did he pay to the lord of the village, who had the right to payment of a fifth of a fifth? Was he allowed to hunt and fish, were the cider press, the tower and the mill far away, was he allowed to have a dovecote, was the tithe heavy and forced labor frequent and painful? How many bushels of salt was he obliged to consume, how much was the tax on drinks, and was there capital punishment for those who were convicted of having tobacco plants in their gardens?

There is an element of fantasy in the scene: the sweating farmer, the two Frenchmen, polite, careful not to patronize. "At all these questions," Barbé-Marbois continues, the man "started to laugh. . . . He told us that justice was neither high nor low in America, but perfectly fair and equal for everyone, and we could not make him understand at all what sort of beings lords of the village were. He continued to think that we were trying to talk to him about a justice of the peace, and he could not distinguish the idea of superiority from that of magistracy."

Foreigners who went South were shocked to see slave quarters at Mount Vernon, though they noted that Washington was benevolent toward his slaves and that, like Jefferson, he disapproved the institution. But how could the father of liberty not free these poor creatures? Did he fear a general insurrection as a result? Did he think liberation should be left to the Congress? That slavery was an evil all foreigners agreed. Yet the problem seemed too vast for discussion. Some slaveowners were brutal, some kind; it was difficult to make an overall judgment, though it was agreed that any slaveowner was unjustified by the tenets of human decency. Nicholas Cresswell, passing through Maryland, noted without comment that he had seen the hindquarters of a Negro chained to a tree "for murdering his overseer."

When foreigners spoke of poverty in America they meant the poverty of white men; they were continually surprised not to find more of it. Perhaps the travelers were comparing what they saw with conditions in Europe, where Americans in their turn had expressed shock at the terrible plight of the London poor, the Paris beggars. In Massachusetts, Barbé-Marbois and his companion, carrying their own supplies, one day discovered they had too much food with them. "We said to our host, 'Give this to the poor.' He hardly understood us, and no poor could be found." Begging was unknown, said the Frenchman. From Boston to Philadelphia he had not seen a single pauper, nor met a "peasant" who was not well dressed or had not a good wagon or at least a good horse. Chastellux declared that in America no very poor people were to be seen. "Everyone enjoys easy circumstances."

A traveler sees what he wishes to see, and the American curiosity concerning strangers was insatiable, especially in rural districts — which meant nearly everywhere. No European peasant, no British yeoman would have dared such questions. Isaac Weld traveled out into Lexington, Kentucky. "Of all the uncouth human beings I met with in America," he writes, "these people from the western country were the most so; their curiosity was boundless. Frequently have I been stopped abruptly by one of them in a solitary part of the road, and in such a manner that had it been another country I should have imagined it was a highwayman that was going to demand my purse. . . . 'Stop, Mister! why I guess now you be coming from the new state.' 'No Sir,' — 'Oh! why then, pray now where might you be coming from?' 'From the low country.' — 'Why you must have heard all the news then; pray now, Mister, what might the price of bacon be in those parts?' 'Upon my word, my friend, I can't inform you.' — 'Aye, aye, I see, Mister, what might your name be?' — A stranger going the same way is sure of having the company of these worthy people, so desirous of information, as far as the next tavern, where he is seldom suffered to remain for five minutes till he is again assailed with the same question."

Isaac Weld must have been a stiff young man. If he refused to talk he was, he says, in danger of finding himself in a quarrel, especially when the company discovered that he was not an American.

For French and English alike it was upsetting to find no distinction in dress between maid and mistress, or between the lower orders and the first magistrate of the state. "Luxury," wrote de Beaujour, "has penetrated to the cottage of the workingman." Moreau was surprised that everyone could read and write, "although almost no French sailor is able to do so." It was noted that newspapers and gazettes were numerous and kept the people well informed; in the country they appeared weekly, in town twice a week and in the large cities twice a day — "morning, noon and night," wrote a Frenchman. From his lodgings in a small Massachusetts town, La Rochefoucauld wrote that the people in the house "busied themselves much with politics, and from the landlord to the housemaid they all read two newspapers a day."

These observations were made along the Atlantic coastline. In the backland — "the great interior country," as Gouverneur Morris called it — no schools existed. Life was rough, the labor backbreaking. Here a boy of fourteen was already a man, proficient with firearms, able to hunt, bring home game to eat, prepared if necessary to join the defense of his household against savages. American history is illumined by the miracle of men who grew up "in the forest" and emerged at manhood speaking excellent English, having been nourished on such prose as the King James Bible, *Pilgrim's Progress*, Addison's essays, Milton, the heroic couplets of Pope. John Marshall at the age of twelve had never seen a schoolhouse. But under somebody's instigation — probably his father's — the boy already had transcribed Pope's *Essay on Man* in toto and knew long passages by heart. On the Back River in Elizabeth City County, Virginia, Chancellor Wythe as a youth was taught Latin and the rudiments of Greek by his mother. All through the eighteenth century, travelers remarked on the purity of the American speech, its grammatical correctness and the absence of local dialects. Nicholas Cresswell in the 1770's went so far as to declare the Americans spoke better English than the English.

Nevertheless these visitors must surely have been partly deaf, or moved only in the best circles. Evidence against them is abundant: in the phonetically spelled letters of soldiers during the war, in glossaries and manuals prepared for the correction of speech. The *Columbian Grammar*, published at Boston in 1795, has a list of Improprieties: "acrost, bekays, chimbley, drowned, larnin', ourn, yourn, theirn; watermilyon; cheer for chair, riz for risen, kivver for cover." During the war, a brave infantryman at Bound Brook composed a "Song of the Minute Men":

Now tew oure Station Let us march and randevouse with pleasure
We have been like Brave minut men to sarve so Great a Treasure
We let them se amediately that we are men of mettle
We Jarsey boys that fere no nois will never flinch for Battle.

New Englanders said *dew* for do, *tew* for too. Noah Webster in his *Dissertations on the English language* (1789) notes the *keow* of New England but defends it as no worse than the London *skey* for sky and *kaynd* for kind. As for the Easterners' habit of saying *this here country, that there man*, Webster declares it coeval with the primitive Saxons. He wishes, however, that persons in the middle states would not say *fotch* for fetch and *cotched* for caught, which latter "is more frequent and equally barbarous." The people at large, remarks Webster, say *admírable, dispútable, compáreable*. And the people, Webster asserts, are right.

It seemed indeed that a new language was being created. Thomas Jefferson was sensitive to it, impatient with reviewers in English journals who set themselves against what they called the adulteration of the language by American words. "The new circumstances in which we are placed," Jefferson wrote to Washington, "call for new words, new phrases." Chastellux in his travels noted that people were apt to tell him, "You speak good American," or "American is not hard to learn." An energetic way, adds Chastellux, of expressing aversion for the English. Benjamin Franklin, whose own books had a tinge unmistakably native, enjoyed hearing a salty local dialect and remarked that "the Boston manner, turn of phrase and even tone of voice and accent in pronunciation, all please, and seem to revive and refresh me."

It was Noah Webster, however, who discovered in the American language more than a diversion or an expression of hatred for Britain. To Webster the American language constituted a philosophy and a most passionate creed. "Now is the time," he wrote (1785), "and *this* the country in which we may expect success in attempting changes favorable to . . . establish a national language, as well as a national government." As an independent people, Webster added, in all things we should be federal, be *national*. It was a word he liked to underline. Webster's *American Spelling Book* went into millions of copies — fifteen million in its author's lifetime, sixty million in a century; his *American Dictionary* made his name a household word. Webster's philosophy of language went far beyond conventional philology. People of large fortunes and family distinction, he said, have a bold, independent way of speaking, as witness New England, where there are no slaves, few servants and little talk of family descent. Here the people address each other very differently than in the South. Instead of saying *you must*, New Englanders ask, *is it not best?* — "or give their opinions with an indecisive tone; *you had better, I believe*." This idea of equality of birth and fortune, says Webster, "gives a singular tone to their language and complexion to their manners."

Nicholas Cresswell, during his travels, writes that the New Englanders "have a sort of whining cadence which I cannot describe." On this peculiarity all agreed, although, like Cresswell, none could spell it out. If Roger Sherman of Connecticut spoke of his neighbor's daughter he pronounced it *datter*, if he spoke of cranberry sauce, he called it *sass;* with his neighbors he extolled the laws of God and *natur*. As a young man, Sherman wrote and printed a series of almanacs which he sold to make money.

> The various Harmony [he wrote] in the Works of Nature
> Manifest the Wisdom of the Creator.

> Learn when to speak and when to silent set
> Fools often speak and shew their want of wit.

Most Americans used the current eighteenth-century pronunciation of *sarve* for serve, *desarve* for deserve, and said *consate* for conceit, *desate* for deceit. They also said *obleege,* and *deef* for deaf. They seem to have flattened the final *a* in America — at any rate they sang lustily, in welcome to General Washington:

> Hail, bright auspicious day!
> Long shall America
> Thy praise resound.

At the College of William and Mary the faculty took especial pains that their students learn correct pronunciation. Gentlemen cared how their children spoke. Robert Carter, the Virginia planter, had advertised for a tutor "educated in good schools upon the Continent" (meaning the American continent), rather than an Englishman or Scotchman — not because of any superiority in scholarship or character but because Carter preferred the native accent. In Philadelphia that stouthearted pre-Revolutionary schoolmaster David James Dove tried to find an assistant "who can pronounce English articulately, and read with emphasis, accent, quantity, and pauses. But if he have not the qualifications, tho' he should. . . dub himself Professor and Orator, he will be rejected as an impostor."

French travelers, even those who spoke English, found they must acquire a new vocabulary, indigenous and colorful: backwoods, back country; catboat, pungy; bullfrog, eggplant, lightning bug, razorback. From the Indians there had been adapted a bewildering succession of proper nouns and place names. Impossible to spell this polyglot American language! French visitors, writing home, did the best they could: *Jancky Dudle . . . Kentokey . . . the town of Norege,* in Connecticut. Gentlemen wrote of those well-known Indian tribes, Scherokys and Tchactas. In Newburyport, Chastellux was properly worsted after the polite visit of a colonel "whose name," wrote the Chevalier, "was pronounced something like Wigsleps."*

Even before 1780 there had been at least seventeen colleges in

---

* Americans too have known bafflement when first confronted with the Massachusetts tribe of Wigglesworth.

America; after the war they sprang up everywhere, from Union College in New York State to Transylvania "beyond the mountains." The best known of the older institutions were of course Harvard, William and Mary, Yale, Columbia and "the colleges at Princeton, New Jersey." Travelers visited these institutions, talked with the professors and were well impressed. In Philadelphia they called at the Library Company and were entertained by members of the American Philosophical Society, a learned sodality established by Dr. Franklin "for the Promotion of Useful Knowledge."

No American would have denied that in his country, learning tended toward the useful. It seemed indeed that utility, the practical application of experimental theory, was part of the *âme républicaine*, Benjamin Franklin its prophet and Philadelphia its natural center. Here was David Rittenhouse with his famous orrery and the telescope he had himself built to view the transit of Venus; here was Bartram's Garden with its botanical collection; Dr. Benjamin Rush with his new treatments for the insane. These were the men whom, after Franklin, educated foreigners endeavored to meet.

Philadelphia boasted its College of Physicians, with the Doctors Morgan, Redman, Shippen, Hutchinson, Kuhn — bold imaginative men, frequently quarrelsome among themselves, as befitted savants whose hearts were in their work. Dr. Adam Kuhn with his gold-headed cane and gold snuffbox, his hair curled and powdered, was a sight for any sickroom. He and his brethren prescribed red bark, laudanum and opium; they applied blisters and clysters, measured out vomits and cathartics, bled their patients for fevers — and for pleurisy "by the quart," one diarist noted later. Women in pregnancy and labor were bled because of plethora, Dr. Shippen said; too much blood. The good doctors came to childbirth with instruments rattling in their bags. It followed that young mothers died later of childbirth fever brought on by infection; in difficult cases the baby was extracted piecemeal with a hook. The horrors of treatment are indescribable: face cancers burned out with plasters, breasts removed while strong men sat on the patient's feet or held her shoulders down.

Small wonder people did not summon the doctor unless they

had to. Neighbors dosed each other with rhubarb and senna, castor oil, Daffy's Elixir, tea made of quashee root or nettles; they made plasters of honey and flour, onion, garlic and deer fat. Elizabeth Drinker of Philadelphia, considered an authority in physic, noted that she had cured a very bad stye with a rotten apple, and a child's deeply bruised foot with cataplasms of cow dung. Often enough people called in quacks; a governor's daughter had her son's lame foot triumphantly cured by an Indian powwow doctor. For the jaundice, an infusion, in white wine, of goose dung and earthworms was said to be helpful.

Filth was thrown into the streets, wells contaminated by backyard privies. Typhoid, malaria, smallpox, the bloody flux, the putrid sore throat (diphtheria) swept through the cities in summer like a scythe. Rickets and scurvy abounded. These were the good old days, so often lamented by moderns of a romantic turn. One is almost surprised that fifty-five delegates survived to maturity and the Federal Convention. A Virginia innkeeper and his wife told Chastellux they had had fourteen children, none of whom lived to the age of two.

Nevertheless physicians worked hard, risked their lives in time of pestilence, studied day and night to learn, dissect, discover, cure. And physicians did not grow rich. The receipt books of the grandest show payments in sugar, wine — "a red cow as per agreement." Dr. Rush bled many patients to death in the yellow fever epidemic of 1793. But he had vision nonetheless and desired to change the entire emphasis of learning in America, and not only in medicine. He proposed the founding of a postgraduate college to prepare youths for public life. Why, demanded Rush, should young men study Greek particles and the conformation of the ruins at Palmyra when they should be acquiring "those branches of knowledge which increase the conveniences of life, lessen human misery, improve our country, promote population, exalt the human understanding, and establish domestic and political happiness"?

Sir Francis Bacon had cherished a like vision, a century and a half before. Yet even Dr. Rush's dream came too soon, too early. The American people were not yet ready. Fitch's steamboat was still something to laugh at; even Dr. Franklin's electrical experiments were generally considered useless except for the installation of lightning rods. General Washington wished to establish a national university, erected and supported by Congress. At the Convention, young Charles Pinckney had proposed it as part of his original plan. But though Pinckney and Madison were to bring it up again in August and September (careful to call it federal, not national), the motion in the end was voted down on the grounds that Congress would have sufficient power itself to found a university.

America in 1787 was on the verge, the very brink of industrial and scientific expansion. Still recovering from war, with the scars visible wherever British armies had marched, the states within a decade were to see vast changes: turnpikes built and canals, fulfilling Washington's dream of opening up the western country. They were to see the utilization of coal, which as yet, men said, served only to put fires *out*. In the 1790's, Eli Whitney would introduce his cotton gin and Samuel Slater set up a spinning factory with the machinery whose plans he had carried in his head from England. Americans of 1787 showed immense pride of country, bombastic and touching. The first bridge over the Charles River at Boston (1786) inspired broadsides, poems:

> I sing the day in which the Bridge
> Is finished and done.
> Boston and Charleston lads rejoice
> And fire your cannon guns.
> The Bridge is finished now I say
> Each other bridge outvies
> For London Bridge compared with ours
> Appears in dim disguise.

Moreau was disturbed by the virulence of state pride, resulting in contempt for other districts, particularly between "Easterners" and Southerners. A grave fault, the Frenchman called it. "The faint differences between the various states," he said, "are not at all marked by politeness. They have the same form of government, the same ideas, the same notions — and the residents of each one have the highest opinion of themselves and their section." A

Philadelphian told Moreau that America wouldn't change places with any country on earth — *no, sir!*

The bragging and the boasting were in truth part of a young vigor, a young defiance. America must shout aloud her name, her independence. All the world must be informed of her grandiose new plans, which encompassed a continent and concerned nothing less than the equality of men. "We are making experiments," Franklin had said.

Little time was left, in all this, for the fine arts. Here, literature was not a trade or a means of livelihood, as in Europe. "Literature in America is an amusement only," wrote Thomas Cooper. Barbé-Marbois, praising the absence of poverty, reluctantly admits that if he has seen no beggar in America, neither has he met a Gluck, a Greuze or Bouchardon, or the author of literary masterpieces. Chastellux attributes this to the absence of rich patrons. Benjamin Franklin confessed that the New World had no place for artists. Such artistic geniuses as had arisen in America, he said, uniformly quitted their country for Europe, where they could be more suitably rewarded.

It was John Adams who made the truest observation. In Paris he viewed the Tuileries, the public squares and gardens, ornamented with "very magnificent statues." Troubled, Adams wrote home to his wife that it was not indeed the fine arts which our country required. "The mechanic arts are those which we have occasion for in a young country as yet simple and not far advanced in luxury. I must study politics and war, that my sons may have liberty to study mathematics and philosophy, geography, natural history and naval architecture, navigation, commerce and agriculture, in order to give their children a right to study painting, poetry, music, architecture, statuary, tapestry and porcelain."

Foreign visitors to the states, for all their philosophical discussions upon this new man, the American, found time to discourse eloquently on American women. Some thought the Boston girls prettiest, others the Philadelphians. On a fine winter day along the north sidewalk of Market Street between Third and Fifth, writes

Moreau with careful historical precision, "one can see four hundred young persons, each of whom would certainly be followed on any Paris promenade." These maidens, so charming and adorable at fifteen, unfortunately will be "faded at twenty-three, old at thirty-five, decrepit at forty or forty-five." And how extraordinary that a woman should leave her hair its natural color! Rouge was proscribed and so was powder. The prudery of young American matrons was unconscionable. Upon a gentleman at an evening party inquiring if French ladies rode horseback and hearing that they did, "like men . . . all the women blushed," writes Barbé-Marbois, "hid themselves behind their fans and finally burst into laughter. They cannot understand how a woman can make her toilet before a man, or even how she can dress herself in the presence of her husband."

All this was very ridiculous, said Moreau. He had seen a woman make her brother leave the room while she changed the diaper of her son, aged five weeks. Certain words were forbidden: garter, leg, knee, shirt. American women divided their bodies in two: from the head to the waist was stomach, the rest was ankles. In God's name how could a doctor guess the location of a female ailment? "He is forbidden the slightest touch," writes Moreau. "His patient, even at the risk of her life, leaves him in the vaguest doubt."

And what a pity the Americans servilely followed the English custom of sending the women from table at the end of dessert! Surely, wrote Chastellux, "every amusement which separates men from women is contrary to the welfare of society, calculated to render one of the sexes boorish and the other dull, and to destroy, in short, that sensibility, the source of which Nature has placed in interchange between the sexes." There was an awful solemnity to young American ladies. When one of them at a soirée was urged to sing, she sat on her chair straight as a poker, her eyes fixed upon the floor. "One waited until her voice began to proclaim that she was not petrified."

The visitors were experiencing at best a provincial society. Men and women had not had time to acquire the poise, the light laughter and badinage of Parisian drawing rooms. The poor young lady who sang no doubt was indeed petrified, and to her marrow. Two French noblemen standing in cheerful elegance before her were as terrifying as a brace of Monongahela wildcats. In these American cities, Chastellux adds, "if society becomes easy and gay there, if they learn to appreciate pleasure when it comes without being formally invited, then one will be able to enjoy all the advantages resulting from their customs and manners without having to envy anything in Europe."

The Frenchmen were only discovering what one is bound to find in a young civilization and a raw new world: rigidity, clannishness, suspicion of the stranger. Easy gaiety and easy laughter, the absence of prudery — did these belong then to rank, to money, to a conscious knowledge of power and place? Simplicity of manners, Quaker plainness, New England ladies with unpowdered hair, young wives and young husbands with austere morals, "men of principle" — one could not look for this and sophisticated elegance all in one place and time. French visitors were bored by the simplicity and stiffness, but they acknowledged a corresponding significance. "These same men," wrote Barbé-Marbois, "who open their doors themselves, who go on foot to judge the people, who buy their own food, are those who have brought about this Revolution." It was these men who, when necessary, raised a musket and marched on the enemy. "And between ourselves," finished Barbé-Marbois, "I am not sure that people who have porters, stewards, butlers, and covered carriages with springs, would have offered the same resistance to despotism."

# XIV

## The Western Territory, the land companies and the Northwest Ordinance. Manasseh Cutler.

> Can it be supposed that this vast country including the Western Territory will 150 years hence remain one nation?
>
> NATHANIEL GORHAM, *in Convention*

THE territory in question was gigantic. From the Appalachian barrier it rolled westward to the Mississippi, from the Great Lakes south to Spanish Florida. Ten states would one day be created from it.* But in the year 1787, west of the mountains there were no admitted states, only chaos and Indian wars, together with the dream of riches and free land.

Before Independence the Western problem had belonged to Britain; it had been Britain who must keep peace with the Indians, fight off French and Spaniards and find a method for gradual, orderly, transmontane settlement. Despairing of this, in 1763 Britain closed the West by proclamation. But with the Peace of '83, the Western empire fell to the states; theirs the responsibility and the reward. It soon became apparent that empire building required a more central, coordinated effort than the states were prepared to give. Congress tried its hand in various acts, resolutions, reports and ordinances.

The trouble was that the states cherished different notions of what should be done with the West, and each state acted for its own advantage. No sooner had England surrendered the territory

* Kentucky, Tennessee, Ohio, Indiana, Mississippi, Illinois, Alabama, Michigan, Wisconsin, West Virginia.

Western Lands Ceded by States, 1782 -1802

Western lands and territories claimed by states

Approximate extent of English colonial penetration and settlement

than seven states claimed it piecemeal as their own. Their original charters granted it to them, said Virginia, New York, Connecticut, Massachusetts, Georgia, the Carolinas. But when problems rose and pressed, when Indians refused to sell their lands or, cheated, turned on their oppressors, the states began ceding their Western territories to the Union. They moved reluctantly; it would be 1802 before the thing was done and Georgia gave up her tremendous claims, which reached to the Mississippi River.

Years of bargaining had preceded these cessions. The Federal Convention knew of it intimately; many a member had battled with the problem in his state legislature. Delegates were familiar with the terms, the bargains in Congress, knew also of those troublesome regions which threatened to break off from large states and establish themeslves independently. The northwest corner of North Carolina now chose to call itself the State of Franklin; Pennsylvania had long been harassed by its western citizens who desired to set up a state of their own. And why not? — argued certain Convention delegates, as Luther Martin of Maryland. Large states were "dangerous members of a federal republic"; Georgia for instance was bigger than "the whole island of Great Britain." Was not the province of Maine (Madison in his note spelled it Mayne) this summer of 1787 holding a convention to consider separation from Massachusetts? Vermont, still outside the Union, sat among her mountains enjoying a happy tax-free life, to the growing irritation of her neighbors. New Hampshire, Massachusetts — and especially New York — had long coveted her territory. Dr. Johnson of Connecticut said sharply one day in Convention that Vermont should be *compelled* to come into the Union.

All up and down the United States these problems reached: boundaries, land claims, statehood. But it was in the West that the question loomed largest and darkest. It was touch and go whether Tennessee and Kentucky would turn from the Union altogether. The question of the Mississippi was vital and struck deep. Spain controlled the west bank of the river. Florida was Spanish, as were New Orleans and all outlets to the sea. Spain owned the huge tract known as Louisiana. To Kentucky and Tennessee, no single policy of state or Union mattered so much as free commerce down the

Mississippi, an ocean port for their goods. If they could not have it, if the Atlantic states would not help them, if Congress remained indifferent, then Kentucky and Tennessee would create their own terms as to their statehood and as to Spain.

The East heard rumors of plots to make Kentucky a Spanish province. One James Wilkinson composed high-sounding memorials about an "honorable" transfer of allegiance. Why, he asked, should an "intelligent being" plant himself "like a vegetable where he was born," refusing a better status if such was offered by his Catholic Majesty, with free commerce down the Mississippi? New England, busy with codfishing and trade by sea, showed herself stubbornly callous to Western interests. In August of 1786, John Jay had urged Congress to surrender the navigation of the Mississippi to Spain for twenty-five or thirty years, in return for certain commercial advantages. When the South heard of it, and the West, they were outraged. These "commercial advantages" would accrue only to the East. Must Westerners then be "sold as vassals to the cruel Spaniards, to be their bondsmen as the Israelites were to the Egyptians"? Patrick Henry declared that Jay's plan invalidated the Union. Even Madison was indignant.

Jay's measure was defeated. Yet how were these matters to be solved, how was this vast new empire to be governed? There were British intrigues along the Mississippi. England would not be sorry to detach the Western Territory from the American Union; Lord Dorchester in Canada had been sympathetic to Wilkinson's efforts. "The Western States," Washington had written, "stand as it were upon a pivot. The touch of a feather would turn them any way." That the problem was old did not make it less exigent; in the summer of 1787 Congress seized upon it anew. The Federal Convention had debated the subject, on and off, since Randolph first introduced the Virginia Plan: "*Resolved*, that provision ought to be made for the admission of States lawfully arising within the limits of the United States. . . ."

Yet it was no business of the Federal Convention to order the internal administration of the Western Territory. That was for Congress. What concerned the Convention — and the United States Constitution — was whether this great interior country, this eventual mass of large new states, was to be admitted to the Union on terms of equality. Had a young state, west of the mountains, a right to the same number of representatives in Congress as the original states? And would not such equality prove a dangerous policy, a swamping of older, experienced government councils by a horde of wild men in fringed leggings, uncouth, untutored, uncivil altogether? Ironically, the Atlantic states looked on their vast Western frontier as Britain once had looked on the American colonies — with paternal suspicion of her own alien young.

There was not time to lose. Over the mountains poured the settlers, following the Wilderness Road through the Cumberland Gap into the bluegrass country, making their way along the Watauga River into East Tennessee, blazing trees and establishing their tomahawk claims in the green valley of the Kanawha. Some took the Warriors' Path northward or led their wagons over Braddock's Road and Forbes's Road through Pennsylvania to the Forks of the Ohio; many came by the Great Genesee Road from New England. It is hard to gauge the numbers; there was no census until 1790. But the over-mountain population, which in 1775 numbered only a few thousand, by 1790 would reach more than 110,000. In 1787, count was kept of the flatboats floating down the Ohio River; more than nine hundred of them, carrying "eighteen thousand men, women and children and twelve thousand horses, sheep and cattle, and six hundred and fifty wagons."

This is the American story, and everywhere it differs. Kentucky's ground was dark and bloody, or so the Indians named it, while north on Lake Erie, New Englanders settled the Western Reserve in orderly manner, laid out their lots and celebrated the Fourth of July as if they were at home in Connecticut. And with the settlers came the speculators and the land hawks, land robbers, land sharks, the gamblers, gougers, outlaws, jobbers. Long before the war with England, the speculators had begun their work; London financiers did not miss the promise of this virgin territory. To the Federal Convention the land companies were as familiar as the regions their names represented. There had been the old Ohio Company back in 1747, the Loyal Land Company, and in the '60's the Indiana Company, the Vandalia and the Grand Illinois venture in which Benjamin Franklin had invested. Their names were many and colorful: the Greenbrier, the Transylvania, the Wabash, the New Wales, the Military Adventurers. The fateful Yazoo companies had not yet appeared. But through some forty years these companies had been forming and dissolving, angling for land grants, first in London, then with the Continental Congress or the state legislatures; offering to dispose of ten thousand acres or five million and, since the war, buying with depreciated currency and holding for future profit.

George Washington had been a principal promoter of the Mississippi Company in 1763. Interested since his youth, at sixteen he went out to survey Lord Fairfax's lands in the Shenandoah Valley. After the war he lobbied vigorously for army officers who desired land grants; the General complained that while Congress debated with Virginia over cession of her holdings, "banditti" went out and jumped the claims. In 1784, Washington decided to see for himself, traveled over the mountains to the Kanawha and bought from old soldiers their warrants to locate. The vastness of the claims amazed the General; he had heard prospective buyers talk of "fifty, a hundred, and even 500,000 acres as a gentleman used to talk of 1000 acres." Washington himself was to die possessed of some forty-one thousand acres of frontier territory.

Others of the Federal Convention were not so fortunate. James Wilson was already over his head in land speculations. He had been president of the Illinois-Wabash Company, his business interests were multiple and far-flung. Wilson's feverish gambling had become an obsession; like Robert Morris he would pay for it with his reputation. Morris was soon to be disastrously involved in Western lands; on paper he owned a small empire.

Yet there is no evidence to show that these men allowed their speculative interests to influence their action in the Federal Convention. Perhaps Williamson of North Carolina phrased it for his colleagues when he later assured Madison that for himself he conceived his opinions were not biased by private interests, but "having claims to a considerable quantity of land in the Western Country, I am fully persuaded that the Value of those lands must be increased by an efficient Federal Government."

There were men of the same opinion who proved less scrupulous. The land companies, if they desired a firm government for the Western Territory, desired it only because firm government was the way to ensure their money. On the thirteenth of July, 1787, there arrived in Philadelphia a representative of this faction, an extraordinary gentleman, early example of a type that was to be notorious in America: the promoter, the money man, standing for big risks and big business.

His name was Manasseh Cutler — the Reverend Doctor Cutler of Ipswich, Massachusetts, ex-army chaplain, who had read law and practiced as a physician, besides being a botanist of no mean attainments. The past eight days Cutler had spent in New York, negotiating with Congress on behalf of the newly incorporated Ohio Company of which he was a founder. He had actually succeeded in securing the right to take up — at about nine cents (specie) per acre — one and a half million acres of choice land at the junction of the Ohio and Muskingum rivers. "We obtained," wrote Cutler, "the grant of near five millions of acres . . . one million and a half for the Ohio Company and the remainder for a private speculation, in which many of the principal characters of America are concerned. Without connecting this speculation, similar terms and advantages could not have been obtained for the Ohio Company."

It was the biggest contract ever made in America; the making of it had involved Congress in the drafting and enacting of the great Northwest Ordinance, passed with a quorum of only eight states on the very day when Cutler crossed the ferry and took the stagecoach for Philadelphia. Cutler was jubilant, his triumph happily untempered by moral reflections on the means that had been used to win over reluctant Congressmen.

Manasseh Cutler was a tall, portly, personable figure, who frequently sported a black velvet suit, black silk stockings, silver knee and shoe buckles. His portrait shows a benevolent face, an open expression and heavy eyebrows. His energy was boundless, his nature by all accounts remarkably convivial and congenial — in brief, he was the perfect lobbyist. A Virginian described Cutler as "an open, frank, honest, New Englandman — an uncommon animal." In reality Cutler seems to have been flexuous as an eel, quick to turn when profit was around the corner. At Philadelphia he wasted no time before meeting members of the Federal Convention; it was his business to see that the United States Constitution, like the Northwest Ordinance, included no measures obstructive to westward expansion — and to the Ohio Company.

The Federal Convention, in close touch with Congress, knew all about the Northwest Ordinance. Rufus King had helped to draft it. Yet King, like others of the Federal Convention, was by no means pleased with the Ordinance as enacted, nor with measures that had preceded it. Congress had been impolitic, said King, to lay out the Territory in states; better first to achieve some kind of balance between East and West. What Massachusetts — and the Federal Convention — could not know was how extraordinarily successful the Northwest Ordinance of 1787 would prove to be. It has been called the third great document of American history, after the Declaration of Independence and the Constitution.

Straight across the Western Territory, bisecting it almost in the middle, the Ohio River ran from the Alleghenies to the Mississippi. Above it the Northwest Territory reached north to the Great Lakes. South of the Ohio a region equally vast would later be divided into states, but with slavery permitted; this however must wait until Georgia and the Carolinas ceded their huge claims. Meanwhile Congress struggled to lay out the Northwest Territory, survey it, mark it into ranges. In their enacted plans the simple, practical details conjure up the old West, the remoteness of the territory and the anxious care of Congress in marking the seven first great ranges:

> The Geographer shall personally attend to the running of the first east and west line . . . The lines shall be measured with a chain; shall be plainly marked by chaps on the trees, and exactly described on a plat; whereon shall be noted by the surveyors at their proper distance, all mines, salt-springs, salt-licks and mill-seats that shall come to his knowledge, and all water-courses, mountains and other remarkable and permanent things, over and near which such lines shall pass, and also the quality of the lands.

The Northwest Ordinance provided that the entire Territory was to be ruled at first by a governor, a secretary and three judges, named by Congress. In the whole region of six and a half million acres, not less than three nor more than five states were to be created. When in any given region the population reached five thousand free male inhabitants, a legislature could be elected and a nonvoting delegate sent to Congress. As soon as one of the five states attained a population of sixty thousand free inhabitants it could be admitted to the Union and write its own constitution. Slavery was prohibited; a bill of rights guaranteed freedom of worship, *habeas corpus*, trail by jury, and security of contracts. "Schools and the means of education shall ever be encouraged," said Article III. There was a property qualification: voters must own fifty acres, legislators two hundred acres. There was also a clause which became famous more for the breach than the observance: "The utmost good faith shall always be observed towards the Indians."

In sum, the new states were to be admitted on an equal footing with the old ones, "at as early periods as may be consistent with the general interest." *

By mid-July the Ordinance had been enacted into law. Nevertheless it lay within the power of the Federal Convention to cripple the growing West in more ways than one. For or against these potential states the Convention from the outset took sides and held them vehemently, the proponents charged with feeling. Actually, jealousy of East for West was no new thing. Even before the problem became continental, Pennsylvania, Virginia, the Carolinas, Massachusetts, New York, when they could, had held to an inequality of representation in their state legislatures; the back counties were kept down.

And now in 1787 the old question took on a new face. Population was shifting so fast a legislator could not keep pace with it. Rhode Island and Massachusetts complained they were losing their citizens to the West or even to Maine. The Southwest was being peopled with astonishing rapidity; Georgia with her faraway Mississippi border could absorb any number. When Read of

* See chapter note, page 311.

Delaware demanded why Georgia was allowed two representatives in the House when she had fewer inhabitants than Delaware, Gouverneur Morris replied that before the Constitution could take effect, Georgia would probably be entitled to that many.

All this signified a new alignment, a possible and disturbing transfer of power. Legislators tried to foretell the trends, predict the commercial future of the Western states; Madison saw them as "altogether agricultural." What actually happened in the ensuing century and a half proved so different from these early prognoses that one marvels the problem was resolved with such safe and equitable vagueness, and that the Constitution in Article IV, Section 3 left the new states free to expand into the vast smoking roaring conglomerate empire they have become.

The Convention had early agreed that in the original states every forty thousand inhabitants were entitled to one representative in the lower house. But with the new rage for Western emigration this suddenly became dangerous. The energy of these over-mountain people was dismaying. States formed and took names without so much as by-your-leave. Transylvania, Westsylvania, Franklin, Vandalia . . . fashioning makeshift governments and makeshift law courts of their own. Soon there might be as many Western states as Eastern. And these people were poor! They would not be able to pay their share in the Union, pay their taxes and inposts, or pay their own militia to hold back the Indians.

Persistently the argument reappeared. Were these ignorant poor settlers to be allowed to outvote the maritime states? Rather let the East take care of its own interest "by dealing out the right of representation in safe proportions": this from Nathaniel Gorham of Massachusetts. George Clymer, the Philadelphia merchant, an "old patriot" — he had signed the Declaration of Independence — thought it "suicide" for the original states to encourage the Western country. Clymer, like his colleague Ingersoll, was one of the Convention's silent members, very experienced politically but more effectual in caucus than on the floor.

Luther Martin spoke heatedly, confusedly. He wished a clause in the Constitution guaranteeing to the United States the still unceded lands: the backlands, vacant lands, he called them. Moreover, must a new district, ready for statehood, wait upon permission from neighboring states? Must Vermont be at the mercy of New York, and the new State of Franklin be dependent upon North Carolina? At home in Annapolis, Martin was shortly to inform his state legislature of the unreasonable hardship imposed by a Constitution which forced states west of the mountains to remain connected with states on the Atlantic side. In Martin's angry opinion, it would justify a recourse to arms "to shake off so ignominious a yoke."

Massachusetts came out against admitting the West on equal terms. Elbridge Gerry's republican principles frequently clashed with his interests as a New England merchant; he expressed himself as convinced the over-mountain states would before long be more thickly populated than the Northern. They would abuse their power, "drain our wealth into the Western country." To guard against it, Gerry wished to see the Constitution limit the admission of new states "in such a manner that they should never be able to outnumber the Atlantic states."

Gerry made a formal motion to this effect, seconded by Rufus King. But Roger Sherman in his flat Yankee voice opined that there was "no probability the number of future states would exceed that of the existing states." Such a contingency was too remote for consideration. "Besides, we are providing for our posterity, for our children and our grandchildren, who would be as likely to be citizens of new Western states as of the old states. On this consideration alone, we ought to make no such discrimination as was proposed by the motion."

But some of our children, retorted Gerry, will stay behind. In this rage for emigration, should we not provide for their interests? And besides, foreigners were resorting to that country, making it uncertain what turn things might take.

Gerry's motion was voted on and went down five to four, with Pennsylvania divided. Gerry, Gorham, King, Martin, Clymer, Butler, Rutledge of South Carolina — all were for curbing the West. But in the entire Convention nobody showed himself so decisive on the point as Gouverneur Morris. That the Westerners would bring on a war with Spain was inevitable, he said; nor would they scruple to involve the whole continent for the sake of the Mississippi River. Morris strongly advised apportioning all

Congressional representatives East *and* West by property rather than by numbers. Pierce Butler had said the same and Rutledge agreed. This would settle everything; this would ensure that the power remained in "safe" hands. And what reason was there to think, Morris later demanded, that the interior country could furnish enlightened statesmen in administration? "The busy haunts of men, not the remote wilderness, was the proper school of political talents. The back members were always most averse to the best measures."

Until the end of the Convention, Morris was to persist, and beyond the Convention. Himself fastidious, mannered, he disliked Westerners, their politics, their ways, their speech; he feared their terrifying potential. "I dread the cold and sour temper of the back counties," he was to write Washington during ratification in Pennsylvania. Morris never let go an inch. Right up through August and early September he worked in committee to alter Article IV, Section 3, so that new states might not come in unconditionally. Morris's ideas extended beyond the Northwest Territory to regions even more debatable; much later he confessed it. "I always thought," he wrote in 1803, "that when we should acquire Canada and Louisiana it would be proper to govern them as provinces, and allow them no voice in our councils. In wording the third section of the fourth Article, I went as far as circumstances would permit to establish the exclusion. . . . Candor obliges me to add my belief that had it been more pointedly expressed, a strong opposition would have been made."

The men who stood out against Morris were few but startlingly effectual: Madison, Sherman, George Mason, James Wilson and, from time to time, Randolph of Virginia. Early in July, Randolph had reminded the Convention that Congress had already pledged the public faith to new states, "that they shall be admitted on equal terms." Randolph referred to an earlier resolution passed by Congress, promising that any new states entering the Union should have "the same rights of sovereignty, freedom and independence as the other states." It was something Gouverneur Morris chose to forget.

James Wilson, forceful, knowledgeable, came out unequivocally for Western equality. Wilson has not been much described by historians. The narrow shoulders and dark clothes, the scholar's spectacles low on his nose, the plump chin and cheeks — these do not invite description in the grand manner. In his portrait the eyes are watchful, as if he were ready to loose his intellectual shaft. Benjamin Rush said of Wilson that his mind was "one blaze of light." In the records of the Convention, when Wilson rises to speak it is as if an electric charge passes down the page. Not the flash induced by a Patrick Henry or the witty quick illumination of a Gouverneur Morris but rather the hard relentless light of intellect. When Wilson speaks he wastes no time and considers no man's feelings.

Concerning the West, he "viewed without apprehension," said Wilson, the time when a few states might contain superior members — the majority of the people wherever found ought in all questions to govern the minority. "If the interior country should acquire this majority, they will not only have the right, but will avail themselves of it whether we will or no." Any government, Wilson implied, can be misled by jealousy. Had not jealousy misled Great Britain? "The fatal maxims espoused by Britain were that the Colonies were growing too fast, and that their growth must be stinted in time." And what were the consequences? "First enmity on our part, then actual separation." Should the same policy be pursued by the East toward the West, the same result would follow. "Further," finished Wilson, "if numbers be not a proper rule [for representation], why is not some better rule pointed out? Congress have never been able to discover a better rule."

Madison also championed the West. He looked ahead; his words showed thought, long consideration. Not the least surprising characteristic of the Federal Convention was that, contrary to the tradition of political assemblies, it let itself be swayed by men of thought and historical perspective. Regarding the Western states, Madison said he was "clear and firm in opinion that no unfavorable distinctions were admissible either in point of justice or policy." In his view, hope of Western contributions to the general treasury had been much underrated. Whenever the Mississippi should be opened to the Western people — which would of necessity be the case as soon as their population allowed it — then imposts on Western trade would be collected "with less expense," said Madison, "and greater certainty than on that of the Atlantic States." In the meantime it might be remembered that Western supplies had to pass through the Atlantic states to reach the sea; they would have to pay accordingly.

Madison spoke out strongly against Gouverneur Morris's motion for conditional admission of new states. The West, he said, "neither would nor ought to submit to a Union which degraded them from an equal rank with other states." Besides, said Madison sharply, the gentleman [Morris] was inconsistent. First he recommended implicit loyalty from South to North, then exhorted all to a jealousy of a Western majority. Did the gentleman then determine the human character by the points of the compass? The truth was that all men having power ought to be distrusted to a certain degree. . . . And "if the Western States hereafter arising should be admitted into the Union, they ought to be considered as equals and as brethren."

George Mason supported Madison. It is interesting that these two Virginians, very different in personality and estate, were so liberal toward the West. Neither of them cherished Gouverneur Morris's prejudice. Mason spoke with feeling. Strong objections, he said, had been drawn from the danger to the Atlantic interests from new Western states. "Ought we to sacrifice what we know to be right in itself, lest it should prove favorable to states which are not yet in existence? If the Western States are to be admitted into the Union as they arise, they must — I will repeat — they must be treated as equals and subjected to no degrading discriminations."

It was not the first subject on which George Mason had appealed to men's principles. Dr. Franklin had remarked in Convention that some of the worst rogues in his acquaintance had been the richest rogues. But the Doctor had also pointed out that governments need men of wealth who can be independent in their thinking. George Mason was a case in point. Westerners — Mason said — "will have the same pride and other passions which we have, and will either not unite with or will speedily revolt from the Union, if they are not in all respects placed on an equal footing with their brethren." As for the expectation of their poverty and inability to contribute to the general treasury, he did not know, finished Mason, but that in time they would be both more numerous and more wealthy than their Atlantic brethren, though not perhaps before they might choose to become a separate people.

Madison crossed out the last clause: *A separate people.* Perhaps he could not bear to see it on paper. Perhaps he wished no one in future to see it, outside the Convention.

It was in the midst of this discussion that the Reverend Manasseh Cutler arrived from New York and put up at the Indian Queen. His mission was clear; to persuade the Federal Convention — as he had persuaded the Congress — that the Constitution must not permit new or old states to breach their contracts in Western land sales. Already, Cutler had sold shares in the Ohio Company to congressmen; he had manipulated it so that General St. Clair was named first governor of the Territory instead of General Putnam, who till then had been the candidate. (St. Clair was president of Congress, a telling factor.) Cutler's diary, discreet but vivid, fills two printed volumes. Everything he wrote about Philadelphia is interesting. To the Reverend Manasseh, Ipswich, Massachusetts, or even Boston, had nothing to compare with the refinements of this biggest and most luxurious metropolis of the Union.

His chamber at the Indian Queen, says Cutler, afforded a fine view of the river and the Jersey shore. The young Negro who showed him to his room was smart in ruffled shirt and powdered hair. The furniture was handsome; two of the latest London magazines lay on the table, and the Negro at once fetched a barber to dress the visitor's hair. Cutler dispatched a note to Caleb Strong of Massachusetts, and in a very short time was introduced to Gorham, Madison, Mason, Governor Martin, Williamson, Rutledge, Charles Pinckney and Alexander Hamilton. They sat convivially till after one in the morning.

Cutler's diary omits the conversation. But this was a man for business, and secrecy rule or no secrecy rule, there is small doubt Cutler maneuvered the talk around to Congress, the Northwest Ordinance, the lush Ohio Valley, the seven ranges and the profits to be made if the new Constitution kept the states from interfering. In New York, congressmen had shown eagerness to buy into the company. It was to be assumed Convention members would be pleased by a like opportunity before the rush for shares began. Cutler's son of nineteen was going out with the first wagons, he himself expected to follow. His scheme, Cutler was ready to explain, enabled the United States to pay off more than four millions of the public debt. Surely, the Federal Convention would put nothing in the way of such a plan?

Manasseh Cutler's personality seems to have been irresistible. No sooner did delegates meet him than they invited him home with them. Next morning the New Englander was up early and walked with Caleb Strong to Elbridge Gerry's house on Spruce Street. The weather was cool, the city quiet at this hour. To Cutler's surprise, Mrs. Gerry, young and pretty, sat at breakfast with the gentlemen, though it was only half past five. Whereas in Boston, wrote Cutler, the ladies could "hardly see a breakfast table at nine without falling into hysterics." Cutler admired the baby, two months old, and remarked in his diary that few old bachelors were so fortunate in matrimony as Mr. Gerry. It was astonishing how easily the conversation went, with guests staying in the house and strangers present. Cutler's diary exclaimed upon it: "What advantages are derived from a finished education and the best of company! How does it banish that awkward stiffness, so common when strangers meet in company! How does it engage the most perfect strangers in all the freedom of an easy and pleasing sociability, common only to the most intimate friends!"

There is something engaging about Manasseh Cutler, with his desire to see, to learn, to improve his manners. Taken through the State House, Cutler found it richer and grander architecturally than any public building he had seen. In the west room downstairs, the Pennsylvania Supreme Court was sitting, the three judges robed in scarlet. Chief Justice McKean had his hat on, which Cutler thought looked odd, though it was customary. The sentries were "very alert in the performance of their duty."

In the afternoon Cutler called on Dr. Franklin in Market Street and felt, he wrote, as if he were about to be introduced to a monarch. But when they went into the garden, there sat the Doctor under his mulberry tree — "a short, fat, trunched old man in a plain Quaker dress, bald pate and short white locks." Franklin rose, begged the visitor to draw his chair closer, showed him a snake with two heads, caught in the Delaware River, and was about to tell a story concerning two-headed reptiles and the Federal Convention when he was stopped by one of the company who bade the Doctor remember the secrecy rule. Notwithstanding Franklin's age, wrote Cutler, his manners were "perfectly easy and everything about him seems to diffuse an unrestrained freedom and happiness. He has an incessant vein of humor, accompanied with an uncommon vivacity which seems as natural and involuntary as his breathing. He urged me to call on him again, which my short tarry will not admit."

Cutler left Philadelphia and went on his way. What had passed between him and the delegates we shall never know; certainly they had not responded as openly (or as venally) as had the Congress at New York. But delegates had offered private hospitality and they had seemed receptive. The Reverend Manasseh could tell his colleagues in New England that things looked promising for the Ohio Company.

But the Federal Convention was by no means finished with the matter of the Western states; this would continue all summer. It was Rufus King who on August twenty-eighth moved that the Constitution include the significant words, adapted from the Northwest Ordinance, that states could pass no laws impairing the obligation of contracts. Gouverneur Morris, however, held out to the very end. Had it not been for him the Constitution would have included a clause providing that new states "should be admitted on the same terms with the original states." During sittings of the Committee of Detail, Morris got the clause deleted. In its final phrasing, Article IV, Section 3 welcomed new states into the Union, providing they were not formed "within the jurisdiction of any other State," without the consent of the local legislatures involved. Quite properly it was left for Congress to "dispose of and make all needful Rules and Regulations respecting the Territory or other Property belonging to the United States."

During the ratification period, following September of 1787, the Western question would loom large. In the *Federalist Papers,*

Madison and Hamilton brought it up as a strong argument for the Constitution. They mentioned the threat of disunion, the possible secession of the West, the jealousies among new states and the rapacity of Europe where our virgin lands were concerned. Quoting Article IV, Madison declared such a provision "absolutely necessary" if the Union was to stand. Full faith and credit must be given in each state to the acts and proceedings of every other state; citizens throughout the Union were entitled to like privileges and immunities. All this the Constitution guaranteed.

United States history can show many threats of disunion. Because of the Civil War, one is used to thinking of these threats as coming from the South. Yet it is well to remember that if the Convention had failed, if the Western Territory had not been admitted on terms of equality, there might have followed a whole series of revolutions, of civil strife and territorial secession as the nation pushed ever farther westward and new states reached maturity. Under such conditions it is not impossible to conceive of the United States proper as ending at the Appalachian Ridge.

In December of 1787, Manasseh Cutler's little band of pioneers, with Cutler's son among them, made their farewells and fired their departing volleys before Manasseh's house at Ipswich. On the black canvas of their covered wagon the letters stood out in white paint: FOR THE OHIO AT THE MUSKINGUM.

## XV

*The Great Compromise. A king for America.*
*Ten-day adjournment. General Washington*
*goes fishing.*

> If the General Government should be left depend-
> ent on the State Legislatures, it would be happy for us
> if we had never met in this room.
> JOHN DICKINSON, *in Convention*

BENJAMIN FRANKLIN, like General Washington, never neglected an opportunity to influence the public. Perhaps it was Franklin who gave the *Pennsylvania Packet* a cheerful but deceptive little item which appeared on July 19, 1787: "So great is the unanimity, we hear, that prevails in the Convention upon all great federal subjects, that it has been proposed to call the rooms in which they assemble — Unanimity Hall."

Actually, delegates were far from unanimity. Three days earlier, the Convention had passed that essential measure which came to be known as the Great Compromise, by which every state was to have two members in the United States Senate. This would offset proportional representation in the House, where the large states of course had the advantage, with one representative to every forty thousand inhabitants. There are critics today who think the Convention erred, and that the Senate, like the House, should have remained proportional. Yet without the Great Compromise it is hard to see how the Federal Convention could have proceeded further; since the beginning it had been cause for battle. The effort to resolve it, Luther Martin wrote later, "nearly terminated in a dissolution of the Convention." It was this question as much as anything which had caused Washington on July tenth to write Hamilton that the crisis was alarming and he "almost despaired."

Perhaps the delegates would never have reached agreement, had not the heat broken. By Monday, July sixteenth, Philadelphia was cool after a month of torment; on Friday, a breeze had come in from the northwest. Over the weekend, members could rest and enjoy themselves, sleep comfortably in their narrow chambers at the lodging houses along Market Street or Second Street hill above the river. Even the mosquitoes were quiescent, though on the streets at noon the horseflies droned and darted.

The small states were jubilant over the Compromise; the large states, alarmed, tried to reorganize, recover their position. Even though the Convention had voted, the rules would have let them broach the subject again. But it was hopeless, the large states were beaten; after July seventeenth they let the question die. From now on matters would move more easily; the little states were readier to meet the big, and willing to yield on many questions. They felt safe, no longer threatened by those towering bullies — Virginia, Pennsylvania, Massachusetts, or any possible combination of the three. Delegates reported hopefully to their friends. The Convention had "nearly agreed on the principles and outlines of a system." Davie of North Carolina wrote that he would shortly come home. Mysteriously, Davie added that "the two great characters you inquire after move with inconceivable circumspection. Their situations, though dissimilar, are both peculiar and delicate."

Possibly, Davie referred to colleagues from the Carolinas. But if he meant Washington, it was true the General remained silent in the Convention, yet showed his sentiments, for or against measures, by smiling or frowning. If the other "great character" was Franklin, his discretion permitted a Convention story to slip out now and then in company. Yet the Doctor's joviality never passed the line of real revelation; Franklin could keep silence when he chose.

It was natural for delegates to observe closely the General and the Doctor, taking note of their reaction and response. Franklin expressed himself as pleased with the Great Compromise; on July eighteenth he sent a message to his friend and protégé Captain John Paul Jones in New York: "The Convention goes on well and there is hope of great good to result from their counsels."

The Doctor was sanguine; it was part of his nature. But in truth the fight between small states and large had gone so deep that echoes would sound for years. Throughout the following winter, delegates reported on it to their state conventions for ratification. Caleb Strong told his colleagues in Boston that the Federal Convention had been "nigh breaking up," but for the Compromise. Luther Martin declared in Annapolis that even Dr. Franklin had conceded to equality in the Senate only when he found no other terms would be accepted. In 1796, during the fight over Jay's Treaty with England, President Washington told a hostile House of Representatives that the sovereignty and political safety of the smaller states depended on the equal senatorial vote. In 1803 — again a crucial time — Jonathan Dayton of New Jersey reminded the Senate that the makers of the Constitution had provided checks against state combinations by granting equal votes in one House, proportional votes in the other. When nullification was agitating in 1830, Charles Pinckney of South Carolina informed Congress that the Federal Convention of 1787 had argued "most pertinaciously for near six weeks" over the Compromise. "Nothing but the prudence and forebearance of the large states," said Pinckney, "saved the Union."

South Carolina was in the middle rank. Yet the small states also forbore, showed patience. Madison in his old age set down a clear testimony in letters to his friends. The threatened contest in the Federal Convention, he said, had not turned, as most men supposed, on the degree of power to be granted to the central government but rather on "the rule by which the states should be represented and vote in the government" — a question "the most threatening that was encountered in framing the Constitution."

About a week after the Great Compromise was passed, the two New Hampshire delegates finally appeared — a good nine weeks late; the Convention knew they had waited until Governor Langdon offered to pay for the journey. One of them, Nicholas Gilman, wrote home that much work remained for the assembly to do: "Feeble minds," he said, "are for feeble measures and some for patching the old garment; while vigorous minds . . . advocate a high-toned monarchy."

High-toned was current slang for high-powered, centralized — the kind of government that Alexander Hamilton was accused of fostering. Yet contemporary uses of the word monarchy are to-day surprising. Why did Gilman of New Hampshire declare that "vigorous minds" (surely the best minds) desired a monarchy? Mrs. Mercy Warren, wife of James Warren and sister of James Otis, was at the moment busy composing a *History of the American Revolution*, eventually to appear in three volumes. Mercy Warren was a redoubtable lady, an old-time Sam Adams patriot who saw the Revolution betrayed at every step; moreover she was fiercely biased on the states-rights side. She wrote to everybody, gleaning information, giving out patriotic advice — and everybody answered, including John Adams in England. To Catharine Macaulay, the London bluestocking, Mrs. Warren wrote during August of 1787 that in America "the young ardent spirits . . . cry out for monarchy." These men, "in pursuit of office and emolument," with the Society of the Cincinnati at their back, make a formidable body, she said, "ready to bow to the sceptre of a King."

Whether or no Mrs. Warren exaggerated, the very fact of her statement shows a trend. Again, however, it is odd to think of minds described as vigorous, young and ardent, crying out boldly for something supposedly abhorrent to the American spirit. Perhaps Hamilton was a case in point. Himself young, ardent, vigorous of mind and ambitious, the idea of an elective monarchy attracted him. He saw no reason why a chief executive with life tenure would interfere with a truly republican government. A generation later, Rufus King in the United States Senate was to remind a young member that the Convention of '87 had looked on a possible American monarchy with something less than horror. Every Convention delegate, said the New Englander, had grown up the loyal subject of a king; they were used to the word. John Adams in 1789 challenged Roger Sherman to say whether our Constitution was not, after all "a monarchical republic, or, if you will, a limited monarchy. The duration of our president," Adams argued, "is neither perpetual nor for life; it is only for four years; but his power during those four years is much greater than that of an avoyer, a consul, a podestà, a doge, a stadholder; nay, than a king of Poland; nay, than a king of Sparta." When Gouverneur Morris was named Minister to France in the early 1790's, George Mason declared his political doctrines made him unfit for the post; Mason had heard Morris, in the Federal Convention, say outright that "we must have a monarchy sooner or later (tho' I think his word was a *despot*) and the sooner we take him, while we are able to make a bargain with him, the better." It is pertinent also to note a bitter little item in the journal of that acerb politician Senator Maclay, representing Pennsylvania in the first Congress held under the Constitution. "June 5, 1789: Yesterday was the anniversary of his Britannic Majesty's birth. It was a high day and celebrated with great festivity on that account. The old leaven anti-revolutionism has leavened the whole lump, nor can we keep the Congress free from the influence of it."

A king for America! . . . Incredible, that post-Revolutionary patriots would permit themselves such a thought. "I am astonished," Jefferson wrote a congressman in the summer of '87, "at some people's considering a kingly government as a refuge." The Federal Convention was more than half over when Williamson of North Carolina made his remark about its being "pretty certain that we should at some time or other have a king." In Williamson's mind a single magistrate would in effect constitute an elective king, and would "feel the spirit of one. He will spare no pains to keep himself in office for life, and will then lay a train for the succession of his children." No precaution should be omitted "that might postpone this event as long as possible."

No fewer than sixty ballots were needed before the method of selecting the President was decided; repeatedly, delegates fell upon it as if never before debated. Five times, the Convention voted in favor of having the President appointed by Congress. Once they voted against that, once for electors chosen by the state legislators, twice against that, and then voted again and again to reconsider the whole business. Madison remained opposed to popular election, one of his arguments being that people would prefer a citizen of their own state, thereby subjecting the small states to a disadvantage.

Equally as many separate ballots were taken on other matters concerning the executive department. Should the President be subject to impeachment? If so, he could not be called monarch; a king cannot be impeached. Gouverneur Morris thought the President should be impeachable. "He may be bribed by a greater power to betray his trust." Morris reminded delegates that though one would have thought the King of England well secured against bribery, Charles II had been bribed by Louis XIV. The American magistrate, however, "is not the king but the prime minister," said Morris. "The people are the king. . . . The way to keep out monarchical government is to establish such a republic as will make the people happy and prevent a desire of change."

Should a President be allowed more than one term, and how long a term? The question stopped the Convention repeatedly; next winter it would appear in ratification debates. As argument for a long term, Alexander Hamilton in the *Federalist Papers* inquired if peace and stability would be served by having half a dozen former Presidents "wandering among the people like discontented ghosts and sighing for a place they were destined never more to possess"? Benjamin Franklin in Convention came out strong for re-eligibility. Why should the chief magistrate feel degraded — as delegates seemed to think — by being returned to the people after office? Such a notion was contrary to republican principles. "In free governments the rulers are the servants," Franklin said, "and the people their superiors and sovereigns. For the former therefore to return among the latter is not to *degrade* but to *promote* them." In Madison's notes the words are underlined.

To the talk of presidential power and privilege, Pierce Butler added an interesting postscript. Butler, it will be remembered, was the aristocratic South Carolinian, born and brought up abroad, who liked to parade his cousinship with the noble English family of Percy, but who nevertheless in his own state had championed the cause of the poor voteless back-county settlers. After the Convention, Butler wrote his son that the powers of the President had been made "full great" — greater than he himself had been disposed to make them. It was his private opinion that these powers would have been less extensive had not many members looked to General Washington as their first President. "So that," Butler concluded, "the man, who by his patriotism and virtue, contributed largely to the emancipation of his country, may be the innocent means of its being, when he is laid low, oppressed."

In the third month of the Convention, the matter of a king for America came to a head. A newspaper reported a movement, persistent and disturbing, to invite the "Bishop of Osnaburgh," second son of George III, to America as king. The rumor flamed from town to town, traced eventually to a Connecticut loyalist who had got up a circular letter suggesting that, as the states did not possess enough wit to govern themselves, the Bishop be sent for. Colonel David Humphreys, Washington's friend, even wrote that the Bishop had been named as first toast at a dinner he attended.

The Convention was quick to act. A note in the *Pennsylvania Journal* mentioned certain "idly circulating reports" which had been received by delegates. "To which," finished the *Journal*, "it has been uniformly answered, tho' we cannot affirmatively tell you what we are doing, we can, negatively, tell you what we are not doing — we never once thought of a king." Nevertheless the *Independent Gazetteer* printed a pertinent anecdote about taking down the CROWN (in large letters) of Philadelphia's Christ Church steeple, which had been injured by lightning. When a bystander asked what was to be done with the crown, "an arch boy," finished the *Gazetteer*, "said they had better wait till the Convention breaks up, and know first what *they* recommended." After the Convention, too, the matter of a monarch for America was to be political capital at election time. In May of 1788, much was made of a certain slip of paper, written out during the Convention by John Francis Mercer, delegate from Maryland, and said to list all the Conventioneers who had been for an American king: McHenry and Luther Martin had copied it. Daniel Carroll of Maryland, named on a preliminary ballot for Congress, was reported to figure on this list of the damned. There were counter-charges, recriminations, votes lost and gained. In the end Mercer denied the whole thing and Carroll went to Congress.

But the tradition of monarchy died hard in America. When the question of the President's title came up in the Senate, John Adams, no monarchist, wanted it to be "His Highness, the President of the United States and Protector of their Liberties." Nothing less, said Adams, would be proportional to the authority and dignity of his office and to the wealth, power and population of the nation. The House refused; Washington and his successors remained plain "Mr. President."

On Thursday, July twenty-sixth, the Convention appointed a small committee — the Committee of Detail, they called it — to set their resolves, suggestions, amendments and propositions into workable arrangement, or, as Washington phrased it in his diary, to "draw into method and form the several matters which had been agreed to by the Convention as a Constitution for the United States." The five members: Randolph of Virginia, Wilson of Pennsylvania, Gorham of Massachusetts, Ellsworth of Connecticut and Rutledge of South Carolina, were by no means expected to produce a finished Constitution. Calling their work a "Report," they based it on the twenty-three Resolutions already passed, and they were given until August sixth — eleven days — to prepare it. Meanwhile the Convention would adjourn.

Newspapers carried notices of the adjournment; there was a flurry of letter-writing by delegates and interested bystanders. A member from North Carolina apologized to the governor of his state for not being able to give out more information. Secrecy was very necessary, he said. "Many crude matters," daily uttered on the floor, "might make an undue impression on the too credulous and unthinking mobility." James Madison's father, irked at receiving no news, wrote suggesting that his son might at least give some information as to what the Convention was *not* doing. John Jay wrote to John Adams that the Convention had "agreed on the leading principles of their plan and named a committee to put it into form; but we know not what it is, and I believe it is best that we should not." Young James Monroe sent Jefferson a vague report and said he feared the country's ruin, should the Convention's recommendations be rejected. He trusted, however, that General Washington's presence would "overawe and keep under the demon of party," and that the General's signature to the new Constitution would "secure its passage through the union."

The General himself got on his horse and rode up-country with his friends, trout fishing. He was still living on Market Street with Robert Morris and his lady, who described their visitor as extraordinarily quiet and self-effacing. It was Washington's habit, returning from the Convention, to slip into the house unannounced. No one knew he was home until they found him working over his papers or sitting quietly, meditating. The General became much interested in Mrs. Morris's household management; she was, he said, "a notable lady in family arrangements." Eventually he bought a mangle from her, secondhand: "I *think* that is what they are called," he wrote his secretary, Tobias Lear.

Washington's reputation has shifted much from generation to generation. During his lifetime he suffered sharp criticism, both as Commander in Chief and more particularly as President, when the French Revolution divided the states into angry faction. With the years, the virulence of party feeling faded and the Washington legend began to grow; it bloomed or withered according to the fashion of the day. Washington has been labeled an American saint, a Parson Weems prig, a general who lost battles, a brilliant commander, a slow-witted country gentleman, a staunch yet shadowy figure made apparently of stone, with false teeth which fitted wretchedly. Charles Wilson Peale, who painted him often, said the General had "a pig eye" (small and gray), features flushed with port and the figure of Apollo. Gilbert Stuart on the other hand said the General's shoulders were high and narrow, his hands and feet too big for his frame. The Houdon bust and the Houdon life mask show a face strikingly handsome, with even brows, a strong bony structure and eyes set deep and wide apart.

Among the differing contemporary descriptions of Washington, one quality seems agreed on; we find it often noted. "There is a remarkable air of dignity about him, with a striking degree of gracefulness," wrote an Englishman in 1780. "He carries himself freely," said Barbé-Marbois, "and with a sort of military grace.

He is masculine looking, without his features being less gentle on that account. I have never seen anyone who was more naturally and spontaneously polite."

In this carriage of Washington's — this "noble, gentle urbanity," one observer called it — was something which went beyond the social graces, influencing profoundly those who met him. Mrs. John Adams visited Washington's encampment near Boston in 1775. Abigail Adams could be sharp-tongued, nor was she given to flattering personal descriptions. Yet on meeting the General she made no apology for quoting Dryden's high-flown lines, which she said "instantly occurred" to her:

> Mark his majestic fabric; he's a temple
> Sacred by birth, and built by hands divine;
> His soul's the deity that lodges there;
> Nor is the pile unworthy of the God.

Trevelyan, the English historian, declares that Washington's influence over his French allies in the war "owed not a little to the dignity and charm of his bodily presence, that outward gift which . . . is seldom despised except by those to whom it is refused." Robert Morris told a neighbor that Washington was "the only man in whose presence he felt any awe." When the General went to the theater, people liked to watch him and note his hearty laugh. After he was President, though titles had been eschewed and though Washington looked, wrote a contemporary, "an unostentatious, plain sedate citizen, notwithstanding people generally addressed him and spoke of him as His Highness the President." A Virginia colonel complained that at his official levees the General's bows were more distant and stiff than those of a king. Washington replied ruefully that his bows were the best he could manage; their stiffness must be due to age or the unskillfulness of his teacher — certainly not to pride and dignity of office, "which God knows has no charm for me."

Some men have a talent for acting or for oratory. Washington's genius it seemed lay in his character. He was passionate, high-tempered, controlled; his family at Mount Vernon did not fear him. There are no tales of cringing children, nor do his letters to the young carry the relentless hortatory tone of Jefferson's to his daughter Martha.

There is an anecdote, in different versions, concerning Gouverneur Morris and the General, that summer of 1787. Perhaps the story is mere legend, but legends can be illustrative of truth. Morris announced in company that he was afraid of no man on earth, whereupon Alexander Hamilton laid a bet that Morris would not dare to greet General Washington by a slap on the back. Brash, cheerful, self-assured, Morris entered a drawing room a few evenings later and found Washington standing by the fireplace. "Well, General!" said Morris, laying a hand on Washington's shoulder. The General said nothing. But at once Morris knew his mistake and was ready, he said afterward, to sink through the floor.

In a Convention of quarrelsome, fiery states it was well to have such a presiding officer, personally remote, in whom the quality of petty jealousy — noticeable enough when he was a young lieutenant — had been conquered and put down. "I do not think vanity is a trait of my character," Washington wrote quite simply. One feels this influence in the Convention; one sees the General presiding, his face grave, attentive, the pockmarks showing faintly when he turned to the light. One feels his anxiety, his deep involvement. "It is not sufficient," Washington had written, "for a man to be a passive friend and well wisher to the cause." One remembers the visitor to Mount Vernon during ratification debates, who remarked that he had never seen the General so keen for anying as he was for the adoption of the new Constitution.

From Washington's diary: Monday July 30, 1787. "In company with Mr. Govr. Morris and in his Phaeton with my horses, went up to one Jane Moore's (in whose house we lodged) in the vicinity of Valley Forge to get Trout." Tuesday, July 31. "Whilst Mr. Morris was fishing I rid over the old Cantonment of the American [Army] of the Winter, 1777 and 8, visited all the Works, wch. were in Ruins, and the Incampments in woods where the grounds had not been cultivated."

The General rode over his old cantonment in the hot July weather. There were plowed fields, now, between the earthworks; the slopes where he rode were dry and dusty. Valley Forge, and all the works in ruins. What could a man feel beyond sadness for the terrible past, a thankfulness for peace, for summertime and the coming harvest. The General returned to his friends and fished the evening stream.

Next day it rained and the party went back to Philadelphia. Convention members had scattered during the adjournment; Sherman and Johnson had gone home in the stage to Connecticut. Pierce Butler was in New York, where he had brought his family from South Carolina — "Philadelphia not being so healthy," he said. General Charles Cotesworth Pinckney had harnessed up his two fine bay geldings and trotted off to Bethlehem, sightseeing. He had bought the horses from Jacob Hiltzheimer, the Quaker merchant, who provided an itinerary for the journey, with names of the best inns.

On Saturday night, August fourth, a concert was advertised at the "Opera House" in Philadelphia, followed by a "Comic Lecture in Five Acts," called *The Generous American*, after which came a Comic Opera in two acts entitled *The Padlock*. It must have been a heavy evening. Washington escaped it. He had gone fishing again, this time near Trenton for perch, and, he wrote, "with more success." People were gratified that the General took time to visit the Trenton Iron Works, described by the *Pennsylvania Packet* as "much the largest and best constructed furnace in America, being charged with fourteen tons of iron, at that time converting into steel. His Excellency was pleased to express his approbation of it."

His Excellency had been interested in the buckwheat, too, around Valley Forge, and had been careful to learn from a farmer how to cultivate it and use it as food for cattle. Made into a wash it was "most excellent," says the General's diary, "to lay fat upon hogs." And mixed with Irish potatoes "very good for Colts that are weaning."

# XVI

*Committee of Detail. The slavery compromise.*

I cannot reconcile myself to the idea of a division
of this Continent, even fifty years hence.
                                    JOHN ADAMS, *1789**

ON Monday, August sixth, the Committee of Detail was
ready with its report. The five members had labored
hard. They by no means considered that they were presenting the final United States Constitution to the Convention.
Merely, this was the Virginia Plan once more amended — another
stage in a summer's progress.

The committee's work can be partially followed in the various
drafts written out by Randolph and Wilson, with alterations in
Rutledge's spidery hand. Among George Mason's papers is a fas-
cinating document in Randolph's handwriting, nothing less than
hints on how to compose a constitution — ideas perhaps gathered as the five men sat in the library room adjoining the Convention chamber. A fundamental constitution, Randolph calls it.
First of all, he says, only essential principles should be inserted, lest
government be clogged by permanent, unalterable provisions
which ought to be shaped to later times and events. Simple, precise language should be used and none but general propositions
stated; "for the construction of a constitution of necessity differs
from that of law."

Concerning a preamble, the committee was dubious. Preambles,
Randolph stated, are for the purpose of designating the ends of
government and human politics — a subject fitter for the schools,
or to be expressed in the first formation of state governments.

* Letter to William Tudor, September 18.

Here, notes Randolph, "we are not working on the natural rights of men not yet gathered into society, but upon those rights, modified by society and interwoven with what we call the rights of states." Nor is it proper to pledge in a preamble the mutual faith of the parties. "This may be done more solemnly at the close of the draught, as in the [Articles of] Confederation." The object of this particular preamble ought to be "briefly to declare that the present foederal government is insufficient to the general happiness, that the conviction of this fact gave birth to this convention, and that the only effectual means which they can devise for curing this insufficiency is the establishment of a supreme legislative, executive and judiciary. . . .

"(In this manner we may discharge the first resolution)," writes Randolph in parentheses. "Let it next be declared that the following are the constitution and fundamentals of government for the United States."

It is always a surprise to find men proceeding with extreme simplicity toward a complex and vastly important end. The committee, for all its experience, worked hard and humbly to define a constitutional preamble. Preambles, after all, had been invented centuries ago. The English Commons had used them to publish their views to the people. Heralds read these preambles on street corners — and Queen Elizabeth had not liked it. Tudor monarchs saw no need for justifying new laws to the people. Laws represented the Crown's initiative and the Crown's authority; they were to be obeyed, not explained.

Yet the problems of government, like the problems of marriage, it would seem must be approached newly with every occasion and every generation. And each generation must find its own words. One recalls Jefferson's quandary in the year 1774, when Virginia wished to convey official concern because the port of Boston had been closed by the British. Sympathy could be shown by a day of fasting and prayer. But how to establish such a day, how to proclaim it? Jefferson and his friends took from the shelves old Rushworth's *Historical Collections* and pored through Parliamentary records of Stuart times — "rummaged over," wrote Jefferson, "for the revolutionary precedents and forms . . . we cooked up a resolution, somewhat modernizing their phrases . . . for a day of fasting, humiliation and prayer."

After the year 1787 there was to be a rash of constitution-making all over Europe, ending almost abruptly in the year 1815. In this constitution-shaping, certain phrases became common currency: the *public welfare*, the *general happiness*. America being the first nation to write out such a constitution, it is interesting to note Randolph's phraseology: government must be "sufficient to the general happiness." Later that summer, the Committee of Style would do handsomely with the words, when they undertook to refine the Constitution into literary shape. For their August report the Committee of Detail had as models the Virginia Resolves, Charles Pinckney's Resolves, Paterson's New Jersey Plan, the Articles of Confederation and all of the state constitutions. "What is the Constitution of the United States," John Adams was to exclaim a year later, "but that of Massachusetts, New York and Maryland! There is not a feature in it which cannot be found in one or the other."

John Adams possessed the historian's disconcerting habit of reverting always to originals. Years after serving on the committee to draft the Declaration of Independence, he remarked coolly that the document contained nothing which had not been hackneyed back and forth in Congress for two years. . . . Now, the Committee of Detail looked to the written models on their table. But beyond and beneath these documents the five committee members — and the Convention — could revert to a long tradition of written corporations, covenants, charters, compacts, from the Massachusetts Body of Liberties and the Fundamental Orders of Connecticut down through Franklin's Plan of Union in 1754, Galloway's Plan in 1774 and the Articles of Confederation. Not all of these covenants and designs had succeeded. Nevertheless they leaned upon that principle which is at the heart of constitutional government and which Roger Williams had expressed long ago as "the civil power, or people consenting and agreeing." The states, in short, were used to assembling their citizens for the purpose of writing out bodies of basic law. "It was agreed," says Governor Winthrop's journal of 1635, "that some men should be appointed to frame a body of grounds of laws, in resemblance to a Magna Charta, which, being allowed by some of the ministers and the general court, should be received for fundamental laws."

The Committee of Detail divided their material into articles and sections, set it down and had it neatly printed overnight by Dunlap in Philadelphia. On August sixth, Rutledge of South Carolina handed out copies in the State House. Attendance was small, delegates were not returned from their ten-day vacation. But what they had now in their hands was a clear design for a government of enumerated powers, bold, "national," and directed at the people as individuals rather than the states as corporate bodies.

The new document contained much that was surprising, even shocking, though it included nothing that had not already been discussed, debated, argued. But to see it laid out so plain, set down by article and section, drew a man's fears, made him once more cautious. By the rules of the Convention, any one of these clauses could be reargued, even voted on again. Five weeks of intensive debate would ensue before delegates could agree, and give the document to a new committee for final polishing.

As soon as copies were distributed, the meeting adjourned; members carried their papers away for discussion. The Maryland delegation met in Daniel Carroll's lodgings: McHenry, Carroll, Luther Martin, John Francis Mercer (newly arrived in Philadelphia) and that genial bachelor Daniel of St. Thomas Jenifer. McHenry was much alarmed at the article giving Congress power to pass navigation acts, collect taxes and imposts and "regulate commerce among the several states." This meant, said McHenry, that "the dearest interests of trade" would be under the control of four large states. What then would become of the Southern export trade, their staples of tobacco, rice, indigo? "We almost shuddered," wrote McHenry, "at the fate of the commerce of Maryland, should we be unable to make a change in this extraordinary power . . . and agreed that our deputation ought never to assent to this article in its present form."

All summer this question was to be agitated; in the end it would be settled by a bargain which, with a kind of brutal expediency, turned on the slavery issue. The Northern states agreed that Congress should not pass any navigation law by a mere majority, but must have a two-thirds vote of each house; agreed also that the import tax on slaves would not exceed ten dollars a head; that slaves would be counted, for purpose of representation and taxes, in the proportion of five slaves to three free white inhabitants — the "federal ratio." In return, the Southern states conceded that the importation of slaves would cease in the year 1808.

Hamilton said later that without the federal ratio "no union could possibly have been formed." It was true, and true also that the Constitution could not have gone through without the slavery compromise. The question before the Convention was not, Shall slavery be abolished? It was rather, Who shall have power to control it — the states or the national government? As the Constitution now stood, Congress could control the traffic in slaves exactly as it controlled all other trade and commerce.

Yet always when the question came up, members spoke out bluntly and with feeling upon the basic moral issue. Roger Sherman said he looked on the slave trade as "iniquitous," but he did not think himself bound to make opposition. Gouverneur Morris declared slavery to be a "nefarious institution, the curse of heaven on the states where it prevailed." Travel through the whole continent!* declaimed Morris angrily. Compare the free regions, their "rich and noble cultivation . . . with the misery and poverty which overspreads the barren wastes of Virginia, Maryland and the other states having slaves." Must the North then send its militia to defend the South against such an institution, should the need arise and slaves rebel against their masters? "Wretched Africans!" exclaimed Morris. "The vassalage of the poor has ever been the favorite offspring of aristocracy!"

This was bold talk. Gouverneur Morris, once launched and on his feet — wooden leg, stout cane, flashing eye — seldom stopped short of his oratorical goal.

Rutledge said flatly that religion and humanity had nothing to do with the question. "Interest alone is the governing principle of nations." The eighteenth century seldom deceived itself concerning the governing principles of rulers or nations; Rutledge did not speak ironically. He meant to turn the discussion from the rights

---

* Morris chose to ignore New York with her twenty thousand slaves.

of human beings to the conveniences of trade and commerce, and he succeeded. The true question, Rutledge said, was "whether the Southern states shall or shall not be parties to the Union." Let the North consult its interest and it would not oppose the increase of slaves to harvest commodities of which it would become the carrier. Ellsworth of Connecticut suggested the decision be left to the states severally: "What enriches a part enriches the whole, and the states are the best judges of their particular interest." Moreover the old Confederacy had not meddled with this point; Ellsworth saw no necessity for bringing it within the policy of the new one. Charles Pinckney said brusquely that South Carolina would not agree to any government which prohibited the slave trade. And if the states were left at liberty, South Carolina by degrees would probably "do of herself what is wished."

It is the perennial catchword: leave the states to themselves and they will be good, they will prove themselves exemplary members of the American family. George Mason, however, would have none of this. On the twenty-second of August he rose to make his famous speech, brought on by Roger Sherman's saying again that though he disapproved the slave trade, abolition seemed to be proceeding gradually. The good sense of the several states would probably by degrees complete it; Sherman thought best to leave the matter as they found it, and not create more objections to the new government.

Mason was in an excellent position to have his say and be listened to by his Southern colleagues. It was common knowledge that his magnificent plantation employed two hundred slaves and that their master would long ago have freed them had it been possible. "This infernal traffic," Mason began, "originated in the avarice of British merchants! The British government constantly checked the attempts of Virginia to put a stop to it."

How much of this statement delegates were ready to accept, one cannot judge. It was all too reminiscent of Jefferson's diatribe in his rough draft of the Declaration of Independence: the "King of Great Britain kept open a market where *men* were bought and sold, and prostituted his negative by suppressing Virginia's legislative attempts to restrain this execrable commerce." (Before adopting the Declaration, Congress struck out every word of this.) But Mason now used the old argument confidently, then went on to speak of slavery not in terms of expedience — "interest," commerce, ships, profit — but in a high moral tone. Slaves, he said, "produce the most pernicious effect on manners. Every master of slaves is born a petty tyrant; they bring the judgment of heaven on a country. . . . Slavery discourages arts and manufactures. The poor despise labor when they see it performed by slaves. . . . The Western people," said Mason indignantly, "are already calling out for slaves for their new lands, and will fill that country with slaves if they can be got through South Carolina and Georgia. I hold it essential in every point of view that the general government should have power to prevent the increase of slavery. . . . I lament," said Mason earnestly, "that some of our Eastern brethren [New Englanders] have from a lust of gain embarked on this nefarious traffic."

The shaft struck home; shipowning delegates were at once on the defensive. Oliver Ellsworth declared icily that as he had never owned a slave he could not judge the effects of slavery on character, and that if the matter must be considered in a moral light, we should go further and free the slaves already in the country. Had not abolition already taken place in Massachusetts? Connecticut was making provision for so doing.

Young Charles Pinckney here voiced the only moral defense of slavery that was expressed in Convention. The institution was justified by the example of all the world, he said, as witness Greece, Rome and the sanction given by the modern states of France, Holland and England. "In all ages," said Pinckney, "one half of mankind have been slaves. If the Southern states were let alone" (again the argument), they would "probably of themselves stop importation."

General Charles Cotesworth Pinckney immediately bolstered his cousin and fellow Carolinian by declaring that even if he himself and all his colleagues agreed to the new government on such terms, they would never obtain the consent of their constituents: "South Carolina and Georgia cannot do without slaves." Abraham Baldwin of Georgia wished the matter left to the states, to which James Wilson coolly replied that if Georgia and South Carolina were as disposed to get rid of the slave traffic in as short a time as had been suggested, they would never refuse to enter the Union merely because importation might be prohibited. John Dickinson with his impressive manner came out for national control of the question. He "considered it as inadmissible on every principle of honor and safety that the importation of slaves should be authorized to the states by the Constitution. The true question was whether the national happiness would be promoted or impeded by the importation, and this question ought to be left to the national government, not to the states particularly interested." As to the arguments about Greece and Rome, those states were made unhappy by their slaves; moreover, both England and France excluded slaves from their kingdoms.

Rufus King said the problem should be considered "in a political light only." Langdon of New Hampshire was strenuous for giving the power of prohibition to the general government. He could not, he said, in good conscience leave it to the states. Rutledge declared the people of the Carolinas and Georgia would "never be such fools as to give up so important an interest." Roger Sherman said it was better to let the Southern states import slaves than to part with these states, "if they make that a *sine qua non*."

In the end a compromise was reached: the Constitution would permit the importation of slaves until the year 1808, after which time it would be forbidden. Thus far, Mason and Dickinson had won their point: a matter that concerned the public good should be transferred from local to central authority, from state to Congress. No delegate had come to Philadelphia hoping for anything so drastic as to outlaw slavery from the United States, even those who hated it most. This was not a legislative body, to make laws. It was the business of delegates to create a Constitution for the country as it existed, and if slavery made a mockery of the words freedom, liberty, the rights of man, then those who thought so could have their say on the floor.

Without disrupting the Convention and destroying the Union they could do no more. The time was not yet come.

# XVII

*Foreigners in Congress. The "ten miles square."*

We read many things in rolls, but we know not
with what passion and earnestness it was done.
SIR JAMES WHITELOCKE, *member of Parliament*

T HE August heat was merciless. From the seventh to the twenty-seventh, Dr. Johnson's diary gives only two cool days. Twice there was rain. Afterward the sun shone through a steamy mist; even the leaves on the trees looked unrefreshed. Those who have lived through Philadelphia summers know these afternoons, and in the mind's eye can view with compassion delegates walking slowly home, wiping their faces with their handkerchiefs and wondering if the swamps of Georgia offered a worse climate.

In the State House, problems seemed to multiply rather than diminish. The matter for instance of admitting foreigners to Congress. To qualify, how long must a man be a citizen? The Committee of Detail in its report said four years for a senator, three for a representative, but the Convention was not ready to agree. Gouverneur Morris wanted fourteen years for senators. It takes seven years to learn to be a shoemaker, he said; "fourteen at least are necessary to learn to be an American legislator . . . We should not be polite at the expense of prudence. It is said that some tribes of Indians carry their hospitality so far as to offer to strangers their wives and daughters." Was this a proper model for us? Morris asked. He would admit them to his house, invite them to his table, provide for them comfortable lodgings — but he would not carry the complaisance so far as to bed them with his wife. As to those philosophical gentlemen — those citizens of the world, as they called themselves — Morris owned he did not wish to see any of them in our public councils. He would not trust them. "The men who can shake off attachments to their own country can never love any other . . . Admit a Frenchman into your senate and he will study to increase the commerce of France; an Englishman, he will feel an equal bias in favor of that of England."

Charles Pinckney was of like mind, without the attendant oratory. Because the Senate has the treaty-making power and the confirming of ambassadors, there would be "peculiar danger and impropriety in opening its doors to those who have foreign attachments." Pinckney recalled that the Athenians had made it death for any stranger to raise his voice in their legislative proceedings. George Mason said he would restrain senatorial eligibility to natives, were it not that many foreigners had "acquired great merit during the Revolution."

Madison said if restrictions were in order they should not be in the Constitution. Congress already had been granted the right of regulating naturalization; let Congress therefore make the necessary laws. Should the new Constitution give stability and reputation to the United States, great numbers of respectable Europeans would be ready to transfer their fortunes hither — "men who love liberty," said Madison, "and wish to partake of its blessings. . . . All such would feel the mortification of being marked with suspicious incapacitations."

Dr. Franklin said he would be very sorry to see anything like illiberality inserted in the Constitution: "The people in Europe are friendly to this country. Even in the country with which we have been lately at war we have now and had during the war a great many friends, not only among the people at large but in both Houses of Parliament. . . . We found in the course of the Revolution that many strangers served us faithfully — and that many natives took part against their country. When foreigners, after looking about for some other country in which they can obtain more happiness, give a preference to ours, it is a proof of attachment which ought to excite our confidence and affection."

Edmund Randolph was not sure whether foreigners were useful to us or not. But he would never agree to disable them from office for a period of fourteen years. Remember, cautioned Randolph, the language of our patriots during the Revolution and the principles laid down in our state constitutions. Under the faith of these invitations many foreigners may have come here and fixed their fortunes among us. He would, said Randolph, go so far as seven years' citizenship requirement for senators, but no farther.

Pierce Butler of South Carolina was decidedly opposed to letting foreigners into Congress without a long residence in this country. These people brought with them, said Butler, not only attachments to other countries but ideas of government "so distinct from ours that in every point of view they are dangerous." Had he himself been called to public life shortly after his arrival in the States, his "foreign habits and attachments would have rendered him an improper agent in public affairs."

The Convention was well aware of its many foreign-born members — from Ireland, Scotland, England, the West Indies. Pierce Butler had come to America as an officer in His Majesty's army; James Wilson at twenty-two had arrived in the midst of the Stamp Act troubles. Both men had served in a public capacity for much of their adult lives. The Convention knew that what these two foreign-born Americans had to say about immigrants could be highly pertinent. Wilson disagreed stoutly with Butler . . . "expressed himself feelingly," wrote McHenry of Maryland. When a man is excited his foreign accent grows more pronounced, Wilson's Scotch burr was always noticeable. He said he rose with feelings which were perhaps peculiar. He had not been born in this country. If the ideas of some gentlemen should be pursued, it might happen that he who had been thought worthy of being trusted with the framing of the Constitution might be excluded from holding a place under it. He considered such exclusion "as one of the most galling chains which the human mind could experience." It was wrong, said Wilson, "to deprive the government of the talents, virtue and abilities of such foreigners as might choose to remove to this country." Wilson was soon to point out, and with pardonable exaggeration, that in the late army, almost all the general officers of the Pennsylvania line had been foreigners — nor had complaint been heard against their fidelity or merit. Moreover, three of Pennsylvania's deputies to the Convention were not native-born: Robert Morris, Thomas Fitzsimons and himself.

Wilson read aloud a clause from the Pennsylvania Constitution of 1776, giving foreigners of two years' residence all the rights of citizenship. The Articles of Confederation, he said, made a citizen of one state a citizen of all: for Wilson, restrictive laws against foreigners constituted a breach of faith. Alexander Hamilton, too, found such laws offensive. "I am in general against embarrassing the Government with minute restrictions," he said. "There is on one side the possible danger that has been suggested — on the other side, the advantage of encouraging foreigners is obvious. . . . Persons in Europe of moderate fortunes will be fond of coming here, where they will be on a level with the first citizens. I move that the section be so altered as to require merely citizenship and inhabitancy."

Madison seconded the motion. The Convention voted and then voted again . . . for Hamilton's motion, for nine years' citizenship, for five years', for four. In the end it stood at seven years a citizen for representatives, and nine for senators. There was no argument about the decision that the chief executive must be native-born.

The battle over where to fix the seat of government was fiercer in Congress than in the Federal Convention. And it had begun years ago. Congress had lost prestige by moving about so much, suffering itself to be chased from city to city: Philadelphia, Trenton, Princeton, York, Lancaster, Annapolis, New York. Southern congressmen, rather surprisingly, did not urge a southern site. They liked the northern climate, they said; when they set out to travel they traveled north and could as easily get to New York and Boston by water as to the Chesapeake. New Jersey and Pennsylvania in 1785 had offered considerable sums of money to have the government fixed at Trenton or Philadelphia. Virginia congressmen had written to Governor Patrick Henry urging that a "foederal-town" be built somewhere apart from a great city, and suggesting Georgetown as suitable, or the Falls of the Delaware.

To the Federal Convention these things were well known. The constant moving of Congress, a member said, had "dishonored the federal government and would require as strong a cure as we can devise." It was pointed out that a permanent place was even more necessary to the new government than to the old. There would be more congressmen than before, many from the interior parts of the country. These could not make their journey easily by water; they would have to come overland. Congress had better stay in New York until a capital site had been selected and the necessary buildings erected. Somebody objected that if the government were once fixed at New York it would never be able to move, especially if the President were a Northern man. To this Gouverneur Morris retorted with his careless highhandedness that such a distrust was "inconsistent with all government" — in short, it made no sense.

The seat of government, it was urged, must not be in the same city with a state government. Jurisdictional disputes might arise, and besides, it would give a provincial tincture to the national deliberations. Yet New York and Philadelphia both had expectations of being the national capital; it would not do to make enemies of these cities. Williamson of North Carolina reminded delegates how deeply the passions of men were agitated by this matter.

Just who it was that suggested the Federal District be ten miles square is hard to determine. But the phrase caught on, to be used next winter with much effect by the anti-Constitutionalists. George Mason, who in the Federal Convention was mild enough concerning the proposals for a national capital, at home in Virginia developed a phobia on the subject. Think — he told his state convention for ratification — only think of giving Congress an unlimited power over such a federal region! "This ten miles square may set at defiance the laws of the surrounding states and may . . . become the sanctuary of the blackest crimes! Here the federal courts are to sit. . . . What sort of a jury shall we have within the ten miles square?" Mason answered his own question: "The immediate creatures of the government! What chance will poor men get? . . . Here the greatest offender may meet protection. If any of the officers or creatures [of the national government] should attempt to oppress the people or should actually perpetrate the blackest deed, he has nothing to do but get into the ten miles square."

What the anti-Constitutionalists made of it was wonderful and ingenious. Patrick Henry boomed his alarums over the tyranny to be exercised by a supreme government in this ten miles square. Luther Martin in the Maryland legislature referred ominously to "the seat of empire." Governor Clinton of New York — friend of Lansing and Yates, enemy of Hamilton — wrote, under the name of Cato, diatribes to the *New York Journal* concerning the ten miles square. The court of the President would be held there, said Clinton. In this place, men would see all the vices of princely courts: "ambition with idleness, baseness with pride, the thirst of riches without labor . . . flattery . . . treason . . . perfidy; but above all the perpetual ridicule of virtue."

The Federal Convention left the decision, finally, to the national legislature. Article I, Section 8 says that Congress shall have power to *"exercise exclusive Legislation in all Cases whatsoever, over such District (not exceeding ten Miles square) as may, by Cession of particular States, and the acceptance of Congress, become the Seat of the Government of the United States."* *

There was a brief but lively debate over fixing the time for Congress to meet. Should it be once a year, with the date left undecided? Nathaniel Gorham said the New England charters and constitutions had long ago provided settled dates, with no inconveniency resulting. Rufus King saw no reason for meeting every year. Too much legislating was a great vice of our system; it should be the states, not the national government, that made the laws. Roger Sherman brought up the hardy old revolutionary argument that frequent meetings of the legislature were an essential safeguard to liberty — as during the Puritan Revolution in England. And besides, most of the state charters in America demanded annual assemblies. Members felt there would surely be business enough to require it; the Western country would create

---

* The political battle over a site for the federal district would continue until 1790, when by dint of a now celebrated bargain, the District of Columbia would be created and President Washington would himself choose a site for the Capitol building.

added problems. George Mason remarked that if not enough legislative business turned up, Congress would have "inquisitorial powers" which must be used. Nobody challenged the statement. Under the Confederation, Congress, with legislative, executive and judicial functions all in one, had made frequent use of its investigative function.

Gouverneur Morris was against convening Congress in December, as suggested. May would be better. "It might frequently happen," he said, "that our measures ought to be influenced by those in Europe, which were generally planned during the winter, and of which intelligence would arrive in the spring." Section 4 of Article I, as finally drafted, declared: *"The Congress shall assemble at least once in every Year, and such Meeting shall be on the first Monday in December, unless they shall by Law appoint a different Day."*

# XVIII

*Test oaths, Deism and tolerance. A standing army.*
*Treason defined.*

> We grow more and more skeptical as we proceed.
> If we do not decide soon, we shall be unable to come
> to any decision.
>                    OLIVER ELLSWORTH, *in Convention*

A S the weeks wore on, certain delegates could not bear to
hear the same questions reopened: the Presidential powers, for instance, and the matter of the President's
negative on new laws. "Postpone the question, postpone!" said
cautious members. "Mr. Rutledge," wrote Madison on August fifteenth, "was strenuous against postponing and complained much
of the tediousness of the proceedings." Three days later Rutledge
renewed his complaint: "remarked on the length of the session,"
noted Madison, "the probable impatience of the public and the
extreme anxiety of many members of the Convention to bring the
business to an end; concluding with a motion that the Convention
meet henceforward precisely at ten o'clock A.M. and that precisely at four o'clock P.M., the President adjourn the House without motion for the purpose, and that no motion to adjourn sooner
be allowed."

Paterson of New Jersey had left Philadelphia late in July and
gone home to his law business. "What are the Convention
about?" he wrote to Ellsworth on August twenty-third. "When
will they rise? Will they agree upon a system energetic and
effectual, or will they break up without doing anything to the
purpose? Full of disputation and noisy as the wind, it is said that
you are afraid of the very windows, and have a man planted

under them to prevent the secrets and doings from flying out."
He hoped, Paterson added, that members would not have as much
altercation upon details as they had had in "getting the principles
of the system."

Since the first day of meeting, the "principles of the system"
had been many times written out and presented to the Convention:
in the Virginia Plan, the Pinckney Plan (never debated); the "Report" of the Committee of the Whole (June thirteenth), the New
Jersey Plan, which Paterson himself had introduced. And on August sixth, as Paterson surely knew, the comprehensive Report of
the Committee of Detail.

All these plans and resolves and propositions and reports had
called for a government in three parts: executive, legislative and
judicial. No one had disputed that basic proposition, revolutionary though it was as applied to a national system. Yet the "altercation upon details" had been in fact a continued and unremitting
struggle over principles. To define treason, determine the seat and
extent of the taxing power and the proportion of representatives
from state to state — these "details," as finally agreed on, were to
change the United States from a confederation to a workable,
lasting Federal Republic. Two balanced powers: Congress and the
Executive, states and central government, with the judiciary as
umpire. It was to be a triumphant conclusion.

But in August of 1787 the Convention could not see so far
ahead. The novelty of their plan, the daring of it, dazzled and
even blinded them at times. They could only grope through details as through a forest, a maze of ever-widening circles. It is
significant that when the Convention adjourned in September and
the Constitution was made public, members expressed themselves
as astonished at what they had achieved. Washington declared it
was "much to be wondered at . . . little short of a miracle." Madison, writing to Jefferson, also used the word "miracle." Charles
Pinckney told his fellow Carolinians they should be "astonishingly
pleased" that a government "so perfect could have been formed
from such discordant and unpromising material."

This however was in the future. Meanwhile in the State House,
aware that the end approached, delegates brought forward their
especial notions: a council to advise with the President, a Vice

President who should preside over the Senate, a law to protect the rights of authors and inventors. George Mason wished Congress to have power over the personal expenditure of citizens in matters of dress, furniture, fabrics, especially those imported from Europe. Sumptuary laws, such regulations were called. It was natural for Mason, the old Revolutionary, to initiate the motion. Nonimportation had been part of the Revolutionary slogan since 1765, part of the Continental Association — of Independence itself. Drafting the famous Virginia Bill of Rights in 1776, Mason had declared that "no free government or the blessings of liberty can be preserved to any people but by a firm adherence to temperance, frugality and virtue." New Hampshire, Massachusetts, Vermont had followed suit. Encourage native manufactures, wear suits and clothes of native make. "Economy, frugality and American manufactures!" declaimed Mason in Convention.

It was a nice marriage of commerce and patriotism. To despise luxury, to dress plainly was republican, American; in Paris, Dr. Franklin had made the most of it. The domestic arrangements of eighteenth-century America would be looked on today as austere at best, if not downright uncomfortable, with bathing at a minimum and a lady's brocade costume worn for years and willed to the next generation. Yet in the Federal Convention were members who inveighed repeatedly against the growing extravagance of their countrymen. High life and high living sapped the moral fiber. Observe the fate of the later Romans! "Luxury with ten thousand evils in her train," wrote Abigail Adams from London.

To George Mason, sumptuary laws deserved a place not only in state legislation but nationally; such a policy would agree, he said, "as well with economical as with republican views." But the Convention preferred to keep the matter under state control.

Late in July it had been agreed that congressmen, judges, the President and other officers must swear on oath to support the Constitution. James Wilson demurred. He had never been fond of oaths, he said, and considered them a left-handed security only. A good government did not need them, "and a bad one could not or ought not to be supported." Every national revolution makes much of oaths and oath-taking; what was loyalty on Monday may well be treason on Tuesday. Moreover the federal nature of the new union confused the issue. General Washington's proc-lamation of 1777, requiring oaths of allegiance from all who had formerly sworn to uphold Britain, had angered certain elements in Congress: allegiance to the United States might diminish a man's allegiance to, say, the sovereign state of Georgia.

Most of the states included a religious qualification in their oaths for officeholders; many of these discriminated against Catho-lics, Jews, Deists and unbelievers. Beyond the cardinal principle that church and state must be separate, religion in America was a matter for local option and had been since the beginning. When the Reverend Hugh Peters of Salem, Massachusetts, had been asked, *circa* 1636, what they did with dissenters in New England, he said they put them over the river. Yet if Virginia had started out as Anglican, Massachusetts as Puritan, Pennsylvania as Quaker, they had gradually won to a wider conception and wider liberty — within Protestant limits, that is — a limit defined with nice but unconscious irony by President Ezra Stiles of Yale Col-lege as "universal, equal, religious, *protestant* liberty." Within these boundaries the states quite early practiced a surprising diversity — presbyter and priest alike would have called it an anarchy — which was to become a strength to the nation rather than a weak-ness. All across the continent would range the church spires of different sects whose congregations lived, if not in harmony, at least in nominal peace. "I am a friend to a variety of sects," said Edmund Randolph, "because they keep one another in order."

The Federal Convention did not discuss religion. The relation-ship of chuch and state, already well established, was no part of its business. Yet there sat no delegate whose ideas of government or political philosophy were not profoundly influenced by his religious beliefs and training. Deism was in the air. Two genera-tions ago it had made the westward crossing, to the immense perturbation of the faithful. Here was a religion free of creed: the Newtonian universe, the classical revival, the discovery of new seas and new lands had enlarged the world but crowded the old dogma rudely. Ezra Stiles, who boasted that he could "freely live and converse in civil friendship with Jews, Romanists and all the sects of Protestants," was constrained to add at the end, "and even with Deists." Dr. Franklin could have defined this creedless religion; with Jefferson and John Adams, the Doctor shared the Deistical outlook. "Natural religion," Deists called their faith. There is a God, they said, but he is to be found through reason rather than through revelation. God created this world but he did not interfere with its workings; a man's heaven and hell were of his own making. Deism was a way of looking at the cosmos; it was a state of mind and the orthodox shuddered at the word, declaring it "all the same with the old philosophical paganism."

Beyond the State House walls, people had no way of knowing if the Convention's "new plan" would require test oaths of government officers. In Pennsylvania the test oath had been a hot issue. The Convention received a letter from a man well known in the city: Jonas Phillips, a merchant who had been politically active as a Revolutionary, had fought with the Philadelphia militia, and helped to found the Mikveh Israel Congregation. "Sires," the letter began; "I, the subscriber being one of the people called Jews of the City of Philadelphia, a people scattered and dispersed among all nations, do behold with concern. . . ." Phillips went on to quote Section 10 of the Pennsylvania Constitution, requiring every state representative to swear that he believed in God and acknowledged the Old and New Testaments to be divinely inspired. To take any such oath, wrote Phillips, "is absolutely against the religious principles of a Jew and is against his conscience." Moreover, it was "well known among all the citizens of the thirteen united States that the Jews have been true and faithful Whigs, and during the late contest with England they had been foremost in aiding and assisting the States with their lives and fortunes. They have supported the cause, have bravely fought and bled for liberty which they cannot enjoy."

Jonas Phillips, in the dark as to the Convention's real doings, or perhaps not daring to mention a national Constitution, put his plea in local terms, referring to the constitution of his own state. If the Honorable Convention, he said, could see fit to alter the said oath and leave out the part concerning the New Testament Scriptures, then the "Israelites will think themselves happy to live under a government where all religious societies are on an equal footing." The letter ends on a note of prayer and praise. "May the people of these States rise up as a great and young lion. May they prevail

against their enemies . . . May God extend peace to them and
their seed after them as long as the sun and moon endureth. And
may the Almighty God of our father Abraham, Isaac and Jacob
endue this noble Assembly with wisdom, judgment and unanimity in their councils. . . ."

It was wonderful and touching; we do not know in what terms
it was answered. We do know that Article VI, after various refinements in committee, exacted from federal and state officers an
oath to support the United States Constitution — *"but no religious Test,"* it added, *"shall ever be required as a Qualification to
any Office or public Trust under the United States."* The clause,
a triumph for toleration, provided rich ammunition for anti-Constitutionalists during the ratification period. Could not God be
acknowledged in the preamble at least? — they demanded. Judge
William Williams of Connecticut suggested as much in a letter to
the *American Mercury* (February, 1788): "We the people of the
United States, in a firm belief of the being and perfections of one
living and true God, the creator and supreme Governor of the
world. . . ."

Luther Martin in the Maryland convention for ratification was
to declare that Article VI had been adopted by the Convention
without much debate. "However," he went on in a high flight of
sarcasm, much italicized in the printed version — "However,
there were some members *so unfashionable* as to think that a *belief of the existence of a Deity*, and of a *state of future rewards
and punishments* would be some security for the good conduct of
our rulers, and that, in a Christian country, it would be *at least
decent* to hold out some distinction between the professors of
Christianity and downright infidelity or paganism."

The Convention still used as its working basis the August sixth
Report of the Committee of Detail, which, like the final Constitution, was divided into articles and sections. Article VII of the
Report listed the powers of Congress, beginning with the "power
to lay and collect taxes," proceeding thence to the famous commerce clause — "power to regulate commerce with foreign nations, and among the several states" — and so on through the establishment of a post office, the coining and borrowing of money

and the setting up of judicial tribunals. There followed directly a clause giving Congress sanction "to subdue a rebellion in any state on the application of its legislature; to make war; to raise armies; to build and equip fleets. . . ."

Rebellion in any state? To certain delegates the phrase was an offense, exacerbated by Gouverneur Morris's flat opinion that it would be unnecessary for Congress to await a state's "application" for aid. "The general government," said Morris, "should enforce obedience in all the cases where it may be necessary." This brought Elbridge Gerry to his feet. One senses the excitement in this slight, nervous man, the frown etched deeply, the hands stiff with tension. He was against "letting loose the myrmidons of the United States on a state without its own consent. More blood would have been spilt in Massachusetts in the late insurrection [Shays's] if the General Government had intermeddled."

Morris's reply was reasonable, maddeningly so. The Convention was acting a very strange part, he said. "We first form a strong man to protect us, and at the same time wish to tie his hands behind him." Surely, Congress might "be trusted with such a power to preserve the general tranquillity." But Gerry was not convinced. He "took notice," wrote Madison, that Article VI contained "no check against standing armies in time of peace."

It was the old bugbear. A tyrant, a Cromwell would arise . . . Gerry trotted out the timeworn arguments against a standing army; all summer he had used them: The people were jealous on this head, and if the new plan permitted it, great opposition would be raised. . . . He himself would never consent to an army of an indefinite number. Two or three thousand troops would be sufficient. If there were no restriction, a few states might well establish military governments. . . . And how was such an army to be trained? Were the states then to be made drill sergeants, preparing their militia for a national army? He had as lief see the citizens of Massachusetts disarmed as to take the command from them and subject it to Congress. It would be regarded as a system of despotism. "Will any man say that liberty will be as safe in the hands of eighty or a hundred men taken from the whole continent as in the hands of two or three hundred taken from a single state? . . . Some people," remarked Gerry gloomily, "will support a plan of vigorous government at every risk."

Did he look at Gouverneur Morris as he said it? "Others of a more democratic cast," continued Gerry, "will oppose it with equal determination. And a civil war may be produced by the conflict!"

With the argument at its height, Ellsworth of Connecticut saw fit to interject a homely note, one of those simple suggestions, quite aside from the point, which can bring an excited meeting safely down to earth. How were these soldiers to be disciplined? "The states will never submit to the same militia laws. Three or four shillings as a penalty will enforce obedience better in New England, than forty lashes in some other places."

Surely, delegates smiled. New Englanders were known as penny pinchers; Southerners always enjoyed a joke at the "Eastern" expense. But Gerry remained morose. To the end of the Convention he was to show himself determined to view with alarm a general government which would usurp power in all directions. He declared that if delegates continued in this vein they would put upon the Constitution "as black a mark as was set on Cain. He had "no such confidence in the general government," said Gerry, "as some gentlemen possessed."

On that Saturday morning, nothing was finally decided, but on the following Monday, August twentieth, the Convention proceeded to the ensuing section of Article VII.* This concerned treason, a live issue in every state, the cause of frequent angry litigation, and in itself capable of determining the outcome of political elections.

How was the Constitution to define treason, and what punishment should be indicated? Was treason to be stipulated as betrayal of a man's particular state and also of the United States, and would not this put in double jeopardy a person accused of treason against his state? George Mason argued that the United States, under the new Constitution, would possess only a qualified sovereignty. Therefore an act against a particular state — like Bacon's

---

* Article III, Section 3 in the Constitution as finally revised.

Rebellion in Virginia — would not be treason against the United States.

Treason is at best a murky legal problem, doubly difficult following a great war. To most of the Convention the words Tory and traitor still were synonymous. State laws were clear enough, permitting Tory property to be confiscated or ruinously taxed. In some states if a citizen could prove that his neighbor had been a loyalist there was a good chance of seizing the man's property or at least of possessing those desirable meadows which lay beyond, say, one's own south pasture. After six years of fighting it is not difficult for greed to operate under the guise of patriotism. Nine states had exiled their loyalists, five had disfranchised them. The Pennsylvania Test Act of 1777 remained in force until March of 1787: under penalty of losing their citizenship, suspects must renounce fidelity to King George, pledge allegiance to Pennsylvania and swear to expose conspiracies. New York, Virginia, the Carolinas, Georgia were equally harsh.

The Convention was aware of all this, acutely aware also that these state laws ran contrary to the peace treaty of 1783, which declared "there shall be no future confiscations made, nor any prosecutions commenced against any person or persons for, or by reason of the part which he or she may have taken in the . . . war; and that no person shall, on that account, suffer any loss or damage either in his person, liberty or property." Nothing could have been plainer. On her side Britain agreed to the free navigation of the Mississippi "from its source to the ocean." His Britannic Majesty would, "with all convenient speed . . . withdraw all his armies, garrisons and fleets from the said United States, and from every post, place and harbour."

Britain, however, still held her posts along the Great Lakes and the Mississippi. Why, she demanded, should one party honor a treaty which the others palpably violated? But the Treaty of '83, retorted North Carolina, was no part of her state law. She would not permit former loyalists to sue in state courts for the payment of debts — another outright breach of the treaty. Also she defined treason as levying war against either "the United States in Congress assembled," or against "the State of North Carolina."

Congress had tried in vain to reason with the states, recommending leniency and mutual observance of the treaty. Virginia, however, objected strenuously; Edmund Randolph had declared that not even the resurrection of the prophets would convince Americans who owed old debts to Britain that they should pay up simply because Congress and the peace treaty recommended it. William Paterson of New Jersey too had been harsh; among Convention delegates were those who, like Governor Alexander Martin of North Carolina, had used loyalist treason as the cornerstone of a political career. (Governor Martin had once remarked that he would like to hang all Tories.) In his state it was treason to have served as an officer under the King, to have been named at any time in a confiscation act, to have remained outside the state more than a year after the passage of the loyalty law. Moreoever, in North Carolina the old English law of petty treason still obtained, it included murder, rape, robbery, house-burning and other offenses. In 1787, court dockets of the state were still crowded with treason prosecutions.

During the long course of English history many crimes had been punished with outrageous cruelty under the name of treason, and many private scores had been thus paid off. Delegates to the Convention knew it; they had heard of times when in England a man's religion had been treason, and for it he could be torn limb from limb — and all properly legal under the constitution. American lawyers were cognizant of the dangers of vague constitutional doctrine on this point. (During the ratification period James Wilson was to remind his state convention that it was an old trick of tyrants willfully to extend the definition of treason, thereby gaining much power over the people.) Gouverneur Morris, Mason and Randolph wished the Constitution to use the time-honored words of the old English Statute of Treasons, enacted in the reign of Edward III (1351). But should "giving aid and comfort to the enemy" be specified, or was it enough to say that treason consisted in "levying war and adhering to the enemy"? Madison was for leaving more latitude to Congress, where the matter would be, he said, as safe as in the state legislatures. John Dickinson demanded exactly what was meant in the old statute by requiring the "testimony of two witnesses." Were these witnesses to testify to the same overt act or different overt acts?

Dr. Johnson of Connecticut contended that treason could not be against both the United States and individual states. Old Franklin in his wisdom now remarked that "prosecutions for treason were generally virulent, and perjury too easily made use of against innocence." James Wilson noted how "extremely difficult" it could be to find proof of treason, as in a traitorous correspondence with an enemy. Randolph was against giving the President power to pardon traitors. The President himself might be part of the plot. On the other hand it would be altogether unfit, said Rufus King, to grant such power to Congress. "In Massachusetts," King said, "one assembly would have hung all the insurgents [in Shays's Rebellion]. The next was equally disposed to pardon them all."

Seven times, on August twentieth, the Convention voted to change the wording of the article involved. Given total power over traitors, Congress could nullify the state laws of treason and invalidate all current state prosecutions and rejections of the peace treaty. On the other hand, this total power of Congress must itself be defined, so that Congress could never expand its scope nor introduce petty treason into the American jurisprudence, nor employ treason as a weapon against political opponents. Treason must be limited to acts of war, acts associated with a national enemy. Gouverneur Morris and Randolph referred again to the old English statute, painstakingly specific as to definition. "It is essential to the preservation of liberty," Morris said, "to define precisely and exclusively what shall constitute the crime of treason."

In the face of great difficulties the Convention achieved such definition. Somehow, quarrels and local jealousies were dissolved, somehow the narrow definition was made and allowed to stand. Nothing specific is said in the United States Constitution about treason against a state. The power of punishment is left to Congress — but punishment is strictly limited. The problem of double jeopardy was resolved by a neat use of the plural pronoun — the only time in the Constitution that the states are thus referred to:

"*Treason against the United States*," says Article III, Section 3, "*shall consist only in levying War against them, or in adhering to their Enemies, giving them Aid and Comfort. No Person shall*

*be convicted of Treason unless on the Testimony of two Witnesses*
*to the same overt Act, or on Confession in open Court.*

"*The Congress shall have Power to declare the Punishment of*
*Treason, but no Attainder of Treason shall work Corruption of*
*Blood, or Forfeiture except during the Life of the Person at-*
*tainted.*"

Corruption of blood was the ancient English phrase, from the
statute of Edward III. By it, dishonor descended to the next generation: a traitor's children could not inherit his titles, honors or
estates. But concerning this old statute the Convention ignored
the first and perhaps most famous stipulation of high treason:
"To compass or imagine the death of the king." The Convention was establishing not a monarchy but a republic; the President would be no sovereign. Elected from the citizenry, he would
return to the citizenry when his term was over. Delegates it seems
were more fearful of granting the President too much power than
of his person being harmed. They feared his sinning rather than
his being sinned against.* But if Section 3 of Article III was a
triumph for the liberties of citizens, it was not to escape censure
next winter, notably by George Mason and Luther Martin. Both
men were to be widely criticized for this. If they objected to the
treason clause, why had they not said so in Convention — why
wait until the matter was settled? In the Maryland convention for
ratification, Martin's tone on this score was high and handsome.
"By the principles of the American Revolution," he said, "arbitrary
power may and ought to be resisted, even by arms if necessary!
The time may come when it shall be the duty of a state, in
order to preserve itself from the oppression of the general government, to have recourse to the sword." Yet under the new Constitution this would make traitors of patriots; it would require
citizens "*tamely* and *passively* to *yield to despotism* or oppose it
at the hazard of the halter!" †

---

* Twenty-one months after the death of President Kennedy Congress on
August 28, 1965, made it a federal offense to assassinate the President. Their
purpose was to put the proceeding in a federal court with a federal prose-
cutor and federal investigating agencies.
† Martin's italics, from his printed speech entitled "Genuine Information
Relative to the Proceedings of the General Convention Held at Philadelphia
in 1787."

"The time may come. . . ." Like Gerry's threat concerning a national army, it was a foreshadowing, a presage. "Civil war!" Gerry had said. In the country many were ready to listen; feeling still ran high against a strong government, a strong Congress, a standing army. It ran high for "liberty," and the less government the better. Next winter during state ratification, the people at large would have their chance to express this feeling.

Yet in the Federal Convention Gerry shouted against the wind. True, it is a tricky business to define the word treason. It means defining not only the crime but the body sinned against — in this case, a Union, a United States strong enough to stand and repel all threats from within as from without. Delegates intended that the United States Constitution reflect this strength. It must *"insure domestic Tranquility, provide for the common defence."* And if in the process, citizens should surrender a little of their cherished liberties, then they must be taught, persuaded that in the end they stood to gain more than they relinquished.

To Madison, Morris, Wilson, Ellsworth and the strong Constitutionalists it must have seemed the road lay very long ahead. Here in their chamber giving onto Philadelphia's Chestnut Street they had sat three months. For three months they had tried by argument and maneuver to win their points, quiet the mistrusting, inspire the reluctant. Yet still suspicion smoldered. And when they should go home to their constituents and the ratification process begin, the battle must be fought all over again. With a weary stubbornness they knew it and set their faces to the fight.

# XIX

## *Who shall ratify? The people or the states?*

> I consider the difference between a system founded
> on the legislatures only, and one founded on the peo-
> ple, to be the true difference between a league or
> treaty and a constitution.
> JAMES MADISON, *in Convention*

AUGUST thirtieth. The Convention had but sixteen working days left. No date had been set for dissolution. But
since the beginning, members had planned to sit no
longer than September. Now at the end of August adjournment
was in sight. It heightened debate, made members uneasy and
tempers short. Of the original fifty-five delegates, eleven had already defected on excuse of illness in the family or private business — or, like Lansing and Yates of New York, frank opposition
to the proceedings.*

The Convention's work was nearly done. And it was high time;
the country waited the outcome. Yesterday the *Pennsylvania Gazette* had reported that "the states neglect their roads and canals
till they see whether those necessary improvements will not become the objects of a national government. Trading and manufacturing companies suspend their voyages and manufactures till
they see how far their commerce will be protected and promoted
by a national system of commercial regulations. The lawful usu-
rer locks up or buries his specie till he sees whether the new
frame of government will deliver him from the curse or fear of
paper money and tender laws."

The *Gazette*, of course, was very pro-Constitution; it did not
mind stretching a point for the good of the cause. But in truth,

* See chapter note, page 311.

time was of the essence; the Convention could not drag on into autumn. On September fifth the Pennsylvania legislature — the Assembly, they called it — was due to convene in the State House; they would need the east room where the Federal Convention was sitting. On August thirtieth delegates reached the last point of the Constitution to be considered. In the Committee Report, Articles XXI, XXII, and XXIII concerned ratification and certain practical steps toward setting up a new government. Article XXI was brief and extremely controversial: "The ratifications of the Conventions of —— States shall be sufficient for organizing this Constitution."

A blank had been left for the number of states. And the number could be vitally significant. Once the document was signed in Philadelphia it must go straight to Congress for its "approbation," after which Congress would recommend it be sent out to the states for ratification at home. But suppose all thirteen states were required to ratify? Obviously, Rhode Island would vote against the Constitution in Congress; so probably would New York and Maryland, whose delegates at the Federal Convention grew daily more hostile.

Concerning the number thirteen there was moreover a basic difficulty to be got round. Legally, the Federal Convention sat to amend the Articles of Confederation, an action which required the agreement of every state in the Union. Strategically, the opposition could make much of this, in Convention, in Congress, or later when the Constitution went out to the states. To agree upon ratification by less than thirteen states would be to acknowledge the new Constitution as a revolution in government, with the old Confederation abrogated and overthrown. Every delegate knew by now that such was actually the case; they could not have arrived at Article XXI without knowing it. Until today, however, this acknowledgment had been passed over or argued away by such strong-government men as Madison, Wilson, Gouverneur Morris. Article XXI brought it to a head.

James Wilson had sat in the Continental Congress which devised and ratified the Articles of Confederation. He knew the implications of ratification by fewer than thirteen states. He must have determined upon the attack direct, for no sooner was Article XXI read aloud than Wilson moved that the blank space be filled with the number seven — that being, he said, a majority of the whole. At once, argument broke out. Maryland moved to postpone the question; very likely her delegation wanted time for an evening caucus, a recruiting of the forces. There was bargaining to and fro, with one member for ten states, another for nine. Wilson, seeing which way the wind blew, raised his number to eight. Madison objected that ratification by seven or eight or even nine states would put the "whole body of the people" under a Constitution which less than a majority had ratified.

That Madison should say this is surprising. Wilson stepped in quickly: only the states which ratified would be bound by the new Constitution. "We must," said Wilson, "in this case go to the original powers of society. The house on fire must be extinguished without a scrupulous regard to ordinary rights."

It was the old Revolutionary argument resurrected; Wilson had heard it often in the Continental Congress during the winter of 1775-1776: when a nation is ill ruled, men must have recourse to a higher law, a law above kings, princes and parliaments. But in the Federal Convention, Wilson avoided the phrase "law of nature," preferring "the original powers of society." Immediately, Pierce Butler came out for ratification by nine states; he "revolted at the idea that one or two states should restrain the others from consulting their safety."

Butler's move was clever. When going outside legality it is well to remind one's colleagues that they are voting not for innovation and dangerous new doctrines but for "safety" and order. Carroll of Maryland now declared for ratification by all thirteen states, which seemed tantamount to wishing the Constitution defeated. He said a confederation which had been unanimously established could not be dissolved without unanimity. Himself a strong-government man, Carroll perhaps thought it strategic (and at this point safe) to side with his dissident Maryland colleagues.

The time had come to adjourn for the day. As the Convention rose, McHenry of Maryland scribbled in his notes, "Proposed to have a private conference with each other tomorrow before meet-

ing of the convention to take measures for carrying out propositions, etc —"

There must have been other conferences and caucuses that
Thursday night. Next morning the Committee's Article XXI, as
amended, "was then agreed to by all the States," wrote Madison,
"Maryland excepted." The blank space had been filled with the
number nine.

There arose now the question of whether the new Constitution
should be ratified by the state legislatures or by the people at
large. The original Virginia Plan had provided for "assemblies of
Representatives . . . expressly chosen by the people." As early as
June fifth a motion to this effect had been favorably voted on in
Committee of the Whole, though Roger Sherman had been
against it and Elbridge Gerry skittish; it was then he remarked
that the people had "the wildest ideas of government in the
world." The states were not accustomed to popular ratification.
By whatever method their several constitutions had been drafted
— by provincial convention, by the local legislature or a combination of both — when it came to ratification, only Massachusetts
and New Hampshire had taken the step of submitting their constitutions to town meetings for approval.

Why not, therefore, let the state legislatures ratify the federal
Constitution? To many minds it seemed a far less hazardous procedure than the calling of thirteen separate conventions. Yet how
to present so new, so novel a system to state legislatures which
were solemnly obligated to uphold the old? Pierce Butler said it
could not be done. The Convention had earlier debated the point
with heat, Randolph pointing out that if the state legislatures were
allowed to ratify, then local demagogues, fearful of losing their
places in a new governmental system, would surely vote against it
or manage somehow to block its passage. "Designing men," Nathaniel Gorham had said, "will find means to delay from year to
year, if not to frustrate altogether the national system." Legislators were well aware how to interrupt an important measure "by
artfully pressing a variety of little businesses."

Gorham, that old political warhorse, knew whereof he spoke,
having served as president of Congress and speaker of the Massa-

chusetts House; at the Federal Convention he had presided over stormy sittings in the Committee of the Whole. Now in his fiftieth year, Gorham had a pleasant manner; it seemed he was propitiatory about everything except the state of Rhode Island, whose recalcitrance never ceased to irritate him. But by whatever system of ratification — were all the states to suffer themselves to be ruined, he asked, if Rhode Island should persist in her opposition?

Ellsworth of Connecticut said outright that a "new set of ideas seems to have crept in since the Articles of Confederation were established. Conventions of the people, or with power derived expressly from the people, were not then thought of. The legislatures were considered as competent." To Madison, however, it was clear that the state legislatures were "incompetent to make the proposed changes." It would be a novel and dangerous doctrine indeed, if a legislature could change the constitution under which it held its existence. "I consider," said Madison, "the difference between a system founded on the legislatures only, and one founded on the people, to be the true difference between a *league* or *treaty* and a *constitution*." George Mason said the same thing, but more emotionally. "Legislators," he declared, "are the mere creatures of the state constitutions and cannot be greater than their creators. . . . Whither then must we resort? To the people . . . . It is of great moment that this doctrine should be cherished as the basis of free government."

On the day Mason said it the Convention voted for popular ratification, nine to one. But they would not let the matter rest. The word ratification brought the new Constitution alarmingly near, suggesting a *fait accompli* and conjuring up every bogey its opponents most feared. Maryland kept on repeating that her state officers were sworn not to let alterations in government be made by any agency but themselves.

All summer the Convention had been fighting this argument, expressed in a dozen different forms: let the states have the power; do not hand it over to Congress and to this vague entity called the people at large. But Madison was adamant. The people, he said, "were in fact the fountain of all power, and by resorting to them, all difficulties were got over." The people "could alter constitutions as they pleased. It was a principle in the [state] bills of rights, that first principles might be resorted to."

This was too high-toned for Luther Martin. With a wry irony he retorted that there was "danger of commotions from a resort to the people and to first principles in which the government might be on one side and the people on the other." Martin was sure that Maryland would not ratify unless rushed into it — hurried by surprise. Rufus King retorted that Massachusetts had sworn not to alter her constitution for a decade, yet she had sent deputies to Philadelphia. She too, said King, must have been thinking in terms of first principles.

First principles meant, among other things, the right to overturn a bad government; to the opposition the words at this late date must have sounded unbearably self-righteous. Elbridge Gerry had sat in the Continental Congress of '76; he had signed the Declaration of Independence. What right had a johnny-come-lately like Rufus King to recite Revolutionary principles? Gouverneur Morris suggested that each state be left to pursue its own system of ratification. Gerry, tried beyond caution, said the new system was full of vices and it was wholly improper to destroy the Confederation without the unanimous consent of those who had created it. He moved that the vote on Article XXII be postponed. George Mason seconded him, declaring (Madison noted), "that he would sooner chop off his right hand than put it to the Constitution as it now stands. He wished to see some points not yet decided brought to a decision before being compelled to give a final opinion on the Article. Should these points be improperly settled, his wish would then be to bring the whole subject before another general convention."

The notion of another general convention was to Madison and his friends anathema; it meant failure, the end of all their work and all their hopes. Gouverneur Morris said curtly that he had long wished for another convention that would have the firmness to provide a vigorous government, "which we are afraid to do." Gerry lost his motion for postponement and Article XXII was voted through. But ten days later Gerry brought the whole thing up again in connection with discussing Article XIX, on the amending power. After the Constitution was ratified and effectual, how many states must be required to vote for a proposed amendment? Two-thirds? Three-fourths? Or was unanimity necessary?

Round and round went the argument. South Carolina showed herself fearful that the articles relating to the slave trade would be affected. This was on September tenth, a Monday. Alexander Hamilton was present; he had come back to Philadelphia and would be there for the signing. Rather surprisingly he took Gerry's side, reverted once more to Article XXI, and said he thought it wrong to allow nine states to institute a new government on the ruins of the existing one. Madison must have been sorely tried by Hamilton in this Convention. Having missed the summer's arguments, the summer's slow skillful buildup by the strong-government men, here was Hamilton back again and arguing with the opposition. But Gerry, perhaps heartened by this support from an unexpected quarter, declared it would be indecent and pernicious to dissolve the solemn obligations of the Confederation in so slight a manner. "If nine out of thirteen can dissolve the compact, six out of nine will be just as able to dissolve the new one hereafter."

Edmund Randolph announced that if no change were made in this part of the plan he would be obliged to dissent from the whole system. Nearly two weeks ago he had made this threat, saying that as the Constitution then stood, there were features so odious he doubted if he would be able to agree to it. Now he declared that "from the beginning he had been convinced that radical changes in the system of the Union were necessary." Under this conviction he had "brought forward a set of republican propositions as the basis and outline of a reform."

Randolph referred of course to the Virginia Plan. But his propositions, Randolph went on, had been widely, irreconcilably departed from. He proposed therefore that state conventions "should be at liberty to offer amendments to the Plan, and that these [amendments] be submitted to a second general Convention with full power to settle the Plan finally." He did not expect to succeed in this proposition, Randolph finished, "but the discharge of his duty in making the attempt would give quiet to his own mind."

Hamilton here suggested a substitute resolution (for Article

XXI) concerning congressional approbation, and a subsequent mode of sending the new Constitution out to the states. Gerry seconded it. But James Wilson, deeply roused, said it was "necessary now to speak freely." Expressing himself in what Madison called "strong terms," Wilson declared against seeking the approbation of Congress. It would be "worse than folly" to rely on Rhode Island's voting *aye* in Congress — or on New York or Maryland. "After spending four or five months in the laborious and arduous task of forming a government of our country, we are ourselves at the close throwing insuperable obstacles in the way of its success."

It was a strong statement, quite plainly true, and it brought Randolph to his feet again, ready to list his specific objections: the small number of representatives in Congress . . . the want of limitation on a standing army . . . the want of some particular restraint on navigation acts . . . the presidential power to pardon treason. . . . Was he then, Randolph demanded, "to promote the establishment of a plan which he verily believed would end in Tyranny?" Madison put a capital T to the word. "He was unwilling," he said [Madison wrote on], "to impede the wishes and judgment of the Convention — but he must keep himself free, in case he should be honored with a seat in the Convention of his State, to act according to the dictates of his judgment. The only mode in which his embarrassments could be removed, was that of submitting the plan to Congress to go from them to the State Legislatures, and from these to the State Conventions having power to adopt, reject or amend; the process to close with another general Convention with full power to adopt or reject the alterations proposed by the state conventions, and to establish finally the government."

Randolph put his plan in the form of a resolution; Franklin seconded it. The two were a strong team, but their motion never reached a vote. George Mason stepped in to urge that the motion lie on the table for a day or two, and won his point. In the end the matter would be settled by strategy, an immensely clever, altogether successful maneuver in committee which avoided a renewal of debate on the floor, yet satisfied the Convention.

Of this maneuver delegates were of course ignorant. After

Mason's motion had been accepted, Charles Pinckney moved that an address to the people be prepared, to accompany the Constitution, and that this be referred to the proper committee.

"Adjourned," wrote Madison at the foot of the page.

## XX

## Drafting the Constitution. The Committee of Style and Arrangement takes hold. September 8-12.

> A free government is a complicated piece of ma-
> chinery, the nice and exact adjustment of whose
> springs, wheels, and weights, is not yet well compre-
> hended by the artists of the age, and still less by the
> people.
>
> JOHN ADAMS TO THOMAS JEFFERSON,
> *Quincy, May 19, 1821*

IN spite of disagreement, indecision, threats of withdrawal and articles not settled, the Convention was ready to put the Constitution into final form and present it to the country. The State House was noisy and busy with men passing to and fro beyond the closed doors of the big east chamber. The Pennsylvania Assembly met according to schedule on September fifth but had politely offered to move upstairs; Convention delegates assured their Pennsylvania brethren they would not be longer than ten days at most. A few days later, Madison recorded that a committee had been chosen by ballot "to revise the style of and arrange the articles which had been agreed to by the House." The five men selected were William Samuel Johnson, Alexander Hamilton, Gouverneur Morris, James Madison, and Rufus King. They were called the Committee of Style and Arrangement.

It is hard to see how there could have been a better choice, though it seems strange that they passed over James Wilson. But Wilson was not personally ingratiating; even in Pennsylvania he was not generally liked, and Southern members of the Convention may have been wary of his uncompromising stand for a strong central government. Yet every one of the five was a strong-government partisan; not a states'-sovereignty man sat on the committee. The omission of George Mason is a little surprising, considering his reputation as a writer of state documents. Perhaps he refused to serve, already knowing it likely he would repudiate the Constitution.

Dr. Johnson was at once named chairman — the perfect man to preside over these four masters of argument and political strategy. Delegates did not forget that in Congress Johnson had been known as "the man the southerners were vastly fond of." His presence on the committee must have been reassuring; the doctor's quiet manner disarmed. In the Convention he had not missed a day since his arrival early in June, and his little way of always being ready to instruct and inform never seemed tedious. In short, men liked the new president of Columbia College; a contemporary had gone so far as to state that in person the doctor was "the *tout ensemble* of a perfect man, in face, form and proportion."

As for Alexander Hamilton, his speech of June eighteenth had not been forgotten, with its monarchical slant; yet delegates knew his grasp of the situation, knew also that his pen was quick and eloquent; nobody could say better what he wanted to say about the constitution of governments. Late in July, Hamilton had launched in the *New York Daily Advertiser* a powerful attack on Governor Clinton's anti-Convention stand. Further, he had corresponded with Washington and Rufus King and quite evidently kept in touch with progress. "Thinking men," he had written to Washington in July, "seem to be convinced that a strong well mounted government will better suit the popular palate than one of a different complexion." Moreover the personal bravado and arrogance that made young Hamilton disliked in certain quarters would be curbed in this committee; his four colleagues were none of them men to be dictated to. And if it was felt that Hamilton, with his air of foreignness, had no love for "the people," it was known that he indubitably loved the Union. Nor did he think, as did many, that a consolidated government, a powerful Union, would curb individual liberties. Hamilton believed, and said so, that America could be both free *and* powerful.

Gouverneur Morris — the "Tall Boy" — stumping in and out with his wooden leg and his polished manners, was in his way as audacious as Hamilton, nor was Morris overly fond of the people at large. Sophistication, that un-American trait, was instinct with Morris and he dared the unpatriotic sentiment that luxury might not be "such a bad thing as people believed." Here was the oftenest heard voice of the Convention, the delegate who talked more than anybody on the floor, and who had the courage to change his mind publicly when he saw himself in the wrong.

Morris had been named amanuensis for the committee's task, which was to be one of style and arrangement, with no substantive changes. People said of Gouverneur Morris that he knew human nature — a characteristic hardly called for in the drafter of a constitution. It was Morris's contention that the writing of history requires more than scholarship, and that the historian would better prepare himself by reading Shakespeare than by reading Hume. But to put historical facts together requires judgment and skill. The skeleton must be clothed with those "muscles," Morris said, that give symmetry, strength and grace to the completed form, which itself will take on color from the historian's own outlook and experience.

The Federal Convention was ignorant of all this when it voted Gouverneur Morris to the Committee of Style and Arrangement. Yet harmony of form is not a bad thing in such a document, and to write a national constitution that can be carried in the pocket is perhaps an achievement of art as well as of judgment.

No one ever said about James Madison, fourth member of the committee, that he knew human nature; to say it would have been beside the point. What Madison knew was political science, governments, constitutions, books, treatises. Here, moreover, was a man who knew himself and moved within the fortunate radius of his nature. Madison's power lay in the grasp of the subject at hand, an ability to compare one political system or idea with another, at lightning speed equating present with past. His convictions were deep and passionate. But by training or by natural endowment he possessed a ruthless tenacity and could await his moment, then rise, his mind free, and without oratory or display put down or reassure the opposition.

During nearly four months Madison had been incredibly diligent and watchful. For the rest of his life he would be explaining and expounding the new Constitution — in Congress, as President of the United States, and years later at Montpelier, answering letters from all over the country. Now he sat in his place at the conference table, tired, serious, a person who had, wrote one who knew him, "a calm expression, a penetrating blue eye — and looked like a thinking man."

The fifth member of the committee, Rufus King, as a congressman had been doubtful of the Annapolis Convention and had come to Philadelphia filled with misgivings; he regarded Congress as the proper body for proposing alterations in the Confederacy. But during the summer King had slowly changed his mind and become a strong supporter of the Constitution. A convert is always fervent; King's part in the Convention had been large. He boasted a tremendous reputation for oratory; Brissot de Warville called him "the most eloquent man of the United States." Daniel Webster was later to testify that as an orator King was "unequaled." But a reputation for oratory, like a reputation for ballet dancing, is hard to convey to succeeding generations; much depends on manner and personality. Rufus King was known to every member of Congress; quite evidently he cut an impressive and uncommonly handsome figure. Pierce of Georgia wrote solemnly that he might "with propriety be reckoned as among the luminaries of the present age."

On the day the Committee of Style was formed, a Saturday, its chairman drove to the Falls of the Schuylkill to dine early with a delegate, Thomas Mifflin, and his charming Quaker wife, Sarah. That evening, Dr. Johnson met with his committee. It was to take them four days to finish their task. Whether they began with the preamble or, as seems more likely, with the body of the document, for sheer strategy one of the cleverest things they did was to delete altogether the controversial Articles XXII and XXIII concerning ratification and put them in the form of two resolves, an appendage designed for the instruction of Congress as to immediate procedure. In the Constitution the final article simply states that "*The Ratification of the Conventions of nine States, shall be sufficient for the Establishment of this Constitution between the States so ratifying the Same.*"

A letter was drafted to "accompany the plan to Congress,"

Johnson said, and to be signed by George Washington as representing the Convention. "SIR," it began; "We have now the honor to submit to the consideration of the United States in Congress assembled, that Constitution which has appeared to us the most advisable."

In its justification of the Convention's work, the letter took the place of a long preamble such as had prefaced the Declaration of Independence. The letter has come down to us in Gouverneur Morris's handwriting — a most skillful and touching document which breathes confidence in what the Convention had achieved, makes no apologies but tells with seriousness and humility just what such a convention of diverse states felt it could and could not do. "It is obviously impracticable," says the second paragraph, "in the foederal government of these States, to secure all rights of independent sovereignty to each, and yet provide for the interest and safety of all. Individuals entering into society, must give up a share of liberty to preserve the rest. The magnitude of the sacrifice must depend as well on situation and circumstance, as on the object to be obtained. It is at all times difficult to draw with precision the line between those rights which must be surrendered, and those which may be reserved; and on the present occasion this difficulty was encreased by a difference among the several States as to their situation, extent, habits, and particular interests."

It was indeed so "encreased." The wonder is that twelve states got through months of discussion without disbanding, and that the Committee of Style could now go on with their task unhampered. The letter to Congress, as it proceeded, used a dangerous word; it said the greatest interest of every American lay in the "consolidation of our Union, in which is involved our prosperity, felicity, safety, perhaps our national existence."

Since May twenty-ninth, when the Virginia Resolves were presented, members had got used to the notion of a consolidated government, though later the word would raise alarm in certain quarters. The letter to Congress ended by saying that although it was not to be expected the Constitution would meet the full and entire approbation of every state, "each will doubtless consider . . . that it is liable to as few exceptions as could reasonably have been expected, we hope and believe. That it may promote the lasting welfare of that country so dear to us all, and secure her freedom and happiness, is our most ardent wish."

There is something refreshing in the eighteenth-century use of the word happiness in public documents. Jefferson's "pursuit of happiness" was an "unalienable right" of mankind, along with life and liberty. Even earlier, in the Virginia Bill of Rights, George Mason had granted to men "certain inherent rights, namely, the enjoyment of life and liberty, with the means of acquiring and possessing property, and pursuing and obtaining happiness and safety." Chastellux, friend of America, had written a treatise *On Public Happiness* (*De la Félicité Publique*). "The true national spirit," he said, "which allies itself perfectly with liberty and happiness."

Alexander Hamilton rang a dozen changes on the phrase. A historian has listed them: "the public weal, the public safety, the public welfare, the public felicity, the general good, the national happiness, the permanent happiness of society." William Penn had been suspicious of the word. Men seemed to agree, he said, that the end of government was happiness, but they differed dangerously in defining the means to that end. In 1786 Madison had written to James Monroe concerning the current maxim "that the interest of the majority is the political standard of right and wrong. Taking the word 'interest' as synonymous with 'ultimate happiness,' in which sense it is qualified with every necessary moral ingredient, the proposition is no doubt true. But taking it in the popular sense, as referring to the immediate augmentation of property and wealth, nothing can be more false. In the latter sense . . . it is only re-establishing, under another name and a more specious form, force as a measure of right."

Madison was no political romantic. The right to possess property, to hold fast to it and to be represented in whatever body determined taxes: this was an essential part of liberty and of the public happiness. In the next century "public happiness" would take the rather bleak name of utilitarianism, and in our own time a judge in court* has spoken of a right to "the orderly pursuit of

* Justice McReynolds in *Meyer* v. *Nebraska,* 1923.

happiness" — a slightly hortatory modification of a glorious hope.

But in the year 1787 the Committee of Style and Arrangement had no such cautions or scruples, their "most ardent wish" being to secure the "freedom and happiness" and the "lasting welfare of that country so dear to us all." The letter to Congress having covered all necessary points of justification for the summer's proceedings, the committee made short work of their new preamble. "*We the People of the United States,*" wrote Morris boldly.

The phrase as Morris put it was very new. On the table before him lay the Convention's twenty-three resolves — fought over, voted upon and many times rewritten — arranged under articles and sections. These articles carried their own preamble, which said nothing at all about the "People of the United States." What the articles had said was, "We the undersigned delegates of the States of New Hampshire, Massachusetts-bay" . . . and so on down the list of thirteen, including (with more hope than judgment) the "Rhodeisland and Providence Plantations." Yet to the committee there was little use in promising Rhode Island's support to this new Constitution, or Maryland's, or New York's. Better to avoid enumeration and let the various states ratify when and if they chose. . . . "*We the People of the United States . . .*"

No member of the committee has said he knew the significance of that phrase, or guessed it would rouse the bitter oratory of such men as Patrick Henry, to whom the Union meant the states, not the people as a nation. To Henry, this phrase, "the People," would permit a national government to ride roughshod over the states and their rights. Nor did members of the committee foresee that in Europe the phrase would serve as an inspiration, a flag of defiance against absolutist kings. If *We the People* should indeed prove an entity, a corporate being, what power that incorporation might one day represent!

Having disposed of an inconvenient problem and got rid of the hazard of naming states that would not care to be named, Morris's pen proceeded . . . "*in Order,*" he wrote, "*to form a more perfect Union, establish Justice, insure domestic Tranquility, provide for the common defence, promote the general Welfare, and secure the Blessings of Liberty to ourselves and our Posterity, do ordain and establish this Constitution for the United States of America.*"

The seven verbs rolled out: to form, establish, insure, provide, promote, secure, ordain. One might challenge the centuries to better these verbs. Did Morris study over them or did they come easily from his pen? A grace was necessary, Morris believed, for good historical writing — a harmony, and "muscles." Morris was setting down a working instrument of government which must be plain, brief and strategically a trifle vague in places, to give play for future circumstance. "It is important not to make the government too complex," Caleb Strong had said in Convention, and Nathaniel Gorham had urged that "the vagueness of the terms constitutes the propriety of them."

In Morris's mind, in the committee's mind echoed the words and arguments of a long summer; the five men came well primed for their task. These twenty-three articles were the result of battle, harangue and compromise. "Always let losers have their words." Sir Francis Bacon said it two centuries before, giving advice to himself as a young lawyer. In creating the United States Constitution, every loser surely had his words; to this fact the system owed its strength. And if the new government was indeed a revolution, it carried an advantage few revolutions have shown: no central power, no "leader" swept it into being. Here was a fusion which owed its validity not least to the dissidents. The Committee of Style, conscious of the fact, did its work accordingly. "*This Constitution,*" wrote Morris in Article VI, ". . . *shall be the supreme Law of the Land.*" Around the ancient phrase (it came from Magna Carta) Congress and the states were to turn as on a hub. Luther Martin had moved that resolution — though he did not say "supreme law of the land." He said "supreme law of the respective states."

The Committee of Style had never heard of the supremacy clause . . . the commerce clause . . . the full faith and credit clause. Such nomenclature came later, when the courts had begun their interpretations. All that Gouverneur Morris could do was to take twenty-three articles and condense them into seven, with their proper sections. He was proud of his work, and many years later told Timothy Pickering the Constitution "was written by the fingers which write this letter," adding that "having rejected redundant and equivocal terms, I believed it to be as clear as our language would permit."

Madison is the best witness of the part Morris played. "The *finish* given to the style and arrangement," Madison wrote, ". . . fairly belongs to the pen of Mr. Morris." Though the articles, said Madison, had been presented to the committee in logical arrangement, still, "there was sufficient room for the talents and taste stamped by the author on the face of it." In one instance at least, Morris made a final attempt to twist a clause to his own thinking — and failed. It was the third section of Article IV, about excluding new territories, in wording which, Morris later confessed, he "went as far as circumstances would permit to establish the exclusion." *

But Gouverneur Morris had every right to take pride in his labors. When the Convention rose and the Constitution was published, delegates would find themselves charged by the opposition with ambiguity of expression. In the Massachusetts convention for ratification Caleb Strong was to make rebuttal in words characteristically simple, and not without their own unadorned dignity and eloquence. He believed, he said, that a great majority of those who formed the Constitution were sincere and honest men, and that if any sections were not altogether explicit, it could not be attributed to design. "For my part, I think the whole of it is expressed in the plain, common language of mankind."

* See page 178.

# XXI

## *A bill of rights rejected.*

Democratical States must always *feel* before they
can *see;* — it is this that makes their governments slow,
but the people will be right at last.
GEORGE WASHINGTON TO LAFAYETTE, *July 25, 1785*

"WE hear," said the *Pennsylvania Packet* on September
sixth, "that the Convention propose to adjourn next
week." Exultantly pro-Constitutional, the *Packet* let
fly in its best style: "The year 1776 is celebrated for a revolution
in favor of Liberty. The year 1787 it is expected will be celebrated with equal joy, for a revolution in favor of Government."
Later the *Packet* gave space to a "paragraph writer" — current
name for columnist — who let himself imagine that the Constitution had been rejected by the states. He described the
nation's plight: "His Excellency Daniel Shays has taken possession of the Massachusetts government and the former encum-
bents are to be executed tomorrow. New Jersey has petitioned to
be taken again under the protection of the British Crown. . . ."

On September twelfth, Dr. Johnson noted in his diary that it
was very hot; for the most part the weather had been blessedly
cool while the Committee of Style did its work. That morning, a
Wednesday, the committee presented their Constitution; Johnson referred to it in the now customary phrase as "the plan." The
Convention, unimpressed, or conscious perhaps that this was their
last chance, proceeded to tear the plan apart as they had done
with every previous version since May. . . . Let the President's
negative be overruled only by two-thirds of Congress, not three-
fourths. . . . Include a provision for jury trials in civil cases.

. . . The first motion won by close vote, the second hung fire; Gerry proposed that the Committee of Style provide such a clause for consideration.

Trial by jury had long been a sacred trinity of words, celebrated as the palladium of liberty and accompanied by panegyric about the rights of man and the ancient privileges come down from our Saxon ancestors. Actually, trial by jury had by no means insured fair treatment in court these many centuries; time was, in England, when juries were easily intimidated by judge or lordly defendant. Nevertheless trial by jury was a phrase to conjure with. This morning it inspired George Mason to say the first word* of the summer about a bill of rights for the Constitution. He wished, Mason said, "the plan had been prefaced with a bill of rights. It would give great quiet to the people." Such a bill could be prepared in a few hours, Mason added, if the committee simply referred to the various state declarations.

Eight of the state constitutions included bills of rights. Mason himself had written Virginia's in 1776. Elbridge Gerry now moved for the preparation of such a bill and Mason seconded him. Roger Sherman, however, said the state declarations were sufficient; after all, they were not repealed by the new Constitution. Mason said no to this; the laws of the United States were now to be the supreme law of the land and therefore paramount to state bills of rights. Ten states to none, the Convention voted against adding a bill of rights to the Constitution. Massachusetts was absent. Gerry must have left the chamber. Even Virginia voted no.

Thus summarily was the question dismissed, a reaction which at first seems extraordinary. So familiar are Americans today with the Bill of Rights that they confuse it with the first seven articles which in September of 1787 made up the whole body of the Constitution. If challenged, many citizens would say the United States Constitution is that document which begins *We the People* and guarantees freedom of speech and religion, *habeas corpus* and so on. Actually, of course, the Bill of Rights consists of the first ten amendments to the Constitution, suggested by the states during

---

* On August twentieth Charles Pinckney had submitted to the Committee of Detail certain provisions which could have amounted to a bill of rights. But nothing came of it and it was never brought to the floor.

the ratification period and passed by the first Congress (1789) under the new government.

When the Constitution was published in the newspapers after the Convention rose, and the Antifederalists gathered their strength for opposition, nothing created such an uproar as the lack of a bill of rights. What had the Convention been thinking of, to neglect a matter so elementary, so much a part of the heritage of free people? Why, the business went back to Magna Carta! Blackstone had defined it, and Lord Coke before him in his *Second Institute*.

The Convention's stand, however, was reasonable, if mistaken. No delegate had been against such rights. Merely they considered the Constitution covered the matter as it stood. And when, shortly after the ten-to-nothing vote, Pinckney and Gerry moved for a declaration "that the liberty of the press should be inviolably observed," Roger Sherman said at once it was unnecessary; the power of Congress did not extend to the press. Seven to four the states again voted no.

There is a fascination in reading the delegates' later defense of their position. To Alexander Hamilton a bill of rights was more than unnecessary. It would be dangerous, he said. "Why declare that things shall not be done which there is no power [in Congress] to do?" Hamilton argued that bills of rights originally were stipulations between kings and their subjects, like Magna Carta, which was "obtained by the barons, sword in hand, from King John."* Whereas in the American government the people, having surrendered nothing and retained everything, have no need of particular reservations. "*We the People of the United States* . . ." Hamilton quoted the preamble — a firmer recognition of popular rights, he said, than volumes of those aphorisms appearing in the state bills of rights, which "would sound much better in a treatise of ethics than in a constitution of government." And while at it, why not declare in the Constitution that government ought to be free, that taxes ought not to be excessive ～～ '

As for James Wilson, he told a meeting of P〔 that a bill of rights would not only have bee〔 impracticable. "Enumerate all the rights of men〔

* *Federalist Papers, Number 84.*

gentleman in the late Convention would have attempted such a thing." The new Constitution in Wilson's view was not a body of fundamental law which would require a statement of natural rights. Rather it was municipal law, positive law — what in medieval days was called *jus civile*. Not a declaration of eternal rights but a code for reference.

Quite evidently the Federal Convention looked on its work as practical, everyday business; all along they had avoided highflown phrases about the rights of man. Such rights, John Dickinson was to argue in the newspapers — trial by jury, no taxation without representation — "must be preserved by soundness of sense and honesty of heart." Compared with these qualities, what, he demanded, are bills of rights? "Do we want to be reminded that the sun enlightens, warms, invigorates, and cheers? or how horrid it would be, to have his blessed beams intercepted, by our being thrust into mines or dungeons? Liberty is the sun of society, and Rights are the beams."

Roger Sherman never changed his stand against a bill of rights. In his forthright way he wrote about it to a New Haven paper, signing himself "A Countryman." "No bill of rights," said Sherman, "ever yet bound the supreme power longer than the honeymoon of a new married couple, unless the rulers were interested in preserving the rights; and in that case they have always been ready enough to declare the rights, and to preserve them when they were declared."

The newspapers were to be flooded with letters and articles on the subject, signed Brutus, Sydney, Agrippa, Cato, Candidus.* Noah Webster, stung by the New York convention's arguments for a bill of rights, addressed the members (via the newspapers) in his best free-swinging sarcasm. To complete their list of unalienable rights, Webster suggested a clause "that everybody shall, in good weather, hunt on his own land, and catch fish in rivers that are public property . . . and that Congress shall never restrain any inhabitant of America from eating and drinking, at seasonable times, or prevent his lying on his left side, in a long winter's night, or even on his back, when he is fatigued by lying on his right."

Dr. Benjamin Rush was to tell the Pennsylvania convention for

Sydney and Brutus were Yates; Governor Clinton was Cato.

ratification that he "considered it an honor to the late convention that this system has not been disgraced with a bill of rights. Would it not be absurd to frame a formal declaration that our natural rights are acquired from ourselves?" Down in South Carolina, General Charles Cotesworth Pinckney delivered the nakedest statement of all. Bills of rights, he told the legislature, "generally begin with declaring that all men are by nature born free. Now, we should make that declaration with a very bad grace, when a large part of our property consists in men who are actually born slaves."

Such were the arguments against a bill of rights for the Constitution. The reasons in favor scarcely need quotation; they are part of our thinking today. There were, however, surprising twists to men's expression of their convictions. Jefferson for instance was indignant at the omission of a bill of rights and hoped "Virginia's opposition would remedy this." But, writing to General Washington from Paris, Jefferson classed the omission of a bill of rights as only one of two things that he disliked strongly in the new Constitution. The other was the perpetual re-eligibility of the President, which he feared would "make that an office for life, first, and then hereditary."

Lesser men had their say; everywhere, people took part. In Portland, Maine, a printer named Thomas Wait, publisher of the *Cumberland Gazette*, maintained "there was a certain darkness, duplicity and studied ambiguity of expression running through the whole Constitution which renders a bill of rights peculiarly necessary. As it now stands, but very few individuals do or ever will understand it, consequently Congress will be its own interpreter."

It was a shrewd and very natural reaction. The Constitution was new and shocking, and minds offended by novelty are apt to complain of darkness or ambiguity in matters not yet digested. Luther Martin in Maryland raised a great outcry, hinting that the lack of a bill of rights was deliberate and scandalous. Oliver Ellsworth replied angrily in the newspapers, signing himself "A Landholder." Why had Mr. Martin never spoken out in the Convention for a bill of rights? "You, sir," wrote Ellsworth, "never signified by any motion or expression whatever, that [the plan] stood in need of a bill of rights, or in any wise endangered the trial by jury. In these respects the Constitution met your entire approbation; for had you believed it defective in these essentials, you ought to have mentioned it in Convention, or had you thought it wanted further guards, it was your indispensable duty to have proposed them." Martin floundered badly in his reply, said that he had indeed prepared and even drafted a bill of rights toward the end of the Convention, but had been advised against presenting it. "Ambition and interest," wrote Martin, had "so far blinded the understanding of some of the principal framers of the Constitution . . . I most sacredly believe their object is the total abolition and destruction of all state governments, and the erection on their ruins of one great and extensive empire. . . ."

With charity and much perceptive good sense, Richard Henry Lee of Virginia, a congressman — no member of the Convention and fiercely anti-Constitutionalist — excused the Convention's fault concerning a bill of rights. Lee said that when men have long and early understood certain matters as the common concerns of the country, they are apt to suppose these things are understood by others and need not be expressed. "And it is not uncommon," Lee added, "for the ablest men frequently to make this mistake. Whereas such rights should be constantly kept in view, in addresses, in bills of rights, in newspapers, and so on."

The Convention records bear Lee out. The framers looked upon the Constitution as a bill of rights in itself; all its provisions were for a free people and a people responsible. Why, therefore, enumerate the things that Congress must not do?

Luther Martin had left Philadelphia on September fourth, giving as his reason pressing business at home, though six months later he told his constituents he had quitted the Convention with a "fixed determination to return if possible before the Convention rose . . . I wished," he said, "to have been present at the conclusion, to have then given [the Constitution] my solemn negative. It is my highest ambition that my name may also be recorded as one who considered the system injurious to my country, and as such opposed it."

But Luther Martin's solemn negative went by default. He stayed home; the Constitution was signed without him. On Friday, September fourteenth, various words were altered in Article I, and the Convention formally agreed to the committee's two resolves as substitution for Articles XXII and XXIII. But delegates could not let go, let down, be finished with the business. Patiently they brought forward their plans, as Dr. Franklin's motion that Congress be empowered to cut canals where needed. James Wilson said it would facilitate communication with the West — and how right he was a later generation would prove. But a Northern member said canals would split the states into parties, and besides, Philadelphia and New York would use canal building as an excuse to establish a bank; already this had been a matter for contention in those cities. George Mason too objected; he feared monopolies. By eight states to three, Franklin's motion was defeated.

Gouverneur Morris wished to strike out, in Section 8 of Article I, the second use of the word punish: "To define and punish piracies and felonies committed on the high seas and punish offences against the law of nations." This would make offenses against the law of nations definable as well as punishable. James Wilson was against it. "To pretend to *define* the law of nations which depends on the authority of all the civilized nations of the world," he said, "would have a look of arrogance and would make us ridiculous." But the states voted six to five for Morris's motion. Madison and Charles Pinckney now brought forward — and lost — a motion that Congress be empowered "to establish an University, in which no preferences or distinctions should be allowed on account of religion." There was debate over Section 9 of Article I, whether Congress should be required to publish an account of the public expenditures, and if this should be annual. In the end the Convention settled on the phrase, "*shall be published from time to time.*"

Saturday, September fifteenth, was the final working day of the Convention. As the meeting opened, Carroll of Maryland reminded the House that no address to the people had been prepared, a matter he considered "of great importance. . . . The people had been accustomed to such on great occasions," Carroll said, and moved that a committee be appointed to prepare the address.

Rutledge of South Carolina objected, "on account of the delay." Also, it would be improper to address the people before it was known whether Congress would approve and support the Constitution. When the time came, Congress could prepare such an address, and the members of this Convention could explain to their constituents at home "the reasons of what has been done." Langdon of New Hampshire moved to add one member each to the representatives of North Carolina and Rhode Island, whereupon Rufus King rose in his wrath to declare there was no official proof that North Carolina had a greater population than at first estimated. "And," finished King, he could "never sign the Constitution if Rhode Island is to be allowed two members — that is, one fourth of the number allowed to Massachusetts."

With this, Gunning Bedford spoke up for an increase in Delaware's representatives, and the matter threatened to get out of hand. It was a long day. The Convention sat till six o'clock. Article after article was considered, words altered. Now at this latest date the admittance of new states came up again, the power of Congress to regulate commerce, the presidential pardon for traitors. As the hours passed, Mason, Randolph and Gerry showed themselves increasingly restive. The United States Senate had too much power, Mason said.

It was the amending clause that brought Mason's dissatisfaction to a head. Article V provided that whenever two-thirds of Congress deemed it necessary, the Constitution could be amended after ratification by three-fourths of the states. Mason said that such a method was "exceptionable and dangerous." He was unhappy also with Congress's power to pass navigation acts by a bare majority; thus enabling, he said, "a few rich merchants in Philadelphia, New York and Boston to monopolize the staples of the southern states."

Edmund Randolph now spoke out, "animadverting," wrote Madison, "on the indefinite and dangerous power given by the Constitution to Congress, expressing the pain he felt at differing from the body of the Convention, on the close of the great and awful subject of their labours, and anxiously wishing for some accommodating expedient which would relieve him of his embarrassments." Randolph thereupon made a motion that amendments to the new Constitution might be offered by the state conventions, which in turn would be submitted to and finally decided on by another general convention. "Should this proposition be disregarded," finished Randolph solemnly, it would be impossible for him to put his name to the instrument. Whether he would oppose it afterwards he would not then decide. But he would not deprive himself of the freedom to do so in his own state, if that course should be prescribed by his final judgment.

George Mason "seconded and followed Mr. Randolph," wrote Madison, "in animadversions on the dangerous power and structure of the government, concluding that it would end either in monarchy or a tyrannical aristocracy; which, he was in doubt, but one or other, he was sure. This Constitution," finished Mason, "has been formed without the knowledge or idea of the people. A second Convention will know more of the sense of the people, and will be able to provide a system more consonant to it." It was improper to say to the people, take this or nothing. As the Constitution now stood he could neither give it his support or vote in Virginia. And he could not sign here what he could not support there. With the expedient of another Convention as proposed, he could sign.

It was a perilous moment. Were Randolph and Mason going to defect, then, and what influence would their defection have on other delegates and on the country at large? Randolph had seemed to favor a strong central government. Had it not been the Randolph Plan which the assembly had debated all these months? As for Colonel Mason, with his white hair and his passionate patriotism, he had sworn to bury his bones in Philadelphia rather than quit the Convention before a workable plan was made. And now Mason insisted on a second convention — to Madison, Hamilton, Washington, Wilson, an impossible contingency.

Charles Pinckney stood up. Before he reached the age of thirty-two, Pinckney was to be elected governor of South Carolina. He was vain, dazzling, troublesome, but this summer he had proved his worth. What he said now was eminently sensible and very outspoken. "These declarations from members so respectable, at the close of this important scene, give a peculiar solemnity to the present moment. . . ."

"Pinckney descanted," wrote Madison, "on the consequences of calling forth the deliberations and amendments of the different states on the subject of government at large. Nothing but confusion and contrariety could spring from the experiment. The states will never agree in their plans — And the deputies to a second Convention coming together under the discordant impressions of their constituents, will never agree."

Pinckney finished by making his own position plain. Madison followed it to the end. "He was not without objections as well as others to the plan [the Constitution]," Pinckney said. "He objected to the contemptible weakness and dependence of the Executive. He objected to the power of a majority only of Congress over commerce. But apprehending the danger of a general confusion, and an ultimate decision by the sword he should give the plan his support."

Elbridge Gerry was next on his feet, ready with his points against the Constitution. There were eleven of them; Gerry probably had a list in his hand. "1. The duration and re-eligibility of the Senate. 2. the power of the House of Representatives to conceal their journals. 3. the power of Congress over the places of election. 4. the unlimited power of Congress over their own compensations. 5. Massachusetts has not a due share of representatives allotted to her. . . ."

It must have been dismaying to listen to Gerry, with his nervous, emphatic manner. Gerry went on with his list, then declared he could "get over all these [objections] if the rights of the citizens were not rendered insecure." He mentioned the raising of armies, the establishment of a tribunal without juries, "which will be a Star Chamber as to civil cases. . . . Under such a view of the Constitution the best that can be done is to provide for a second general Convention." For himself, Gerry said, he was determined to withhold his name from the Constitution.

Nobody answered, or if they did, it is not recorded. Randolph's proposition for a second Convention came to the vote. "All the States answered — no," wrote Madison.

"On the question to agree to the Constitution as amended. All the States aye.

"The Constitution was then ordered to be engrossed.

"And the House adjourned."

# XXII

## *The Constitution is signed. The dissidents.*

> It was done by bargain and compromise, yet notwithstanding its imperfections, on the adoption of it depends (in my feeble judgment) whether or no we shall become a respectable nation, or a people torn to pieces by intestine commotions, and rendered contemptible for ages.
>
> NICHOLAS GILMAN, *delegate from New Hampshire,* TO JOSEPH GILMAN, *September 18, 1787*

THE weekend had been cloudy; on Friday and Saturday it rained. But Monday, September seventeenth, dawned clear and cold, there was a pleasing touch of autumn in the air. Walking from their lodgings below Fifth Street, members, as they approached the State House, could see the big clock on the east wall, its base nearly on the ground, its face high under the eaves; one had to look upward to tell the time. For most delegates this would be their last day on Chestnut Street and in the familiar building; consciousness of it sharpened a man's perception. . . . The neat brick pavement and gutters, washed clean by the rain, the tall pumps, the sentries at the door. Dr. Franklin's sedan chair lumbering into view, the prisoners carrying their stout burden up the State House steps. . . . Already the scene took on a quality of nostalgia, as of something customary, something lived with but soon to be abandoned.

The big square east room was bright; morning sun streamed through the high south windows. A lofty ceiling blanketed the sound of footsteps and voices overhead, where the Pennsylvania Assembly was sitting; only the scrape of a chair could be heard now and again, or men talking in the hallway as they passed toward the stairs. Out of fifty-five Convention members who had attended at one time or another, forty were present this morning. The largest delegation was Pennsylvania's, with eight. Virginia had five of her original seven, Massachusetts three. Caleb Strong had gone home to New England.

Members took their seats while the Constitution, now engrossed (copied out on parchment in a fine clerkly script), was read aloud. At its close, Dr. Franklin "rose," noted Madison, "with a speech in his hand, which he had reduced to writing for his own conveniency, and which Mr. Wilson read in the words following:

"Mr. President,

"I confess that there are several parts of this constitution which I do not at present approve. . . ."

It was a beginning well calculated to disarm the reluctant; old Franklin had not lost his touch. "But I am not sure I shall never approve them," the speech went on. "For having lived long, I have experienced many instances of being obliged by better information or fuller consideration, to change opinions even on important subjects, which I once thought right, but found to be otherwise. It is therefore that the older I grow, the more apt I am to doubt my own judgment, and to pay more respect to the judgment of others. Most men indeed as well as most sects in religion, think themselves in possession of all truth, and that wherever others differ from them it is so far error . . . But though many private persons think almost as highly of their own infallibility as of that of their sect, few express it so naturally as a certain French lady, who in a dispute with her sister, said 'I don't know how it happens, Sister, but I meet with nobody but myself, that's always in the right' — *Il n'y a que moi qui a toujours raison.*

"In these sentiments, Sir, I agree to this Constitution with all its faults, if they are such."

He doubted, the Doctor went on to say, if a second convention could do any better; after all they too would have their local interests and their selfish views. Indeed, said Franklin, it astonished him to find the Constitution approaching so near to perfection as it did. "And I think it will astonish our enemies, who are waiting with confidence to hear that our councils are confounded . . . and that our states are on the point of separation, only to meet hereafter for the purpose of cutting one another's throats."

Benjamin Franklin was pleased with his speech, he sent copies out to friends. Throughout, it has the Franklin charm; these are the words of an old man, gentle, accommodating, yet with the vigor and knowledge of a long life behind them. "I consent, Sir, to this Constitution," said Franklin, "because I expect no better and because I am not sure that it is not the best. The opinions I have had of its errors, I sacrifice to the public good. I have never whispered a syllable of them abroad. Within these walls they were born, and here they shall die."

Franklin went on to plead with delegates not to air their objections publicly and thus undermine the summer's work and lose the advantage with foreign nations which an appearance of unanimity would achieve. "Sir," he said, "I cannot help expressing a wish that every member of the Convention who may still have objections to it, would with me, on this occasion doubt a little of his own infallibility — and to make manifest our unanimity, put his name to this instrument."

Not every delegate was won by Franklin's magic. McHenry of Maryland wrote sourly in his notes: "Dr. Franklin put a paper into Mr. Wilson's hand to read, containing his reasons for assenting to the constitution. It was plain, insinuating, persuasive — and in any event of the system guarded the Doctor's fame." To the end of Franklin's life and beyond the end, people would be jealous of his renown and suspicious of his motives. Ironically enough, in McHenry's notes Franklin's influence seems plain enough. Having decided to sign, McHenry wrote out his reasons under headings: "1stly I distrust my own judgement, especially as it is opposite to the opinion of a majority of gentlemen whose abilities and patriotism are of the first cast; and as I have had already frequent occasions to be convinced that I have not always judged right . . ."

Dr. Franklin finished his speech by offering a motion which had been drawn by Gouverneur Morris and put into the Doctor's hands, said Madison, "that it might have the better chance of success." The motion was a calculated trick of language to beguile dissenters; it suggested that the Constitution be signed by the delegates, but in the following form: "Done in Convention, by the unanimous consent of *the States* present the 17th of September." This meant that delegates were not individually committed to uphold the Constitution, thus making it easier for the dissidents. Before the motion was voted on, Nathaniel Gorham said that if it was not too late, he would like to suggest that the clause in Article I, giving a representative in Congress to every forty thousand inhabitants, be changed to one in every thirty thousand.

It was a matter upon which the Convention had seriously disagreed; a larger representation would benefit the big states to the disadvantage of the small. Washington stood up to put the question. It must have surprised members when the General, after his summer's silence, suddenly launched into speech. He declared, wrote Madison, "that although his situation had hitherto restrained him from offering his sentiments on questions depending in the House, and it might be thought, ought now to impose silence on him, yet he could not forbear expressing his wish that the alteration proposed might take place. It was much to be desired that the objections to the plan recommended might be made as few as possible — The smallness of the proportion of representatives had been considered by many members of the Convention, an insufficient security for the rights and interests of the people. He acknowledged that it had always appeared to himself as among the exceptionable parts of the plan; and late as the present moment was for admitting amendments, he thought this of so much consequence that it would give much satisfaction to see it adopted."

The General's plea, the General's influence were irresistible. Unanimously, the states agreed.

The moment for signing was drawing near; the dissidents must speak now or never. To defy such figures as Washington and Franklin presented a terrifying hazard. Washington would be the nation's first President; in going against a Constitution which the General strongly approved, any aspirant for office under the new government cut his own throat. Yet there were a man's constituents at home to think of. In every state, powerful factions existed, opposed to the Constitution, desirous of a second convention. Edmund Randolph was young, much of his career lay before him.

But Virginia politics, Virginia affairs had always been paramount with Randolph; his deepest loyalties were local. Years later he was to declare, paraphrasing Patrick Henry's famous speech, "I am not really an American. I am a Virginian." Moreover it was difficult for Randolph to make up his mind and to stand by a decision when he had made it — a trait surprising in a man so vigorous; it would seem the young Governor was more showy than decisive. His own vacillations caused Randolph much anxiety; concerning the Constitution he was to shift back and forth, blow cold and hot until George Mason would be moved to refer to him as "young Arnold."

On that last day of the Federal Convention, Randolph must have brooded over Franklin's words while the discussion proceeded. Then Randolph rose, and, wrote Madison, "with an allusion to the observations of Dr. Franklin, apologized for his refusing to sign the Constitution, notwithstanding the vast majority and venerable names that would give sanction to its wisdom and its worth. He said however that he did not mean by this refusal to decide that he should oppose the Constitution without doors. He meant only to keep himself free to be governed by his duty as it should be prescribed by his future judgment. He refused to sign, because he thought the object of the Convention would be frustrated by the alternative which it presented to the people."

"Nine states," declared Randolph, "will fail to ratify the plan and confusion must ensue."

Just which nine Randolph meant, he did not indicate. "With such a view of the subject," he finished, he ought not, he could not, by pledging himself to support the plan, restrain himself from taking such steps as might appear to him "most consistent with the public good."

Randolph was leaving himself free to act as he chose in the Virginia convention for ratification. Gouverneur Morris was next to speak. He too had objections, "but considering the present plan as the best that was to be attained," wrote Madison, "he should take it with all its faults. The majority had determined in its favor and by that determination he should abide."

"The moment this plan goes forth," finished Morris, "all other considerations will be laid aside — and the great question will be, shall there be a national government or not? And this must take place or a general anarchy will be the alternative."

Williamson of North Carolina, aware that his colleague Blount had decided not to sign, now suggested that signing be confined to the letter going to Congress with the plan. This might satisfy members who disliked the Constitution. For himself he did not think a better plan was to be expected, and he had no scruple in putting his name to it.

In the room were six delegates who had attended faithfully all summer, had voted when voting was in order and had some of them served their turn in committees — but who had not seen fit to say one word on the floor. Blount of North Carolina was among them; the others were Judge Blair of Virginia, Gilman of New Hampshire, Bassett of Delaware, Few of Georgia, and Ingersoll of Philadelphia. Blount now rose to offer his first and only word. Though he had declared he would not sign, he said — and thus pledge himself in support of the plan — he "was relieved by the form proposed and would without committing himself attest the fact that the plan was the unanimous act of the states in Convention." Ingersoll still held back — from modesty, according to a member of the Convention, though this is hard to credit in a lawyer of marked success.

Alexander Hamilton "expressed his anxiety," wrote Madison, "that every member should sign . . ." "A few characters of consequence," Hamilton said, "by opposing or even refusing to sign the Constitution, might do infinite mischief by kindling the latent sparks which lurk under an enthusiasm in favor of the Convention which may soon subside. No man's ideas are more remote from the plan than my own are known to be. But is it possible to deliberate between anarchy and convulsion on one side, and the chance of good to be expected from the plan on the other?"

Dr. Franklin said he trusted that Mr. Randolph did not think himself alluded to in the remarks he had offered this morning. When drawing up his paper he had not known that any particular member would refuse to sign, and he hoped so to be understood. He had a high sense of obligation to Mr. Randolph, said Franklin, "for having brought forth the plan in the first instance, and for the assistance he had given in its progress, and hoped that he would yet lay aside his objections, and by concurring with his brethren, prevent the great mischief which the refusal of his name might produce."

But Randolph would not yield. "He repeated," wrote Madison, "that in refusing to sign the Constitution, he took a step which might be the most awful of his life, but it was dictated by his conscience, and it was not possible for him to hesitate, much less, to change. He repeated also his persuasion, that the holding out this plan with a final alternative to the people, of accepting or rejecting it in toto, would really produce the anarchy and civil convulsions which were apprehended from the refusal of individuals to sign it."

Elbridge Gerry was next. As the only Northerner in the Convention who refused to sign, his position was difficult. But Gerry had a reputation for quarrelsomeness; he seemed happiest in opposition. "A man of sense but a Grumbletonian," a contemporary said, ". . . of service by objecting to every thing he did not propose."

On this final day of the Convention, Gerry "described," wrote Madison, "the painful feelings of his situation, and the embarrassment under which he rose to offer any further observations on the subject which had been finally decided." He feared civil war, Gerry said; in Massachusetts particularly, "there are two parties, one devoted to democracy, the worst he thought of all political evils, the other as violent in the opposite extreme. From the collision of these in opposing and resisting the Constitution, confusion was greatly to be feared." He had thought the plan should have been proposed "in a more mediating shape, in order to abate the heat and opposition of parties. As it had been passed by the Convention, he was persuaded it would have a contrary effect. He could not therefore, by signing the Constitution, pledge himself to abide by it at all events." Alluding to the remarks of Dr. Franklin, he could not but view them "as levelled at himself and the other gentlemen who meant not to sign."

If anyone replied to Gerry it is not recorded. Madison's notes grew shorter every day. But General Charles Cotesworth Pinckney at once expressed disapproval of Dr. Franklin's ambiguous method of signing. He "thought it best to be candid and let the form speak the substance." He would himself sign the Constitution "with a view to support it with all his influence, and wished to pledge himself accordingly." Dr. Franklin demurred, saying that it was "too soon to pledge ourselves, before Congress and our constituents shall have approved the plan."

Of the six wordless delegates, a second now was moved to break silence. Jared Ingersoll said he did not consider a man's signature as a pledge to support the Constitution at all events. Rather, it was "a recommendation of what, all things considered, was the most eligible."

Franklin's motion on the form of signing won by ten votes. The dissidents had all spoken out, had had their say. Surprisingly, George Mason did not rise again. On the blank pages of his draft of the Constitution — the one returned by the Committee of Style on September twelfth — Mason had written out his objections; they cover three pages. "There is no declaration of rights," they begin, and go on to the "dangerous" powers of the President and Senate . . . the President had no council, the Vice President as head of the Senate "dangerously" blended the executive and legislative powers . . . and so on through the list. Actually, Mason had expected to present these objections to the Convention but — he later wrote to Jefferson — he "was discouraged from doing so by the precipitate, and intemperate, not to say indecent manner, in which the business was conducted, during the last week of the Convention, after the patrons of this new plan found they had a decided majority in their favour; which was obtained by a compromise between the Eastern and the two Southern states, to permit the latter to continue the importation of slaves for twenty odd years; a more favourite object with them, than the liberty and happiness of the people."

After the Convention, Mason sent General Washington the list of objections, which, he wrote, "a little moderation and temper in the latter end of the Convention might have removed." Plainly, Mason was worried about the effect of his not signing. "Col. Mason left Philada. in an exceedingly ill humor indeed," Madison wrote to Jefferson. "A number of little circumstances arising in part from the impatience which prevailed towards the close of the business, conspired to whet his acrimony. He returned to Virginia with a fixed disposition to prevent the adoption of the plan if possible. He has some lesser objections. Being now under the necessity of justifying his refusal to sign, he will of course muster every possible one."

Nobody in Virginia or out of it questioned George Mason's devotion to his ideals. Washington's senior by seven years, Mason had long cherished a romantic view of liberty and republicanism. Back in '78 when Mason's own creation, the Virginia constitution, had been adopted, he wrote a friend that "we seem to have been treading upon enchanted ground." But in September of 1787, George Mason no longer walked as if enchanted. He had always distrusted a strong central government; now he saw one in the making. Very likely his gout troubled him in this crisis, or the stomach complaint that visited him in times of stress. (After one difficult session in the Virginia legislature he had written Washington that he had been "near fainting in the House" . . . from "mere vexation and disgust.") Whence this rush to settle the United States Constitution and be done with the business? Why must delegates move so fast? Mason foresaw the new government eventually "vibrating," he wrote, "between a monarchy and a corrupt oppressive aristocracy."

The moment had come to sign the Constitution. Before the members moved to the table, a motion was made and passed that the official journals and others papers of the Convention be put into General Washington's hands, to be retained by him "subject to the order of Congress, if ever formed under the Constitution."

It was now past three o'clock. Members ranged themselves according to the geography of states, beginning with New Hampshire and going southward. New Hampshire, Massachusetts . . . Connecticut . . . New York . . . New Jersey . . . Pennsylvania . . . Delaware, and so down to Georgia. Four men who fiercely opposed the Constitution were absent: Luther Martin, Yates and Lansing of New York, young Mercer of Maryland who had gone home in the middle of August. Nine men who approved were also absent: Ellsworth of Connecticut, Strong of Massachusetts, Houstoun and Pierce of Georgia, Governor Martin and Davie of North Carolina, Houston of New Jersey, and McClurg and George Wythe of Virginia. John Dickinson too was absent; he had not been feeling well and had gone home to Wilmington. George Read of Delaware had a letter authorizing him to sign for Dickinson. One man — old Roger Sherman — could boast that he had signed as well the Continental Association of 1774, the Declaration of Independence, and the Articles of Confederation. New York had but a single signer: Alexander Hamilton — a situation which caused Washington to write that night in his diary: "Met in Convention, when the Constitution received the unanimous assent of 11 States and Colo. Hamilton's from New York."

Madison wrote to Jefferson: "It will not escape you that three names only from Virginia are subscribed to the Act." They were Washington, Blair and Madison. "James Madison, Jr.," his signature reads. It was a sparse showing for the great commonwealth which considered itself the prime mover in this business. Benjamin Franklin was helped forward from his place; afterward it was said the old man wept when he signed. Following Pennsylvania six states remained; they moved slowly to the table.

"Whilst the last members were signing it," wrote Madison, "Doctr. Franklin looking towards the Presidents chair, at the back of which a rising sun happened to be painted, observed to a few members near him, that painters had found it difficult to distinguish in their art a rising from a setting sun. I have, said he, often and often in the course of the session, and the vicissitudes of my hopes and fears as to its issue, looked at that behind the President without being able to tell whether it was rising or setting: But now at length I have the happiness to know that it is a rising and not a setting sun."

Major Jackson, the Secretary, received his instructions to carry the document tomorrow to Congress in New York, engrossed, fully executed and signed. Members would each receive a printed copy; at long last the injunction of secrecy was removed. Madison's weary hand set down his final terse, triumphant sentence:

"The Constitution being signed by all the Members present except Mr. Randolph, Mr. Mason and Mr. Gerry who declined giving it the sanction of their names, the Convention dissolved itself by an Adjournment sine die."

On the same day, General Washington finished the entry in his diary. "The business being closed," he wrote, "the members adjourned to the City Tavern, dined together and took a cordial leave of each other; after which I returned to my lodgings, did some business with, and received the papers from the Secretary of the Convention, and retired to meditate on the momentous work which had been executed, after not less than five, and for a large part of the time Six, and sometimes 7 hours sitting every day, [except] Sundays and the ten days adjournment for more than four months."

# THE FIGHT
# FOR RATIFICATION

# XXIII

*The Constitution goes before the country.*

What hopes was there that so many jarring and
bigotted sovereigns would descend from any of their
fancied independencies for the common advantage?
JAMES WHITE, *Congressman*, TO
WILLIAM BLOUNT, *October 25, 1787*

TWO days after the Convention rose, the *Pennsylvania
Packet* published the Constitution, complete in four pages,
all other news abandoned. On the front page in six lines of
bold type the preamble stood out:

WE THE PEOPLE OF THE UNITED STATES
OF AMERICA . . .

At the end came the Convention's Letter to Congress, with its
closing appeal: "That [the Constitution] may promote the lasting
welfare of that country so dear to us all, and secure her freedom
and happiness, is our most ardent wish." The letter bore Washington's signature. "By unanimous order of the Convention" was
written underneath.

Newspapers everywhere published the Constitution as soon as
they could lay hands on it. So many columns had never been
given over to a political subject in America. Correspondents
wrote in, angry, approving or frightened as the case might be.
The country was shocked, startled. This Constitution, this three-
headed government, was no mere amendment of the Confederation! Its provisions were novel, unlooked-for. Why had the Federal Convention insisted upon secrecy — because they knew the
people would not consent to such drastic changes? The states
were as suspicious as the Convention itself had been when on May

twenty-ninth Randolph had confounded delegates with his fifteen Resolves. The summer's arguments, the vital questions asked and answered, the challenges, counter-ripostes, the final compromises and bitterly contested resolutions—the country could know none of these.

It was all to be done over again. And this time the argument would not be contained neatly within four walls. The whole country must know and read, scorn, reject or accept. A man's future, his political or business career, might well be jeopardized by the stand he took. Gerry and Randolph hurried to publish their protest; on October fourth the *Pennsylvania Packet* printed Mason's objections, the whole long list: The Constitution had no bill of rights . . . in the House of Representatives there was only the shadow of representation, not the substance . . . the federal judiciary would destroy and absorb the state judiciaries . . . the President had no council; the office of Vice President was unnecessary and dangerous. . . .

But beyond and below men's reasoned objections, their feelings were stirred, even outraged. This new Constitution was patterned after the English system surely. Under it the United States would no longer be a confederation of free sovereign states but a consolidation, an empire. The very word *consolidation* was an offense against "first principles," against the principles of the Revolution that Americans had fought for. The spirit of '75—had it then vanished with victory? Had this New World changed and altered to something different?

The Constitutionalists published their counterarguments: in October a series began in the New York newspapers, signed PUBLIUS. These were the *Federalist Papers*, written by Madison, Hamilton and John Jay, one day to be known as the final eloquent exposition of the United States Constitution, and to serve as an aid to the courts, to Congress and the President. But at the time, though widely reprinted, PUBLIUS did not create much stir. Its arguments were reasoned, quiet, intellectual in content, and what citizens looked for was fireworks, denunciation, thunder. Both sides readied their ammunition, rallied their cohorts. Ten delegates from the Federal Convention who were members of Congress went posthaste to New York. Federalists, they were called;

the opposition were the Antifederalists, though the latter said it was a misnomer, claiming they were the true Federalists, and the Convention men should be named Consolidationists, Nationalists.

Congress was quick to act. Too quick, said the Antifederalists; such haste was extreme, intemperate. Only eight days after receiving the Constitution, Congress passed a recommendation that the states call conventions for ratification. The official letter as dispatched was bland, wary; it never once included the word Constitution. "Having received the report of the Convention lately assembled at Philadelphia," wrote Congress: "*Resolved unanimously* that the said report, together with the resolutions and letter accompanying the same, be transmitted to the several legislatures."

It was a trick; there had been nothing unanimous about it, said Richard Henry Lee, representative from Virginia, adding that the word was meant to apply not to unanimous approbation but only to the transmission of the Constitution — its sending-out. "The greatness of the powers given," Lee declared, "and the multitude of places to be created, produce a coalition of monarchy men, military men, aristocrats and drones, whose noise, impudence and zeal exceed all belief."

It was an odd choice of words to describe Washington, Madison, Hamilton and others who could be expected to hold office under the new government. But the Lees were not renowned for temperate speech, and in Virginia the old anti-Washington faction still existed, with Lee and Patrick Henry at the head of it. Concerning the Constitution, Lee seemed almost hysterical. It was, he said, highly and dangerously oligarchic. "Either a monarchy or an aristocracy will be generated." Like William Grayson, his Virginia colleague in Congress, Lee had been elected to the Federal Convention. Both men had refused to serve, on the grounds that congressmen should not sit to judge a document of their own making. Lee had fought under Washington, signed the Declaration of Independence and had been a close friend of Samuel Adams ever since the two had met in the first Continental Congress — when John Adams said Lee was "a masterly man." Lee was passionate in his Antifederalism; as with Patrick Henry it went to the bone. And despite his distinguished birth and bearing, Lee liked to castigate "the artful and ever active aristocracy," which he held responsible for the new Constitution. "If our countrymen are so soon changed," he wrote, "and the language of 1774 is become odious to them, it will be in vain to use the language of freedom, or attempt to rouse them to free inquiries."

Colonel Grayson, equally ardent in opposition, had been educated in England, had fought in the Continental line and had become a lawyer and debater of an elegant wit, cool and fearless. He looked upon the Constitution "as a most ridiculous piece of business — something like the legs of Nebuchadnezzar's image . . . formed by jumbling a number of ideas together. The temper of America," Grayson said, "is changed beyond conception."

Lee and Grayson, with Patrick Henry, were to lead the Antifederalists in Virginia. Already, Henry was sending hot messages to Kentucky, letting them know the new system would cater to the East, not the West. By this Constitution, Henry claimed, Kentucky would lose the free navigation of the Mississippi, which would be turned over to Spain. It was a telling argument, at once plausible and rabble-rousing. The new government was planning, said Henry, to set up an established religion. Moreover, the benefits promised were delusive. And what was this language which said "*We, the people,* instead of *We, the states?*" "Mr. Henry," Madison told Jefferson, "is the great adversary who will render the event precarious. He is I find with his usual address, working up every possible interest into a spirit of opposition."

The Antifederalists had powerful leaders. Even Washington admitted it: in New York the Clintonians, with Melancton Smith the congressman, most skillful of Hamilton's opponents; also Lansing, Yates, and Marinus Willett, once a renowned Son of Liberty, to whom the Continental Congress had presented "an elegant sword," for bravery in battle. Then too there was General John Lamb, once known to the Revolutionary Army as the "restless genius." Fearful of the presidential power and tired of hearing about the virtues of "our illustrious chief, this Cincinnatus who laid down his laurels and returned to the plow," Lamb admitted it was well enough about General Washington. But what of *General Slushington,* who might succeed him?

Down in Maryland, Luther Martin loosed his customary stream of invective, mixed with shrewdness and supported by such men as William Paca, signer of the Declaration and already three times governor of his state, also the stormy Samuel Chase, one day to be impeached as Justice of the United States Supreme Court. Chase wrote to the newspapers urging caution, a more deliberate consideration. The people of Maryland must not be surprised into any public measure. They must hear both sides.

In Massachusetts, those old patriots Samuel Adams, James Winthrop and General James Warren were Antifederalists by instinct; their very bloodlines ran against consolidation. Together with congressmen Nathan Dane and Benjamin Austin, they made a formidable phalanx. (Somebody said Dane was a born insurrectionist and should have been named Jack Cade.) But it was Virginia that boasted the most impressive Antifederal contingent, a strong combination of planter aristocracy and the Kentucky frontier, with George Mason, Patrick Henry, the colonels Grayson and Lee; Benjamin Harrison, who had been governor; and James Monroe, humbly born, not yet thirty, but who at eighteen had enlisted in the Continental Army, fought at Harlem, White Plains and Trenton, and was destined to serve as fifth President of the United States. "I am truly sorry," wrote Madison to Archibald Stuart from New York, "to find so many respectable names on your list of adversaries to the Federal Constitution."

Signers of the Declaration, state governors, judges of the superior courts, a future President — no one could say the Antifederalists were led by mere demagogues or petty local politicians, though in certain states, as New York, Pennsylvania, Maryland, Virginia and Massachusetts, there was to be much of faction in the fight, with state politics calling the tune. But the Federalists held the advantage of a definite program, affirmative and daring. The Antifederalists on the other hand were open to the charge of being disgruntled patriots, onetime leaders of the Revolution, restless at seeing themselves pushed aside by "the Conventioners and their new system." The Antifederalists at this early stage were thought to have numbers on their side almost overwhelmingly. Citizens who had never seen the Constitution or never heard it discussed could not very well be Constitutionalists, and this included a large part of the country.

Antifederalists worked on the people's fears; they viewed

with alarm, harped on the novelty, the experimental nature of the program. As Davie of North Carolina said, "It is much easier to alarm people than to inform them." In this matter, fear was close to the surface, easily aroused. The back country feared the seaboard, and the seaboard was responsible for the Constitution. Southerners feared the commercial power and ambition of the "Northern Hive." Give Northern states and Northern cities the reins and they would undertake to drive the nation! Farmers everywhere hated the cities, as farmers have done forever. Antifederalists played upon this hatred. Patrick Henry was to speak of "the tyranny of Philadelphia," which he likened to "the tyranny of George III. . . . I believe," Henry said, that under the Constitution "this similitude will be incontestably proved."

There was fear of the Vice Presidency — "a dangerous and useless office." The notion of a Federal City — the "ten miles square" — was sure bait for panic. A Baptist preacher in North Carolina, candidate for his state ratification convention, told a meeting of frontier parishioners that the Federal City would be "walled in or fortified. Here an army of 50,000 or perhaps 100,000 men will be finally embodied and will sally forth and enslave the people, who will be gradually disarmed." As for a national army, the prospect was not only terrifying but offensive, running counter, said Antifederalists, to every principle of the Republic.

And the Constitution included no bill of rights. Citizens came back to it repeatedly, though months would pass before Massachusetts showed the way to achieve such amendments by recommendation rather than by rejecting the Constitution. Beyond this signal and extraordinary lack of a bill of rights, Antifederalists saw a plot. Had not the Convention insisted on secrecy throughout four entire months? "The evil genius of darkness presided at the Constitution's birth. It came forth under the veil of mystery."

The loudest outcry was directed against federal power of taxation. How were these monies to be gathered in? By *Continental tax collectors*, with bayonet and sword? The states should tax themselves, said Antifederalists. And if in the end the government were allowed to tax the states, it should be done only after requisition was tried, as under the Articles of Confederation.

The Federalists had already met these arguments and were ready with their replies. The Convention in Philadelphia had been a forum, a college in preparation for this larger debate. Benjamin Franklin in his wisdom knew it. "To get the bad customs of a country changed," he wrote, "and new ones, though better, introduced, it is necessary first to remove the prejudices of the people, enlighten their ignorance, and convince them that their interests will be promoted by the proposed changes; and this is not the work of a day."

The first reaction, and, as it proved, the most violent, showed itself in Pennsylvania. On September eighteenth, a Convention delegate, Thomas Mifflin of Philadelphia, read the new Constitution aloud to the legislature (the Assembly) in the State House.

From the first word of Article I, it was plain the document controverted everything that Pennsylvania's own radical Constitution (of '76) stood for, such as a one-chamber legislature, annual elections, a President chosen by the legislature. These were "popular" features and no mistake. For eleven years, the Pennsylvania constitution had been the focus of intense party dispute, mass meetings, riots and upheavals that had almost the aspect of civil war. George Bryan, Irishman, friend of Sam Adams, led the radical element with his colleagues Matlack and Cannon, though Dr. Franklin himself presided over the Assembly.

Since July there had been rumors that the new Constitution included features which would altogether overset the Pennsylvania system. Yet when, on September twenty-eighth, George Clymer (a Convention delegate) rose in his place to propose a series of resolves in favor of a state convention for ratification, the Assembly showed itself not only surprised but dismayed. Why the haste, why the hurry? demanded back-country members: Smilie of Fayette County; Robert Whitehill, whose farm lay on the far side of the Susquehanna near Harrisburg; Findley of Fayette, who had declined election to the Federal Convention because delegates were not paid and he could not, he said, afford to leave his farm. Findley was much respected in the party. He had the aspect of a frontiersman, with his hard-bitten face and shaggy brows; long dark hair fell to his coat collar. Outside the city, said Whitehill, not one Pennsylvanian in twenty knew anything about the new Constitution.

Nothing had been heard from Congress in New York. Who knew if Congress so much as approved the system? The Assembly was due to adjourn tomorrow, a Saturday, at noon. A general election was coming in November. Why not wait and let the new legislature discuss whether or not a convention should be held?

This of course was dead against Federalist strategy: delay might allow the opposition to elect an Antifederalist Assembly. Amid much confusion the final question was put off until four that afternoon. But when four o'clock came the Assembly found itself short of a quorum. Nineteen Antifederalists had stayed away. The sergeant at arms, dispatched to find them, came back to report the members were locked in their lodgings in "Mr. Boyd's house on Sixth Street," and refused to budge.

That night, crowds surged through the city, the taverns were full of noisy partisans on both sides. From subsequent reports of these activities, it is hard to distinguish who was on which side and why, though Philadelphia artisans and mechanics were for the Constitution because it would improve trade with Europe. Early on Saturday morning, September twenty-ninth, a mob hurled stones through Boyd's windows, broke in the door, seized two assemblymen and carried them, fighting, to the State House, where they were thrust down in their seats, with clothes torn and faces — said one account — "white with rage." A quorum being thus achieved, it was decided, amidst approval from the gallery, that seated members who had answered to their names were a legitimate part of the House, no matter how they got there. Smilie of Fayette objected to the applause and laughter from spectators. "This is not the voice of the people," he said.

Very likely he was right, if "the people" meant farmers, inland dwellers. The question was put and the vote taken concerning a ratification convention, to convene November twenty-first in Philadelphia. It passed, forty-five to two. The seventeen absentees must have regretted that their dissent would not be registered.

With a ratification convention in the near future, the two sides were busier than ever in Pennsylvania. CENTINEL launched his series in the *Gazetteer*. "Citizens!" he said. "You have the peculiar felicity of living under the most perfect system of local government in the world. Suffer it not to be wrested from you — the inevitable consequence of the new Constitution." Were Pennsylvania freemen, asked CENTINEL, to let themselves be subjected "to the supremacy of the *lordly and profligate few*"? Was Pennsylvania infatuated by *the splendor of names*, the fatal glare and fascination of the words *Franklin, Washington?* CENTINEL even hinted that Franklin was senile and Washington a bit silly. With "Machiavellian art and consummate cunning the conspirators have practised upon our *illustrious chief*." Mr. John Adams, too, had deceived the public with his book, which proposed a Senate composed of "the better sort, the well-born." * JOHN HUMBLE, in the *Gazetteer*, confidently informed the public that the United States contained six hundred wellborn and three million lowborn. In newspaper offices the italic type faces must have been worn at the edges. *"James the Caledonian,"* wrote CENTINEL; *"Robert Morris* the Cofferer with his aide-de-camp, *Gouvero*, assisted by the deranged brain of *Publius*, a *New-York* writer."

New York, used as an adjective, is always opprobrious in Philadelphia. "Very bold and menacing language," commented Madison. The struggle continued; a large part of Pennsylvania seemed involved. James Wilson made a masterly address in the State House yard; it was printed and widely disseminated. Wilson spoke plainly, directly, indulging in no "Wilsonian oratory," as they called it in New England. Do not fear a baneful aristocracy in the Senate, Wilson said. Remember that body can pass no law without the consent of the House of Representatives. Moreover, the Senate is fettered by the presidential negative. Nor need citizens be afraid the general government aims to "reduce the state governments to mere corporations and eventually to annihilate them." On the contrary, the general government would depend for its very existence upon the state governments, as was shown by the method settled upon for electing both Houses. As for the much-dreaded federal power of taxation — how else could that body provide for the general safety, support the dignity of the Union, and discharge its debts?

That the Constitution should meet with opposition was in no

---

* What Adams's *Defence* had actually urged was that "the rich, the wellborn and the able" be controlled by placing them "by themselves in a senate — to all intents an ostracism.

way unexpected, Wilson said. "It is the nature of man to pursue his own interest, and I do not mean to make any personal reflection when I say that it is the interest of a very numerous, powerful and respectable body" (Wilson meant the Pennsylvania Assembly) "to counteract and destroy the excellent work done by the late Convention . . . Every person who either enjoys or expects to enjoy a place of profit under the present establishment will object to the proposed innovation — not, in truth, because it is injurious to the liberties of his country, but because it affects his schemes of wealth and consequence."

This was plain speaking indeed. But the people listened, heard Wilson out. One cannot but admire their patience, the willingness of citizens to learn, ascertain the truth about this new government. Never had so educational a debate been sustained in America, though the shafts on both sides were bitter and often far from just. It was suggested at one point that if Antifederalists did not like their name, let them be called Shaysites; the Federalists could be called Washingtonians.

On November thirtieth the Pennsylvania convention for ratification met in the State House and sat for five weeks. Day after day, James Wilson was on his feet, tireless, astute, answering the honorable gentleman from Westmoreland County, the honorable gentleman from Fayette. The more effectual Wilson showed himself, the more the opposition hated him. *James de Caledonia* was proud, they said, and carried himself like an aristocrat. PLAIN TRUTH retorted, via the *Gazetteer*, that a man in spectacles has to hold his head up, in order to see through the glasses and keep them from falling off his nose. As the weeks wore on, Wilson from time to time abandoned his customary logic to tell movingly of the difficulties that had beset the Federal Convention, how on some days "the great and interesting work seemed to be at a stand, at another it proceeded with energy and rapidity." In the end, "many members beheld it with wonder and admiration." There was a new liberty in the air! Wilson told his fellow citizens; he would call it, he said, "federal liberty."

Dr. Benjamin Rush worked hard at these meetings. So did Justice McKean (both of them signers of the Declaration). McKean had a rough wit which he used with effect. The arguments of

Antifederalists, he said, made a sound like the working of small beer; their fears were chimerical: "If the sky falls we shall catch larks, if the rivers run dry we shall catch eels."

On December twelfth, Pennsylvania ratified the Constitution by a vote of forty-six to twenty-three. The opposition lacked neither fervor nor conviction, but the Federalists had been too much for them. Yet with ratification, the Pennsylvania Antifederalists lost none of their anger, their agitation. On December twenty-seventh, an outdoor rally was held at Carlisle, to celebrate the Constitution. There was a bonfire, and speeches. A mob of Antifeds (now so called), armed with clubs, rushed toward the fire and attacked James Wilson. When Wilson fought back they knocked him down and began to beat him as he lay. He would have been killed, it was said, had not an old soldier thrown himself on Wilson's body and taken the blows.

In spite of haste, Pennsylvania did not achieve the honor of being the first state to ratify. Little Delaware ratified with a unanimous vote on December sixth, by which time Pennsylvania's vote was fairly sure. New Jersey followed ten days later, also unanimously. It was generally conceded that with Pennsylvania in the Union, these small states could do no less. Georgia came next, on January second — a region which had never been looked on by Federalists as a hazard. "If a weak State," Washington had written, "with the Indians on its back and the Spaniards on its flank does not see the necessity of a General Government, there must I think be wickedness or insanity in the way."

A few days after Georgia's capitulation, Connecticut came along with a vote of one hundred and twenty-eight to forty-two. Caught between large states, Connecticut had little choice. In her list of delegates she lived up to her Congregational reputation: eighty names came straight out of the Old Testament. From Aaron to Zebulon the roll call ranged, solemn and resounding: Abraham and Abijah, Amos and Asaph; Eli, Eliphalet, Eleazer, Apaphras; Gideon, Isaac, Jabez; Jeremiah and Joshua and Jedidiah; Nehemiah, Moses, Lemuel, Ichabod, Daniel; Seth and Solomon and Selah: in Connecticut the clergy were very influential. Oliver Ellsworth knew his audience and took his allegories from

Scripture, pointing out the Canaanitish nations, which by their situation were rendered easy prey. And what was to defend Connecticut "from the rapacity and ambition of New York, when she has spread over that vast territory which she claims and holds? . . . On our other side there is a large and powerful state. Have we not already begun to be tributaries? If we do not . . . unite, shall we not be like Issachar of old, a strong ass crouching down between two burdens? New Jersey and Delaware have seen this, and have adopted the Constitution unanimously."

Roger Sherman too had done his work, addressing his church-going neighbors with characteristic plainness in the *New Haven Gazette:* "You do not hate to read newspaper essays on the new constitution more than I hate to write them. Then we will be short . . . which I have often found the best expression in a dull sermon, except the last."

After Connecticut the next arena was to be the great and powerful Commonwealth of Massachusetts, which scheduled her convention for January 9, 1788, with the largest delegation of all, thirteen counties represented and the western farmers primed for opposition to the "despotism" of Boston merchants. Virginia had put off her convention till May, New York until July. Rhode Island had no intention of holding a convention — certainly not until twelve states had made their decision.

The nation prepared its delegations, while pens and voices continued busy in the cause. "Much will depend upon literary abilities," Washington had said. "The recommendation by good pens should be *openly*, I mean publickly, afforded in the Gazettes." The General need not have troubled. The newspapers were flooded. The *Boston Daily Advertiser*, pleased at the situation, urged both sides to battle:

> Come on brother scribblers, 'tis idle to lag!
> The Convention has let the cat out of the bag.

"The Constitution," Madison wrote to Jefferson on December ninth, "engrosses almost the whole political attention of America." Very early, Washington had sent Jefferson a copy of the Constitution. Madison did the same, dispatching with it a tremendous letter, describing in detail the work of the Federal Convention. It was "impossible," Madison said, "to consider the degree of concord which ultimately prevailed as less than a miracle."

Jefferson replied at once. "I like much the idea of framing a government which should go on of itself peaceably," he said, "without needing a continual recurrence to the state legislatures. I like the organization of the government into Legislative, Judiciary and Executive. . . . I will now add what I do not like. First, the omission of a bill of rights. . . ."

This was in December. In February, Jefferson wrote Madison that he wished "the 9 first conventions may receive, and the last 4 reject [the Constitution]. The former will secure it finally, while the latter will oblige them to offer a declaration of rights in order to complete the union. We shall thus have all its good, and cure its principal defects . . ."

There was in Jefferson a wonderful perversity, a flexibility that brought his enemies to angry frustration. The wish he expressed to Madison proved prophetic, though the dissident states were to achieve their Bill of Rights short of rejecting the Constitution. Before very long, Jefferson began to show approval of the Constitution, even enthusiasm. "It is a good canvas," he wrote, "on which some strokes only want retouching. . . . The operations which have taken place in America lately, fill me with pleasure. . . . The example of changing a constitution, by assembling the wise men of the State, instead of assembling armies, will be worth as much to the world as former examples we have given them. The Constitution . . . is unquestionably the wisest ever yet presented to men."

As for John Adams, when American newspapers reached London, announcing that Congress had approved the Constitution, he sat down and wrote joyfully to Jefferson: "As we say at sea, huzza for the new world and farewell to the old one!" To Rufus King, just after Christmas, Adams declared the new Constitution was, "if not the greatest exertion of human understanding, the greatest single effort of national deliberation that the world has ever seen." Adams argued with Jefferson. "We agree perfectly," he wrote, "that the many should have a full fair and perfect representation. You are apprehensive of monarchy: I, of aristocracy.

You are apprehensive the President when once chosen, will be chosen again and again as long as he lives. So much the better, it appears to me."

Of all the letter-writers, none was more assiduous than Washington. Even before he left Philadelphia in September, the General had sent the Constitution to Lafayette. "If it be good," he wrote, "I suppose it will work its way. . . . If bad it will recoil on the framers." And scarcely had he set foot in Mount Vernon when the General was writing to Patrick Henry, tactfully, persuasively. "I wish the Constitution . . . had been made more perfect. But I sincerely believe it is the best that could be obtained at this time . . . it appears to me that the political concerns of this country are in a manner suspended by a thread . . . and, if nothing had been agreed on by the Convention, anarchy would soon have ensued."

Patrick Henry wrote back in words milder than milk, far different from the heated missives he dispatched to other parts of the country. Federalists and Antifederalists reported to the Chief. Randolph tried to explain his position. George Mason sent his objections, which Washington forwarded to Madison, who in turn wrote back that Mason's reasons should have been urged earlier, at the Federal Convention, or not at all. Mount Vernon on its quiet river bluff seemed indeed the heart and focus of the struggle. And the country knew this, showed it in a hundred small homely ways. The *Pennsylvania Packet*, even before it printed the Constitution, had carried on its front page Charles Willson Peale's advertisement of a mezzotint depicting "His Excellency . . . in a neat oval frame (the inner frame gilt)." Peale must have made a good thing of it; there were citizens ready to support the Constitution, sight unseen, because Washington had helped to write it.

Gouverneur Morris wrote buoyantly to Mount Vernon — more so than the occasion warranted. Eastward of New York, he said, the states could be relied on to support the Constitution; "for I make no account," said Morris, "of the dissension in Rhode Island." But Washington remained anxious, alert, by no means confident of a favorable outcome. Madison too was apprehensive. As the winter progressed it seemed to him the quarrel went deeper than mere disagreement as to certain clauses, or the necessity of a bill of rights. "I have for some time been persuaded," Madison wrote to Edmund Pendleton in February, "that the question on which the proposed Constitution must turn, is the simple one: whether the Union shall or shall not be continued. There is, in my opinion, no middle ground to be taken. The opposition, with some, has disunion, assuredly, for its object; and with all, for its real tendency."

Benjamin Franklin, very old, detached, philosophical, observed proceedings around the country, including the riots in his own Pennsylvania. Then he wrote to friends in Europe. "I send you," he said, "the proposed new federal Constitution for these states. I was engaged four months of the last summer in the Convention that formed it. . . . If it succeeds, I do not see why you might not in Europe carry the project of good Henry the Fourth into execution, by forming a Federal Union and one grand republic of all its different states and kingdoms; by means of a like Convention; for we had many interests to reconcile."

Beyond the interests to reconcile, striking deeper than commercial dislocation or debates on imposts and excises — beyond the pocket and the purse, the country felt this struggle. If there was envy from state to state there was another feeling — pride, the growing notion that this new Constitution of government carried with it something of meaning for America and perhaps even for the world.

It was at this time that St. John Crèvecoeur, settled in New York, wrote to Jefferson that if the Constitution failed, he would try to leave the country. "Old as I am I could even fight for the admission of this new federal government — now or never."

# XXIV

*Massachusetts. The people speak.*

> Mr. President, . . . I beg your leave to say a few
> words to my brother plow joggers in this house.
> JONATHAN SMITH *of Berkshire County,*
> *in the Massachusetts Convention*

THREE hundred and fifty-five delegates met in the Brattle Street Church, Boston; the gallery was crowded with spectators. The convention had tried the State House but found it too small. Throughout a month of meetings there were prayers every morning. Samuel Adams, a delegate, saw to that. John Hancock, governor of the state, was elected president of the convention. Like Sam Adams, Hancock remained enormously powerful in Massachusetts, "heart and soul opposed" to the Constitution, wrote a delegate. But Hancock stayed away from the convention, giving for excuse his usual convenient attack of gout. Notoriously avid of popularity, the Governor wished to time his appearance to that moment when the vote would be sure and the issue certain.

The Commonwealth was considered predominantly Antifederalist. Citizens reared in the town-meeting tradition despised all delegated authority. And the new Constitution was a government of representatives, some of whom (the senators) were to sit for six years — anathema to the democratic spirit, which looked on annual elections as the basis of liberty. Election of delegates to the convention had shown solid Federalist majorities in the coastal counties of Sussex, Essex, Plymouth and Barnstable. The inland counties were Antifederalist, especially Worcester, also Hampshire and Berkshire to the west, where the skies had not yet cleared after Captain Shays and his little army of rebels. The Massachusetts convention numbered, indeed, twenty-nine men who had fought with Shays, some of them officers. Among delegates the captains were as numerous as the colonels and esquires would be in the Virginia convention, later on.

To these plain captains and inland farmers, any praise of the Constitution from the wellborn was enough to damn it. Antifederalist writers had been sounding off all autumn in their newspapers against "the hideous daemon of aristocracy . . . the NOBLE order of Cincinnatus, holders of public securities, bankers and lawyers, who were for having the people gulp down the gilded pill blindfolded." The Province of Maine, greatly desiring independent statehood, feared the new Constitution would prevent her separation from Massachusetts. Out in Berkshire County, farmers believed that the ballot box, an old hat, had been stuffed in favor of Federalist candidates. "We wish for nothing," wrote a Berkshireman in his own ingenious orthography, "but a firm Stable inirgetick Government both Federal and State . . . but when we see a certain Set of Men among us not only ravenously Greedy to Swallow the new Fedderal Constitution them Selves but making the greatest exertions to ram it down the Throats of others without giving them time to taste it . . . it is to us truly alarming."

Elbridge Gerry, who might have been a useful spokesman for the Antifederalists, was not elected to the convention; he came from Boston, a Federalist district. Gerry had presented his list of objections to the Massachusetts legislature in October; they had been greatly influential. "*Damn him — damn him!*" a Cambridge Federalist wrote to General Knox. "Every thing looked well and had the most favorable appearance in this state, previous to this — and now I have my doubts." By invitation, Gerry attended the Massachusetts convention to answer questions *ex officio* — an unsuccessful maneuver; the Convention was not half through when Gerry "left in dudgeon," a delegate reported to Washington. But Rufus King sat, and Nathaniel Gorham and Caleb Strong. Together with ex-Governor Bowdoin, Judge Dana and the brilliant lawyer Theophilus Parsons, they made a powerful Federalist bloc. As Gorham wrote to Madison, the convention included "three judges of the supreme court, fifteen members of the [Massachusetts] senate, twenty from among the most respectable of the clergy, ten or twelve of the first characters at the bar, judges of probate, high sheriffs of counties."

The opposition was numerous and fervent; it is said they had a majority of two hundred and one, as the convention opened. But compared with the Constitutionalists they were ill managed, excitable, wordy. Federalists, profiting by experience, treated their opponents with noticeable respect; every man had his say. Maine had sent a truly oratorical delegation: General Thompson, known for his obstinacy and his flowery periods; Samuel Nason, a saddler and storekeeper from the Sebago Lake district, who had nearly missed coming to the convention, his town having at first decided against sending a delegate. But Nason — as a neighbor wrote later — "come down full charged with Gass and Stirred up a 2nd Meeting and procured himself Elected, and I presume will go up charged like a Baloon."

Dr. Taylor of Worcester, Nason and William Widgery of Maine were designated by Rufus King as "the champions of our opponents." Wigdery was to be especially eloquent concerning the despised Section 8 of Article I — that Congress *"shall have Power To lay and collect Taxes, Duties, Imposts and Excises."* "Who, sir," demanded Widgery, "is to pay the debts of the yeomanry and others? All we hear is that the merchant and farmer will flourish, and that the mechanics and tradesmen are to make their fortunes directly, if the Constitution goes down. Sir, when oil will quench fire, I will believe all this, and not till then. . . . Is the seat of government to be carried to Philadelphia? . . . Some gentlemen have given out that we are surrounded by enemies, that we owe debts, and that the nations will make war against us and take our shipping. Sir, I ask, is this a fact?"

It was hard for country members. How could they know truth from rumor, how argue against men who had sat in the Federal Convention, or against experienced politicians like Rufus King, George Cabot, Fisher Ames, the judges Dana and Sumner? Samuel Adams remained quiet, biding his time. Delegates were sharp with each other, even more outspoken than they had been at Philadelphia, though personal altercation at no time rose to the heights it would attain in Virginia and New York. The opposition argued that Congress "with the purse-strings in its hands would use the sword with a vengeance." William Widgery feared that Congress would withhold its journals, keeping the people in ignorance of its doings.

But for the most part the farmers, the captains and the '75 men based their arguments on generalities, "first principles"; they said this new Constitution endangered their freedoms. "Britain never tried to enslave us until she told us we had too much liberty. The Confederation wants amendments; shall we not amend it?" Or they launched into resounding double periods, reverting to the good old days. "Had I a voice like Jove," said Nason of Maine, "I would proclaim it throughout the world — and had I an arm like Jove I would hurl from the world those villains that would attempt to establish in our country a standing army! I wish, sir, that gentlemen of Boston would bring to their minds the fatal evening of the 5th of March, 1770, when by standing troops they lost five of their fellow-townsmen. I will ask them, what price can atone for their lives? . . . Sir, we had patriots then who alarmed us of our danger, who showed us the serpent and bade us beware of it. Shall I name them? I cannot avoid it. . . . We had a Hancock, an Adams, and a Warren."

There was no need for the words *Boston Massacre*. The bare date was enough, and it still had power to conjure. Sam Adams had been the hero of that day. It seemed indeed that Antifederalists based their arguments not on political expediency or the need for a balanced government but on morality, Christianity, the being against sin. Why, they demanded, did not the Constitution take a stand against slavery, beyond merely outlawing the trade after 1808? Major Lusk of West Stockbridge described the miseries of the poor African natives, kidnapped and sold for slaves. "O! Washington," exclaimed Thompson of Maine, "what a name he has had. How he has immortalized himself! But he holds those in slavery who have as good a right to be free as he has. He is still for self, and in my opinion, his character has sunk fifty percent." There was indignation at the absence of religious qualification for government officers. One Antifederalist said he "shuddered at the idea that Roman Catholics, papists and pagans might be introduced into office, and that popery and the Inquisition may be established in America." Another declared he desired no rulers who did not believe in God or Christ. "A person cannot be a good man without being a good Christian."

The Federalists were patient, enduring like men who knew their minds and their strategy. As time wore on it seemed the opposition could scarcely bear to hear the Federalists out. When Fisher Ames, Nathaniel Gorham and Cabot of Beverley presented analogies between ancient history and the present state of affairs, Benjamin Randall of Suffolk said this quoting of history was "no more to the purpose than to tell how our forefathers dug clams at Plymouth." Abraham White of Bristol County declared the people ought to be jealous of all rulers; as for himself he "would not trust a flock of Moseses. . . . Suppose the Congress should say that none shall be electors but those worth 50 or 100 pounds sterling. Cannot they do it? Yes . . . they can. And if any lawyer can beat me out of it I will give him ten guineas."

The prime interchange of the convention was instigated by an old Worcester County farmer named Amos Singletry — the first white male child born in his town. Self-taught, with no schooling whatever, Singletry had sat in the state legislature for years. "Mr. President," said Singletry, ". . . some gentlemen have called on them that were on the stage in the beginning of our troubles, in the year 1775. I was one of them. And I say that if anybody had proposed such a Constitution as this in that day, it would have been thrown away at once. It would not have been looked at. . . . Does not this constitution . . . take away all we have — all our property? Does it not lay all taxes, duties, imposts, and excises? And what more have we to give? . . . These lawyers and men of learning, and moneyed men that talk so finely, and gloss over matters so smoothly, to make us poor illiterate people swallow down the pill, expect to get into Congress themselves. They expect to be the managers of this Constitution, and get all the power and all the money into their own hands. And then they will swallow up us little fellows, like the great Leviathan, Mr. President; yes, just as the whale swallowed up Jonah."

The reply was immediate. Jonathan Smith represented Lanesborough, in the Berkshire Hills; his speech comes through clearly, indicative of his manner, slow and quiet. As Smith rises in his place one sees the speaker as sturdy, serious, and fairly young.

"Mr. President," Smith began, "I am a plain man, and get my living by the plow. I am not used to speak in public, but I beg your leave to say a few words to my brother plow joggers in this house. I have lived in a part of the country where I have known the worth of good government by the want of it. There was a black cloud that rose in the east last winter, and spread over the west . . ."

Shays's Rebellion: the words were not pronounced. But immediately, Smith was interrupted, challenged, called to order. Samuel Adams defended him, bidding the convention "let him go on in his own way." After a telling description of the distresses incident upon Shays's uprising, Smith declared the anxiety had been so great that people would have been glad to "snatch at anything that looked like a government," thereby inviting what might well have resulted in a tyranny. "Now, Mr. President," continued Smith, "when I saw this Constitution, I found that it was a cure for these disorders. I got a copy of it, and read it over and over. I had been a member of the Convention to form our own state constitution, and had learnt something of the checks and balances of power, and I found them all there. I did not go to any lawyer, to ask his opinion. We have no lawyer in our town, and we do well enough without. I formed my own opinion, and was pleased with this Constitution."

Here, says the reporter, Smith indicated Singletry. "My honorable old daddy there," Smith continued, "won't think that I expect to be a Congress-man, and swallow up the liberties of the people. I never had any post, nor do I want one. But I don't think worse of the Constitution because lawyers, and men of learning, and moneyed men, are fond of it. I don't suspect that they want to get into Congress, and abuse their power. . . . Some gentlemen think that our liberty and property are not safe in the hands of moneyed men, and men of learning. I am not of that mind.

"Brother farmers, let us suppose a case, now: Suppose you had a farm of fifty acres, and your title was disputed, and there was a farm of five thousand acres joined to you, that belonged to a man of learning, and his title was involved in the same difficulty.

Would you not be glad to have him for your friend, rather than stand alone in the dispute? Well, the case is the same. These lawyers, these moneyed men, these men of learning, are all embarked in the same cause with us, and we must all swim or sink together. And shall we throw the Constitution overboard because it does not please us alike? . . . Some gentlemen say, don't be in a hurry. Take time to consider, and don't take a leap in the dark. I say, Take things in time, gather fruit when it is ripe. There is a time to sow and a time to reap. We sowed our seed when we sent men to the Federal Convention. Now is the harvest. Now is the time to reap the fruit of our labor. And if we don't do it now, I am afraid we shall never have another opportunity."

On January twentieth, Madison, in close touch with events, wrote Washington from New York that the news from Massachusetts "begins to be very ominous." Neither side as yet dared to hazard the final question and the vote. Governor Hancock had not made his appearance. Rufus King told General Washington that "as soon as the majority is exhibited on either side I think his health will suffice him to be abroad."

Nothing could be done without Hancock, and Samuel Adams knew it. Years ago, it had been Adams who brought the rich young Hancock into the Liberty Party. They had enjoyed an uneasy friendship ever since, punctuated with periods of open political enmity; during Shays's Rebellion Adams had supported Governor Bowdoin's strong military measures against the insurgents. But now Adams was ready to vote for the Constitution and to bring Hancock round, provided certain amendments were offered. Several prominent Federalists, almost in despair of success, composed a series of these amendments to be presented to the convention, not as a condition for ratification but as recommendations to Congress. There were nine amendments and they were by no means a bill of rights, being concerned rather with limiting the federal power of taxation, limiting the federal power over elections and making sure that Congress could "erect no company of merchants with exclusive advantages of commerce."

But no matter what the amendments offered (and only one of them became part of the final Bill of Rights), as strategy they were brilliant — the opening wedge, first use of an expedient that was to win the consent of Antifederalists in many states.

It was decided that Hancock should be the man to present these amendments to the convention. (Sam Adams entitled them the "Conciliatory Proposition.") Theophilus Parsons wrote a speech of presentation, and with Adams, Sedgwick and others, called upon Hancock at his splendid house on Beacon Hill, where he received them with his legs swathed in flannel bandages. By flattery and bargain the Governor was brought round. Former Bowdoin supporters were guaranteed to Hancock at the next gubernatorial election. Moreover, in the quite likely event that Virginia refused ratification, Hancock would be nominated by Massachusetts as first President of the United States. (It was said that Hancock had never recovered from losing the position of Commander in Chief to Washington in 1775.) "Hancock," wrote Madison to Jefferson, "is weak, ambitious, a courtier of popularity, given to low intrigue, and lately reunited by a factious friendship with Samuel Adams."

On January thirtieth, Hancock permitted himself a dramatic entry into the convention. In full view of the floor and "a vast many people attending in the galleries," the Governor was carried up the aisle to the chair, his feet still wrapped in bandages. He read — as though having written it himself — Parsons's speech with the "Conciliatory Proposition." A motion was made for its acceptance, seconded by Adams, who said that though he had earlier declared his doubts about the Constitution, his mind had been eased by His Excellency's Conciliatory Proposition; he felt the amendments would do the same for the convention and "the people without doors. A proposal of this sort, coming from Massachusetts . . . will have its weight. It is of the greatest importance that America should still be united in sentiment."

On that day and for six ensuing days, Hancock's Proposition was debated. Antifederalists at first declared the Massachusetts convention had no right to suggest amendments; these were beyond their sphere. Some gentlemen might vote for them — he "would not say Judases." (This from General Thompson.) On February fifth the Antifederalist ranks broke, when William Symmes, the bright young Andover lawyer, capitulated, in spite of contrary instructions from his constituents. His hand on his breast, Symmes said he stood acquitted in his conscience for what he was about to do; he hoped and trusted his constituents would acquit him also. (They did not. The reaction of his neighbors proved so violent that Symmes was forced to move away from Andover.) Barrell of Maine spoke too. He said he felt shame to speak in the presence of such giants of rhetoric, yet he knew that his constituents expected something more from him than a merely silent vote. He would wish this Constitution had not been hurried on, "like the driving of Jehu," and gave in detail eight reasons for his Antifederalist stand. He greatly desired an adjournment, that he might have time to go home and present to his constituents the arguments he had heard in convention. Failing that, he was tempted, Barrell said, to risk the displeasure of his country, and adopt the Constitution without their consent.

On that same day, February fifth, Samuel Adams proposed further amendments. Liberty of the press and rights of conscience must be guaranteed, also the prohibition of standing armies and of unreasonable search and seizure. These proposals threw the convention at once into disorder, not because either side disagreed in principle but because Antifederalists believed that if Samuel Adams considered such precautions necessary, it must mean the Constitution provided for a government even more arbitrary than they had feared.

Adams, much chagrined, withdrew his motion. It was time to put the final question: Should the Constitution be adopted, with recommendations for amendments as specified? In their statement to Congress, their preamble, Massachusetts used the ancient, moving words:

> Acknowledging with grateful hearts the goodness of the Supreme Ruler of the Universe in affording the people of the United States . . . an opportunity, deliberately and peaceably, without fraud or surprise, of entering into an explicit and solemn compact with each other, by assenting to and ratifying a new Constitution . . .

The vote was close: one hundred and eighty-seven ayes to one hundred and sixty-eight noes, a margin of only nineteen. Before the Convention broke up, seven more Antifederalists had their say. Fierce old Abraham White led off — he who had sworn he would not trust a flock of Moseses. As the majority had won, said White, he would go home and do his utmost to induce his constituents to live in peace under the new Constitution, and cheerfully submit to it. Widgery of Maine said that although he had opposed adoption he had been overruled by a majority of wise and understanding men. He would try to sow the seeds of union and peace among the people he represented, and endeavor to avert any protests, because he believed this convention to be "as full a representation of the people as can be convened." Now that Massachusetts had adopted the Constitution, Widgery prophesied that "not only nine, but the whole thirteen would come into the measure."

Whitney, Cooley, Nason, Dr. Taylor, Major Swain said much the same, rising one by one with their retractions and their pledges of good faith. They had been fairly beaten, they had "fought like good soldiers," they said. But, beaten, they would "sit down contented, hoping the minority might be disappointed in their fears, and the majority reap the full fruition of the benefit they anticipate . . . cheerfully and heartily they would support the Constitution."

Amid the clamor of bells and the boom of cannon, delegates trooped out of the Brattle Street Church and over to Faneuil Hall, where, said a newspaper, "the toasts given were truly conciliatory, and were, we believe, drank with sincerity by every one present. All appeared to be willing to bury the hatchet of animosity, and smoke the calumet of union and love." Cartoons and pamphlets and poems were distributed in the streets. Massachusetts, confident that her action would lead the nation to ratification, took joy in her achievement. And with some justification; it has since been conceded that if the Constitution had lost in Massachusetts, it would never have been ratified.

To the tune of Yankee Doodle, Boston citizens sang their convention ballad:

> The 'Vention did in Boston meet,
> The State House could not hold 'em,
> So then they went to Fed'ral Street,
> And there the truth was told 'em. . . .

And ev'ry morning went to prayer,
And then began disputing,
Till oppositions silenced were,
By arguments refuting.

Then 'Squire Hancock like a man,
Who dearly loved the nation,
By a conciliatory plan,
Prevented much vexation.

He made a woundy Fed'ral speech,
With sense and elocution;
And then the 'Vention did beseech
T'adopt the Constitution.

.  .  .  .  .  .  .  .  .  .  .  .  .  .  .  .  ●

Now politicians of all kinds,
Who are not yet decided,
May see how Yankees speak their minds,
And yet are not divided.

So here I end my Fed'ral song,
Composed of thirteen verses;
May agriculture flourish long
And commerce fill our purses!

# XXV

## Virginia and New York. The federal procession.

The plot thickens fast. A few short weeks will determine the political fate of America.

WASHINGTON TO LAFAYETTE, *May 28, 1788*

WITH Massachusetts, six states had ratified. Maryland came along in April, with a vote of sixty-three to eleven. Thirteen amendments were appended, after the example set by Massachusetts. But Maryland added a protest, signed by twelve delegates, among them Luther Martin. "We consider," it said, "the proposed form of government very defective, and that the liberty and happiness of the people will be endangered if the system be not greatly changed and altered."

Late in May, South Carolina ratified, one hundred and forty-nine to forty-six. Their convention list shows solid blocks of aye voters from the seaboard and nays from outlying counties whose names are eloquent of their remoteness and the unsettled condition of the country: the "Lower Districts betwen Broad and Saluda Rivers"; the "District called the New Acquisition."

Virginia Antifederalists were disappointed; they had hoped for support from South Carolina. New Hampshire, next in order, had difficulty deciding. If she voted aye, the Constitution won a majority of nine. "The delay in our blacksliding State," wrote Nicholas Gilman to the president of New Hampshire, "has rendered [adoption] much more doubtful in my mind than . . . at any period since the completion of the plan." New Hampshire debated, adjourned without voting, then met again and on June twenty-first decided for the Constitution, fifty-seven to forty-six. Only one speech has come down to us. Joshua Atherton of Amherst delivered himself against the abomination of the slave traffic and the fact that the Constitution did not outlaw it. Imagine, he said, the situation reversed! Suppose "these man-stealers" making a landing on the New Hampshire coast, proceeding inland and carrying off to Africa "the whole or a part of the inhabitants of the town of Exeter. Bedewed with tears of anguish . . . brother is cleft from brother, sister from sister. The scene," finished Mr. Atherton brokenly, "is too affecting. I have not fortitude to pursue the subject."

If Antifederalists had not indulged in such flights of oratory, perhaps they might have carried more votes in convention. Always it seemed easy for some hardheaded Federalist to cut down his opponent with a few commonsense suggestions. Why — for instance — should we fear our congressmen? Are they not our own creatures, elected by ourselves? Why must it be assumed that Congress will be more corrupt than the voters who are responsible for sending them to govern? And will not the President as well as the much-dreaded senators be returned to the people, to live among their neighbors and bear their reproaches, should they misconduct themselves in office?

The Constitution continued to make converts in the state conventions. Often enough, Antifederalists seemed relieved to confess they had changed their minds and that further information had calmed their fears and resolved their doubts.

While New Hampshire met and adjourned and delayed, Virginia was holding her convention at Richmond, in the new Academy on Shockoe Hill. The country looked to the Old Dominion, wondering which way she would go. Virginia's territory reached to the Mississippi; it included the District of Kentucky and West Virginia. Her population was a fifth of the population of the entire Union. Should Virginia ratify, she would be the ninth state, or so she thought; New Hampshire's final vote was still three weeks away. If Virginia refused, New York, North Carolina and Rhode Island would doubtless follow her lead.

This was to be the ablest of all the ratification conventions and the best prepared, a gathering studded with stars, with names and faces known throughout the state and beyond — well-speaking gentlemen on both sides, well-dressed, wellborn. More than a fourth were military men; among them James Monroe, Nicholas, Stephen; Bland, Carrington, Cabell; Colonel Grayson, Richard Henry Lee and his cousin Light-Horse Harry of the same name. They had fought the British, they had fought the Indians, and in political conviction they were ranged on both sides.

Washington was not present but remained at Mount Vernon, receiving and sending letters, messages. All that month of June the driveway was busy with express riders. The General had not put himself forward for nomination, nor had it been urged on him by Federalist leaders. His absence did not detract from his influence; the nation knew of his approval. The Honorable Hugh Blair Grigsby, writing an account of the convention while there were delegates still living, puts it down as a simple historical fact that in 1788, neither Washington nor Madison "stood in the estimation of Virginia on the same platform with Patrick Henry and George Mason as statesmen." *

Toward the rear of the hall sat the fourteen Kentuckians, wearing pistols and hangers; to reach here they had ridden through Indian country. The Antifederalist ranks were very strong, led by such men as Mason, Benjamin Harrison, Theodorick Bland, John Tyler (father of the President), the Cabells, Edmund Ruffin, James Monroe, Grayson and Richard Henry Lee. Washington, pondering over their names, said it was "a little strange that the men of large property in the South should be more afraid that the Constitution will produce an aristocracy or a monarchy, than the genuine democratical people of the East." Chief among Antifederalists was Patrick Henry, tall, thin, stooped, and at fifty-two looking on himself as aged and broken in health. He wore spectacles, concealed his reddish-brown hair by a brown wig, not too well-fitting. His blue eye was still keen, his long face alive with feeling; the old magic waited to be called up at will. "I fear that

---

* Grigsby's account of the Virginia convention, in two volumes, is wonderfully vivid. Himself a fervent Antifederalist and a reporter of proven accuracy, Grigsby wrestles in footnotes with the Constitutionalists. "This argument was hardly fair," he says. Or, "An obvious sophism. . . . It was a little prudish to blame the Assembly for doing what they had a right to do."

overwhelming torrent, Patrick Henry," wrote General Knox to Rufus King when the convention was well under way.

From the first day, Henry was the nerve center of the room. "The Henryites," they called his followers. Every Federalist came girded against them. And the Federalist ranks were impressive. One of them, Judge Edmund Pendleton, served as presiding officer. White-haired, painfully crippled, he struggled to his feet on crutches; his hip had been dislocated by a fall from a horse. Pendleton's dress was elegant; his infirmity only added somehow to the dignity of his bearing. "The Confederation did not carry us through the war," he said. "Common danger and the spirit of America did that."

When the convention went into the Committee of the Whole, another Federalist presided. Chancellor Wythe, it will be recalled, had attended the Federal Convention briefly, called home by the illness of his wife. Everybody in Richmond knew him; Wythe had taught law to Madison's father and to Thomas Jefferson; Henry Clay would one day be his pupil. Behind a bald forehead, thick gray hair fell loose to his neck. He wore a single-breasted coat with a standing collar, a white cravat buckled behind. He was a small man and brisk, his carriage erect, graceful.

Madison was present, this time without his notebook. Grigsby describes him with hair powdered, ending in a long queue, "handsomely arrayed in blue and buff. His low stature," says Grigsby, "made it difficult for him to be seen from all parts of the house; his voice was rarely loud enough to be heard throughout the hall. He always rose to speak as if with a view of expressing some thought that had casually occurred to him, with his hat in his hand and his notes in his hat; and the warmest excitement of debate was visible in him only by a more or less rapid and forward see-saw motion of his body." Madison, as always masterful in debate, called the meeting back to earth from the impassioned flights of Henry or Randolph's anxious personal apologia.

Yet of all the Constitution's supporters, George Nicholas of Albermarle County was considered — by Grigsby at least — most formidable to Patrick Henry. Nicholas at thirty-four was an extraordinary figure, short and stout to the point of deformity; a local caricaturist drew him as a plum pudding with legs. Someone remarked that since Sir Nicholas Bacon in Chancery, no lawyer had ever been so fat. Well educated, perfectly self-possessed, Nicholas could keep his audience attentive for two hours at a stretch, his only gesture the right forefinger stabbing.

George Mason came dressed in black silk; on certain days he was to be seen approaching the Academy arm in arm with Patrick Henry, walking from the Swan tavern. James Monroe, Antifederalist, at thirty came almost unknown to this assembly. He was the son of a Scotch carpenter; his demeanor appeared stiff, a little awkward. Monroe's brother-in-law, Beau Dawson, sumptuously dressed and powdered, always the republican, hated a consolidated government. Francis Corbin, a Federalist, was rich, educated in England, with polished manners and the prestige of an ancient name. Colonel James Innes, six feet tall and so heavily built he could not sit in a common chair nor ride an ordinary horse, possessed a voice that blasted through the hall. Yet he was a courteous man, incisive in debate. To settle this new government, he said, "is as important as the revolution which severed us from the British empire."

John Marshall, now in his thirty-third year, was a great strength to the Constitutionalists. Ruddy and handsome, with wild black hair, a piercing dark eye, as a concession to the occasion he had draped his tall frame in a new coat which however had cost but a pound and looked it. The assembly knew Marshall, respected him for his soldierly record in the Revolution and loved him for his sociability — which, says Grigsby primly, at times verged on excess.

With such dramatis personae, the Virginia convention could not lack color. Always, one is conscious of the fourteen Kentuckians, sitting watchful, biding their time. Always, too, one remembers that out of one hundred and seventy members, the barest majority will carry the Constitution. It is a scene romantic, passionate, the very best "theater." Yet all of it is true, factual, and seldom has American history shown a political scene more seriously enacted. Patrick Henry rose and hurled his bolts: "Whither is the spirit of America gone? Whither is the genius of America fled? . . . We drew the spirit of liberty from our British ancestors. But now, Sir, the American spirit, assisted by the ropes and chains of consolidation, is about to convert this country into a powerful and mighty empire. . . . There will be no checks, no real balances, in this government. What can avail your specious, imaginary balances, your rope-dancing, chain-rattling, ridiculous ideal checks and contrivances?"

It was here, or hereabouts, that Mr. Best of Nansemond County, "an intelligent gentleman," says Grigsby, "involuntarily felt his wrists to assure himself that the fetters were not already pressing his flesh. The gallery on which he was sitting seemed to become dark as a dungeon." The true orator's power possessed Patrick Henry. Even Madison confessed himself nonplussed, and said that when Mr. Henry stood up to reply to him, a pause, a shake of the head or a striking gesture would undo an hour's work before a word was uttered. At impassioned moments Henry would raise a hand and twirl his wig two or three times round his head. The galleries were always packed when Henry spoke; once he was on his feet for seven hours: "Who authorizes gentlemen to speak the language of We, the people, instead of We, the states? . . . The people gave them no power to use their name. . . . Even from that illustrious man who saved us by his valor, I would have a reason for this conduct!" Advocates of the Constitution, said Henry, brought forward fears, awful prognostications of evils to come, should the Constitution fail of ratification. Yet had there been a single tumult in Virginia? Where was any disposition in this country to revolt against the dominion of laws?

Colonel Grayson too was skillful with this argument of imaginary Federalist fears, playing upon it: "Pennsylvania and Maryland are to fall upon us from the north like the Goths and Vandals of old . . . the Indians are to invade us from our rear . . . And the Carolinians from the south, mounted on alligators, I presume, are to come and destroy our cornfields and eat up our little children! These, Sir, are the mighty dangers which await us if we reject the Constitution." To Grayson as to Patrick Henry, a consolidated government meant government by force. Genuine self-government could be maintained only by giving Congress the regulation of commerce, and then infusing new strength and spirit into the state legislatures. This, said Grayson, was the proper course to hold "till the American character be marked with some certain

features. We are yet too young to know what we are fit for. . . .
I never heard of two supreme coordinate powers in one and the
same country before. I cannot conceive how it can happen. It sur-
passes every thing that I have read of concerning other governments, or that I can conceive by the utmost exertion of my faculties."

Clause by clause, the Virginians went through the Constitution
. . . A federal bench would swallow up and destroy the state
courts . . . the tax power should not be used by the federal government until requisitions first were tried. "I will never give up
that *darling* word, requisitions," said Henry, and the reporter underlined it. Madison lost patience. In his own state, among his intimate friends, Madison used a different tone, different arguments
than in Philadelphia. There were here strong local loyalties to
combat, and a local feeling, a deep proud provinciality. John Tyler, whose estate, Greenway, lay on the James River, one day declared mournfully that should Constitutionalists prevail, then ships,
as they passed his door on foreign voyages, would carry another
flag than Virginia's — that pennant which in a day of doubt and
dread he had seen when it was first hoisted above the Capitol at
Richmond.

Antifederalists brought up the old argument that the nation was
too big, too widely extended for a central government as proposed: congressmen from New Hampshire would never understand or sympathize with the needs of Virginia or the Carolinas.
Madison replied soothingly, and with a touch of his prophetic gift:
"Let it not be forgotten there is a probability that that ignorance
which is complained of in some parts of America will be continually diminishing. . . . Does not our own experience teach us
that the people are better informed than they were a few years
ago? The citizen of Georgia knows more now of the affairs of
New Hampshire than he did, before the Revolution, of those of
South Carolina. When the representatives from the different states
are collected together . . . they will interchange their knowledge
with one another, and will have the laws of each state on the table."

Madison seemed tired, edgy. Once he interrupted Henry in full
flight, and twice in a single day the reporter wrote that Madison's
voice failed him: "Here Mr. Madison spoke of the distinction be-

tween regulation of police and legislation, but so low he could not be heard. . . . Mr. Madison made several other remarks, which could not be heard." After one strenuous debate, Madison fell ill and went to bed for three days.

The reporter, David Robertson, had been brought in by Constitutionalists — the first time a shorthand man had been employed in Virginia. Antifederalists were suspicious, they said this was a Federalist maneuver. Actually, Robertson was excellent, his reports full and clear. He used the first person singular except when events moved too fast or when he succumbed to emotion; Grigsby says Robertson's face was at times "bedewed with tears." "Here," writes Robertson, "Mr. Henry strongly and pathetically expatiated on the probability of the President's enslaving America, and the horrid consequences that must result." The *Pennsylvania Packet* said Robertson's presence alarmed Henry, "as he wished to speak the language of his soul." Robertson was from Petersburg. But Richmond seemed infested with Northerners. Robert Morris was in town, often seen conferring with Federalist leaders, though in fact he came to collect debts owing him. Eleazer Oswald arrived from Philadelphia, where he published that flaming Antifederalist newspaper the *Independent Gazetteer;* he brought messages of support from the Clintonians. Gouverneur Morris, too, was present.

Among the stars and the patriot orators, it was Edmund Randolph who supplied the prime shock and surprise of the convention. The handsome young Governor was much beloved in his state. The great part he had played in Philadelphia was known to many; his refusal to sign the Constitution had become common knowledge; the *Virginia Gazette* in January, 1788, carried a letter with his reasons. But since then, Randolph had begun to waver; already he had been attacked in a newspaper for inconsistency. Yet no one knew for certain what the Governor's final decision would be. Late in April, Washington had told Lafayette that if Randolph supported the Constitution he would "do it feebly." Nor was Madison sure of his colleague; Randolph's county, strongly Antifederalist, had confidently sent him to the convention.

On June fourth, the first day of full debate, the Governor rose and made his declaration. It took him some time to reach his point. Plainly on the defensive, Randolph said he had not come hither to apologize. . . . He was not a candidate for popularity. . . . If the Constitution were put before him as in Philadelphia — wholly to adopt or wholly to reject — he would again refuse his signature. But Massachusetts had urged amendments to be enacted by Congress *after* full ratification. For himself, he had originally been for *previous* amendments, to be approved by the several states before they ratified. But the postponement of this convention to so late a date made this impossible, "without inevitable ruin to the Union." Eight states had adopted the Constitution; they could not recede. He stood, then, to express his earnest endeavors for a firm, energetic government, and to concur in any practical scheme of amendments. Randolph, in short, was for the Constitution.

From this day on, no matter how it was argued, the base of difference between Federalists and Antifederalists in the Virginia convention would be "previous amendments" or "subsequent amendments" — whether the Constitution should be ratified as it stood, with amendments to be enacted later; or whether new state conventions should be called to alter the document before ratification.

Randolph had spoken convincingly; a convert's argument is always heartfelt. But Patrick Henry had no intention of letting his adversary off without a challenge as to this change of front. The gentleman's alteration of opinion, Henry said, "was very strange and unaccountable. . . . Did he not tell us that he withheld his signature? He was not then led by the illumined, the illustrious few. . . . What alterations have a few months brought about! . . . Something extraordinary must have operated so great a change in his opinions."

Randolph and the convention understood Henry's hints very well, with their implication that Washington's persuasion — or worse, Washington's promise of future favors under the new government — had brought about this change. Much later, when Washington named Randolph as United States Attorney General, Randolph would be at pains to defend himself from this same charge. Furiously, Randolph answered Patrick Henry. He disdained the honorable gentleman's aspersions and insinuations. "If our friendship must fall," said Randolph, "let it fall like Lucifer, never to rise again! . . . He has accused me of inconsistency. . . . Sir, if I do not stand on the bottom of integrity and pure love for Virginia, as much as those who can be most clamorous, I wish to resign my existence."

There was more on both sides, in the best Old Dominion manner. That night, Colonel Cabell, Henry's friend, "waited on Randolph" — Grigsby's phrase — and the affair was fortunately settled, "without a resort to the field." Hereafter, Randolph was superb in debate; even Grigsby admits it. He spoke far better than he had spoken at Philadelphia, forgot personal feuding and gave what was surely the best performance of his life.

On June twenty-fourth, by prearrangement with his supporters, Chancellor Wythe moved a resolution for ratification, with a bill of rights and subsequent amendments, thus forestalling Patrick Henry, who had come to the assembly that day with his own very different resolution to present. Wythe, rising to speak, "looked pale and fatigued," says Grigsby, and so agitated that even those near him could not understand what he said. Patrick Henry, for his part, showed "a fierce humor, strangely mixed with grief and shame." *Subsequent* amendments, Henry said, were a novelty and an absurdity. To enter into a compact of government, and then afterward to settle the terms of this compact was an idea dreadful, abhorrent to his mind. Look at Massachusetts, which had ratified by only nineteen votes! Look at Pennsylvania, where the people were plainly not represented in their convention. If this plan were accepted by the convention, said Henry, he would conceive it his duty to have nothing more to do with the Constitution, and to quit this assembly and go home.

The clerk read aloud Henry's Declaration of Rights and his other amendments; they were nearly the same as the ones ultimately accepted by the convention. But Henry's "previous amendments" implied the calling of new ratification conventions by every state in the Confederacy. Randolph, picking up Henry's final remark about having nothing more to do with the Constitution, rose and accused him of threatening secession. This was a charge which many Federalists believed true, including Madison and Washington. Henry at once denied it. The dissolution of the Union was terrible to his mind, he said.

The day ended with Patrick Henry prophesying the "awful immensity of the dangers with which [the new system] was pregnant" and envisioning "the angels on high, looking down and reviewing America's future." It was at this opportune moment that a thunderstorm arose, the hall grew dark, lightning glared, rain dashed against the windows. Doors slammed, says Grigsby, like a peal of musketry. Men rushed from their seats to the center of the room, and the meeting adjourned.

Only one day of debate remained. The Virginia legislature was due to assemble, and required the Academy hall. For the past week, legislators had been drifting into town, to Madison's alarm. These men claimed closeness to the people; they might misquote their constituents and prejudice things unfavorably. Madison, moreover, believed that Antifederalists wished to spin out the convention until they could hear from the New York convention, or until weary members might adjourn without making any decision.

Each night for the past three weeks, both sides had made careful, detailed estimates of the votes they could count upon, the changes that a day's work might have caused. The fourteen Kentuckians were a source of jealous contention. With the vote running so close, even two of them might turn the tide. Throughout the convention, Patrick Henry had been extremely effectual on the great issue of the Mississippi River, though he was aware, he said, that he had been accused of "scuffling for Kentucky votes." Reminding delegates that only two years ago John Jay had urged Congress to surrender the Mississippi to Spain for a generation, Henry called on members who had been in Congress at the time and demanded that they rise and give the facts of that shameful bargain. Four delegates rose: Madison, Henry Lee, Grayson, Monroe.

Under the new Constitution, Section 8 of Article I authorized Congress "to regulate Commerce with foreign Nations and among the several States." There was danger, here, that navigation of the river might be sacrificed. Henry's picture of the Mississippi Valley, prosperous and happy under a future Confederacy, ruined and deserted under the Constitution, dismayed the assembly. In the end, however, four out of the fourteen Kentuckians voted on the Federalist side.

On Wednesday, June twenty-fifth, Edmund Pendleton, from the chair, ordered Wythe's original motion put to the question. Shortly before the vote was taken, Patrick Henry spoke his last word. If he should find himself in the minority, he would have, he said, those painful sensations which arise from a conviction of being overpowered in a good cause. But he would be a peaceful citizen. "I wish not to go to violence, but will wait with hopes that the spirit which predominated in the Revolution is not yet gone, nor the cause of those who are attached to the Revolution not yet lost. I shall therefore wait in expectation of seeing that government changed, so as to be compatible with the safety, liberty and happiness of the people."

It was generous, it had a touch of magnificence. Randolph spoke next, very briefly, and his last word did not equal Henry's. Randolph spoke solely in self-justification. His part in the Federal Convention, he said, had been inspired by strongest affection for the Union. The objections which he then had to the Constitution still stood. Yet the accession of eight states reduced deliberation to the single question of Union or no Union. Should some future annalist desire to vilify his name, let him state those truths.

The Constitution was now put to the vote, including a Declaration of Rights which contained twenty articles, and subsequent amendments to the same number.* By eighty-nine to seventy-nine the Constitution won. It had been close, very close indeed. That night angry Antifederalists, determined to create measures for resisting the new system, held a mass meeting in Richmond, with Patrick Henry presiding. But Henry told his wrathful colleagues that he had done his best against the Constitution "in

---

* Out of this Declaration of Rights, ten articles would be enacted into law by the first Congress under the Constitution — though in different, briefer phraseology. The twenty amendments would be rejected. One of them provided that no army be kept up in times of peace without the consent of both Houses. One article would have hampered the Supreme Court into virtual powerlessness; one declared that no direct tax could operate in any state if the state had previously collected its own quota.

the proper place [the Convention]." The question, said Henry, was now settled; "as true and faithful republicans you had all better go home."

Henry's admirers claim that he was probably more responsible than any or all others for the adoption of the first ten amendments to the Constitution — the Bill of Rights. And there is no doubt that Henry's part in this went beyond mere rhetorical challenges and thunderbolts. In final form the Constitution was the product of both sides, pro and anti. The opposition's part is difficult to assess, though none can question its value. Even Washington conceded it. "Upon the whole," he wrote, "I doubt whether the opposition to the Constitution will not ultimately be productive of more good than evil; it has called forth, in its defence, abilities which would not perhaps have been otherwise exerted that have thrown new light upon the science of Government, they have given the rights of man a full and fair discussion, and explained them in so clear and forcible a manner, as cannot fail to make a lasting impression."

News of Virginia's capitulation reached Poughkeepsie on July second, when the New York convention had been under way for two weeks. It was a crushing blow. During the winter, the Clintonians had tried to keep in communication with a state from which they had hoped much. Governor Clinton was unanimously elected president of the convention, his able supporters being Robert Yates, John Lansing, Thomas Tredwell. Hero of this opposition was Melancton Smith of Dutchess County, who spoke often and well, with a touch of humor that was appealing. For the Constitutionalists there were John Jay and James Duane. The old names were conspicuous: Roosevelt, Ten Eyck, Van Cortlandt, De Witt. But Alexander Hamilton waged his memorable contest against what seemed truly insuperable odds and numbers. His argument was brilliant, his persistence almost superhuman.

The debate, basically the same as elsewhere, need not be repeated here, though local considerations were especially influential: Constitutionalists harped upon Massachusetts and Pennsylvania, close by, powerful, and now committed to the Union. Should

New York fail to ratify, none remained to keep her company but North Carolina, Rhode Island and Vermont (not yet a state). It was a risk impossible to assume.

On July twenty-sixth, New York ratified by thirty to twenty-seven, a majority of three. Her capitulation was grudging, filled with conditions even beyond a bill of rights and a list of thirty-two subsequent amendments. Lansing moved (and lost) a resolution that New York have the right to withdraw from the Union after a number of years, should her suggested amendments not be previously submitted to a general convention. A circular letter, strongly recommending such a convention, was sent out to all thirteen legislatures.

By August, 1788, eleven states had ratified: Delaware, Pennsylvania, New Jersey, Georgia, Connecticut, Massachusetts, Maryland, South Carolina, New Hampshire, Virginia, New York. Rhode Island and North Carolina would come along in their time. As soon as a majority of nine was assured, state by state held joyful celebration, animosity for the moment forgotten. Perhaps this is endemic to America; once the vote is counted, everybody wants to be in the parade. There was rioting in Albany by Antifederalists, a public burning of the Constitution. Yet in New York City, ten horses had pulled the ship *Hamilton* through the streets — a frigate of thirty-two guns, full-rigged and manned with thirty seamen, "every thing complete and in proportion," a contemporary wrote. Providence, Rhode Island, attempted a Federalist demonstration; it was circumvented when Antifeds, greatly in the majority, advanced upon the scene, forcibly converted the preparations into a July Fourth celebration and helped the Federalists to consume their roasted ox.

The Federal processions were wonderfully ingenious. The ship *Federal Constitution*, the ship *Union*, mounted on wagons, were drawn by horses which bore on their foreheads the names of ratifying states. Philadelphia chose July Fourth for her celebration, and it outdid all the rest. At sunrise a full peal of bells rang out from Christ Church steeple; the ship *Rising Sun*, anchored off Market Street, discharged her cannon in salute to the day. At the wharves all vessels were decorated, and along the harbor from South Street to the Northern Liberties ten ships were ranged, each bearing at its masthead a broad white flag inscribed with the name of a state in gold: *New Hampshire . . . Massachusetts . . . Pennsylvania . . .* A brisk south wind, coming up with the dawn, fluttered the pennants all day.

By eight in the morning the procession was assembling; at nine-thirty it began to move. The First City Troop of Light Dragoons led off, resplendent in their blue coats faced with red, their white saddleclothes edged in blue. After them rode a horseman carrying a flag to symbolize Independence. Next came Thomas Fitzsimons — a member of the Federal Convention — riding Count Rochambeau's steed and bearing a standard with the date of the French Alliance: *Sixth of February, 1778*. Then a horseman carrying a staff twined with olive and laurel, to celebrate the Peace Treaty of 1783; after him a herald with a trumpet, proclaiming a New Era. Next came the Convention of the States, personified by Peter Muhlenberg on horseback; behind him a band of music, playing for dear life a grand march composed for the occasion by Alexander Reinagle.

On they marched, the horses stepping high through streets swept clean for the occasion, under trees neatly trimmed. One rider carried a banner inscribed *Washington, the Friend of his Country*. A big car rumbled by in the shape of an eagle, painted bright blue. On the eagle's breast thirteen stars were emblazoned above thirteen red and white stripes. Six horses drew the vehicle, on which a staff was fixed, holding the Constitution, framed, and crowned with the cap of liberty. Seated within the car, glorious in their robes of office, were Chief Justice McKean and the justices Atlee and Rush.

All along Third Street, up Callowhill to Fourth and west on Market Street went the Grand Procession, a mile and a half of it. Spectators crowded the footways, stood at open windows and on the roofs of the houses, gazing down at the tramping bright lines of marchers. The consuls and representatives of foreign states passed "in an ornamental car drawn by four horses." Barbé-Marbois was among them. . . . A citizen and an Indian chief sat side by side in their carriage, "smoking the Calumet of Peace together — the Sachem's head adorned with scarlet and white plumes, ten strings of wampum round his neck."

But the crowning glory was the Grand Foederal Edifice, set on a carriage drawn by ten white horses. Thirteen Corinthian columns, ten of them complete, three left unfinished, supported the dome. The frieze showed thirteen stars, and surmounting the dome the figure of *Plenty* bore a cornucopia. *In Union the Fabric stands firm*, said a device around the pedestal. Ten gentlemen sat within the Edifice; they represented the citizens at large, to whom the Constitution had been committed for ratification.

Architects and house carpenters followed on foot, to the number of four hundred and fifty; behind them, sawmakers and filecutters with their flag — a gold saw on a pink shield. The Agricultural Society was led by "Samuel Powell, Eq." After him, farmers drove four-ox plows, and a sower spread his seed. . . . The Manufacturing Society, its insignia a beehive, with bees issuing in the rays of a rising sun. The Society's horse-drawn platform was thirty feet long and carried spindles and a carding machine, with women workers drawing cotton, "suitable for blue jeans or federal rib." The float, the whirring machines were viewed "with astonishment and delight." Citizens could soon be clothed in cotton, a new fabric, proper for both winter and summer, and not attractive to moths.

On they came: brickmakers and clockmakers, fringe and ribbon weavers; saddlers and cordwainers; boat builders, sailmakers, ship joiners, ropemakers, carvers, gilders, coopers; blacksmiths and coachmakers, skinners and glovers; goldsmiths and gunsmiths, the brewers and bakers dressed in spotless white; tailors, perukemakers, barber-surgeons and staymakers. "Mr. Francis Serre, with his first journeyman, carried an elegant pair of lady's stays." Watchmen marched, calling the hour: "*Ten* o'clock, and a glorious star-light morning." (This, said the *Pennsylvania Gazette*, meant the ten states that had ratified.)

It was wonderful and heartwarming and edifying, including the ranks of marching clergy, "of almost every denomination, united in charity and brotherly love. A circumstance," added the *Gazette*, "which probably never occurred in such extent." The Federal ship *Union,* on its carriage, mounted twenty guns, "an elegant piece of workmanship," carved and painted, manned by a crew of twenty-five. Boys trimmed sail as the ship moved along; the pilot was received on board, and as the procession approached Union Green — named for the occasion — a sailor threw the lead-line and cast anchor.

Union Green lay at the foot of Bush Hill, Mr. William Hamilton's estate. Here, under awnings, tables had been set out, with a "plentiful cold collation." James Wilson made a speech, after which ten toasts were drunk, in American porter, beer and cider, each toast being announced by a trumpet and answered by a discharge of artillery from the ship *Rising Sun* in the harbor. The crowd drank to "The people of the United States." They toasted "Honor and Immortality to the Members of the late Convention." Lastly, with a large benevolence, they drank to "The Whole Family of Mankind."

By six o'clock it was over. "Seventeen thousand" celebrants *"soberly* retired to their respective homes," said the official account, written by Francis Hopkinson, chairman of the committee of arrangement. Hopkinson had labored mightily, including the composition of an *Ode* in four verses, distributed to the crowd as the procession moved along:

> Hail to this festival! — all hail the day!
> Columbia's standard on her roof display!
> And let the people's motto ever be,
> "United thus, and thus united, free!"

The weather had been cloudy, but toward late afternoon the sun came out, and in the evening, "the sky was illuminated by a beautiful aurora borealis." Afterward, people remarked upon the spectators' silence while the procession passed. Benjamin Rush the Philadelphia physician, signer of the Declaration of Independence, called it a "solemn silence," as though citizens were awed, moved by a joy intense and profound. No victory during the late war, Rush said, had brought such deep-seated happiness to every countenance. The sight of the Federal ship *Union,* "complete in all its parts and moving upon dry land conveyed emotions . . . that cannot be described . . . The union of twelve states in the *form,* and of ten states in the *adoption*, of the Constitution in less than ten months, under the influence of local prejudices, opposite interests, popular arts, and even the threats of bold and desperate men, is a solitary event in the history of mankind.

" 'Tis done," Rush wrote. "We have become a nation."

# Chapter Notes

## CHAPTER FOURTEEN

*Page 175.* The Northwest Ordinance was based on a plan drafted by Jefferson in 1784, before he went to France — a plan which provided for government by the people, direct and immediate, also the admission of new states as equals of the old. It was superseded by the Ordinance of '87, criticized by historians as being far less liberal than Jefferson's plan, playing into the hands of the land companies. Nevertheless the Territory grew and prospered until it became eventually the five states of Ohio, Indiana, Illinois, Michigan, and Wisconsin.

## CHAPTER NINETEEN

*Page 225.* After the Convention rose, Yates and Lansing wrote to Governor Clinton of New York, giving their reasons for quitting Philadelphia. Their letter, a clear expression of the anti-Constitutionalist stand, said in part:

It is with the sincerest concern we observe . . . that we have been reduced to the disagreeable alternative, of either exceeding the power delegated to us, and giving our assent to measures which we conceive destructive to the political happiness of the citizens of the United States, or opposing our opinion to that of a body of respectable men, to whom those citizens had given the most unequivocal proofs of confidence. . . . Thus circumstanced, . . . we gave the principles of the constitution . . our decided and unreserved dissent; but we must candidly confess, that we should have been equally opposed to any system, however modified, which had in object the consolidation of the United States into one government. . . .

We were of the opinion, that the leading feature of every amendment [to the Confederation] ought to be the preservation of the individual states, in their uncontrouled constitutional rights. . . . A general government . . . must unavoidably, in a short time, be productive of the destruction of the civil liberty of such citizens who could be effectively coerced by it . . . the extremities of the United States could not be kept in due submission and obedience to its laws. . . . the expence of supporting it would become intolerably burdensome . . . the interests of a great majority of the inhabitants . . . must necessarily be unknown.

We were not present at the completion of the new constitution; but before we left the convention, its principles were so well established, as to convince us, that no alteration was to be expected, to conform it to our ideas of expedience and safety. . . .

We have the honor to be, With the greatest respect, Your excellency's Most obedient, and Very humble servants,

ROBERT YATES,
JOHN LANSING, JUN.

# The Constitution of the United States*

We the People of the United States, in Order to form a more perfect Union, establish Justice, insure domestic Tranquility, provide for the common defence, promote the general Welfare, and secure the Blessings of Liberty to ourselves and our Posterity, do ordain and establish this Constitution for the United States of America.

## Article. I.

Section. 1. All legislative Powers herein granted shall be vested in a Congress of the United States, which shall consist of a Senate and House of Representatives.

Section. 2. The House of Representatives shall be composed of Members chosen every second Year by the People of the several States, and the Electors in each State shall have <the> Qualifications requisite for Electors of the most numerous Branch of the State Legislature.

No Person shall be a Representative who shall not have attained to the Age of twenty five Years, and been seven Years a Citizen of the United States, and who shall not, when elected, be an Inhabitant of that State in which he shall be chosen.

Representatives and direct Taxes shall be apportioned among the several States which may be included within this Union, according to their respective Numbers, which shall be determined by adding to the whole Number of free Persons, including those bound to Service for a Term of Years, and excluding Indians not taxed, three fifths of all other Persons. The actual Enumeration shall be made within three Years after the first Meeting of the Congress of the United States, and within every subsequent Term of ten Years, in such Manner as they shall by Law direct. The Number of Representatives shall not exceed one for every thirty Thousand, but each State shall have at Least one Representative; and until such enumeration shall be made, the State of New Hampshire shall be entitled to chuse three, Massachusetts eight, Rhode-Island and Providence Plantations one, Connecticut five, New-York six, New Jersey four, Pennsylvania eight, Delaware one, Maryland six, Virginia ten, North Carolina five, South Carolina five, and Georgia three.

* After the engrossed parchment sent by the Federal Convention to Congress on September 18, 1787. Reproduced in *The Records of the Federal Convention*, Max Farrand, ed., vol. II, pp. 651-666.

When vacancies happen in the Representation from any State, the Executive Authority thereof shall issue Writs of Election to fill such Vacancies.

The House of Representatives shall chuse their Speaker and other Officers; and shall have the sole Power of Impeachment.

Section. 3. The Senate of the United States shall be composed of two Senators from each State, chosen by the Legislature thereof, for six Years; and each Senator shall have one Vote.

Immediately after they shall be assembled in Consequence of the first Election, they shall be divided as equally as may be into three Classes. The Seats of the Senators of the first Class shall be vacated at the Expiration of the second Year, of the second Class at the Expiration of the fourth Year, and of the third Class at the Expiration of the sixth Year, so that one third may be chosen every second Year; and if Vacancies happen by Resignation, or otherwise, during the Recess of the Legislature of any State, the Executive thereof may make temporary Appointments until the next Meeting of the Legislature, which shall then fill such Vacancies.

No Person shall be a Senator who shall not have attained to the Age of thirty Years, and been nine Years a Citizen of the United States, and who shall not, when elected, be an Inhabitant of that State for which he shall be chosen.

The Vice President of the United States shall be President of the Senate, but shall have no Vote, unless they be equally divided.

The Senate shall chuse their other Officers, and also a President pro tempore, in the Absence of the Vice President, or when he shall exercise the Office of President of the United States.

The Senate shall have the sole Power to try all Impeachments. When sitting for that Purpose, they shall be on Oath or Affirmation. When the President of the United States <is tried> the Chief Justice shall preside: And no Person shall be convicted without the Concurrence of two thirds of the Members present.

Judgment in Cases of Impeachment shall not extend further than to removal from Office, and disqualification to hold and enjoy any Office of honor, Trust or Profit under the United States: but the Party convicted shall nevertheless be liable and subject to Indictment, Trial, Judgment and Punishment, according to Law.

Section. 4. The Times, Places and Manner of holding Elections for Senators and Representatives, shall be prescribed in each State by the Legislature thereof; but the Congress may at any time by Law make or alter such Regulations, except as to the Places of chusing Senators.

The Congress shall assemble at least once in every Year, and such Meeting shall be on the first Monday in December, unless they shall by Law appoint a different Day.

Section. 5. Each House shall be the Judge of the Elections, Returns and Qualifications of its own Members, and a Majority of each shall constitute a Quorum to do Business; but a smaller Number may adjourn from day to day, and may be authorized to compel the Attendance of absent Members, in such Manner, and under such Penalties as each House may provide.

Each House may determine the Rules of its Proceedings, punish its Members for disorderly Behaviour, and, with the Concurrence of two thirds, expel a Member.

Each House shall keep a Journal of its Proceedings, and from time to time publish the same, excepting such Parts as may in their Judgment require Secrecy; and the Yeas and Nays of the Members of either House on any question shall, at the Desire of one fifth of those Present, be entered on the Journal.

Neither House, during the Session of Congress, shall, without the Consent of the other, adjourn for more than three days, nor to any other Place than that in which the two Houses shall be sitting.

Section. 6. The Senators and Representatives shall receive a Compensation for their Services, to be ascertained by Law, and paid out of the Treasury of the United States. They shall in all Cases, except Treason, Felony and Breach of the Peace, be privileged from Arrest during their Attendance at the Session of their respective Houses, and in going to and returning from the same; and for any Speech or Debate in either House, they shall not be questiond in any other Place.

No Senator or Representative shall, during the Time for which he was elected, be appointed to any civil Office under the Authority of the United States, which shall have been created, or the Emoluments whereof shall have been encreased during such time; and no Person holding any Office under the United States, shall be a Member of either House during his Continuance in Office.

Section. 7. All Bills for raising Revenue shall originate in the House of Representatives; but the Senate may propose or concur with Amendments as on other Bills.

Every Bill which shall have passed the House of Representatives and the Senate, shall, before it become a Law, be presented to the President of the United States; if he approve he shall sign it, but if not he shall return it, with his Objections to that House in which it shall have originated, who shall enter the Objections at large on their Journal, and proceed to reconsider it. If after such Reconsideration two thirds of that House shall agree to pass the Bill, it shall be sent, together with the Objections, to the other House, by which it shall likewise be reconsidered, and if approved by two thirds of that House, it shall become a Law. But in all such Cases the Votes of both Houses shall be determined by yeas and Nays, and the Names of the Persons voting for and against the Bill shall be entered on the Journal of each House respectively. If any Bill shall not be returned by the President within ten Days (Sundays excepted) after it shall have been presented to him, the Same shall be a Law, in like Manner as if he had signed it, unless the Congress by their Adjournment prevent its Return, in which Case it shall not be a Law.

Every Order, Resolution, or Vote to which the Concurrence of the Senate and House of Representatives may be necessary (except on a question of Adjournment) shall be presented to the President of the United States; and before the Same shall take Effect, shall be approved by him, or being disapproved by him, shall be repassed by two thirds of the Senate and House of Representatives, according to the Rules and Limitations prescribed in the Case of a Bill.

Section. 8. The Congress shall have Power To lay and collect Taxes, Duties, Imposts and Excises, to pay the Debts and provide for the common Defence and general Welfare of the United States; but all Duties, Imposts and Excises shall be uniform throughout the United States;

To borrow Money on the credit of the United States;

To regulate Commerce with foreign Nations, and among the several States, and with the Indian Tribes;

To establish an uniform Rule of Naturalization, and uniform Laws on the subject of Bankruptcies throughout the United States;

To coin Money, regulate the Value thereof, and of foreign Coin, and fix the Standard of Weights and Measures;

To provide for the Punishment of counterfeiting the Securities and current Coin of the United States;

To establish Post Offices and post Roads;

To promote the Progress of Science and useful Arts, by securing for limited Times to Authors and Inventors the exclusive Right to their respective Writings and Discoveries;

To constitute Tribunals inferior to the supreme Court;

To define and punish Piracies and Felonies committed on the high Seas, and Offences against the Law of Nations;

To declare War, grant Letters of Marque and Reprisal, and make Rules concerning Captures on Land and Water;

To raise and support Armies, but no Appropriation of Money to that Use shall be for a longer Term than two Years;

To provide and maintain a Navy;

To make Rules for the Government and Regulation of the land and naval Forces;

To provide for calling forth the Militia to execute the Laws of the Union, suppress Insurrections and repel Invasions;

To provide for organizing, arming, and disciplining, the Militia, and for governing such Part of them as may be employed in the Service of the United States, reserving to the States respectively, the Appointment of the Officers, and the Authority of training the Militia according to the discipline prescribed by Congress;

To exercise exclusive Legislation in all Cases whatsoever, over such District (not exceeding ten Miles square) as may, by Cession of Particular States, and the Acceptance of Congress, become the Seat of the Government of the United States, and to exercise like Authority over all Places purchased by the Consent of the Legislature of the State in which the Same shall be, for the Erection of Forts, Magazines, Arsenals, dock-Yards, and other needful Buildings; — And

To make all Laws which shall be necessary and proper for carrying into Execution the foregoing Powers, and all other Powers vested by this Constitution in the Government of the United States, or in any Department or Officer thereof.

Section. 9. The Migration or Importation of such Persons as any of the States now existing shall think proper to admit, shall not be prohibited by the Congress prior to the Year one thousand eight hundred and eight, but a Tax or duty may be imposed on such Importation, not exceeding ten dollars for each Person.

The Privilege of the Writ of Habeas Corpus shall not be suspended, unless when in Cases of Rebellion or Invasion the public Safety may require it.

No Bill of Attainder or ex post facto Law shall be passed.

No Capitation, or other direct, Tax shall be laid, unless in Proportion to the Census or Enumeration herein before directed to be taken.

No Tax or Duty shall be laid on Articles exported from any State.

No Preference shall be given by any Regulation of Commerce or Revenue to the Ports of one State over those of another: nor shall Vessels bound to, or from, one State, be obliged to enter, clear, or pay Duties in another.

No Money shall be drawn from the Treasury, but in Consequence of Appropriations made by Law; and a regular Statement and Account of the Receipts and Expenditures of all public Money shall be published from time to time.

No Title of Nobility shall be granted by the United States: And no Person holding any Office of Profit or Trust under them, shall, without the Consent of the Congress, accept of any present, Emolument, Office, or Title, of any kind whatever, from any King, Prince, or foreign State.

Section. 10. No State shall enter into any Treaty, Alliance, or Confederation; grant Letters of Marque and Reprisal; coin Money; emit Bills of Credit; make any Thing but gold and silver Coin a Tender in Payment of Debts; pass any Bill of Attainder, ex post facto Law, or Law impairing the Obligation of Contracts, or grant any Title of Nobility.

No State shall, without the Consent of <the> Congress, lay any Imposts or Duties on Imports or Exports, except what may be absolutely necessary for executing it's inspection Laws: and the net Produce of all Duties and Imposts, laid by any State on Imports or Exports, shall be for the Use of the Treasury of the United States; and all such Laws shall be subject to the Revision and Controul of &lt;the&gt; Congress.

No State shall, without the Consent of Congress, lay any Duty of Tonnage, keep Troops, or Ships of War in time of Peace, enter into any Agreement or Compact with another State, or with a foreign Power, or engage in War, unless actually invaded, or in such imminent Danger as will not admit of delay.

## Article. II.

Section. 1. The executive Power shall be vested in a President of the United States of America. He shall hold his Office during the Term of four Years, and, together with the Vice President, chosen for the same Term, be elected, as follows

Each State shall appoint, in such Manner as the Legislature thereof may direct, a Number of Electors, equal to the whole Number of Senators and Representatives to which the State may be entitled in the Congress: but no Senator or Representative, or Person holding an Office of Trust or Profit under the United States, shall be appointed an Elector.

The Electors shall meet in their respective States, and vote by Ballot for two Persons, of whom one at least shall not be an Inhabitant of the same State with themselves. And they shall make a List of all the Persons voted for, and of the Number of Votes for each; which List they shall sign and certify, and transmit sealed to the Seat of the Government of the United States, directed to the President of the Senate. The President of the Senate shall, in the Presence of the Senate and House of Representatives, open all the Certificates, and the Votes shall then be counted. The Person having the greatest Number of Votes shall be the President, if such Number be a Majority of the whole Number of Electors appointed; and if there be more than one who have such Majority, and have an equal Number of Votes, then the House of Representatives shall immediately chuse by Ballot one of them for President; and if no Person have a Majority, then from the five highest on the List the said House shall in like Manner chuse the President. But in chusing the President, the Votes shall be taken by States, the Representation from each State having one Vote; A quorum for this Purpose shall consist of a Member or Members from two thirds of the States, and a Majority of all the States shall be necessary to a Choice. In every Case, after the Choice of the President, the Person having the greatest Number of Votes of the Electors shall be the Vice President. But if there should remain two or more who have equal Votes, the Senate shall chuse from them by Ballot the Vice President.

The Congress may determine the Time of chusing the Electors, and the Day on which they shall give their Votes; which Day shall be the same throughout the United States.

No Person except a natural born Citizen, or a Citizen of the United States, at the time of the Adoption of this Constitution, shall be eligible to the Office of President; neither shall any Person be eligible to that Office who shall not have attained to the Age of thirty five Years, and been fourteen Years a Resident within the United States.

In Case of the Removal of the President from Office, or of his Death, Resignation, or Inability to discharge the Powers and Duties of the said Office, the Same shall devolve on the Vice President, and the Congress may by Law provide for the Case of Removal, Death, Resignation or Inability, both of the President and Vice President, declaring what Officer shall then act as President, and such Officer shall act accordingly, until the Disability be removed, or a President shall be elected.

The President shall, at stated Times, receive for his Services, a Compensation, which shall neither be encreased nor diminished during the Period for which he shall have been elected, and he shall not receive within that Period any other Emolument from the United States, or any of them.

Before he enter on the Execution of his Office, he shall take the following Oath or Affirmation: — "I do solemnly swear (or affirm) that I will faithfully execute the Office of President of the United States, and will to the best of my Ability, preserve, protect and defend the Constitution of the United States."

Section. 2. The President shall be Commander in Chief of the Army and Navy of the United States, and of the Militia of the several States, when called into the actual Service of the United States; he may require the Opinion, in writing, of the principal Officer in each of the executive Departments, upon any Subject relating to the Duties of their respective Offices, and he shall have Power to grant Reprieves and Pardons for Offences against the United States, except in Cases of Impeachment.

He shall have Power, by and with the Advice and Consent of the Senate, to make Treaties, provided two thirds of the Senators present concur; and he shall nominate, and by and with the Advice and Consent of the Senate, shall appoint Ambassadors, other public Ministers and Consuls, Judges of the supreme Court, and all other Officers of the United States, whose Appointments are not herein otherwise provided for, and which shall be established by Law: but the Congress may by Law vest the Appointment of such inferior Officers, as they think proper, in the President alone, in the Courts of Law, or in the Heads of Departments.

The President shall have Power to fill up all Vacancies that may happen during the Recess of the Senate, by granting Commissions which shall expire at the End of their next Session.

Section. 3. He shall from time to time give to the Congress Information of the State of the Union, and recommend to their consideration such Measures as he shall judge necessary and expedient; he may, on extraordinary Occasions, convene both Houses, or either of them, and in Case of Disagreement between them, with Respect to the Time of Adjournment, he may adjourn them to such Time as he shall think proper; he shall receive Ambassadors and other public Ministers; he shall take Care that the Laws be faithfully executed, and shall Commission all the Officers of the United States.

Section. 4. The President, Vice President and all civil Officers of the United States, shall be removed from Office on Impeachment for, and Conviction of, Treason, Bribery, or other high Crimes and Misdemeanors.

## Article. III.

Section. 1. The judicial Power of the United States, shall be vested in one supreme Court, and in such inferior Courts as the Congress may from time to time ordain and establish. The Judges, both of the supreme and inferior Courts, shall hold their Offices during good Behaviour, and shall, at stated Times, receive for their Services, a Compensation, which shall not be diminished during their Continuance in Office.

Section. 2. The judicial Power shall extend to all Cases, in Law and Equity, arising under this Constitution, the Laws of the United States, and Treaties made, or which shall be made, under their Authority; — to all Cases affecting Ambassadors, other public Ministers and Consuls; — to all Cases of admiralty and maritime Jurisdiction; — to Controversies to which the United States shall be a Party; — to Controversies between two or more States; — between a State and Citizens of another State; — between Citizens of different States, — between Citizens of the same State claiming Lands under Grants of different States, and between a State, or the Citizens thereof, and foreign States, Citizens or Subjects.

In all Cases affecting Ambassadors, other public Ministers and Consuls, and those in which a State shall be Party, the supreme Court shall have original Jurisdiction. In all the other Cases before mentioned, the supreme Court shall have appellate Jurisdiction, both as to Law and Fact, with such Exceptions, and under such Regulations as the Congress shall make.

The Trial of all Crimes, except in Cases of Impeachment, shall be by Jury; and such Trial shall be held in the State where the said Crimes shall have been committed; but when not committed within any State, the Trial shall be at such Place or Places as the Congress may by Law have directed.

Section. 3. Treason against the United States, shall consist only in levying War against them, or in adhering to their Enemies, giving them Aid and Comfort. No Person shall be convicted of Treason unless on the Testimony of two Witnesses to the same overt Act, or on Confession in open Court.

The Congress shall have Power to declare the Punishment of Treason, but no Attainder of Treason shall work Corruption of Blood, or Forfeiture except during the Life of the Person attainted.

## Article. IV.

Section. 1. Full Faith and Credit shall be given in each State to the public Acts, Records, and judicial Proceedings of every other State. And the Congress may by general Laws prescribe the Manner in which such Acts, Records and Proceedings shall be proved, and the Effect thereof.

Section. 2. The Citizens of each State shall be entitled to all Privileges and Immunities of Citizens in the several States.

A Person charged in any State with Treason, Felony, or other Crime, who shall flee from Justice, and be found in another State, shall on Demand of the executive Authority of the State from which he fled, be delivered up, to be removed to the State having Jurisdiction of the Crime.

No Person held to Service or Labour in one State, under the Laws thereof, escaping into another, shall, in Consequence of any Law or Regulation therein, be discharged from such Service or Labour, but shall be delivered up on Claim of the Party to whom such Service or Labour may be due.

Section. 3. New States may be admitted by the Congress into this Union; but no new State shall be formed or erected within the Jurisdiction of any other State; nor any State be formed by the Junction of two or more States, or Parts of States, without the Consent of the Legislatures of the States concerned as well as of the Congress.

The Congress shall have Power to dispose of and make all needful Rules and Regulations respecting the Territory or other Property belonging to the United States; and nothing in this Constitution shall be so construed as to Prejudice any Claims of the United States, or of any particular State.

Section. 4. The United States shall guarantee to every State in this Union a Republican Form of Government, and shall protect each of

them against Invasion; and on Application of the Legislature, or of
the Executive (when the Legislature cannot be convened) against domestic Violence.

## Article. V.

The Congress, whenever two thirds of both Houses shall deem it
necessary, shall propose Amendments to this Constitution, or, on the
Application of the Legislatures of two thirds of the several States, shall
call a Convention for proposing Amendments, which, in either Case,
shall be valid to all Intents and Purposes, as Part of this Constitution,
when ratified by the Legislatures of three fourths of the several States,
or by Conventions in three fourths thereof, as the one or the other
Mode of Ratification may be proposed by the Congress; Provided that
no Amendment which may be made prior to the Year One thousand
eight hundred and eight shall in any Manner affect the first and fourth
Clauses in the Ninth Section of the first Article; and that no State,
without its Consent, shall be deprived of it's equal Suffrage in the
Senate.

## Article. VI.

All Debts contracted and Engagements entered into, before the
Adoption of this Constitution, shall be as valid against the United
States under this Constitution, as under the Confederation.

This Constitution, and the Laws of the United States which shall be
made in Pursuance thereof; and all Treaties made, or which shall be
made, under the Authority of the United States, shall be the supreme
Law of the Land; and the Judges in every State shall be bound thereby,
any Thing in the Constitution or Laws of any State to the Contrary
notwithstanding.

The Senators and Representatives before mentioned, and the Members of the several State Legislatures, and all executive and judicial Officers, both of the United States and of the several States, shall be
bound by Oath or Affirmation, to support this Constitution; but no
religious Test shall ever be required as a Qualification to any Office or
public Trust under the United States.

## Article. VII.

The Ratification of the Conventions of nine States, shall be sufficient
for the Establishment of this Constitution between the States so ratifying the Same.

Done in Convention by the Unanimous Consent of the States present the Seventeenth Day of September in the Year of our Lord one thousand seven hundred and Eighty seven and of the Independence of the United States of America the Twelfth IN WITNESS whereof We have hereunto subscribed our Names,

Attest William Jackson,
   Secretary.

Go. WASHINGTON — Presidt.
and deputy from Virginia.

New Hampshire { JOHN LANGDON
                NICHOLAS GILMAN

Massachusetts { NATHANIEL GORHAM
             RUFUS KING

Connecticut { WM: SAML. JOHNSON
           ROGER SHERMAN

New York: . . . ALEXANDER HAMILTON

New Jersey { WIL: LIVINGSTON
          DAVID BREARLEY.
          WM. PATERSON.
          JONA: DAYTON

Pennsylvania { B FRANKLIN
           THOMAS MIFFLIN
           ROBT MORRIS
           GEO. CLYMER
           THOS FITZSIMONS
           JARED INGERSOLL
           JAMES WILSON
           GOUV MORRIS

Delaware { GEO: READ
         GUNNING BEDFORD jun
         JOHN DICKINSON
         RICHARD BASSETT
         JACO: BROOM

Maryland { JAMES MCHENRY
         DAN OF ST THOS JENIFER
         DANL CARROLL

Virginia { JOHN BLAIR —
        JAMES MADISON Jr.

North Carolina { WM. BLOUNT
           RICHD. DOBBS SPAIGHT.
           HU WILLIAMSON

South Carolina { J. RUTLEDGE
           CHARLES COTESWORTH PINCKNEY
           CHARLES PINCKNEY
           PIERCE BUTLER.

Georgia { WILLIAM FEW
{ ABR BALDWIN

In Convention Monday, September 17th. 1787.

Present

The States of

New Hampshire, Massachusetts, Connecticut, Mr. Hamilton from New York, New Jersey, Pennsylvania, Delaware, Maryland, Virginia, North Carolina, South Carolina and Georgia.

Resolved,

That the preceding Constitution be laid before the United States in Congress assembled, and that it is the Opinion of this Convention, that it should afterwards be submitted to a Convention of Delegates, chosen in each State by the People thereof, under the Recommendation of its Legislature, for their Assent and Ratification; and that each Convention assenting to, and ratifying the Same, should give Notice thereof to the United States in Congress assembled.

Resolved, That it is the Opinion of this Convention, that as soon as the Conventions of nine States shall have ratified this Constitution, the United States in Congress assembled should fix a Day on which Electors should be appointed by the States which shall have ratified the same, and a Day on which the Electors should assemble to vote for the President, and the Time and Place for commencing Proceedings under this Constitution. That after such Publication the Electors should be appointed, and the Senators and Representatives elected: That the Electors should meet on the Day fixed for the Election of the President, and should transmit their votes certified signed, sealed and directed, as the Constitution requires, to the Secretary of the United States in Congress assembled, that the Senators and Representatives should convene at the Time and Place assigned; that the Senators should appoint a President of the Senate, for the sole Purpose of receiving, opening and counting the Votes for President; and, that after he shall be chosen, the Congress, together with the President, should, without Delay, proceed to execute this Constitution.

By the Unanimous Order of the Convention.

GO: WASHINGTON Presidt.

W. JACKSON Secretary.

# The Bill of Rights

## Article I

Congress shall make no law respecting an establishment of religion, or prohibiting the free exercise thereof; or abridging the freedom of speech, or of the press; or the right of the people peaceably to assemble, and to petition the Government for a redress of grievances.

## Article II

A well regulated Militia, being necessary to the security of a free State, the right of the people to keep and bear Arms, shall not be infringed.

## Article III

No Soldier shall, in time of peace be quartered in any house, without the consent of the Owner, nor in time of war, but in a manner to be prescribed by law.

## Article IV

The right of the people to be secure in their persons, houses, papers, and effects, against unreasonable searches and seizures, shall not be violated, and no Warrants shall issue, but upon probable cause, supported by Oath or affirmation, and particularly describing the place to be searched, and the persons or things to be seized.

## Article V

No person shall be held to answer for a capital, or otherwise infamous crime, unless on a presentment or indictment of a Grand Jury, except in cases arising in the land or naval forces, or in the Militia, when in actual service in time of War or public danger; nor shall any person be subject for the same offence to be twice put in jeopardy of life or limb; nor shall be compelled in any criminal case to be a witness against himself, nor be deprived of life, liberty, or property, without due process of law; nor shall private property be taken for public use, without just compensation.

## Article VI

In all criminal prosecutions, the accused shall enjoy the right to a speedy and public trial, by an impartial jury of the State and district wherein the crime shall have been committed, which district shall have been previously ascertained by law, and to be informed of the nature and cause of the accusation; to be confronted with the witnesses against him; to have compulsory process for obtaining witnesses in his favor, and to have the Assistance of Counsel for his defence.

## Article VII

In suits at common law, where the value in controversy shall exceed twenty dollars, the right of trial by jury shall be preserved, and no fact tried by a jury, shall be otherwise reexamined in any Court of the United States, than according to the rules of the common law.

## Article VIII

Excessive bail shall not be required, nor excessive fines imposed, nor cruel and unusual punishments inflicted.

## Article IX

The enumeration in the Constitution, of certain rights, shall not be construed to deny or disparage others retained by the people.

## Article X

The powers not delegated to the United States by the Constitution, nor prohibited by it to the States, are reserved to the States respectively, or to the people.

# *Author's Note*

LORD CHANCELLOR JOWITT remarked that in writing about a criminal trial, a biased history inevitably emerges unless one includes every word of testimony on both sides. Often enough while writing this book I had like misgivings. The things omitted, the things skimped and hurried over, haunted me at midnight. Originally I had copious footnotes, explaining — for instance — that though Madison made a certain statement on Tuesday, he would contradict it twenty years later. I deleted all of these. It is hard enough for a reader to follow a summer of Convention speeches, without wading through exegeses at the foot of the page. I much regret the omission of pre-Convention debates in Congress and the letters of such men as William Grayson, who desired to strengthen the government but who wished to do so in and through Congress, not by means of a separately elected convention.

Simply, I had not room. Nor do I discuss historical studies which develop the question of judicial review, or compare the British legal system with the American. Concurrent powers, the supremacy clause, the commerce clause — Convention members did not use these words. The Judiciary Act of 1789, the legal reforms of 1803; my narrative had no space for them, nor even to argue at length the terrible question of slavery and why the Federal Convention could not take a stronger stand against it. I regret that Antifederalist arguments could not have been further pursued in my brief chapters on ratification. Yet to give both sides of all these questions, beyond what Convention delegates said, would have required four volumes, not one.

The first half of my book, to the adjournment of July twenty-sixth, treats the Convention chronologically, day by day, as indicated in chapter headings. After "Journey through the American States," I felt the narrative needed a change of pace. Delegates therefore are quoted on any given question — the West, or a standing army — right through the summer, from May to September, without dates and without the words, "he said earlier . . . he was to say later." It is again, a brave reader who will labor through four months of speechmaking, without suffering the further detail of daily and weekly dates or moving back and forth in time.

Besides Major Jackson's official record, the Convention had six reporters: Madison, Yates, King, McHenry, Pierce, Hamilton. All of them wrote objectively; as far as I can see, none colored his report to suit his political bias. Reports differ only in style, and here at times they differ vitally. Madison reports in the third person, past tense: "Mr. Hamilton . . . was obliged therefore to declare himself unfriendly to both plans." Yates on the other hand gives the speaker's name and then uses the first person: "I shall now show that both plans are materially defective" — a technique which is not only more accurate reporting but dramatic and immediate. I usually follow Madison's rendering simply because it is by far the fullest; fortunately, in mid-paragraph he is apt to break down into natural first person speech. But Madison occasionally omits a salient point, which Yates, King or McHenry supplies. In moving from one reporter to another, I have not always identified each reporter by name; in earlier versions of my manuscript I tried this and it proved impossibly confusing. When a delegate rises, it is important the reader think of him as speaking, not merely as being reported. Hence I have not reproduced eighteenth-century capitalization and spelling except in quoting from the finished Constitution. Reporter's italics are given so that the reader may share the speaker's — or the reporter's — urgency.

In quoting the letters of delegates and others, for the most part I use modern spelling and capitalization, so as not to distract from the writer's meaning. Occasionally, when the orthography of a diary or letter seems especially characteristic of the man — as with Washington or John Adams — I have let it stand. I regret

having no room to explain the background of delegates' ideas —
the classical education which caused repeated harping upon the
Amphictyonic Council, that species of exhortation which Mr.
Randal of Massachusetts later declared "no more to the purpose
than to tell how our forefathers dug clams at Plymouth."

Yet despite sins of omission and commission, if I have presented
the Federal Convention in terms comprehensible to my readers,
and in terms as truly dramatic as the records show it to be, I shall
have done what I set out to do, and can rest content.

Because my book reveals no undiscovered material and attempts
no new interpretation, I have kept scholarly apparatus to a minimum. Citations for quotations are in my files, should anyone care
to see them. I include no general bibliography. The source material for this period is known to every student: Max Farrand's
*The Records of the Federal Convention* (4 vols.), 1931-1937;
C. C. Tansill's *Documents Illustrative of the Formation of the
Union of American States*, 1927; J. R. Strayer, ed., *The Delegate
from New York* (notes of John Lansing), 1939; F. N. Thorpe's
*The Federal and State Constitutions* (7 vols.), 1909; E. C. Bur-
nett's *Letters of the Members of the Continental Congress* (8
vols.), 1921-1936, and such excellent compendia as Henry Steele
Commager's *Documents of American History*, 1944, or Commager
and Allan Nevins's *Heritage of America*, 1939.

We live in an age of superb historical editing. Every student is
indebted to Julian P. Boyd for the seventeen volumes of Thomas
Jefferson's papers; I am told there will eventually be more than
fifty volumes. Lyman H. Butterfield's edition of *The Adams
Papers* (9 vols. to date, 1961) and his *Letters of Benjamin Rush*
(2 vols.), 1951; the Yale edition of the papers of Benjamin Franklin (10 vols. to date, 1951), Leonard W. Labaree and others, eds.
— all these set an example for exact and imaginative historical
editing. Among the older school of editors I used John C. Fitz-
patrick's *The Writings of George Washington* (39 vols.), 1931-
1944, which, to the student's delight, has an index for every volume. I used Harold C. Syrett and Jacob E. Cooke's *The Papers
of Alexander Hamilton* (7 vols. to date, 1961); Gaillard Hunt's

*The Writing of James Madison* (9 vols.), 1910; Lester Cappon's *The Adams-Jefferson Letters* (2 vols.), 1959, and of course Jared Sparks and Paul L. Ford.

For the ratification chapters I used perforce those maligned volumes, Jonathan Elliot's *The Debates in the Conventions on the Adoption of the Federal Constitution* (5 vols. in 2), 1941, which must serve the student until the heralded appearance of Robert E. Cushman's documentary *History of the Ratification of the Constitution and the First Ten Amendments.* For other source material I used David Robertson's *Debates and Other Proceedings of the Convention in Virginia*, taken by shorthand on the spot, published in 1805; Hugh B. Grigsby's *History of the Federal Convention of 1788* (2 vols.), 1890-1891; Paul L. Ford's *Pamphlets on the Constitution of the United States*, 1888, and his *Essays on the Constitution*, 1892. Also J. B. McMaster and F. B. Stone, *Pennsylvania and the Federal Constitution, 1787-1788*, 1888; and Samuel B. Harding's *The Contest over the Ratification of the Federal Constitution in the State of Massachusetts*, 1896.

Although my book was written almost entirely from primary source material, I cannot close without expressing my indebtedness to some of the earlier historians of the general scene. Charles Warren's *The Making of the Constitution*, 1928, was constantly useful, as also those classics on constitutional history written by Andrew C. McLaughlin between 1905 and 1928. For my purpose they were indispensable, as were the works of that old controversial master, Charles A. Beard; also Allan Nevins's *The American States during and after the Revolution*, 1924, and Franklin F. Jameson's *The American Revolution Considered as a Social Movement*, 1926. Merrill Jensen's *The Articles of Confederation* (1940), and his *The New Nation* (1950) were greatly helpful; also Jackson T. Main's *The Antifederalists*, 1961; Alpheus T. Mason's *The States Rights Debates*, 1964. Clinton Rossiter's *The Grand Convention* appeared after my book was in galleys; I should like to refer the student to his skillful and comprehensive bibliography. Adrienne Koch's excellent edition of Madison's *Notes of Debates in the Federal Convention of 1787* was published too late for me to use.

# Acknowledgments

ACADEMIC scholars are wonderfully generous in the matter of reading the book manuscripts of their friends. I want to thank Julian Boyd for his painstaking reading and challenging criticism, especially as our interpretations differed in many points. John Powell battled through my manuscript not once but twice; here is a scholar with an unrivaled tolerance for historical discussion, at once demanding and stimulating. Caroline Robbins read my manuscript, and throughout the years of writing gave me unfailing friendly support. I want to thank those who shared with me their scholarly skills: Wallace Davies, Patricia Davis, Jean Wheeler, Frances Harrold.

Charles G. Dorman, David H. Wallace and John C. Milley of the National Independence Historical Park assisted with the Philadelphia scene. Among my friends the librarians I am especially beholden to Howell Heaney of the Free Library of Philadelphia, and the staffs at the Bryn Mawr College and Haverford College Libraries. Martha Sellers is an even better typist than she was twenty-five years ago when she began the tedious copying and recopying which a long manuscript entails.

Lastly, I want to thank my editorial consultant and friend, Barbara Rex, who has borne with me now through six books. Unlike many critics, Barbara does not try to make over a manuscript in her own image. She grasps the author's conception, sometimes before the author himself is fully aware of it, and by tact or *force majeure* brings it into the open. When a page or paragraph does not make its point, Barbara says so. Authors are clamorous and defensive. It is not easy for a critic to persist until the writer has done — at the least — his best with that difficult exercise, the building of English sentences.

# Index

ADAMS, ABIGAIL, 46, 137, 194
Adams, Henry: on L. Martin, 119
Adams, John: on history, xii; on
generals, 6; on state sovereignty,
9; difficulties of government, 11;
in London, 11, 26, 136-138; on constitutions, 11, 199, 234, 275; on
Franklin, 17; on Antifederalists,
18; Jefferson writes to, 30; on
G. Morris, 42; on J. Dickinson, 58;
as advocate on law, 63-64; on
Gerry, 64; on property, 71; on
voting in Salem, 76; sense of destiny, 88; on New Englanders, 91;
on Sherman, 93; on Hamilton, 108;
Martin refers to, 124; on fine arts,
165; on monarchy, 188-189, 279; on
presidential title, 192; on possible
disunion, 197; on Declaration of
Independence, 199; as Deist, 216;
on Richard Henry Lee, 269; on
Constitution, 279
Adams, John Quincy, on Hamilton's speech, 114
Adams, Samuel: on Franklin, 17;
opposes Convention, 18; friend of
Gerry, 45, 64; on property, 71;
on liberty, 138; on Constitution,
282, 284, 288-289; friendship with
Hancock, 288
Albany Plan of Union, ix
Ames, Fisher, 284, 286
Annapolis Convention, 35, 39; background, 9; influence of Shays's Rebellion on, 10; Virginia delegates
refer to, 25
Antifederalists, 8, 10, 18, 86, 226, 245,
269-272, 280, 294; in Pennsylvania,
273-277; in Massachusetts, 282-291;

in Virginia, 293, 295-305; in New
York, 305-306
Articles of Confederation: government under, 4; powers of government, 5; requisitions, 5; R. King
on, 8; background and formation,
8; quoted, 8; commerce under, 9;
revision, 24, 226, 285; poverty of
states under, 27; larger states under,
32; Randolph on defects, 39; lawyers and, 63; Gerry as signer of,
64; on ratification, 67; Madison on,
67; G. Read on, 75; fate of, 77;
Wilson on, 81; Sherman's suggestions about vote, 94, 263; states'
sovereignty under, 105; amending
of, 225
Ashfield, Massachusetts, 11
Atherton, Joshua, 294
Austria, 135

BACON, SIR FRANCIS, xi, 56, 163
Baily, Francis, 155
Baldwin, Abraham, wishes slavery
left to states, 203
Baltimore, Maryland, 151
Barbé-Marbois, Marquis de, 142, 149,
307; on forests, 146; on poor, 150,
165; on liberty, 150, 167; on innkeepers, 154; on travel, 154-157;
on women, 166; on Washington,
193-194
Barrell, Nathaniel, 290
Bartram, John, 144, 162
Bassett, Richard, silence in Convention, 259
Bedford, Gunning, Jr.: description
and background, 35, 82, 130; for
small states, 82, 130, 139; supports

Bedford, Gunning, Jr. (*cont.*)
New Jersey Plan, 105; for increase
in Delaware's representatives, 250
Bill of Rights, 244-248, 272, 279, 281,
288, 304-305; text, 325-326
Bingham, Mrs. W., entertains Washington, 21
Blair, John: as delegate, 18; silence
in Covention, 259
Blount, William: on state sovereignty, 12; silence in Convention,
259; refuses to sign, 259; letter
from James White, 265
Boston, Massachusetts, 150, 160, 164-
165, 208, 250, 275
*Boston Daily Advertiser*, 278
Bowdoin, James; 283, 288-289
Brearley, David: on legislative election, 84; on redistricting Union,
84, 86; supports New Jersey Plan,
105
Brissot de Warville: on Philadelphia,
52; on American climate and people, 144; on scale of living, 151;
on travel, 153-154; on R. King, 237
Bryan, George, 8, 273
Bryce, James, 80; on Wilson, 56; on
Hamilton, 109
Burke, Edmund, 12, 99
Burr, Aaron, 111
Butler, Pierce: on national government, 41; on executive, 59; background and description, 59, 191,
207; on Federal courts, 65-66;
against legislative negative, 83; on
property, 83; on state differences,
92; on lower house power, 95; on
British Parliament, 101; on congressmen, 120-121; on foreigners
in Congress, 207; on ratification,
227, 228

CABOT, GEORGE, 284, 286
Canada, 25, 31, 81, 170, 178
Carmarthen, Francis Osborne, Mar-
quess of, 137
Carroll, Daniel, 191, 200, 227, 249
Carter, Robert, 161
Caswell, Richard, 27, 102
CENTINEL (pseudonym), 274-275

Chase, Justice Samuel: on ratification,
271
Chastellux, François Jean, Marquis
de, 142, 165; on Philadelphia, 52,
97; in forest, 149; on poverty, 151;
on pioneers, 151, 163; on language,
159-161; on society, 166-167; treatise on public happiness, 239
Cincinnati, Society of the: convention in Philadelphia, 19; criticism
of, 20, 283; Washington dines with,
22; Mrs. Warren on, 188
City Tavern, 97, 98, 104, 139, 264
City Troop: greets Washington, 16;
Washington reviews, 22; in Federal Procession, 307
Clinton, George, 8; as New York
political leader, 109-110, 300; on
national capital, 210; as Antifederalist, 235, 270, 305; as Cato, 246f
Clymer, George: fears Western
states, 176; silence in Convention,
176; on ratification, 273
Coke, Sir Edward, xi, 12, 245
*Columbian Grammar*, 159
Congress (under Articles of Confederation), 6, 94; members, 11;
migration of, 12, 208-209; meets
in State House, 23, 50; Dickinson
in, 58; continues business, 62, 66;
and law, 63-64; Livingston in, 65;
on property in 1774, 71; W. S
Johnson and, 97; attitude toward
England, 136-137; and the West,
168-173, 181; Northwest Ordinance, 174-175; on Treaty of 1783,
220-221; and ratification, 226-227,
268; letter from Convention to,
238-240
Congress of the United States, *See*
Representatives, House of; Senate
Connecticut, 92; on requisitions, 5;
Ellsworth answers critics of, 129-
130; Chastellux comments on, 149;
population, 150; ratifies Constitution, 277-278
Constitution: text, 313-324; provision
for amendment, 66; ratification, 67-
68, 110, 226, 233; Crèvecoeur on,
142-143; provisions for West, 170-

171, 176-181; on admission of new states, 183; Randolph notes on, 197-198; on composition, 198-199; on rebellion and treason, 218; preamble, 238-240; provisions for amending, 250-252; final objections to, 249-252, 257-262; the signing of, 262-263; published in *Pennsylvania Packet*, 265; reaction in country to, 265-281, 282-292; on commerce, 303

Constitutionalists, 268, 295. *See also* Federalists

Convention of 1787: general atmosphere, x, xii; Congress sanctions, 4; promoters of, 5-6; opposition to calling, 11; delegates, xviii-xix, 11; W. Grayson on, 12; possibility of failure, 15, 86, 120, 127, 138, 140, 185; Convention reporters, 29-30, 328; credentials of states, 25, 33; rules, 36-37, 128-129; Committee of the Whole, 40, 66, 69, 88, 101, 104, 180; on states' rights, 44; Mason on Convention's duties, 62; on executive power, 55-56; on judicial power, 62-66; on ratification, 67-69, 224-233; on property, 72-73; on slavery, 72; on suffrage, 73-74; Washington in, 77, 118; vote on Senate, 79, 138; vote on legislative veto, 83-84; Sherman's Compromise, 94-96; vote for legislators' terms and salaries, 100-101; supporters of state sovereignty, 105; rejects New Jersey Plan, 117; stalemate over proportional representation, 120, 128, 185; vote on congressional terms, 122; vote on senators' pay, 123; public interest in, 139; and the West, 169-170, 183-184; on admission of new states, 177-183; Great Compromise, 185-187; on presidential election, term, powers, 189-192; Committee of Detail, 192, 197-200, 205, 213, 217; Convention adjourns, 192, 196, 263-264; Committee of Style, 199, 234, 242, 243-244; slavery compromise, 200-

204; foreigners in Congress, 205-208; on national capital, 208-210; altercations near end, 212-213, 224-225, 251; on test oaths, 214-217; on rebellion in states, 218-219, 224; on treason, 219-223; on ratification, 225-233; drafting constitution, 234-242; Bill of Rights, 244-248; discusses canals, 249; on national university, 249; on "laws of nations," 250; final discussions, 249-252, 257-262; on amending Constitution, 250-253; the dissidents, 254-262; delegates sign, 262-263

Cooper, Thomas, 141, 148, 155-156, 165

Corbin, Francis, 297

Cresswell, Nicholas, 159-160

Crèvecoeur, Michel-Guillaume (Hector St. Jean de), 80, 142-143, 153, 281

*Cumberland Gazette,* 247

Curwen, Samuel, 136

Cutler, Manasseh, 173-174, 181-184

DANA, FRANCIS, 283, 284

Davie, William R.: for equal representation in Senate, 130; sees end of Convention, 186; approves but does not sign, 262; on country's reaction, 272

Dayton, Jonathan: age, 4; against Virginia Plan, 130; on Great Compromise, 187

Declaration of Independence, 23, 31, 36, 44, 45, 55, 58, 63, 64, 71, 75, 81, 93, 116, 199, 202, 238, 263

Deism, 215-216

Delaware, 104; delegation, 19, 132; state's ambitions, 26, 86; suffrage in, 73; first to ratify, 277

Delegates: list of, xviii-xix; age, 4; background and experience, 4; number, 11; arrive slowly, 12, 17, 22-23; Virginia's, 18; dress, 23; attendance, 24, 54, 200, 205, 225; credentials, 24, 33; expense of life in Philadelphia, 26-27; those who refuse to sign, 34, 257-262; reac-

Delegates (cont.)
tion to Virginia Resolves, 38; number of lawyers, 63; Pierce's notes on, 98; social life, 98; unanimity of, 185; on Great Compromise, 186-187; New Hampshire delegates arrive, 187-188; during adjournment, 196; altercations near end, 212-214, 225-227, 249-252; on signing, 262-263; take leave, 264
Denmark, 135
Dickinson, John: suffered at mob's hands, 10; on national government, 41, 185; on reason and experience, 44; on monarchy, 58; background, 58; on property, 70; on Senate election, 77-79; on legislative veto, 82; on slave trade, 204; on treason, 221; on Bill of Rights, 246; authorizes Read to sign for him, 263
Dove, David James, 161
Drinker, Elizabeth, 163
Duane, James, 7, 305

Ellsworth, Oliver: on large states, 10; supports New Jersey Plan, 105; amends first Virginia Resolve, 118; criticizes Martin's speech, 124; on Sherman's Compromise, 129; answers critics of Connecticut, 129; on slavery question, 202-203; on difficulty of decisions, 211; on army discipline, 219; attacks Martin on Bill of Rights, 247-248; approves but does not sign, 262; for ratification, 229, 277-278
England, 125, 132-137, 204, 206; trade with, 10; in United States interests, 25, 133-134, 170, 179, 220; government, 57-58, 61, 79; George III, 59, 137, 142, 189, 191; king's negative, 60; lawyers in, 63; suffrage in, 70; Magna Carta, 71, 200, 245; General Pinckney in, 76; Wilson on government, 79; union with Scotland, 96; Hamilton admires, 110, 112, 113; rivalry with France, 133-134; population, 135; English visitors to America, 141-152, 155-

158; treason in, 121, 220-223. See also Parliament
Europe, 46, 48-51, 71, 81, 105, 121, 132-136, 144-145, 155-157, 206, 274
Executive, 55-65; first discussed, 55; Wilson on, 56-57, 62; Randolph on, 57; presidential veto, 59, 243, 275; Butler on, 59, 191; Franklin on, 59-62, 190; Mason on, 62, 118-119; vote on, 62; under English kings, 64; Dickinson on, 58, 62; vote on executive veto, 64; Hamilton on, 113, 115, 188, 190; presidential term and powers, 189-192; G. Morris on presidential impeachment, 190

Federal Procession, 306-310
Federalist Papers, 183-184, 190, 245f, 268
Federalists, 268, 271-272, 280, 293; in Pennsylvania, 274-276; in Massachusetts, 282-286, 288; in Virginia, 295-305
Few, William: on early adjournment, 127; silence in Convention, 259
Findley, William, 273
Fitch, John, 50, 163
Fitzsimons, Thomas, 307
Florida, 168-169
France, 11, 108, 125, 132-135, 204, 206; French visitors to America, 141-152, 153-159, 161-167
Franklin, Benjamin: age, 4, 98; on Tories, 16; career, 16-17; threatens secrecy rule, 22; suggests chaplain, 27; Jefferson on, 29; his sedan chair, 34, 254; on democracy, 47-48; on unicameral legislature, 48; on executive veto, 59-61, 62; on judges, 66; on state conflicts, 95-99; salaries of legislators, 100, 120; proposes prayers for session, 125-126; on compromise, 130, 186-187; on Europe, 126; on taxation, 140; writing style, 159-160; founder of American Philosophical Society, 162; as scientist, 163-164; on

weather, 180; Cutler calls on, 182-183; influences public, 185; on presidential term, 190; on foreigners in Congress, 206; as Deist, 215-216; on treason, 222; on canals, 249; approves Constitution, 255-256; suggests change in representation, 257; urges all members signing, 259-261; "rising sun" speech, 263; on ratification, 273, 281
Franklin, State of, 169, 177. *See also* North Carolina
Fundamental Orders of Connecticut, ix

GATES, HORATIO, 6
*Gazetteer* (*Independent*), 274-275, 276, 300
Georgia: delegates arrive, 17; state's ambitions, 26, 175; trouble with Creeks, 31; as small state, 32, 84, 92, 130; unicameral legislature, 48; ratifies Constitution, 277; Washington on, 277
Germain, Lord George, 40
Germany, 134-135, 145
Gerry, Elbridge: letter from King, 18; on Society of the Cincinnati, 20; his financial affairs, 27; refuses to sign, 34, 260, 263; on national government, 32, 41; on democracy, 44-45, 47; on Shays's Rebellion, 45, 73, 78; house on Spruce Street, 50, 182; on judges, 64; background and description, 64; on amendments to Constitution, 66; on ratification, 67, 228, 230-231, 283; on election of representatives, 70, 74; on Senate, 78; as politician, 78; on legislative veto, 80; sense of destiny, 88-89; on representative term, 99-100; on money bills, 101; supports New Jersey Plan, 105; on corruption in legislature, 121; on delegates' conflicts, 128, 138; on admission of new states, 218-219; on treason, 223-224; on Bill of Rights, 244-245; objections to Constitution, 252, 260, 268

Gilman, Nicholas: on Convention's work, 187-188, 254; silence in Convention, 259; on ratification, 293
Gorham, Nathaniel: description, 35; in Committee of Whole, 40, 101, 113; on weather, 113, 118; on legislative corruption, 121; on strong Union, 128; on large states, 140; on West, 168; concern for Eastern interests, 176; on time of Congressional meeting, 210; on ratification, 228-229, 283-284, 286
Government, ideas on: Wilson, 33, 43, 74-75; Madison, 33; Hamilton, 33, 112; Wythe, 33; discussion, 34, 73, 118; Randolph, 38-40; Dickinson, 78-79; J. Adams, 138
Grayson, William: Revolutionary principles, 8; on Congress, 12, 327; as Antifederalist, 269-270, 295, 298-299; background, 270
Great Britain. *See* England
Greece, 113, 143, 163, 204
Grigsby, Hugh Blair: reports Virginia ratification Convention, 295-302

HAMILTON, ALEXANDER: age, 4, 108; on Continental tax power, 5; on reform of Articles of Confederation, 5-6; during Revolution, 7; description, 7, 108-111, 188, 235; ideas of government, 7, 8, 112; promotes Convention, 8; in New York politics, 14, 110; persuades Washington to attend Convention, 20; as Convention reporter, 30; on sovereignty, 33, 113; leaves Convention, 54, 115; defends Tories, 64; as Nationalist, 70, 110-111, 113; opposed by Yates and Lansing, 86, 109; criticizes New Jersey and Virginia Plans, 106, 113, 132; proposes own plan, 112-114; as Anglophile, 110; on democracy, 112-114; on monarchy, 113, 115, 188; reactions to speech, 114-116; signs Constitution, 115, 263; against chaplain for

HAMILTON, ALEXANDER (*cont.*)
Convention, 126; on foreign influence, 132; on presidential term, 190; on slavery compromise, 201; on foreigners in Congress, 207; on ratification, 231-232, 305; on Committee of Style, 235; on Bill of Rights, 245; urges every delegate to sign, 259

Hancock, John: in Massachusetts convention, 282, 288-289

Henry, Patrick, 66, 81; Revolutionary principles, 8; opposes Constitution, 14, 270, 295-305; refuses to be delegate, 18; as speaker, 80; on Jay's Treaty, 170; on national capital, 209-210; anti-Washington, 269; "tyranny of Philadelphia," 272; Washington urges his support, 280; description, 295; in Virginia ratification Convention, 295-305; on Bill of Rights, 305

Hobbes, Thomas, 143

Holland, 11, 59, 134

Holmes, Oliver Wendell, Jr., x, xii

Hopkins, Stephen, 71

Hopkinson, Francis: career, 31; discusses troubles of states in 1787, 31; to Jefferson on Convention, 31; to Jefferson on Fitch's steam engine, 50; on Federal Procession, 309

House of Representatives. *See* Representatives, House of

Houston, William C., approves but does not sign, 262

Houstoun, William, approves but does not sign, 262

Humphreys, Col. David, 191


INDIAN QUEEN, 38, 50, 52, 99, 139, 181

Indians, 26, 31, 60, 143-144, 153, 161, 168, 175

Ingersoll, Jared: silence in Convention, 35, 259; description, 35; social life, 50; on signing Constitution, 259, 261

Innes, Col. James, 297

JACKSON, MAJOR WILLIAM: elected Secretary of Convention, 30, 32; carries Constitution to Congress, 263

Jay, John: on property, 72; Washington writes to, 87; treaty with Spain, 170, 303; reports to J. Adams on Convention, 192; supports Constitution, 305

Jefferson, Thomas: on delegates, 4; arranges loan in France, 11; on Rhode Island, 13; sends Madison books, 14; criticizes secrecy rule, 22; on Washington, 29; on Franklin, 29; Hopkinson describes state of United States and Convention, 31; Madison writes to on delegates, 37; and *philosophes*, 46; on Shays's Rebellion, 46, 73; on monarchy, 46, 189; and Declaration of Independence, 71; on property, 72; Madison letter on Convention hopes, 89; compares North and South, 92; on Sherman, 93; objections to strong central government, 105; on Hamilton, 109; on Virginia's Act of Religious Freedom, 133; on England, 137; in Paris, 11, 46, 137-138, 145; on American language, 159; protests closing of Boston port, 198-199; on slave trade, 202; as Deist, 215; on Bill of Rights, 247; receives copies of Constitution, 279; suggests Northwest Ordinance, 311

Jenifer, Daniel of St. Thomas, 99, 200

Johnson, Samuel, 143

Johnson, William Samuel: description and background, 97; on Hamilton's speech, 114; on delegates' conflict, 128; on Vermont, 169; goes home, 196; on treason, 222; on Committee of Style, 234-235; president of Columbia College, 235

Jones, John Paul, 187

Jowitt, William Allen, 327

Judicial power: Dickinson on, 62; King on, 62; Wilson on, 65; Sherman on, 65; Butler on, 65-66; jury trials, 243-244; Judiciary Act of 1789, 327

KENTUCKY, 10, 148, 151, 157, 169-171, 270, 271, 294, 295, 297, 303
King, Rufus: age, 4; on government under Articles, 8; quoted, 8; on slow arrival of delegates, 12; on delegates, 18; as Convention reporter, 30; description, 35-36; on rules, 37, 237; on judicial power, 62; on executive power, 62; on federal courts, 65; on ratification, 67, 230, 283; proposes vote on Virginia Plan, 117; against equal representation in Senate, 130; rebukes Bedford, 131; on Northwest Ordinance, 174; on admission of new states, 183; on slavery question, 204; on time of Congressional meeting, 210; on treason, 222; on Committee of Style, 234-235; anger with Rhode Island, 250; on Hancock, 288
King's College, 42
Knox, Gen. Henry: persuades Washington to attend Convention, 20; description, 89-90; hopes for Convention, 90; as general, 155; on P. Henry, 295-296
Kuhn, Adam, 162

LAFAYETTE, MARQUIS DE: Washington reports to, 77, 280; in Revolution, 141-142; in upstate New York, 148-149; on American inns, 155
Lamb, John, 270
Land Companies, 171-172, 181-182. See also Ohio Company
Langdon, John: description, 13; on slavery, 204; on additional representatives, 250
Lansing, John Jr.: as Convention reporter, 30; refuses to sign, 34, 262; opposes Hamilton, 86; promotes New Jersey Plan, 104-105; opposition to Convention, 105, 115, 270, 305-306, 311-312; criticizes Virginia Resolves, 118; leaves Convention, 140, 225, 311

Lee, Richard Henry: on delegates, 4; on representatives, 73; on Bill of Rights, 248; opposes Constitution, 269-270, 295; background and career, 269
Legislature, 44, 275; on two branches, 48; popular election of representatives, 48, 69, 74; vote on legislative veto, 83; based on taxation, 95; proportional representation, 185-187; on legislators' requirements, 100-101, 205; state legislatures to ratify Constitution, 228-233
Livingston, William: background and description, 65
Louisiana, 169, 178
Loyalists. See Tories
Lusk, Maj. T., 285

MACAULAY, CATHERINE, 188
Maclay, William, 189
McClurg, James: as delegate, 18; approves but does not sign, 262
McHenry, James: as Convention reporter, 30; leaves Convention, 54; concern for commerce provisions, 200; on Franklin's approval of Constitution, 256
McKean, Chief Justice Thomas, 181; on ratification, 276-277; on Federal Procession, 307
Madison, James: as speechmaker, ix; age, 4; promotes Convention, 5-6; on commerce under Articles, 9-10; description, 13, 29, 237, 296; arrives in Philadelphia, 13; background, 14; on vices of political system, 14; hopes for Convention, 15; on P. Henry, 18, 270; persuades Washington to attend, 20; writes Virginia's credentials, 26; as Convention reporter, 29-30, 260; on state sovereignty, 33, 82; to Jefferson on delegates, 37; influence on draft of Virginia Resolves, 38; on federal vs. national government, 43; on using force vs. states, 48; on executive power, 62-63, 64; on judicial appointment, 66; on ratifi-

Madison, James (*cont.*)
cation, 67, 227-229, 280-281, 288;
as nationalist, 70, 78, 225-226; on
property, 71, 122; on election of
representatives, 75; on Senate, 77-
78, 122; sense of destiny, 88-89; on
states' differences, 92, 125, 128-129;
number of speeches, 93; length of
representatives' terms and salaries,
99-100, 120-121; on Committee of
Style, 234, 236-237; political ideas,
239-240; on G. Morris as writer of
Constitution, 242; sponsors national
university, 249; on Mason's refusal
to sign, 261-262, 280; reports to
Jefferson, 263, 278-279; on Hancock, 289; in Virginia ratification
convention, 296-305
Maine. *See* Massachusetts
Marshall, John, 147, 158; as Federalist, 297
Martin, Alexander, 221; approves
but does not sign, 262
Martin, Luther: opposes Constitution, 34, 86, 119, 248-249, 270;
on British government, 58; short-
sighted view, 78; supports New
Jersey Plan, 105; description and
character, 119; criticizes Virginia
Plan, 119, 123-124; fears dissolution of Convention, 140, 185;
against large states, 169; on admission of Western states, 176-
177; on Great Compromise, 187;
meets with Maryland delegates,
200; on national capital, 210; on
religion, 217; on treason, 223; on
ratification, 230, 293; on Bill of
Rights, 247-248; does not sign, 262
Maryland: quarrel with Virginia
over navigation rights, 9; population, 9; trade, 10; state Constitution, 101; unrest in, 123; delegates
hostile, 226-227; ratification, 293
Mason, George: as delegate, 18;
financial affairs, 27; as Convention
reporter, 30; refuses to sign, 34,
250, 261-262, 263; on rules, 37; on
democracy, 47, 74; background
and description, 47, 262, 297; on
slavery, 47, 95, 202-203; on Philadelphia social life, 52; on monarchy, 54, 189; on executive, 62;
on Convention's duties, 62; on
elections of representatives, 74-75;
on hopes for Convention, 88; supports New Jersey Plan, 105; on
legislative corruption, 121; on senators' pay and power, 123, 250;
on admission of Western states,
180-181; on national capital, 209-
210; on sumptuary laws, 214; author of Virginia Bill of Rights,
214, 239, 244; on treason, 221, 223;
on ratification, 229-230, 232, 295,
297; not on Committee of Style,
234-235; on monopolies, 249; on
amending Constitution, 250; wants
another Convention, 251-252; objections to Constitution, 261-262,
268, 280
Massachusetts: trade, 10; Shays's Rebellion, 10, 31; delegation, 19; population, 19; credentials of delegates, 24; as colony, 43; legislature,
70; circular letter of 1768, 71; suffrage qualifications, 73; governor,
73; during Revolution, 76, 214; as
large state, 84, 107, 128, 131, 177;
climate, 148; people, 156; problem
of Maine, 169, 283-284; attitude
toward West, 177; religion in, 215;
state constitution ratified, 228, 230;
on ratification, 282-292, 293, 302
*Massachusetts Centinel*, 102
Mercer, John Francis: late arrival,
24, 200; lists pro-monarchy delegates, 191; goes home, does not
sign, 262
Mifflin, Thomas, 237, 273
Mississippi, 25, 31, 92, 168-170, 177,
179, 220, 270, 294, 303
Monroe, James, 295, 297; Revolutionary principles, 8; reports to
Jefferson on Convention, 192-193;
letter from Madison, 239
Moreau de St. Méry, 142; on Philadelphia, 97, 148; on customs, 150,

152; on people, 153; on state differences, 164; on women, 166
Morris, Gouverneur: as speechmaker, ix; age and physical description, 4, 42; reads letter from Rhode Island, 37; quoted on government, 40-41; character and career, 42; on national government, 42; on representatives, 73, 176, 256; number of speeches, 93; on Hamilton's Plan, 114; on effect of Convention, 139, 258; on property, 139; fears Western influence, 177-178; on admission of new states, 183; Madison accuses of wanting monarchy, 189; on impeachment of President, 190; anecdote about Washington, 195; on slavery, 201; on senatorial term, 205; on national capital, 209; on time for congressional meeting, 210; on rebellion in states, 218; on treason, 221-222; on ratification, 230, 280; on Committee of Style, 234-238, 240-242; on "laws of nations" and piracy, 249; describes Constitution, 300
Morris, Robert: suffers at mob's hands, 10; entertains Washington, 21-22, 193-194; debts and financial affairs, 21-27, 172; career, description, 22; hospitality, 50

Nason, Samuel, 284, 285, 291
New England, 150, 155, 159-160, 167, 170, 171, 214, 215
New Hampshire: on requisitions under Articles of Confederation, 5; delays sending delegates, 12, 186-187; credentials (justificatory preamble), 24; suffrage in, 73; climate, 148; attitudes in, 214; state constitution ratified, 228
New Haven Gazette, 278
New Jersey: Fundamental Laws, ix, on requisitions, 5; troops during Revolution, 7; customs, 9; delegation, 19; Livingston governor of, 65; leads small states, 102, 107; climate, 148; as national capital site,

208; loyalist leanings, 243; ratifies Constitution, 277
New Jersey Plan, 102, 104-108, 115, 213; compared with Virginia Resolves, 104-106; Madison opposes, 116-117; Convention rejects, 117
New York, 11, 27, 70-71, 105, 111, 250, 275, 278; on requisitions, 5; on customs, 9; Congress sitting, 11-12; population, 19; credentials of delegates, 24; "seditiors," party in legislature, 31; suffrage qualifications, 73; divisions in state politics, 109-110; opposition to Constitution in, 115, 270; ratification by, 226, 232, 294, 305-306
New York Daily Advertiser, 235
New York Journal, 210
Nicholas, George, 296-297
Noailles, Louis, Vicomte de, 142
Norris, Isaac, speaker of Pennsylvania Assembly, 58
North Carolina: trade and customs, 9; population, 19, 250; delegates' expenses, 27; governor's salary, 74; legislature, 74; delegates report to governor, 102-103, 192; wealth, 130-131; State of Franklin, 169, 177; harsh to Tories, 220-221; for ratification, 272
Northwest Ordinance, 173-175, 181, 183, 311; King moves resolution, 174; against slavery, 35

Ohio Company, 173-174, 181-182, 183. See also land companies
Ohio country, 25-26, 148, 171, 173-174, 181. See also West
Osnaburgh, Bishop of, 191
Otto, Louis Guillaume, 142

Paine, Thomas: in Europe, 18, 135-136; Common Sense, 133
Parliament (British), 23, 74, 94, 135; under Elizabeth, 40, 198; as model for United States, 57, 198; House of Lords, 77, 78, 94, 112, 121; Franklin on, 60-61; Septennial Act,

Parliament (British) (*cont.*)
100; money bills, 101; venality,
120-121, 135. *See also* England
Parsons, Theophilus, 283, 289
Paterson Plan. *See* New Jersey Plan
Paterson, William: as Convention
reporter, 30; on democracy, 45; on
admission of new states, 66; on suffrage, 84; against national government, 84; sponsor of New Jersey
Plan, 102, 104-107; description, 107;
goes home, 211; on altercations in
Convention, 211-212; on debts to
Britain, 221
Peale, Charles Wilson, 51, 193, 280
Pendleton, Edmund, 281, 304; description, 296; as Federalist, 296
Penn, William, 239
Pennsylvania, 17, 35, 92, 107, 122-123,
131; paper money, 9; trade, 10;
militia, 12; Franklin represents, 16;
delegation, 19, 35; population, 19,
143; legislature meets, 23, 226, 234,
254; Wilson on, 33; as colony, 43,
60; unicameral legislature, 48, 273;
suffrage in, 73; as large state, 82,
84; Frenchmen admire, 141; Englishmen comment, 148-152, 155-
156; on price of land, 151; and the
West, 169-171; as national capital
site, 208; religion in, 215-217; ratification of Constitution in, 273-277,
302
*Pennsylvania Gazette*, 225, 308
*Pennsylvania Journal*, 191
*Pennsylvania Packet*, 19-20, 51, 77,
185, 196, 243, 267-268, 280, 300
Peters, Hugh, 215
Philadelphia, 11, 12, 19, 250, 275;
weather, 3, 23, 34, 96-97, 102, 123,
186, 205, 243, 254; on moving of
Congress, 12; Washington arrives,
16, 21; State House, 19; high cost
of living in, 26; prisoners, 34, 49,
50, 52; streets, 49; social life, 50,
52; bookstores, 50; Library Hall,
50; Philosophical Society, 50; Carpenters Hall, 50, 52; Peale's Museum, 51; river front, 51; market

and food, 51; furniture, 51; sanita-
tion, 52; taverns, 52; people (society), 52, 165-167; churches, 52;
the watch, 52
Phillips, Jonas, 216
Pierce, William Leigh: threatens secrecy rule, 22; as Convention reporter, 30; on Sherman, 93; notes
on delegates, 98; anecdote on
Washington, 98-99; on King, 237;
approves but does not sign, 262
Pinckney, Charles: age, 4; financial
affairs, 27; Pinckney's Plan, 39, 213;
on election of senate, 43; urges
vigorous executive, 55; should Convention fail, 68; on popular elections, 74; on legislative veto, 80;
on New Jersey Plan, 107; on slavery, 202, 203; criticizes British
government, 121; on national university, 164, 249; on Great Compromise, 187; on foreigners in Congress, 206; on outcome of Convention, 213, 252; suggests address to
people, 233; his Bill of Rights, 244f,
245; on another Convention, 252
Pinckney, Gen. Charles Cotesworth:
background, 75-76; on popular
elections, 76; on senators' salaries,
120; visits Bethlehem, 196; on
slavery, 203; on Bill of Rights,
247; on signing the Constitution,
260-261
Portugal, 135
Presbyterians, 19
Presidency. *See* Executive
Price, Richard, 89
Priest, William, 149, 153
Priestley, Joseph, 141, 148
Property, 69-72; Butler on, 83; Gerry
on, 95; G. Morris on, 139-140

QUAKERS, 16-17, 49, 52, 61, 133, 141,
145, 167, 215

RANDOLPH, EDMUND, 18, 20, 27, 280;
refuses to sign, 34, 258, 260, 263;
description and background, 37-39,
257-258; offers resolves, 38, 267-

268; on national government, 41; on democracy, 45; on executive, 57, 58-59; on New Englanders, 91; on Senate, 100-101; promotes Virginia Resolves, 108; rebukes Bedford, 131; on Western states, 178; on how to compose constitution, 197-198; on foreigners in Congress, 206-207; on religion, 215; on debts to Britain, 221; on treason, 221-222; on ratification, 228, 258; objections to Constitution, 231-232, 251-252, 257-258; supports Constitution in Virginia convention, 300-304

Ratification, 226-233, 244-245; in Pennsylvania, 273, 277, 302, 305; in Georgia, 277; in New Jersey, 277-278; in Connecticut, 277-278; in Massachusetts, 278, 282-292, 302, 305; in Virginia, 278, 294, 305; in Rhode Island, 278, 294, 306; in New York, 294; 305-306; in Delaware, 277, 278; in Maryland, 293; in South Carolina, 293; in New Hampshire, 293-294; in North Carolina, 294, 306; in Vermont, 306

Read, George: on national government, 75, 86; background, 75; applauds Hamilton's speech, 114; objects to Georgia's representation, 175-176; authorized to sign for Dickinson, 263

Representatives, House of: See also legislative power; voting against popular election, 77; length of term, 99; salaries, 100; proportional representation, 117, 175, 185-187, 250; power of, 275

Revolution: principles of, 6, 8, 70-71, 81, 88, 105, 214, 230; Virginia refers to in credentials, 25; government under, 70, 73; Gen. Pinckney during, 76; Salem, Massachusetts, during, 76; Gerry during, 78; war debts, 108; French sympathy for, 133; French as allies, 141-142

Rhode Island: refusal to send delegates, 3, 13; Sherman on, 10; Jefferson on, 13; Hopkinson on, 31; merchants repudiate lack of participation, 37; must join Union, 86; Dr. Benjamin Rush on, 89; paper money troubles, 123; M. Otto on, 142; opposes Constitution, 226; representation of, 250; Antifederalist demonstration, 306

Robertson, David: reports Virginia ratification convention, 300

Rochambeau, Jean Baptiste de Vimeur, Comte de, 141-142

Roosevelt, Theodore: on Hamilton and Jefferson, 109

Rousseau, Jean Jacques, 71

Rush, Benjamin: hopes for Convention, 89; on Rhode Island, 89; on Franklin, 89; as physician, 162-163; on Wilson, 179; on Bill of Rights, 246-247; work for ratification, 276; on Federal Procession, 307, 309

Russia, 134

Rutledge, John: on delegates' discussion, 55; on judicial appointment, 65; sense of destiny, 80; on legislative vote, 94-95; alterations to Constitution draft, 197; presents copies to delegates, 200; on slavery, 201-202, 204; on length of sessions, 211; on address to people, 250

St. Clair, General Arthur, 181

Schuyler, Phillip, 109-110, 111

Scotland, 66, 96, 143

Secrecy, Rule of, 22-23, 31, 54, 77, 98, 102, 139, 181, 183, 192, 265, 272

Senate: See also legislative power; on election, 44, 77, 79, 100-101; on money bills, 101; on representation, 117; on term, 122, 205-206; on compromise, 185-187; power of, 275

Separation of powers, 213; J. Wilson on, 33; Wythe on, 33; Randolph proposes, 40

Seven Years' War, 6, 141, 171

Shays's Rebellion, 10, 116, 123, 218, 243, 276, 283, 287-288; Gerry on,

Shays's Rebellion (*cont.*)
45, 67; Jefferson on, 46; and lawyers, 64; as treason, 222
Sheffield, Lord, 26
Sherman, Roger: as speechmaker, ix; on small states, 10; on legislative power, 44; on democracy, 47; on executive, 56-57; on courts, 65; on ratification, 67, 228, 278; on senate election, 77; description, 93; speeches in Convention, 93; legislative compromise, 94; on senators' term, 100; supports New Jersey Plan, 105; on stalemate, 138; his language, 160; on admission of new states, 177; goes home, 196; on slave trade, 201-202, 204; on time for congressional meeting, 210; on Bill of Rights, 244-246
Short, William, 89
Singletary, Amos, 286-287
Slater, Samuel, 164
Slavery, 71, 86, 95, 285; Mason on, 47; Wilson proposes three-fifths rule, 95; on attitudes of slaveowners, 156-157; compromise of Convention, 200-204
Smilie, John, 273-274
Smith, Jonathan, 282, 286-287
Smith, Melancton, 270; as Antifederalist, 305
Smith, William, 46
South Carolina: trade and customs, 9, 83; executive, 73; population, 76; attitude toward New England, 91; wealth, 130; on slavery, 202, 231; on ratification, 293
Spaight, Richard Dobbs: suggests reconsideration rule, 36; on senators' terms, 100
Spain, 134, 135; trade, 10; United States interest in, 25-26, 81, 168-170, 177
Stamp Act, 16, 71, 88, 207
State House, 50; description, 23, 31, 48, 254; Franklin arrives, 34; Cutler visits, 182; legislature to meet, 226, 234; ratification contest in, 274

States: jealousies under Articles of Confederation, 9, 10, 11; poverty, 27; troubles in 1787, 31, 225-226; sovereignty, 32-33, 43, 69, 81-82, 104-105, 113; small states, 48, 69, 84, 122, 186; admission of, 66, 80, 175-177; large states, 84, 186; conflict between, 92, 164, 175; Franklin on small vs. large states, 95; slavery and the, 200-204
Stiles, Ezra, 215
Stuart, David, 87
Stuart, Gilbert, 28, 193
Strong, Caleb: description, 35; introduces Cutler, 181; on Great Compromise, 187; on style of Constitution, 242; approves but absent for signing, 262; on ratification, 283
Suffrage, 73-75
Sumner, Increase, 284
Symmes, William, 289-290

TALLEYRAND, CHARLES MAURICE, Prince de: on Hamilton, 109
Ten Miles Square (Federal City), 208-210, 272
Tennessee, 169-171
Thompson, General: on Massachusetts convention, 284, 285, 289
Treason, 219-223
Treaty of Paris, 1783, 11, 92, 168, 220
Trenton Iron Works, 196
Tories: Franklin on, 17; Washington on, 45; defense of, 64; on Livingston, 66; on American king, 191; and test oaths, 220
Trevelyan, George Otto, on Washington, 15, 194
Tyler, John, 295, 299

UNITED STATES, 118; debts of, 11, 134, 221; Pinckney on classes of society, 121; geography and climate, 144-146, 153; forests, 146-147, 153; customs, 148-150; food, 149; houses, 150; people, 150, 153; democracy in, 154; travel in, 153-155; poverty in, 157, 176; education in, 158, 161; language in, 155,

161; general condition in 1787, 164; pride of, 165; art and culture, 165; social life, 165-167; the West, 168-184; growth of, 171, 175; threats of disunion, 184; domestic economy, 214; religion in, 215-216; reaction to Constitution, 265-281

VAN BUREN, MARTIN, 62
Vermont, 169, 177, 214
Vice Presidency, 272; criticism of, 269
Virginia, 17, 107, 131, 163, 214, 244; quarrel with Maryland over navigation rights, 9-10; delegation to Convention, 18-19, 263; population, 19, 294; credentials (justificatory preamble), 25-26; interests in Ohio country, 26, 294; as colony, 43, 220; as large state, 82, 84; poverty in, 151; on national capital, 208-209; religion in, 215; ratification, 294-305
*Virginia Gazette*, 300
Virginia Resolves (Plan), 18, 66-67, 82, 101-102, 115, 213, 228, 238; Randolph presents, 38-39, 267-268; Randolph suggests separation of powers, 40; Paterson criticizes, 107; Convention follows, 117, 197; Randolph urges return to Plan, 231-232
Voltaire, 17, 71

WARREN, JAMES, 188, 271
Warren, Mercy, 188
Wadsworth, Jeremiah, describes Sherman, 93
Washington, George: on requisitions, 5; promotes Convention, 6; on Continental Army's plight, 6; on Continental Congress, 6-7; on politics, 7; on powers of government under Articles, 7; description and character, 7, 27-29, 193-195; on Rhode Island, 13; Trevelyan on, 15; relationship with Madison, 15; arrives in Philadelphia, 16; on Society of the Cincinnati,

20; reluctance to attend Convention, 20; health, 21; social life, 21, 22, 50, 77, 86, 98, 193, 196; his finances and estate, 27; elected president of Convention, 27-29, 31, 32; silence in Convention, 29, 186, 257; Jefferson on, 29; on state sovereignty, 32-33, 87; relinquishes chair, 40; on G. Morris, 42; on Shays's Rebellion, 45, 73; as probable first executive, 61, 257, 270; as nationalist, 70; on property, 71, 77; reports to Lafayette, 77, 280, 293; worried about Mount Vernon, 87; hopes for Convention, 87, 140, 185, 195; anecdote on secrecy rule, 98-99; on Hamilton, 110-111; resumes chair, 117; on Europe, 135; as slaveowner, 156, 285; on national university, 164; on West, 164, 170, 172; on Great Compromise, 187; influence of, 193, 257; on titles and position, 194; anecdote with G. Morris, 195; visits Valley Forge, 195-196; on cattle food, 196; chooses capital site, 210f; "miracle" of Constitution, 238, 265, 324; on democracy, 243; suggests increasing proportion of representatives, 257; notes signing, 263; reports end of Convention, 264; criticized by Antifederalists, 275; on Georgia, 277; on ratification, 278, 280-281, 295; Gen. Thompson on, 285; on Randolph, 300; on opposition to Constitution, 305
Webster, Daniel, on R. King, 237
Webster, Noah, 159, 246
Weld, Isaac, 146-147, 157-158
West, 168-184; Britain's interests. in, 25; Hopkinson on, 31; Wilson's speculation in lands, 56; settlers, 72, 143, 158; voting problems in, 86; congressmen from, 120; communication with, 249. *See also* Ohio country
White, Abraham, 286, 291
Whitehill, Robert, 273
Whitelocke, Sir James, 170

Whitney, Eli, 164

Widgery, William, 284-285, 291

Wilkinson, James, 170

William and Mary, College of, 36, 161-162

Williamson, Hugh: on Convention's expenses, 27; concern for Western states, 125; expense of chaplain, 126-127; as land speculator, 172; on monarchy, 189; concern for national capital, 209; on signing of Constitution, 259

Wilson, James: as speechmaker, ix; suffered at mob's hands, 10, 64, 277; on separation of powers idea, 33; on government of individual vs. states, 43; on executive, 55; background, 55-56, 207; defends Tories, 64; on judicial appointment, 65; on ratification, 67, 226-227, 275-276; on state sovereignty, 69, 81, 85; as nationalist, 70, 74, 78, 80, 104; on popular election, 74; on senate, 79, 130; character, 80, 178-179; description, 179; on Federal liberty, 81; sense of destiny, 98; number of speeches, 93; proposes three-fifths rule for slaves, 107; on pay for congressmen, 120; on small states vs. large

states, 129; as land speculator, 172; on Western states, 178-179; helps compose Constitution, 197; on slave trade, 203-204; on foreigners in Congress, 207-208; on test oaths, 214; on treason, 221-222; on Bill of Rights, 245-246; on canals, 249; on "laws of nations," 249; speech in State House yard, 275-276; in Federal Procession, 309

White, James, 265

Wythe, George: as delegate, 18; leaves Convention, 27, 54; on separation of powers, 33, 40; description, 36, 296; reports on Rules Committee, 36; as nationalist, 78; his education, 158; approves but does not sign, 263

YATES, ROBERT, 39, 270; as Convention reporter, 30; refuses to sign, 34, 115; on Virginia Resolves, 38; defends Tories, 64; on Dickinson's speech, 79; opposes Hamilton, 86; supports New Jersey Plan, 105; on Hamilton's speech, 113-114, 115; leaves Convention, 140, 225, 311; writes as Sydney and Brutus, 246f; as Antifederalist, 305, 311-312